Lecture Notes in Computer Science 11412

Commenced Publication in 1973
Founding and Former Series Editors:
Gerhard Goos, Juris Hartmanis, and Jan van Leeuwen

More information about this series at http://www.springer.com/series/7408

Eric Knauss · Michael Goedicke (Eds.)

Requirements Engineering: Foundation for Software Quality

25th International Working Conference, REFSQ 2019
Essen, Germany, March 18–21, 2019
Proceedings

 Springer

Editors
Eric Knauss (iD)
Department of Computer Science
and Engineering
Chalmers University of Technology
Gothenburg, Sweden

Michael Goedicke
paluno – The Ruhr Institute for Software
Technology
University of Duisburg-Essen
Essen, Germany

ISSN 0302-9743   ISSN 1611-3349   (electronic)
Lecture Notes in Computer Science
ISBN 978-3-030-15537-7   ISBN 978-3-030-15538-4   (eBook)
https://doi.org/10.1007/978-3-030-15538-4

Library of Congress Control Number: 2019934740

LNCS Sublibrary: SL2 – Programming and Software Engineering

This Springer imprint is published by the registered company Springer Nature Switzerland AG
The registered company address is: Gewerbestrasse 11, 6330 Cham, Switzerland

Preface

With great pleasure we welcome the participants and readers to the proceedings of the 25th REFSQ event. REFSQ is the International Working Conference on Requirements Engineering: Foundation for Software Quality. And yes, this was an anniversary: 25th conference in the series! Congratulations, REFSQ!

Good software quality is a goal everybody would easily subscribe to. But as we all know, this is hard to achieve. Thus, requirements engineering is a well-established discipline within the software engineering community. Experts from academic and industrial backgrounds gathered to report the state of the art in the area as well as to discuss proposals to advance the current knowledge about all aspects of requirements engineering. This strong relationship between industry and academia is fundamental for an applied research field such as represented by REFSQ and facilitates results of the highest impact, both through research on practically relevant problems and fast technology transfer to industry.

Requirements engineering is a critical factor in developing high-quality and successful software, systems, and services, especially today, where the speed of development has increased dramatically. Information systems as produced and provided by the big players in search engines, e-commerce, and social networks have development processes that use a fast deployment cycle. Today, it is not unusual that the time from inception to deployment of a change or a new feature takes as little as one week to ten days and that new versions of software are deployed at rates of several deployments per hour. Such pace is at odds with traditional processes that aim to understand, refine, design, and implement a change to a software system and make sure that all works as planned. Through our special theme "Laying the Foundation for Speed and Flexibility in Development" we brought this discussion to the center of attention in the REFSQ community. Which new approaches to understand requirements and guarantee quality can be offered to match this space? Where must we overcome overly tight schedules?

REFSQ has a strong history of being a working conference, that is, an event where excellent contributions from research and practice are extensively discussed and elaborated in various presentation and discussion formats. Normal presentations of established research as well as research previews that report on new developments and emerging results are challenged by a dedicated discussion leader and a critical audience. One important feature is a distinct day for focusing on results and challenges from industrial practice, facilitating a rich exchange between practitioners and academic researchers. This main program is complemented by a set of tutorials, workshops, a doctoral consortium as well as a session with life studies and posters and tools.

The REFSQ 2019 conference was organized as a three-day symposium. The sessions contribute to the topic of the conference in various ways. Thus, we are proud to conclude that REFSQ is a genuine event series in supporting vital scientific and practical results in promoting the field of requirements engineering in a substantial way.

This would have not been possible without numerous teams of authors performing the research, experiments, and putting a lot of thought into the respective subjects. It means a lot to formulate research hypotheses, find the right – in many cases empirical – experiments and finally convince the representatives of the community that the presentation of the results is a worthwhile piece of knowledge for extending the field!

Thus we are pleased to present this volume comprising the REFSQ 2019 proceedings. It features 22 papers from the various fields of requirements engineering research and practice. The Program Committee (PC) carefully reviewed 66 submissions and selected eight technical design papers, five scientific evaluation papers, and nine research previews. Also, the conference was truly international since we had authors, PC members, and reviewers from all continents. We would like to express our gratitude to all these individuals who put so much effort in creating, reviewing, and finally preparing outstanding contributions to the requirements engineering field.

REFSQ 2019 would not have been possible without the engagement and support of these many individuals. The various committees are listed herein. But as editors of this volume, we would like to thank the REFSQ Steering Committee members, in particular Kurt Schneider, for his availability and for the excellent guidance provided. Special thanks go to Klaus Pohl for his long-term engagement for REFSQ. We are indebted to Jennifer Horkoff and Erik Kamsties, the REFSQ 2018 co-chairs, for their extremely helpful advice to all questions popping up at inconvenient times. We are grateful to all the members of the PC for their timely and thorough reviews of the submissions and for the time dedicated to their discussion, both online and face-to-face during the PC meeting. In particular, we thank those PC members who volunteered to serve in the role of shepherd or gatekeeper to authors of conditionally accepted papers. We would like to thank the members of the local organization at the University of Duisburg-Essen for their ongoing smooth support, determination, and being available at all times. We are grateful to the chairs, who organized the various events included in REFSQ 2019.

Finally, we would especially like to thank Vanessa Stricker for her excellent work in coordinating the background organization processes, and Grischa Liebel for his support in preparing this volume.

The volume here consists of presentations of research results or new ideas that we hope the reader will find interesting to follow and help to pursue his/her own work in requirements engineering – especially in order to support the fast pace we observe in our industry.

February 2019

Eric Knauss
Michael Goedicke

Organization

Program Committee Chairs

Eric Knauss   Chalmers | University of Gothenburg, Sweden
Michael Goedicke   University of Duisburg-Essen, Germany

Steering Committee

Kurt Schneider (Chair)   Leibniz Universität Hannover, Germany
Barbara Paech (Vice Chair)   Universität Heidelberg, Germany
Michael Goedicke   University of Duisburg-Essen, Germany
Eric Knauss   Chalmers | University of Gothenburg, Sweden
Erik Kamsties   University of Applied Sciences and Arts Dortmund,
                                 Germany
Jennifer Horkoff   Chalmers | University of Gothenburg, Sweden
Klaus Pohl   Universität Heidelberg, Germany
Anna Perini   Fondazione Bruno Kessler Trento, Italy
Paul Grünbacher   Johannes Kepler University Linz, Austria
Fabiano Dalpiaz   Utrecht University, The Netherlands
Maya Daneva   University of Twente, The Netherlands
Oscar Pastor   Universitat Politècnica de València, Spain
Samuel Fricker   University of Applied Sciences and Arts Northwestern
                                 Switzerland, Switzerland

Program Committee

Raian Ali   Bournemouth University, UK
Joao Araujo   Universidade NOVA de Lisboa, Portugal
Fatma Başak Aydemir   Utrecht University, The Netherlands
Richard Berntsson Svensson   Chalmers | University of Gothenburg, Sweden
Dan Berry   University of Waterloo, Canada
Nelly Condori-Fernández   Universidade da Coruña, Spain
Fabiano Dalpiaz   Utrecht University, The Netherlands
Maya Daneva   University of Twente, The Netherlands
Oscar Dieste   Universidad Politécnica de Madrid, Spain
Joerg Doerr   Fraunhofer, Germany
Alessio Ferrari   ISTI-CNR, Italy
Xavier Franch   Universitat Politécnica de Catalunya, Spain
Samuel A. Fricker   FHNW, Switzerland
Vincenzo Gervasi   University of Pisa, Italy
Martin Glinz   University of Zurich, Switzerland
Paul Grünbacher   Johannes Kepler University Linz, Austria

Renata Guizzardi	Universidade Federal do Espirito Santo, Brazil
Irit Hadar	University of Haifa, Israel
Andrea Herrmann	Free Software Engineering Trainer, Germany
Jennifer Horkoff	Chalmers | University of Gothenburg, Sweden
Hermann Kaindl	Vienna University of Technology, Austria
Erik Kamsties	University of Applied Sciences and Arts Dortmund, Germany
Alessia Knauss	Veoneer AB, Sweden
Anne Koziolek	Karlsruhe Institute of Technology, Germany
Kim Lauenroth	adesso AG, Germany
Emmanuel Letier	University College London, UK
Grischa Liebel	Reykjavik University, Iceland
Nazim Madhavji	University of Western Ontario, Canada
Fabio Massacci	University of Trento, Italy
Raimundas Matulevicius	University of Tartu, Estonia
John Mylopoulos	University of Toronto, Canada
Joyce Nakatumba-Nabende	Makerere University, Uganda
Andreas L. Opdahl	University of Bergen, Norway
Barbara Paech	Universität Heidelberg, Germany
Elda Paja	University of Trento, Italy
Liliana Pasquale	University College Dublin, Ireland
Oscar Pastor Lopez	Universitat Politècnica de València, Spain
Anna Perini	Fondazione Bruno Kessler Trento, Italy
Klaus Pohl	Paluno, University of Duisburg-Essen, Germany
Jolita Ralyté	University of Geneva, Switzerland
Bjorn Regnell	Lund University, Sweden
Mehrdad Sabetzadeh	University of Luxembourg, Luxembourg
Camille Salinesi	CRI, Université de Paris 1 Panthéon-Sorbonne, France
Nicolas Sannier	University of Luxembourg, Luxembourg
Klaus Schmid	University of Hildesheim, Germany
Kurt Schneider	Leibniz Universität Hannover, Germany
Norbert Seyff	FHNW, Switzerland
Paola Spoletini	Kennesaw State University, USA
Angelo Susi	Fondazione Bruno Kessler - Irst, Italy
Michael Unterkalmsteiner	Blekinge Institute of Technology, Sweden
Michael Vierhauser	University of Notre Dame, USA
Yves Wautelet	Katholieke Universiteit Leuven, Belgium
Roel Wieringa	University of Twente, The Netherlands
Krzysztof Wnuk	Department of Software Engineering, Blekinge Institute of Technology, Sweden
Tao Yue	Simula Research Laboratory and Nanjing University of Aeronautics and Astronautics, Norway
Didar Zowghi	University of Technology, Sydney, Australia

Additional Reviewers

Yuliyan Maksimov	Fabian Kneer	Jan Ole Johanssen
Melanie Stade	Matthias Koch	Anja Kleebaum
Sofija Hotomski	Karina Villela	Anne Hess
Sebastian Adam	Anne Hess	Yuliyan Maksimov
Ibtehal Noorwali	Astrid Rohmann	

Organizers

Sponsors

Platin

DAIMLER

Gold

Silver

Contents

Automated Analysis

Decision Support for Security-Control Identification Using Machine Learning

Seifeddine Bettaieb[1], Seung Yeob Shin[1(✉)], Mehrdad Sabetzadeh[1], Lionel Briand[1], Grégory Nou[2], and Michael Garceau[2]

[1] SnT Centre, University of Luxembourg, Luxembourg City, Luxembourg
{seifeddine,shin,sabetzadeh,briand}@svv.lu
[2] BGL BNP Paribas, Luxembourg City, Luxembourg
gregory.nou@bgl.lu, mgarceau@cipherquest.com

Abstract. [**Context & Motivation**] In many domains such as healthcare and banking, IT systems need to fulfill various requirements related to security. The elaboration of security requirements for a given system is in part guided by the controls envisaged by the applicable security standards and best practices. [**Problem**] An important difficulty that analysts have to contend with during security requirements elaboration is sifting through a large number of security controls and determining which ones have a bearing on the security requirements for a given system. This challenge is often exacerbated by the scarce security expertise available in most organizations. [**Principal ideas/results**] In this paper, we develop automated decision support for the identification of security controls that are relevant to a specific system in a particular context. Our approach, which is based on machine learning, leverages historical data from security assessments performed over past systems in order to recommend security controls for a new system. We operationalize and empirically evaluate our approach using real historical data from the banking domain. Our results show that, when one excludes security controls that are rare in the historical data, our approach has an average recall of ≈95% and average precision of ≈67%. [**Contribution**] The high recall – indicating only a few relevant security controls are missed – combined with the reasonable level of precision – indicating that the effort required to confirm recommendations is not excessive – suggests that our approach is a useful aid to analysts for more efficiently identifying the relevant security controls, and also for decreasing the likelihood that important controls would be overlooked.

Keywords: Security requirements engineering · Security assessment · Machine learning

1 Introduction

Many IT systems, e.g., those used in the healthcare and finance sectors, need to meet a variety of security requirements in order to protect against attacks. The

E. Knauss and M. Goedicke (Eds.): REFSQ 2019, LNCS 11412, pp. 3–20, 2019.
https://doi.org/10.1007/978-3-030-15538-4_1

elaboration of these requirements is heavily influenced by the security controls prescribed by standards and best practices such as the ISO 27000 family of standards [14], NIST SP 800 guidelines [24], and OSA security patterns [25]. These controls define a wide range of technical and administrative measures for the avoidance, detection and mitigation of security risks [10]. An example security control from ISO 27002 is: "The integrity of information being made available on a publicly available system should be protected to prevent unauthorized modification." If an application has information assets with public access points, this control may be elaborated into detailed security requirements aimed at avoiding information tampering.

For a specific IT system in a particular context, only a subset of the controls in the security standards and best practices have a bearing on the security requirements. An important task that analysts need to do is therefore to decide which controls are relevant and need to be considered during requirements elaboration. Since the controls are numerous, performing this task entirely manually is not only cumbersome but also error-prone, noting that deciding whether a certain control is relevant often correlates with several contextual factors, e.g., the assets that are associated with a given system, the threats that the system is exposed to, and the vulnerabilities that the system leads to. Overlooking any of these factors can lead to wrong decisions about the security controls, and potentially serious consequences. This problem is made even more acute by the scarcity of expertise in security risk analysis in most organizations.

Our work in this paper is motivated by the need to provide automated decision support for identifying the security controls that are pertinent to a specific system. To this end, we observe that, in security-critical sectors, e.g., finance, security assessment is an increasingly systematic activity, where security assessment data is collected and recorded in a structured way [7]. Many system providers and security consulting firms now have detailed data models in place to keep track of the security-related properties of the systems that they analyze and the decisions they make regarding security. This raises the prospect that existing (historical) data about security assessments can be put to productive use for decision support. What we do in this paper is to examine the feasibility and effectiveness of this prospect in a real setting.

The starting point for our work was a year-long field study at a major international bank. Our study aimed at developing insights into industry practices for assessing IT security risks. The study focused specifically on early-stage security assessments during the system inception and requirements elaboration phases. This study led to a precise characterization of the historical data that we had at our disposal for building automated decision support. While the data model resulting from our field study inevitably has bespoke concepts that are specific to our study context, the majority of the concepts are general and aligned with widely used standards, particularly ISO 27001 and 27002. This helps provide confidence that our data model is representative of a wider set of security practices than our immediate study context.

With a data model for security assessments at hand, we explore the use of several *Machine Learning (ML)* algorithms for identifying the security controls that are most relevant to a given system and context. To this end, we define a set of features for learning from historical security assessment data. We empirically evaluate the accuracy of our approach using real data. Our results show that, when one excludes security controls that are rare, i.e., apply to too few systems in the historical data, our approach on average has a recall of ≈95% and precision of ≈67%. Since recall is high and the number of false positives is not excessive, as suggested by precision, we conclude that ML is a promising avenue for increasing the efficiency of identifying relevant security controls, and also reducing the likelihood that important controls would be missed. In situations where one has to deal with rarely used security controls, ML alone is not sufficient; this necessitates future investigations into how ML can be complemented with other techniques, e.g., guided manual reviews, expert rules and case-based reasoning, in order to provide comprehensive coverage of the security controls.

The rest of the paper is organized as follows: Sect. 2 provides background and compares with related work. Section 3 summarizes the outcomes of our field study on security assessment. Section 4 presents our ML-based approach for recommending relevant security controls. Sections 5 and 6 report on our evaluation. Section 7 discusses threats to validity. Section 8 concludes the paper.

2   Background and Related Work

This section discusses the industry standards and the existing research strands related to our work.

2.1   Information Security Standards

Our collaborating partner has its IT security practices grounded in the ISO 27000 family of information security standards [14]. This commonly used series of standards provides a systematic approach for handling information security. Among these standards, ISO 27001 and 27002 relate most closely to our work in this paper. ISO 27001 specifies a set of requirements for developing and maintaining an information security management system. The standard further envisages requirements for the assessment and control of the security risks posed by security breaches in IT systems. ISO 27002 complements ISO 27001 by providing guidelines for selecting, implementing, and managing controls for security risks. The standard has a total of 128 security controls. These controls span 11 security categories, e.g., security policy, asset management, and access control. When elaborating the security requirements for a system, one has to identify the controls that are relevant to the system at hand. As noted earlier, performing this task without automated assistance is both tedious and prone to errors. Our work in this paper takes aim at providing suitable automated support for the above task.

2.2   Security Requirements Engineering

Security requirements have been widely studied for IT systems, e.g., [6,12,16, 19,22,30,32]. The most closely related research threads to our work are those concerned with early-stage security risk analysis. Two notable techniques to this end are STRIDE and DREAD, both originating from Microsoft [20]. These techniques have been used and improved by many corporations over the years [22]. STRIDE is a method for classifying security threats, whereas DREAD is a method to rate, compare and prioritize the severity of the risks presented by each of the threats classified using STRIDE. Our work is complementary to STRIDE and DREAD, first in that we focus on risk mitigation as opposed to risk classification and triage, and second in that we take an automation angle rather than dealing exclusively with manual security analysis.

Some prior research attempts to assist security engineers through capturing domain expertise in a reusable form. For example, Schmitt and Liggesmeyer [29] propose a model for structuring security knowledge as a way to improve the efficiency of specifying and analyzing security requirements. Sindre and Opdahl [31] develop a systematic approach for security requirements elicitation based on use cases, with a focus on reusable methodological guidelines. In contrast to the above work, we explore how historical data from past security assessments can be mined and reused within a corporate context for building automated decision support. We further demonstrate the effectiveness of our approach through systematic empirical means by applying the approach to an industrial case study.

2.3   Applications of Machine Learning in Requirements Engineering

ML has generated a lot of traction in Requirements Engineering for supporting a variety of tasks, e.g., extracting user-story information [28], identifying non-functional requirements [3], and requirements classification [17]. To the best of our knowledge, we are the first to attempt applying ML for generating automated recommendations for security controls using historical data.

3   Field Study on Security Assessment

This section describes the results of a field study conducted with the goal of building insights into how IT security assessments are done in practice. We started our study with meetings with IT security specialists at our collaborating partner (a bank). Subsequently, the first author spent approximately a year onsite at the partner's headquarters, learning about the details of the security assessment process followed there and the data model that underlies this process.

The security assessment process at our partner is a customized procedure shaped around the guidelines of the ISO 27000 standards [14]. A central goal of this process is to derive, for a given system, a set of ISO-specified controls that need to be elaborated further into security requirements.

In Fig. 1(a), we show an overview of the security assessment process gleaned from our field study, and in Fig. 1(b) – a (simplified) version of the underlying

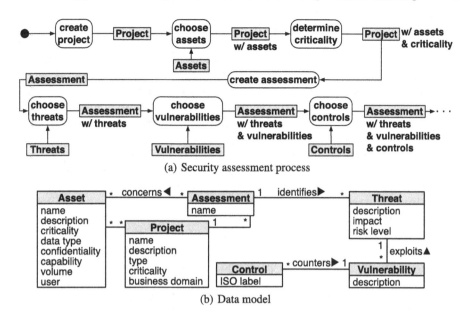

(a) Security assessment process

(b) Data model

Fig. 1. Main outcomes of our field study; note that the outcomes have been scoped to the analytical task pursued in this paper (i.e., decision support for security controls).

data model. While we present the security assessment process in a sequential manner, in practice, the process is iterative. This means that before they are finalized, the choices and the decisions made during assessment may undergo multiple rounds of improvement based on the findings at the different steps of the process. The data model of Fig. 1(b) is populated incrementally as the assessment workflow unfolds, with each step of the workflow adding new information. As we describe in Sect. 4, we use this data model as the basis for defining features for learning from past security assessment records.

As shown in Fig. 1(a), security assessment starts with the "create project" step. A new project represents a system-to-be that is at the inception and requirements gathering stage. In this step, the basic information about a project is specified, e.g., project description and business domain. Next and in the "choose assets" step, the analysts define and link the assets relevant to a given project. In general, an asset can be defined as a resource with economic value that is held or controlled by an individual, corporation, or country [13]. The step is followed by the "determine criticality" step where the analysts, in collaboration with the business stakeholders, decide about project criticality. The more critical a project is, the more is the need to evaluate potential threats and vulnerabilities systematically. To evaluate the criticality of a project, the analysts fill out a security questionnaire comprised of 12 multiple-choice questions. Each question covers a possible aspect of exposure, e.g., the level of exposure to external attacks. Once the questionnaire has been completed, the analysts exercise expert judgment to decide the project criticality level and update the project information accordingly.

The "create assessment" step captures various contextual information about the assets that have been linked to a project. The (data) type of an asset is determined by the content that the asset stores, processes, or transfers. The classification of asset types at our partner is based on their in-house domain expertise and the guidelines of the national data protection authority. The confidentiality of an asset is determined by how sensitive its content is. This attribute is a value on an (ordinal) scale ranging from public to secret. The criticality of an asset is a quantitative score indicating risk exposure. This score determines whether the potential risk posed by an asset is significant enough to warrant additional security analysis. The score is derived from the following asset attributes through a combination of expert judgment and rules: (1) the capability attribute, capturing the output channels to which the content of an asset can be sent, (2) the volume attribute, capturing the volume of data that an individual transaction can read, write, or delete from an asset, and (3) the user attribute, estimating in a logarithmic scale the number of users that can access an asset. We note that for an individual project, our partner may conduct multiple assessments from different perspectives and involving different groups of analysts. In this paper, when we refer to an assessment, we mean the collection of *all* assessment activities performed over a given project. Consequently, the assessment information collected per project is the union of the outcomes of all the assessment activities performed.

Once the contextual information for the assets in a project has been specified, the analysts move on to the identification of threats and vulnerabilities, and subsequently, the security controls. A threat refers to anything that has the potential to cause serious harm to a system, e.g., unauthorized disclosure of confidential information [13]. Threats are identified in the "choose threats" step of the process of Fig. 1(a). In this step, the analysts carefully examine a threat catalog consisting of 22 threat items and decide which ones are applicable. If a threat is deemed applicable to a project, the analysts qualify the threat more precisely within the context of that project. Specifically, for each applicable threat, the analysts provide a description, choose an appropriate risk level, and determine whether the threat impacts confidentiality, integrity, availability, or traceability. Next, in the "choose vulnerabilities" step, the analysts decide about the applicable vulnerabilities. A vulnerability represents a weakness that can be exploited by a threat, leading to the risk of asset damage or exposure [13]. An example vulnerability would be "oversight in defining access control rules to shared information". At our partner, vulnerabilities are identified using a predefined catalog with 156 entries. This catalog encompasses all the vulnerabilities known to the partner in its application domain.

Finally, in the "choose controls" step, the analysts select the appropriate security controls for the project being assessed. The source for the security controls at our partner is the ISO 27002 standard [13]. We thus refer to these controls as ISO controls. The catalog of ISO controls used by our partner constitutes 134 entries. In the remainder of this paper, we develop and evaluate automated decision support for choosing ISO controls. In particular, assuming that the assessment process steps prior to choosing the controls have been already performed for a project, we propose an approach based on ML for recommending the ISO controls relevant to the project.

Before we move on to presenting our approach, it is important to note that, for simplicity and succinctness, we have scoped the security assessment process and data model in Fig. 1 to what is needed for recommending ISO controls. In particular, we have left out of this figure and our explanation thereof a number of activities, e.g., risk mitigation and residual risk analysis, which take place after ISO-control selection.

4   Approach

Our approach for recommending ISO controls is based on ML. In this section, we present the main principles and considerations behind the approach.

4.1   Source Data for Building a Classification Model

To build a classification model, we utilize the database of historical assessment records at our collaborating partner. This database covers all the systems assessed by the partner in the past nine years. From this database, we extract various attributes. Our attributes, which are based on the data model of Fig. 1(b), are discussed next.

4.2   Machine Learning Features

We engineered our features for learning through a joint endeavor with the IT security specialists at our partner. Table 1 presents our feature set alongside our intuition as to why each feature may be a useful indicator for the relevance of ISO controls. Essentially, we chose a feature for inclusion in the set if we deemed the feature to be characterizing an important aspect of security assessment. For instance and as shown in Table 1, the criticality attribute of a project is used as a feature. In contrast, the name attribute of a project is not, since the name has no impact on the identification of ISO controls. The ISO controls (not shown in the table) are treated as class attributes. We build one classifier per ISO control. The class attribute for each ISO control is thus a binary value indicating whether or not the control is relevant to a given project.

4.3   Dealing with Imbalance

An important issue we have to take account of in our approach is imbalance in our security assessment data. In particular, we observe that the absence of ISO controls is much more prevalent than their presence across the projects. This imbalance is caused by the relatively infrequent use of several ISO controls. When a class – in our context, a particular ISO control being applicable – is

Table 1. Our features for machine learning.

Feature	(D) Definition and (I) Intuition
Project type	(D) The type of a project (total of 3 types: usual business, large scale and integration project). (I) Each project type implies a different scale and a specific process for handling risks
Project criticality	(D) The criticality of a project (total of 3 levels: very critical, critical, and non-critical). (I) The more critical a project, the more stringent are the security controls
Business domain	(D) The area of business under which a project falls (total of 48 domains, e.g., web banking, wealth management). (I) The feature relates to how severe the consequences of a breach are. For example, a breach may have more severe implications in wealth management than in certain other domains due to the involvement of vital client information
Business domain category	(D) The category for a group of business domains (total of 4 categories, e.g., the HR category, which encompasses all the human-resource-related business domains). (I) The feature provides an extra layer of abstraction for distinguishing different business domains
Security answers (A1..A12)	(D) The answers provided by the analysts to the questions on a static security questionnaire (total of 12 questions). An example question is: "What is the project's level of exposure to external attacks?" All answers are on a three-point scale: low, significant, very high. (I) The answers serve as an indicator for the seriousness of potential security breaches
Number of assets	(D) The number of assets linked to a project. (I) Increasing the number of assets may lead to an increased attack surface, thus warranting more rigorous controls
Number of critical assets	(D) The number of critical assets in a project. (I) Critical assets are specific entities with major importance. If these assets are compromised, the effects are more serious than those for regular assets. Critical assets may necessitate more security controls
Number of assets per category (C1..C9)	(D) The number of assets in an asset category (total of 9 categories, e.g., mobile application or database). (I) Each asset category has a different impact on the security controls in a project. For example, a client database being compromised would typically have more serious consequences than, say, a mobile application being inaccessible
Number of users	(D) The maximum number of users who can access the data of a project. (I) The potential risk of data exposure is correlated to the number of users accessing the data
Data type	(D) The most sensitive type of data in an asset (total of 4 types, e.g., personal data). (I) The more sensitive the data, the more impact a breach would have
Capability	(D) The capability of extracting data (total of 3 modes: screen, print, and electronic). Screen means that a user can view the data on a screen. Print means that a user can print the data on paper. Electronic means that a user can store the data onto an electronic device. (I) Data exposure risks increase as one goes from screen to print to electronic data extraction. The security controls required may thus be impacted by the extraction capability
Volume	(D) The volume of data that can be read, written, or deleted by one data transaction (total of 3 types: record-by-record, percentage-per-day, and unlimited). Record-by-record means that a user can access only one record at a time. Percentage-per-day means that a user can access a certain percentage of the dataset in one day. Unlimited means that a user has unlimited access. (I) The risk of data exposure correlates with volume. Volume may thus have an influence on the security controls
Confidentiality	(D) The maximum confidentiality level of the assets in a project (total of 4 levels: public, restricted, confidential, secret). (I) The higher the confidentiality level, the more severe are the consequences of a breach. The security controls may thus be influenced by the level of confidentiality
Threats (T1..T22)	(D) The presence or absence of a threat (total of 22 threats). (I) Threats exploits vulnerabilities. The presence of a threat has a direct influence on the security assessment decisions, including those related to the security controls
Threat impact (S1..S4)	(D) Impact scores based on all the threats in a project. Separate scores are computed for confidentiality (S1), integrity (S2), availability (S3), and traceability (S4). (I) The scores relate to the impact of security breaches and thus may influence the controls
Risk (R1..R22)	(D) Estimated risk of each threat on a scale of 1–8 (negligible to extremely high). (I) The risk posed by a threat influences security decisions, including those about the security controls
Vulnerability (V1..V154)	(D) The presence or absence of a vulnerability (total of 154 vulnerabilities). (I) Security controls counter vulnerabilities, and are naturally affected by which vulnerabilities apply

rare, ML classification models have a tendency to predict the more prevalent classes [1]. In our context, this means that, unless steps are taken to counter imbalance for rarely used ISO controls, any classification model that we build may invariably find the rare ISO controls inapplicable. To tackle imbalance, we examine two commonly used methods, namely synthetic minority over-sampling technique (SMOTE) [4] and cost-sensitive learning (CSL) [8].

4.4   Choice of Classification Algorithm

We elect to use interpretable ML techniques to provide analysts not only with security control recommendations, but also the rationale behind how the security controls were selected. An interpretable model would explain how and why a specific decision was made concerning a particular security control. For instance, the model would indicate that a particular ISO control is selected mostly because a certain combination of threats and vulnerabilities is present. We note that, in this paper, we do not attempt to validate the resulting ML models with domain experts. Nevertheless, scoping our work to interpretable ML is important, because experts are unlikely to accept decisions for which they are not provided an explanation.

5   Case Study

We evaluate our approach through an industrial case study from the banking domain. The case study is a follow-on to our field study of Sect. 3 and was conducted with the same industry partner.

5.1   Research Questions

Our case study aims to answer the following research questions (RQs):

RQ1 (classification): *Which classification algorithm is the most accurate at recommending security controls?* The accuracy of our approach is partly driven by the selected ML algorithm. In RQ1, we examine standard classification algorithms based on the existing best practices in the literature [23], and compare the accuracy of the resulting classifiers.

RQ2 (features): *Which features are the most influential for recommending security controls?* Features used in constructing an ML-based classifier typically have different degrees of importance toward the classifier's decision making. In RQ2, we evaluate the importance of the features in Table 1.

RQ3 (usefulness): *What is the overall utility of our approach?* For our approach to be useful in practice, the decision support must propose sufficiently accurate security controls in practical time. RQ3 measures the accuracy of our security recommendation system at the level of projects alongside the execution time of the main steps of our approach.

5.2 Implementation

Our recommendation system is built using the Weka framework [11]. Weka supports a broad spectrum of ML techniques. We ran our experiments on a computer equipped with an Intel i7 CPU with 16 GB of memory.

5.3 Case Study Data

Our raw data is a database of 274 assessment projects conducted over a span of nine years, from 2009 until present. Of these assessment projects, we excluded 47 because they either were not carried through to completion, or were built for testing and training purposes. This leaves us with 227 assessment projects for evaluating our approach.

Among the controls introduced by ISO 27002, some never or too rarely appear in our data. Based on our ML expertise and feedback from security engineers, we excluded the ISO controls that had been used less than 5 times within the selected 227 assessment projects. The applicability of such ISO controls cannot be predicted meaningfully using ML. In summary, our experimental dataset provides values for all the features in Table 1 and 77 ISO controls across 227 assessment projects.

5.4 Experimental Setup

To answer the RQs in Sect. 5.1, we performed three experiments, EXPI, EXPII and EXPIII, as described below.

EXPI. This experiment answers RQ1. We select the following interpretable ML algorithms as candidates for building our recommendation system: Naive Bayes [15], Logistic Regression [18], J48 [27], CART [2], JRip [5], and PART [9]. EXPI compares the accuracy of these six alternatives using the features of Table 1.

We start EXPI with hyper-parameter optimization (HPO) for the six alternatives considered. In doing so, we also account for the data imbalance problem described in Sect. 4.3. As noted in this earlier section, we consider two techniques for handling imbalance: SMOTE and CSL. SMOTE resolves imbalance by adding new artificial (synthetic) minority samples to the dataset. CSL mitigates the bias of the classifier toward the majority class by assigning a larger penalty to either false positives or false negatives. In our context, we levy a larger penalty on false negatives, i.e., ISO controls that apply to a project but are erroneously classified as not relevant. The proportional prevalence of the majority versus the minority (rare) class in our experimental dataset rounds up to 12 to 1. Specifically, our dataset contains 17952 instances of the majority and 1548 instances of the minority class. We use the same ratio for CSL by setting the cost values of false negatives and false positives to 12 and 1, respectively. Note that the cost values of true positives and true negatives are zero.

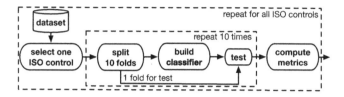

Fig. 2. 10-fold validation for all ISO-control classifiers.

For HPO, we use a step-wise grid search algorithm [21] that starts with a first coarse grid search and then refines the areas of good accuracy with additional finer-grained grid searches. For example, to find an optimal value of a real-type hyper-parameter, at the first search iteration, $i = 1$, we vary the parameter value within the valid range of the parameter by $s_i = 0.1$ step width. After finding the best parameter value, b_i, at the first search iteration, we adjust the step width, s_{i+1}, by $s_i \times 0.1$ (e.g., 0.01 at the second iteration) and adjust the search range for the parameter to $[b_i - s_i, b_i + s_i]$ for the next iteration. We continue the iterations until the difference between the best accuracy values found at the ith and $i - 1$th iterations are less than 0.01. Note that our HPO searches all the possible values in the valid ranges of the integer- and enum-type parameters at the first iteration, and then uses the best-found values at the subsequent iterations for tuning real-type parameters.

Following HPO, we measure through cross validation the accuracy of the alternative ML algorithms for predicting ISO controls. The cross validation process is illustrated in Fig. 2. The "repeat 10 times" block in the figure applies standard 10-fold cross validation [23] to the classifier built for an individual ISO control. This is repeated for all the ISO controls through the "repeat for all ISO controls" block. At the end, the "compute metrics" step calculates the EXPI accuracy metrics described in Sect. 5.5.

EXPII. This experiment answers RQ2. We evaluate the importance of the features in Table 1 based on the best-found configuration in RQ1. For each of the ISO-control classifiers, we rank the features using a standard metric for feature evaluation, as we discuss in Sect. 5.5. We then identify and aggregate the most influential features across all the ISO controls.

EXPIII. This experiment answers RQ3 by examining how much useful assistance one can expect from ML for identifying the ISO controls relevant to a given assessment project. Specifically, EXPIII performs the leave-one-out validation process shown in Fig. 3. The "leave one project out" step takes one project out from the dataset. The remaining dataset is then utilized for training the classifiers of all the ISO controls. Subsequently, the withheld project is used for testing the trained classifiers, as shown in "repeat for all ISO controls" block of the figure. This is repeated for all the projects in the dataset, as indicated by the "repeat for all projects" block. At the end of the process, we compute

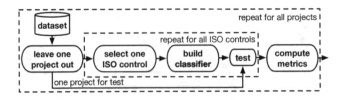

Fig. 3. Leave-one-out validation for all projects.

the EXPIII accuracy metrics described in Sect. 5.5. We note that these accuracy metrics are only indicative of in-vivo usefulness; the metrics have to be considered in their application context for a more definitive evaluation. Doing so requires user studies and is beyond the scope of this current paper.

5.5   Metrics

In EXPI, for a given ISO control c, we define the precision and recall metrics as follows: (1) precision $P^c = TP/(TP + FP)$ and (2) recall $R^c = TP/(TP + FN)$, where TP, FP, and FN are the sum of the true positives, false positives, and false negatives, respectively, across the 10 folds of cross validation for ISO control c. A true positive is a project to which c is relevant and is correctly predicted as such; a false positive is a project to which c is not relevant but is incorrectly predicted to have c as a control; a false negative is a project to which c is relevant but is incorrectly predicted to not have c as a control. These metrics are used for comparing the accuracy of different ML algorithms.

In practice, the decision as to whether an ISO control is applicable should be made as simple as possible to minimize the effort needed from the analysts. The most critical factor here is recall, since the presence of false negatives implies that important ISO controls may be missed. A recall that is too low would thus undermine the usefulness of the approach, meaning that the analysts would be better off doing the selection of the relevant controls entirely manually. To allow the analysts to focus only on the recommended controls, we prioritize recall over precision.

In EXPII, we use the gain ratio metric [26]. This metric, which is commonly used for ranking ML features, is a modification of the information gain metric, aimed at reducing bias on multi-valued features.

In EXPIII, we define precision and recall around a project. This is in contrast to EXPI, where these notions were defined around an ISO control. Let p be the project withheld from the set of all projects in a given round of leave-one-out validation. We define (1) precision P^p as $TP/(TP + FP)$ and (2) recall R^p as $TP/(TP + FN)$, where TP is the number of relevant ISO controls correctly predicted as such for project p, FP is the number of ISO controls that are not relevant to project p but are incorrectly predicted as being relevant, and FN is the number of relevant ISO controls incorrectly predicted as not being relevant to project p. These precision and recall metrics are used for measuring overall accuracy at a project level.

6   Results

In this section, we answer the RQs of Sect. 5.1 based on the results of our case study.

6.1   RQ1

Table 2 shows the results of EXPI, described in Sect. 5.4. Specifically, the table reports the average precision and recall – average P^c and R^c, defined in Sect. 5.5, across all ISO controls – of the six alternative ML classification algorithms considered.

As we argued previously, in our application context, recall has priority over precision. The results of Table 2 thus clearly suggest that J48, which yields an average recall of 94.95% and average precision of 65.90%, is the best choice among the ML classification algorithm considered. For all classification algorithms, including J48, handling imbalance via CSL leads to substantially more accurate classification, when compared to doing so via SMOTE. When J48 is applied alongside CSL with a cost ratio of 12 to 1 for false negatives versus false positives (see Sect. 5.4), the optimal hyper-parameters are as follows: *pruning confidence = 0.001* and *minimal number of instances per leaf = 7.*

Table 2. Comparison of the average precision and recall of different ML classification algorithms with optimized hyper-parameters.

Algorithm	CSL		SMOTE	
	P^c (avg.)	R^c (avg.)	P^c (avg.)	R^c (avg.)
J48	65.90	**94.95**	77.11	78.15
CART	55.11	92.42	76.03	64.20
JRip	64.32	91.35	74.68	79.49
PART	69.19	92.89	73.63	76.74
Logistic regression	64.32	51.54	68.77	58.91
Naive Bayes	33.35	61.59	17.02	50.93

> *The answer to* **RQ1** *is that* J48 combined with CSL leads to the most accurate classification. Using this combination, we obtained an average recall of 94.95% and average precision of 65.90% in our case study.

We answer RQ2 and RQ3 using J48, CSL, and the best hyper-parameter values mentioned above.

6.2   RQ2

As explained in EXPII of Sect. 5.4, we use gain ratio for estimating the importance of our features (Table 1). Based on the gain-ratio scores of the features across all the ISO-control classifiers, we make the following observations:

1. There are 12 vulnerabilities that have a zero gain ratio in all the classifiers. A subsequent investigation revealed that the vulnerabilities in question are not present in any of the past projects. We excluded these vulnerabilities from the dataset. The impact of this exclusion on precision and recall is negligible.

2. With the above 12 vulnerabilities removed, we observed that different ISO-control classifiers use different but overlapping subsets of features. This indicates that the decision about the relevance of different ISO controls is influenced by different factors. The feature subsets were picked automatically by J48's internal feature selection mechanism as implemented in Weka (this mechanism is also based on gain ratio).

In light of the second observation above, we answer RQ2 by measuring the overall importance of the features across all the classifiers. To do so, we first aggregated the top five most important features based on the rankings obtained from the different classifiers. We then computed the importance of a set F of features of the same type (e.g., vulnerability features: V1 to V154 in Table 1) as the percentage of the number of classifiers having some feature of F in their top five most important features. Table 3 shows the results. For example, all (100%) of the classifiers have some vulnerability in their top five most important features. The domain experts in our study stated that the results of Table 3 were consistent with their intuition about the most important factors in determining the relevance of ISO controls.

Table 3. Most important features for ISO-control classification.

Vulnerability	Risk	# of assets per category	Threat impact	Threat	Security answer	# of critical assets
100%	62.80%	16.00%	15.38%	12.80%	2.50%	1.20%

> *The answer to* **RQ2** *is that* overall and in descending order of magnitude, vulnerabilities, risks, the number of assets per category, threat impacts, threats, security answers, and the number of critical assets are the most influential feature groups. This finding is consistent with the intuition of the security specialists in our case study.

6.3   RQ3

Figure 4 summarizes through a box-plot the results of EXPIII, described in Sect. 5.4. Specifically, the boxplot shows the distributions of precision, P^p, and recall, R^p, as defined in Sect. 5.5. On average, our approach has a recall of 94.85% and precision of 67.38% when tasked with identifying the ISO controls relevant to a given project. The high recall suggests that the analysts can focus most of their attention on the recommended

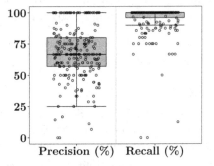

Fig. 4. Precision and recall distributions resulting from leave-one-out validation.

ISO controls, since the recommendations most likely contain all the relevant controls. The precision is reasonable too: On average, our approach recommends 9.4 ISO controls – both true and false positives – for a project. Of these, one can expect an average of 6.3 recommendations to be correct and 3.1 to be incorrect. The domain experts in our study confirmed that, given the small number of recommended ISO controls, they can vet the validity of the recommendations efficiently.

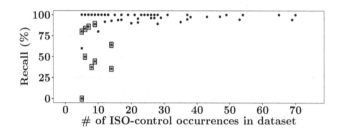

Fig. 5. Recall values of the ISO classifiers.

From Fig. 4, we further observe that the recall (R^p) for eight out of the total of 227 projects in our dataset is below 75%. Upon a follow-up investigation, we determined that the root cause for low recall in these projects is that the majority (and in two cases, all) of the ISO controls relevant to these projects have low prevalence in the dataset. In Fig. 5, we plot the recall of each ISO-control classifier (R^c) against the prevalence of the respective ISO control in the dataset. The ten datapoints encircled by □ represent the ISO controls that bring about low recall in the above-mentioned eight projects. A complementary insight from Fig. 4 is that recall is highly stable for those ISO controls that occur ≥ 15 in our dataset. As noted previously, handling less frequent ISO controls requires complementary techniques and is the subject of future work.

With regard to execution time, we make the following remarks: Generating J48 classification models for all the ISO controls subject to our experiments took 215 s in total; this gives an average training time of 2.8 s per ISO control. With the classifiers built, issuing recommendations for a given project takes an average of 1.7 s. These results suggest that our approach is scalable.

> *The answer to* **RQ3** *is that,* based on our case study results, our approach shows promise in terms of usefulness. In particular, our approach has a high recall (94.85%) and acceptable precision (67.38%) in identifying the ISO controls relevant to a security assessment project. Further, the execution times for training and classification are small. This suggests that our approach will scale to larger datasets.

7   Threats to Validity

The validity considerations most relevant to our work are construct and external validity, as we discuss below.

Construct Validity: Our evaluation metrics are scoped to the security controls for which there are at least five occurrences in the historical data. Below this threshold, applying ML is unlikely to be meaningful. Our evaluation examines whether ML is a suitable technique for our analytical purpose only when ML is applicable. Other techniques – not explored in this paper – are required for dealing with the security controls to which ML cannot be meaningfully applied.

External Validity: Generalizability is an important concern for any single case study, including the one in this paper. While the historical information we draw on for learning is aligned with commonly used ISO standards and is thus representative of a broader set of security assessment practices in industry, additional case studies are essential for examining whether our approach remains effective in other application contexts. In particular, the nature and source of security controls in other contexts and how accurately the pertinence of these controls can be determined through automation requires further investigation.

8   Conclusion

In this paper, we proposed an approach based on machine learning for assisting analysts with the task of deciding what security controls are relevant to a given system and context. This task is an important prerequisite for the proper elaboration of security requirements in the early stages of development. We evaluated our approach using real security assessment data from the banking domain. The results suggest that our approach provides effective decision support for security controls whose application is not too rare in the existing data. For these controls, our approach yielded an average recall of $\approx 95\%$ and average precision of $\approx 67\%$. As far as we are aware, we are the first to have applied machine learning for supporting the selection of security controls.

In the future, we would like to study whether complementary techniques such as case-based reasoning can be utilized for handling security controls with too few occurrences in the existing data. Another important future direction is to provide decision support for the identification of threats and vulnerabilities. Broadening our approach to cover these aspects requires going beyond the structured assessment information that is stored according to a pre-defined schema. In particular, we will need to additionally consider and extract security-related information from textual development artifacts, e.g., system and asset descriptions. Finally, we would like to conduct a qualitative evaluation of the interpretable machine-learning models in our current case study, and further perform new case studies to investigate the usefulness of our approach in domains other than banking.

Acknowledgments. Financial support for this work was provided by the Alphonse Weicker Foundation.

References

1. Batista, G.E., et al.: A study of the behavior of several methods for balancingmachine learning training data. ACM SIGKDD Explor. Newslett. **6**, 20–29 (2004)
2. Breiman, L., et al.: Classification and Regression Trees. Wadsworth International Group, Belmont (1984)
3. Casamayor, A., et al.: Identification of non-functional requirements in textual specifications: a semi-supervised learning approach. IST **52**(4), 436–445 (2010)
4. Chawla, N.V., et al.: SMOTE: synthetic minority over-sampling technique. JAIR **16**, 321–357 (2002)
5. Cohen, W.W.: Fast effective rule induction. In: ICML 1995 (1995)
6. Dalpiaz, F., Paja, E., Giorgini, P.: Security Requirements Engineering: Designing Secure Socio-Technical Systems. MIT Press, Cambridge (2016)
7. Dowd, M., et al.: The Art of Software Security Assessment: Identifying and Preventing Software Vulnerabilities. Pearson Education, London (2006)
8. Elkan, C.: The foundations of cost-sensitive learning. In: IJCAI 2001 (2001)
9. Frank, E., Witten, I.H.: Generating accurate rule sets without global optimization. In: ICML 1998 (1998)
10. Furnell, S.: End-user security culture: a lesson that will never be learnt? Comput. Fraud Secur. **2008**, 6–9 (2008)
11. Hall, M., et al.: The WEKA data mining software: an update. ACM SIGKDD Explor. Newslett. **11**, 10–18 (2009)
12. Ionita, D., Wieringa, R.: Web-based collaborative security requirements elicitation. In: REFSQ Workshops (2016)
13. ISO/IEC 27002:2005 Code of Practice for Information Security Controls. ISO Standard (2005)
14. ISO/IEC 27000:2018 Information Security Management Systems. ISO Standard (2018)
15. John, G.H., Langley, P.: Estimating continuous distributions in Bayesian classifiers. In: UAI 1995 (1995)
16. Jufri, M.T., et al.: Risk-assessment based academic information system security policy using octave allegro and ISO 27002. In: ICIC 2017 (2017)
17. Kurtanović, Z., Maalej, W.: Mining user rationale from software reviews. In: RE 2017 (2017)
18. le Cessie, S., van Houwelingen, J.C.: Ridge estimators in logistic regression. Appl. Stat. **41**(1), 191–201 (1992)
19. Li, T.: Identifying security requirements based on linguistic analysis and machine learning. In: APSEC 2017 (2017)
20. Meier, J.D., et al.: Improving web application security: threats and countermeasures. Technical report, Microsoft (2012)
21. Mitchell, T.M.: Machine learning and data mining. Commun. ACM **42**(11), 30 (1999)
22. Myagmar, S., et al.: Threat modeling as a basis for security requirements. In: SREIS 2005 (2005)
23. Nasrabadi, N.M.: Pattern recognition and machine learning. J. Electron. Imaging **16**(4), 049901 (2007)

24. NIST Special Publication 800–30: Guide for Conducting Risk Assessments. NIST Standard (2012)
25. OSA: Open Security Architecture. http://www.opensecurityarchitecture.org. Accessed Sep 2018
26. Quinlan, J.R.: Induction of decision trees. Mach. Learn. **1**(1), 81–106 (1986)
27. Quinlan, R.: C4.5: Programs for Machine Learning. Morgan Kaufmann, Burlington (1993)
28. Rodeghero, P., et al.: Detecting user story information in developer-client conversations to generate extractive summaries. In: ICSE 2017 (2017)
29. Schmitt, C., Liggesmeyer, P.: A model for structuring and reusing security requirements sources and security requirements. In: REFSQ Workshops (2015)
30. Sihwi, S.W., et al.: An expert system for risk assessment of information system security based on ISO 27002. In: ICKEA 2016 (2016)
31. Sindre, G., Opdahl, A.L.: Eliciting security requirements with misuse cases. REJ **10**, 34–44 (2005)
32. Türpe, S.: The trouble with security requirements. In: RE 2017 (2017)

Is the SAFE Approach Too Simple for App Feature Extraction? A Replication Study

Faiz Ali Shah$^{(\boxtimes)}$, Kairit Sirts, and Dietmar Pfahl

Institute of Computer Science, University of Tartu, Tartu, Estonia
{faiz.ali.shah,kairit.sirts,dietmar.pfahl}@ut.ee

Abstract. [**Context and motivation**] Automatic extraction and analysis of app features from user reviews is helpful for software developers to better understand users perceptions of delivered app features. Recently, a rule-based approach called SAFE was proposed to automatically extract app features from user reviews. SAFE was reported to obtain superior performance in terms of precision and recall over previously proposed techniques. However, the procedure used to evaluate SAFE was in part subjective and not repeatable and thus the whole evaluation might not be reliable. [**Question/problem**] The goal of our study is to perform an external replication of the SAFE evaluation using an objective and repeatable approach. [**Principal ideas/results**] To this end, we first implemented SAFE and checked the correctness of our implementation on the set of app descriptions that were used and published by the authors of the original study. We applied our SAFE implementation to eight review datasets (six app review datasets, one laptop review dataset, one restaurant review dataset) and evaluated its performance against manually annotated feature terms. Our results suggest that the precision of the SAFE approach is strongly influenced by the density of the annotated app features in a review dataset. Overall, we obtained an average precision and recall of 0.120 and 0.539, respectively which is lower than the performance reported in the original SAFE study. [**Contribution**] We performed an unbiased and reproducible evaluation of the SAFE approach for user reviews. We make our implementation and all datasets used for the evaluation available for replication by others.

Keywords: App feature extraction · SAFE approach ·
App review mining · Review summarization

1 Introduction

User feedback is an important source of information for software developers to enhance software quality [1]. In the context of mobile applications, i.e., *apps*, app marketplaces such as AppStore and PlayStore have become useful channels distributing millions of apps to their users. These marketplaces allow users to

© Springer Nature Switzerland AG 2019
E. Knauss and M. Goedicke (Eds.): REFSQ 2019, LNCS 11412, pp. 21–36, 2019.
https://doi.org/10.1007/978-3-030-15538-4_2

submit feedback in the form of reviews. User reviews contain valuable information such as feature evaluation, feature requests or bug reports that is helpful for developers for improving their apps [9]. However, the enormous volume of reviews received every day for a popular app make the manual analysis of these reviews impractical. Earlier studies have performed automatic analysis of user reviews to find out new app features requested by users [7] or to discover the sentiment of app features extracted from user reviews [2,3,13]. One major challenge in these studies has been the automatic extraction of app features from user reviews which is difficult for several reasons. First, there is great variability in how users express identical features and secondly, review texts often contain non-standard language such as slang, typos, and incorrect grammar.

Several approaches have been proposed to extract app features automatically from app user reviews. These approaches include topic models [3], set of patterns/rules [2,5], and supervised sequence tagging models [12]. The recently proposed rule-based approach SAFE [5] uses 18 Part-of-Speech (POS) patterns and five sentence patterns for automatically extracting app features from app descriptions and user reviews. Johann et al. reported the precision and recall of SAFE to be 0.559 and 0.434, respectively, for app feature extraction from app descriptions which is superior over the technique of Harman et al. [4]—an earlier rule-based approach developed for the same purpose. Moreover, SAFE was also reported to outperform the topic-modeling approach of Guzman et al. [3] for the extraction of app features from user reviews with a reported precision and recall of 0.239 and 0.709, respectively [5].

To evaluate the SAFE performance for app descriptions in their original study, Johann et al. created a labeled dataset, in which app features have been manually annotated. However, they did not create such a dataset to evaluate the performance of extracting app features from user reviews. Instead, the authors of the original SAFE study used a coding tool that showed a review text along with a list of SAFE-extracted app feature terms to coders who then had to decide whether the extracted app features were true or false. In case any true app features had not been extracted by SAFE (i.e., false negatives) from a user review, coders had to add them manually by writing them in a corresponding text box. This procedure to spot false negatives (FNs) is subjective and could introduce researcher bias because coders might have accidentally skipped entering some true app features not extracted by SAFE, thus lowering the number of false negatives and thus boosting performance. In summary, the evaluation of the SAFE approach for user reviews as conducted in the original study has the following two issues: (a) the evaluation is not repeatable because the true app features in the user reviews were not reported and (b) the evaluation procedure is potentially biased as it bases the identification of true and false positives on subjective decisions of coders after the list of SAFE-extracted app features has been shown to them. In order to validate the performance of the SAFE, we conducted an external replication [6] of the SAFE evaluation on user reviews, using an unbiased and repeatable procedure. Our goal is to answer the following research question:

RQ: What is the expected performance of SAFE on user reviews?

This research question had to be answered in two steps. Since exact implementation of the SAFE approach has not been published, we first implemented the SAFE method and validated our implementation using the annotated app description dataset made publicly available by the authors of the original SAFE study. This lead us to the first sub-question of RQ.

RQ-A: Does our implementation of the SAFE approach have the same performance as the original implementation of the SAFE approach when applied to app descriptions?

After confirming that our SAFE implementation on the app description dataset achieves a performance close to the one reported in the original SAFE study, we applied SAFE to the following eight annotated review datasets: GUZMAN dataset[1], GUZMAN+ dataset (an extension of the GUZMAN dataset), and four dataset variants derived from the SHAH dataset [14], and LAPTOP and RESTAURANT review datasets[2]. In the rest of this paper, we use the word "features" to collectively refer the features of a software app, laptop product, or restaurant services. Features contained in these review datasets have been manually annotated by humans. The application of our SAFE implementation to these datasets answered the second sub-question of RQ.

RQ-B: Does our implementation of the SAFE approach have the same performance as the original implementation of the SAFE approach when applied to review datasets?

The evaluation results show that the SAFE performance in terms of f1-score for all review datasets is lower than the performance reported in the original SAFE study. Our analyses further reveal that the precision of the SAFE approach is influenced by the density of true features in a review dataset.

The rest of the paper is structured as follows. In Sect. 2, we provide a brief introduction of SAFE approach. Section 3 describes our methodology that include details of our SAFE implementation and its validation, followed by the description of the evaluation method and characteristics of four annotated review datasets. Section 4 discusses the results. In Sect. 5, threats to validity are examined. Section 6 summarizes the previous work related to our study. Conclusions are presented in Sect. 7.

2   SAFE Approach

The SAFE approach is a rule-based method recently proposed by Johann et al. [5] for the extraction of app features from both app descriptions and user reviews. The authors of the SAFE approach performed a manual analysis of descriptions of 100 apps in Google Play Store and identified frequent textual patterns which are used to denote app features of these apps. The 18 Part-of-Speech (POS)

---

[1] The dataset was obtained from the authors of study [3].

[2] http://alt.qcri.org/semeval2014/task4/index.php?id=data-and-tools.

patterns found in the app descriptions are shown in Table 1 together with their frequencies. In addition, the authors also identified five sentence patterns where the app features are mentioned as enumeration, conjunctions and feature identifiers [5]. The exact specification of the five sentence patterns was not presented in the original study. We will describe our interpretation of these patterns in Subsect. 3.1 where we describe our implementation of the SAFE approach.

SAFE first applies a number of pre-processing steps that remove sentences containing URLs, quotations, email addresses, and explanations (text between brackets). Then some parts of the remaining sentences are removed, including subordinate clauses, stop words, bullet points, and symbols such as "*" or"#". Then SAFE patterns are applied to sentences for the extraction of 2-to-4-word candidate app features. In the final step, the list of candidate app features is cleaned by removing duplicates and noise such as identical words pairs, e.g., "document document", which may be extracted using a POS pattern ⟨NOUN-NOUN⟩.

Table 1. List of SAFE POS patterns with frequency of occurrence [5]

#	POS pattern	Freq	#	POS pattern	Freq
1	⟨Noun-Noun⟩	183	10	⟨Adjective-Adjective-Noun⟩	20
2	⟨Verb-Noun⟩	122	11	⟨Noun-Preposition-Noun⟩	18
3	⟨Adjective-Noun⟩	119	12	⟨Verb-Determiner-Noun⟩	14
4	⟨Noun-Conjunction-Noun⟩	98	13	⟨Verb-Noun-Preposition-Noun⟩	14
5	⟨Adjective-Noun-Noun⟩	70	14	⟨Adjective-Noun-Noun-Noun⟩	12
6	⟨Noun-Noun-Noun⟩	35	15	⟨Adjective-Conjunction-Adjective⟩	12
7	⟨Verb-Pronoun-Noun⟩	29	16	⟨Verb-Preposition-Adjective-Noun⟩	11
8	⟨Verb-Pronoun-Noun⟩	29	17	⟨Verb-Pronoun-Adjective-Noun⟩	11
9	⟨Verb-Adjective-Noun⟩	26	18	⟨Noun-Conjunction-Noun-Noun⟩	10

3 Research Method

In this section, we present the main elements of the research method of our replication study. In Subsect. 3.1, we describe the details of our SAFE implementation. In Subsect. 3.2, we describe how we match SAFE-extracted features with true features. In Subsect. 3.3, we present the characteristics of the annotated review datasets that we used for our unbiased and repeatable evaluation of the SAFE approach. Finally, in Subsect. 3.4, we present the experimental setup of our study.

3.1 SAFE Implementation

Since the SAFE implementation used by the authors of the original study is not publicly available, we created our own implementation of the SAFE approach[3]

---

[3] https://github.com/faizalishah/SAFE_REPLICATION.

based on the information detailed in [5]. Like the original study, we used the Python programming language and the Natural Language ToolKit (NLTK)[4] for SAFE implementation. However, since not all details of the implementation of the SAFE approach have been published in the original study, we had to make some decisions on our own. The details of those decisions are discussed in the following paragraphs.

Table 2. List of SAFE sentence patterns [5]

#	Sentence pattern
1	⟨Noun-<u>Conj</u>-Noun: Noun⟩
2	⟨Verb|Noun: (Noun-<u>Comma</u>)$^+$-<u>Conj</u>-Noun⟩
3	⟨Verb|Noun-<u>Conj</u>-Noun|Verb: Noun-<u>Conj</u>-Noun⟩
4	<u>⟨Verb-Noun-Noun-to-Adv</u>-Verb-<u>Conj</u>-Verb-on-Noun-of-Noun-including
	: (Noun-Noun-<u>Comma</u>)$^+$-Noun-<u>Conj</u>-Noun⟩
5	⟨Verb-(<u>Comma</u>-Verb)$^+$-<u>Conj</u>-Verb-Noun: <u>IN</u> (Noun-<u>Comma</u>)$^+$-<u>Conj</u>-Noun-Noun⟩

After performing the pre-processing steps as described in the original study, the SAFE implementation applies linguistic patterns to extract the candidate app features. Following the original study, we first apply the sentence patterns and then the POS patterns. Since the original study does not state in which order the individual POS patterns shall be applied, we decided to apply them in the order in which they are presented in Table 1 (see Sect. 2). Also, the original SAFE study does not explicitly state the format of the sentence patterns. In Table 2, we present the list of sentence patterns used in our SAFE implementation for extracting app features.

The syntax of the patterns is following that of regular expressions. Once a sentence pattern finds a match in the analyzed text, it extracts the app features and represents them using one of the POS patterns. This might require deletion of words found in the matching pattern. For example, conjunctions and commas are always dropped. We indicate in Table 2 the words that are deleted with an underscore.

All patterns have the format ⟨LeftTerm1-Conj1-RightTerm1 : LeftTerm2-Conj2-RightTerm2⟩. The colon symbol ":" denotes where the right-hand side of the first conjunction ends and the left-hand side of the subsequent conjunction begins. Based on the sentence pattern, the following POS patterns are then generated by taking the cross-product of the left-hand and right-hand terms of each conjunction, i.e., the following set of POS patterns will be generated: ⟨LeftTerm1, LeftTerm2⟩, ⟨LeftTerm1, RightTerm2⟩, ⟨RightTerm1, LeftTerm2⟩, and ⟨RightTerm1, LeftTerm2⟩. In the first two sentence patterns Conj1 and Conj2 are empty, respectively. In those cases, the left-hand and right-hand

---

[4] https://www.nltk.org/.

terms of the missing conjunction fall together and the cross-product is simplified accordingly.

An additional complication is introduced by the fact that several of the 18 POS patterns are overlapping. For instance, the shorter POS pattern ⟨Verb-Noun⟩ may overlap with some of the longer POS patterns such as ⟨Verb-Noun-Noun⟩ or ⟨Verb-Noun-Preposition-Noun⟩. Thus, applying these patterns in a sequential order would extract overlapping candidate app features. Since we do not know how this is handled in the original SAFE study, in our implementation, when the overlapping features are extracted from a review sentence, only the longest feature term is preserved. Since we only preserve the longest feature terms, the results of feature extraction would not depend on the order in which POS patterns were applied. Moreover, the original version of the SAFE implementation uses a custom list of stop words which is not publicly available. Therefore, we use our own list of custom stop words for our implementation[5].

3.2   Strategy for Matching SAFE-Extracted and True Features

To compute the performance (precision and recall) of our SAFE implementation on an evaluation set, the number of true positives (TPs), false positives (FPs), and false negatives (FNs) must be counted by matching the SAFE-extracted features against the true features (i.e., those features that were labeled by humans). However, the original SAFE study does not give information about how exactly the extracted and true features were matched to count TPs, FPs, and FNs.

In our study we adopted the token-based subset matching strategy for evaluating our SAFE implementation. In token-based subset matching strategy, an extracted feature is counted as true positive (TP) either when the extracted feature words are a subset of the true feature words or the words of a true feature are a subset of the extracted feature words. In addition, the extracted feature must appear in the same review sentence in which the true feature was annotated. For instance, when the extracted app feature is "create document" and the true app feature annotated in a review text is "create new document" then the extracted app feature "create document" would be counted as a TP because the extracted app feature word-set {create, document} is a subset of the true app feature word-set {create, new, document}. In contrast to this, when the extracted app feature is "create document" from a review sentence but the app feature "create document" has not been annotated in the same review sentence then the extracted app feature "create document" would be counted as a false positive (FP). Finally, the true features, which were not matched with any extracted features will be counted as false negatives (FNs).

We consider this matching strategy justified, because the annotation of true app features in a review text is to a certain degree subjective and it would be too demanding to expect from an extraction method to identify the exact same words as app features as were annotated in the evaluation dataset. The

---

[5] https://github.com/faizalishah/SAFE_REPLICATION/blob/master/SAFE/List_StopWords.

difficulty to annotate identical app features in one and the same user review by two or more annotators has been observed, for example by Guzman et al. [3] who reported an agreement of 53% between two coders. We had a similar experience when annotating our SHAH user review dataset [14]. We should not assume that automatic app feature extraction works better than human annotators do.

3.3   User Review Datasets

In the original SAFE study, no evaluation set was created for the evaluation of SAFE on user reviews. This makes the evaluation of SAFE on user reviews not reproducible even if the original SAFE implementation would be available. Thus, to be able to perform a reproducible evaluation of the SAFE approach, we had to find user reviews in which app features have been annotated. We use four English review datasets that are publicly available and have been used in previous studies, i.e., GUZMAN, SHAH, LAPTOP, and RESTAURANT. The review datasets vary with regards to several characteristics, i.e., domain, annotation guidelines used, the number of annotators, the number of review sentences, and the number of annotated features. This diversity of datasets enables us to analyse the performance of the SAFE approach under different viewpoints and, hence, to obtain a more reliable evaluation for user reviews. We should point out that two of the review datasets, LAPTOP and RESTAURANT, do not contain reviews from app users. We included those review datasets because the SAFE patterns are purely syntactic and thus should not be sensitive to the choice of domain – be it software apps (GUZMAN and SHAH datasets), products (LAPTOP), or services (RESTAURANT).

In Table 3, we characterize each review dataset based on the following information:

(a) the total number of reviews;
(b) the total number of sentences in all reviews;
(c) the total number of 2-to-4-word annotated features;
(d) the density of 2-to-4-word annotated features over review sentences;
(e) the total number of annotated features;
(f) the density of all annotated features over review sentences.

GUZMAN REVIEW DATASETS. The original GUZMAN dataset (See footnote 1) was used as an evaluation set in the study conducted by Guzman et al. [3]. It contains annotated app reviews of seven apps belonging to six different categories: Angry Birds (Games category), DropBox and EverNote (Productivity category), TripAdvisor (Travel category), PicsArt (Photography category), Pinterest (Social category) and WhatsApp (Communication category).[6] In Table 3, we do not show the data of individual app categories but the aggregated summary of the GUZMAN dataset.

According to Guzman et al., the dataset initially consisted of 2800 user reviews (i.e., 400 user reviews per app). After annotation by human coders it

---

[6] Review titles with their annotated app features were removed for our study.

Table 3. Characteristics of the annotated review datasets

Dataset	#Reviews	#Sentences	#2-4-word features	2-4-word features density	#All features	All features density
GUZMAN	1479	4367	1421	.325	2350	.538
GUZMAN+	2800	8267	1421	.172	2350	.284
SHAH-I	3500	5970	352	.059	644	.108
SHAH-II	3500	5970	441	.074	756	.127
SHAH-I ∪ SHAH-II	3500	5970	575	.096	1017	.170
SHAH-I ∩ SHAH-II	3500	5970	242	.041	419	.070
LAPTOP	-	3845	1134	.295	3012	.783
RESTAURANT	-	3841	1157	.301	4827	1.25

turned out that there were 1321 user reviews left without annotation of a single app feature. Only those 1479 user reviews containing at least one annotated app feature were included in the published GUZMAN dataset and used for evaluation. The removed 1321 user reviews were not made publicly available.

In the context of Guzman et al.'s original study, it might have made sense to only use reviews containing annotated app features for evaluation purposes but in a real-world setting, taking a random sample of user reviews from App Store would normally be a mix of reviews mentioning app features (related to specific app features) and reviews that are praising or criticizing the app/versions/updates as a whole but not mentioning any specific app features. In order to also capture the real-world situation in our analysis, we artificially created a new version of the GUZMAN dataset which we named GUZMAN+. The GUZMAN+ dataset contains both types of reviews, i.e., with and without app features, and is thus comparable to other review datasets used in our analysis. Since we did not know which reviews were removed from the original GUZMAN dataset, we simply randomly sampled 1321 reviews without app features from the annotated SHAH dataset and added them to the annotated GUZMAN reviews. As expected, the ratio between number of app features and number of sentences in GUZMAN+ (see Table 3) goes down by almost 50% as compared to the original GUZMAN dataset.

SHAH REVIEW DATASETS. In the context of a previous study we created the SHAH dataset [14]. All reviews in the SHAH dataset were independently annotated by two coders.[7] The Dice coefficient score between the two annotation sets was low (i.e., 0.28), indicating a low agreement between the two coders. Because of that, we decided to use four different versions of the SHAH dataset in this study, i.e., **(1)** SHAH-I, **(2)** SHAH-II, **(3)** SHAH-I ∪ SHAH-II, and **(4)** SHAH-I ∩ SHAH-II. Among the four versions of the SHAH dataset, SHAH-I and SHAH-II contain the annotations of only the first and only the second coder, respectively. The

---

[7] Both coders were software engineering bachelors students at the University of Tartu.

SHAH-I ∪ SHAH-II dataset contains the annotations of both coder 1 and coder 2. In the case of overlapping annotations, only the longer annotation was retained. Finally, the SHAH-I ∩ SHAH-II dataset only contains the annotations annotated by both coders. As we did for the SHAH-I ∪ SHAH-II dataset, when annotations were overlapping we only retained the longer annotation. From all SHAH datasets we removed all app features that were referring to the app itself [14].

The summary statistics of all four versions of the SHAH dataset are shown in Table 3. Overall, in comparison to the GUZMAN, LAPTOP, and RESTAURANT datasets, the SHAH dataset contains a smaller number of app features. Among the four versions of the SHAH dataset, as expected, the SHAH-I ∪ SHAH-II dataset contains the highest number of app features. However, even in this dataset the ratio between the number of app features and the number of sentences (i.e., the features density) is clearly lower than in the other review datasets.

LAPTOP AND RESTAURANT REVIEW DATASETS. The LAPTOP and RESTAURANT review datasets (See footnote 2) are standard benchmark datasets contributed by the SEMEVAL research community.[8] Both datasets have been used in studies that aimed at performing the task of feature extraction (called "aspect terms") from user reviews and its evaluation [8,11]. Both datasets are distributed in predefined training and test splits, which is relevant in the context of machine learning based methods. For our purpose, we merged the training and test sets into single LAPTOP and RESTAURANT datasets, respectively.

The characteristics of the LAPTOP and RESTAURANT datasets in Table 3 show that the ratio between the number of all annotated features and the number of sentences is clearly higher than for the app review datasets. The ratio between the number of 2-to-4-word features and the number of sentences, however, follows the same pattern as most app review datasets with an exception of the GUZMAN dataset which has a comparable ratio.

3.4   Experimental Setup

This section explains the settings used for the SAFE approach evaluation. To answer sub-question RQ-A of our research question RQ, we analyse the performance of our SAFE implementation (as described in Sect. 3.1) when applied to the ten annotated app descriptions made available in the original SAFE study. If the performance of our SAFE implementation in terms of precision, recall, and f1-score is comparable to that reported in the original study, we consider our SAFE implementation to be suitable for tackling sub-question RQ-B of our research question RQ. To answer RQ-B, we apply our SAFE implementation to eight annotated review datasets (see Table 3). The performance measures (precision, recall and F1-score) of SAFE are computed on each review dataset for the annotated 2-to-4-word features and for all annotated features using the token-based subset matching strategy (see Sect. 3.2).

---

[8] http://alt.qcri.org/semeval2018/.

4   Results and Discussion

In this section, we present the results to our research question RQ in two steps. First we present and discuss the results related to sub-question RQ-A, then we present and discuss the results to sub-question RQ-B.

4.1   Validation of SAFE Implementation (RQ-A)

The correctness of our SAFE implementation can be validated by applying it on the same evaluation set used in the original SAFE study. We contacted the main author of the original study and learned that in the original study, only the dataset containing the app descriptions had annotated app features but not the dataset containing the app reviews. Since the authors of the original study shared their annotated dataset of app descriptions, we were at least able to apply our SAFE implementation to the same app description dataset and thus validate our implementation.

Table 4 shows the evaluation results on the annotated app description dataset of our SAFE implementation (on the right) as well as the evaluation results reported by Johann et al. (on the left). Our SAFE implementation achieves exactly the same precision and recall as the original SAFE implementation only for one app description (Google Docs). On two app descriptions (Forest and Dropbox), we achieve higher precision and recall than the original SAFE implementation. For Google Drive app description, we achieve identical recall but higher precision compared to the original SAFE implementation. On the rest of the six app descriptions, we obtain lower precision and recall than the original implementation of SAFE. These differences in performance between the two implementations might be related to the unspecified details brought out in Sect. 3.1. Additionally, there could be differences in matching the extracted app features with true app features that can lead to different results (see Sect. 3.2).

Based on the results of individual app descriptions we cannot claim that our SAFE implementation is the same as the original SAFE method. However, on average over all app descriptions, our SAFE implementation achieves only slightly lower precision and recall than the original SAFE implementation. Since based on the average f1-score the difference between the two implementations is only 0.011, we believe that we can still perform useful analyses with our implementation.

4.2   Evaluation of SAFE Approach (RQ-B)

In this section, we answer the sub-question RQ-B of our research question RQ by comparing the performance reported in the original SAFE study with the performance achieved with our implementation of the SAFE approach on the eight annotated datasets described in Sect. 3.3.

The performance of our implementation of the SAFE approach is presented in Table 5. We evaluated the SAFE approach separately against 2-to-4-word features and against all features. The left-hand side of the table shows the SAFE

Table 4. Comparison of results obtained with the original SAFE implementation and our SAFE implementation on app description dataset.

App name	Original SAFE implementation			Our SAFE implementation		
	Precision	Recall	F1 score	Precision	Recall	F1 score
Forest: Stay focused, be present	.462	.400	.429	.636	.467	.538
Yahoo Mail	.737	.389	.509	.680	.436	.531
Printer Pro	.214	.250	.231	.190	.333	.242
Gmail	.714	.400	.513	.611	.524	.564
Google Drive	.875	.389	.538	1.0	.389	.560
CloudApp Mobile	.722	.481	.578	.478	.423	.449
Google Docs	.667	.462	.545	.667	.462	.545
Dropbox	.300	.300	.300	.400	.333	.364
Fantastical 2 for iPhone	.500	.697	.582	.302	.500	.377
iTranslate Voice	.500	.278	.357	.316	.286	.300
Average	**.559**	**.434**	**.458**	**.528**	**.415**	**.447**

performance evaluated for 2-to-4 word features. The right-hand side of the table presents the SAFE performance evaluated for all features.

The original SAFE study used only 2-to-4-word app features for evaluation since the POS and sentence patterns defined in the SAFE approach can only extract app features composed of two to four words. The original study reported precision and recall of 0.239 and 0.709, respectively, for the SAFE approach [5]. As shown in Table 5, the performance of our SAFE implementation on each of our evaluation datasets when evaluating on 2-to-4-word features varies but is consistently lower than the performance reported in the original study (average precision is 0.120, average recall is 0.539, and average fl-score is 0.184).

When comparing the precision of our SAFE implementation with that reported in the original study, one observes that the evaluation on three of our datasets, i.e., GUZMAN, LAPTOP, and RESTAURANT, is relatively close to the reported precision of 0.239 in the original study. The reason for this phenomenon could be that the density score of the annotated 2-to-4-word features is clearly higher for these three review datasets as compared to the other five review datasets. The sensitivity of SAFE precision to features density is also clearly visible when we look at the evaluation results using all annotated features (right-hand side of Table 5). Also, the fact that the evaluation results when using all features has consistently higher precision values supports the hypothesis that higher features density yields higher precision when using the SAFE approach.

When looking at the recall values, the interpretation is less straightforward than for precision. The highest recall of 0.624 when evaluating on 2-to-4-word

Table 5. Evaluation of SAFE extracted features on annotated review datasets

Dataset	2-4 word features			All features		
	Precision	Recall	F1-score	Precision	Recall	F1-score
GUZMAN	.201	.462	.280	.317	.426	.363
GUZMAN+	.096	.462	.159	.151	.426	.223
SHAH-I	.056	.624	.103	.080	.463	.136
SHAH-II	.064	.544	.115	.090	.443	.149
SHAH-I ∪ SHAH-II	.084	.550	.146	.118	.433	.185
SHAH-I ∩ SHAH-II	.040	.612	.074	.055	.522	.099
LAPTOP	.208	.490	.292	.359	.319	.337
RESTAURANT	.211	.569	.308	.492	.318	.386
Average	**.120**	**.539**	**.184**	**.207**	**.419**	**.235**

app features is obtained for the SHAH-II dataset but it is still considerably lower than the recall of 0.709 reported in the original study. Also, when comparing the recall values across the app review datasets it seems that whenever precision is low (correlating with low app features density) recall is respectively higher. However, this observation can neither be made for the LAPTOP and RESTAURANT datasets nor for the GUZMAN+ dataset. While the obvious explanation for the capped GUZMAN+ recall of 0.462 is that due to the construction of GUZMAN+ it has exactly the same set of annotated app features as GUZMAN, it is less clear why the recall values for the LAPTOP and RESTAURANT datasets are still relatively high. We speculate that other factors than features density have an impact on recall, e.g., the nature of the annotation guidelines used and the subjective interpretation of the annotation guidelines by the coders.

When comparing the precision of 2-to-4-word features with the precision of all features, Table 5 shows that the precision values consistently improve while the recall values go down. This happens because in each dataset the set of 2-to-4-word features is a strict subset of all features. As a consequence, some of the extracted features counted as false positives (FPs) when evaluated against 2-to-4-word features might be counted as true positives (TPs) due to the subset matching strategy that we use to match the extracted features with the true features. The impact is stronger on review datasets where the number of annotated features is higher, such as RESTAURANT, LAPTOP, and GUZMAN.

Based on our analysis of the performance of the SAFE approach we can make several observations about its usefulness to developers who might wish to analyze reviews in order to better understand user needs. The first observation is that due to the purely syntactic-based extraction patterns defined in the SAFE approach, its applicability is not restricted to a specific domain. We have demonstrated this by including review datasets from other domains such as those represented by the LAPTOP and RESTAURANT datasets. Interestingly, the performance of the SAFE approach in terms of f1-score is better on the LAPTOP and RESTAURANT datasets when compared to five realistic app review datasets (i.e., GUZMAN+

and all SHAH datasets). As mentioned before, this seems to be due to the higher density of features in the LAPTOP and RESTAURANT datasets.

Johann et al. [5] comment their evaluation by writing:

> As for the accuracy and benchmark values, we refrain from claiming that these are exact values and we think that they are rather indicative. We think that the order of magnitude of precisions and recalls calculated, as well as the differences between the approaches is significant.

Although we were not able to demonstrate that our implementation exactly matches the one used in the original study, our evaluation results give a reason to suspect that the true estimates of precision and recall of the SAFE approach are in fact lower than suggested by Johann et al. This fact again raises the question of how useful can SAFE approach be for the developers just as it is. The problem with low precision even when the recall is relatively high is that the extracted features contain a lot of noise and if the system does not provide any ranking of "usefulness" over the extracted features, it will be very difficult to spot the useful info from the noise. As Johann et al. [5] themselves say when discussing their results:

> Nevertheless, we think that the achieved accuracy of SAFE—even if it out-performs other research approaches—is not good enough to be applied in practice. We think that a hybrid approach (a simple, pattern and similarity based as SAFE together with a machine learning approach) is probably the most appropriate. For instance, machine learning can be used to pre-filter and classify reviews before applying SAFE on them.

In addition to the idea of first classifying reviews or sentences before applying SAFE we would also propose another way that could potentially improve the usefulness of the SAFE method via machine learning. Assuming that the SAFE approach obtains reasonably high recall when extracting app features from app reviews, one could imagine training a classifier to learn to discriminate between correctly (TPs) and incorrectly (FPs) extracted app features. In such a way it might be possible to retain the high recall while improving the precision.

5 Threats to Validity

The main threat to the validity of our study is that we were not able to exactly replicate the evaluation results of our SAFE implementation on the app description dataset provided by the authors of [5]. This means that although we have carefully checked our implementation but our implementation of the SAFE approach is not exactly the same as used in the original study.

One likely reason for the differences in the performance measures is that we might have decided certain implementation details, which were not specified in the SAFE paper (described in Sect. 3.1), differently than the original authors. For instance, we might have interpreted the sentence patterns differently than intended by the original authors and thus implemented them differently. Similarly, the proposers of the SAFE approach use a custom list of stop words in their

SAFE implementation. This list has not been published. Thus, we had to define our own list of custom stop words and the impact of our choice on the achieved performance values is not known. We intend to make our implementation as well as the custom list of stop words publicly available so that others could replicate and validate our results.

The differences in performance measures might also stem from a different way of counting TPs, FPs and FNs. The authors of the original SAFE study do not explain the matching strategy (exact match or partial match) used to match the SAFE extracted app features against the true app features. In our study, we adopted token-based subset matching strategy for the evaluation of SAFE on user reviews. It is possible that in the original study, the matching was performed differently.

The validity of our results depends partly on the reliability of the annotations of the review datasets. Since we not only used our own annotations (i.e., datasets SHAH-I and SHAH-II) but applied SAFE implementation to other review datasets published in the literature; so we believe that the existing limitations of reliability for the mentioned tasks is not a major threat to validity of our results.

6   Related Work

Recently, Johann et al. proposed a rule-based approach called SAFE that uses POS and sentence patterns for extracting app features from app descriptions and user reviews [5]. The SAFE approach has achieved better performance over the technique of Guzman et al. [3]. However, some aspects of the implementation of the SAFE approach as well as some aspects of its evaluation on user reviews are nor precisely described in the original study. Therefore, we decided to conduct an external replication with a fully published replication package allowing others to reproduce our results.

Several other approaches to extract app features from app reviews have been proposed. We list some of them in the following.

The study of Guzman et al. [3] used an unsupervised LDA topic modeling approach for automatic extraction of app features from user reviews of seven apps (three from App Store and four from Play Store). The performance of the approach is evaluated by matching the extracted app features against the human labeled app features in their labeled dataset. In our study, we used the same labeled dataset (i.e., GUZMAN dataset) for evaluation purpose.

The study of Gu et al. [2] classifies review sentences into categories, such as feature evaluation, praise, feature requests, bug reports and others, and then app features are extracted using 26 manually designed rules only from those sentences that belong to the feature evaluation category. In comparison to the approach of Gu et al., the SAFE approach for app feature extraction is not limited to feature evaluation sentences and it can extract app features from sentences mentioning feature requests, opinions related to features, and bug reports related to features alike.

Keertipati et al. extracted nouns as candidate app features from app review sentences but they did not perform an evaluation to check whether the extracted app features actually represent true app features [7]. On the other hand, Vu et al.'s study [15] instead of directly extracting app features, extracted all potential keywords from user reviews and rank them based on the review rating and occurrence frequency.

In one of our own previous studies, we developed the prototype of a web-based tool to identify competing apps and to compare them based on the users' sentiments mentioned on the common set of app features [13]. This tool extracts two-word collocations as candidate app features without evaluating the extracted app features against true app features. Similar to the original study on the SAFE approach, the evaluation of the performance of the tool prototype with regards to app feature extraction performance was partly biased and subjective and thus not reproducible.

A recent study of Malik et al. [10] used syntactic relations between the features and opinion words for identification of "hot" app features from user review but the dataset used for the evaluation is not publicly available.

7   Conclusion

The SAFE approach is a recently proposed simple rule-based method for automatic extraction of app features from app descriptions and app reviews. For the evaluation of SAFE on app descriptions, the authors of the original SAFE study created and publicly shared an evaluation dataset. However, for evaluation on user reviews no evaluation dataset exists and the evaluation was instead performed using a coding tool. The procedure adopted for the evaluation of the SAFE approach on user reviews is subjective and might have suffered from researcher bias. Due to its subjective nature it is also not reproducible. Therefore, in this study, we performed an unbiased and reproducible evaluation of the SAFE approach with the goal to investigate the true performance of the SAFE approach when applied to user reviews.

We implemented the SAFE approach and once we had confirmed that our implementation achieves comparable average performance when applied to app descriptions as reported in the original study, we applied SAFE to eight different review datasets. The results show that the performance of the SAFE approach when evaluated against 2-to-4-word app features is clearly lower than the performance reported in the original SAFE study. Inspecting the characteristics of the used review datasets it became clear that the precision of the SAFE approach is strongly sensitive to the density of app features in the review datasets.

We conclude that due to very low precision and only moderate recall, SAFE is too simple to be useful in practice for extracting app features from app reviews. In order to make it usable in practice, methods, potentially involving machine learning, for improving the precision while retaining the recall should be studied.

Acknowledgment. We are grateful to Emitza Guzman and Christoph Stanik for sharing the datasets. This research was supported by the institutional research grant IUT20-55 of the Estonian Research Council and the Estonian Center of Excellence in ICT research (EXCITE).

References

1. Groen, E.C., et al.: The crowd in requirements engineering: the landscape and challenges. IEEE Softw. **34**(2), 44–52 (2017). https://doi.org/10.1109/MS.2017.33
2. Gu, X., Kim, S.: What parts of your apps are loved by users? In: 2015 30th IEEE/ACM International Conference on Automated Software Engineering (ASE), pp. 760–770, November 2015. https://doi.org/10.1109/ASE.2015.57
3. Guzman, E., Maalej, W.: How do users like this feature? A fine grained sentiment analysis of app reviews. In: 2014 IEEE 22nd International Requirements Engineering Conference (RE), pp. 153–162. IEEE (2014)
4. Harman, M., Jia, Y., Zhang, Y.: App store mining and analysis: MSR for app stores. In: Proceedings of the 9th IEEE Working Conference on Mining Software Repositories, MSR 2012, pp. 108–111. IEEE Press, Piscataway (2012). http://dl.acm.org/citation.cfm?id=2664446.2664461
5. Johann, T., Stanik, C., Maalej, W.: SAFE: a simple approach for feature extraction from app descriptions and app reviews. In: 2017 IEEE 25th International Requirements Engineering Conference (RE), pp. 21–30. IEEE, September 2017. https://doi.org/10.1109/RE.2017.71
6. Juristo, N., Gómez, O.S.: Replication of software engineering experiments. In: Meyer, B., Nordio, M. (eds.) LASER 2008-2010. LNCS, vol. 7007, pp. 60–88. Springer, Heidelberg (2012). https://doi.org/10.1007/978-3-642-25231-0_2
7. Keertipati, S., Savarimuthu, B.T.R., Licorish, S.A.: Approaches for prioritizing feature improvements extracted from app reviews. In: Proceedings of the 20th International Conference on Evaluation and Assessment in Software Engineering, p. 33. ACM (2016)
8. Liu, P., Joty, S., Meng, H.: Fine-grained opinion mining with recurrent neural networks and word embeddings. In: Proceedings of the 2015 Conference on Empirical Methods in Natural Language Processing, pp. 1433–1443 (2015)
9. Maalej, W., Nabil, H.: Bug report, feature request, or simply praise? On automatically classifying app reviews. In: Proceedings of RE 2015, pp. 116–125. IEEE, August 2015
10. Malik, H., Shakshuki, E.M., Yoo, W.S.: Comparing mobile apps by identifying 'Hot' features. Futur. Gener. Comput. Syst. (2018)
11. Poria, S., Cambria, E., Gelbukh, A.: Aspect extraction for opinion mining with a deep convolutional neural network. Knowl.-Based Syst. **108**, 42–49 (2016)
12. Sänger, M., et al.: Scare–the sentiment corpus of app reviews with fine-grained annotations in German. In: LREC (2016)
13. Shah, F.A., Sabanin, Y., Pfahl, D.: Feature-based evaluation of competing apps. In: Proceedings of the International Workshop on App Market Analytics - WAMA 2016. pp. 15–21. ACM Press, New York (2016). https://doi.org/10.1145/2993259.2993267
14. Shah, F.A., Sirts, K., Pfahl, D.: The impact of annotation guidelines and annotated data on extracting app features from app reviews. arXiv preprint arXiv:1810.05187 (2018)
15. Vu, P.M., Nguyen, T.T., Pham, H.V., Nguyen, T.T.: Mining user opinions in mobile app reviews: a keyword-based approach. In: Proceedings of ASE 2015, pp. 749–759. IEEE (2015)

Making Sense of Requirements

Enabling Users to Specify Correct Privacy Requirements

Manuel Rudolph$^{(\boxtimes)}$, Svenja Polst, and Joerg Doerr

Fraunhofer IESE, Kaiserslautern, Germany
{manuel.rudolph,svenja.polst,
joerg.doerr}@iese.fraunhofer.de

Abstract. Privacy becomes more and more important for users of digital services. Recent studies show that users are concerned about having too little control over their personal data. However, if users get more possibilities for self-determining the privacy effecting their personal data, it must be guaranteed that the resulting privacy requirements are correct. This means, they reflect the user's actual privacy demands. There exist multiple approaches for specifying privacy requirements as an end user, which we call specification paradigms. We assume that a matching of specification paradigms to users based on empirical data can positively influence the objective and perceived correctness. We use the user type model by Dupree, which categorizes users by their motivation and knowledge. We experimentally determined the best match of user types and paradigms. We show that participants with less knowledge and motivation make more mistakes and that a strong limitation of selection options increases objective and perceived correctness of the specified privacy requirements.

Keywords: Privacy requirements specification · User types ·
Specification interfaces · Objective correctness · Perceived correctness

1 Introduction

Since the dawn of the Internet age, users have been increasingly sending (personal) data to services that process and analyze data. At the same time, users become increasingly aware and partially afraid of data misuse and their need for a better privacy protection raises [1, 2]. Even if the need arises, many users do not configure their privacy settings for Internet services. One major cause is that users have problems in adequately specifying their own privacy requirements, which we showed in a previous study [3]. Users rate the specification as too complicated and time consuming. In practice, services provide different specification interfaces, which offer the user a variety of options, specification processes and guidance during the specification of privacy requirements. We refer to those different types of interfaces as specification paradigms. In order to achieve ideal results, we need to provide users a specification paradigm that matches their needs and capabilities best. We assume that the appropriate selection of the specification paradigm for a user can have a positive effect on the acceptance of the tool itself, and can increase its effectiveness. Thus, we investigated the effectiveness of the privacy requirement specification (objective and perceived

© Springer Nature Switzerland AG 2019
E. Knauss and M. Goedicke (Eds.): REFSQ 2019, LNCS 11412, pp. 39–54, 2019.
https://doi.org/10.1007/978-3-030-15538-4_3

correctness of the specified requirements), efficiency (necessary time span for speci-fication) and user satisfaction (how much users like the paradigm). Our results regarding user satisfaction and efficiency were published in [20]. In this article, we focus on the effectiveness. The susceptibility to mistakes should always be of particular interest. Users are very different with respect to their capabilities (e.g., knowledge, available time and cognitive capacity) and preferences (interaction processes they like). Thus, there will probably not be a specification paradigm that delivers the best results for all user types. We use the model of Dupree for clustering users into user types [5]. Whether a paradigm fits a user depends on his specific characteristics. The lack of work on matching specification paradigms to user types motivated this work. Our main contributions in this article are observations and recommendations for best suitable specification paradigms for specific user types regarding effectiveness. They are derived from an experiment in which we asked users representing different personas to solve tasks with four specification paradigms. We measured mistakes produced by the users and the users' perception of correctness.

In this paper, we present the used specification paradigms and their derivation from literature and practice in Sect. 2. In Sect. 3, we discuss available user type model in literature and discuss the selection of the Dupree model. Next, we explain the design and execution of our experiment in Sect. 4. We present and discuss the results in Sect. 5. Finally, we conclude and discuss future work in Sect. 6.

2   The Variety of Privacy Specification Interfaces

Users specify their privacy requirements as policies in different systems using speci-fication interfaces. Depending on the system, different types of specification interfaces are offered, which we call specification paradigms. These differ in following aspects:

- Specification process: With which interactions do users set their privacy require-ments in the interface?
- Number of decisions: How many decisions do users have to take in the specification?
- Degree of guidance: How much support is given to users during specification?

In the following, we identified relevant privacy specification approaches and interfaces in the state of the art and practice and derived appropriate specification paradigms.

2.1   Related Work Regarding End-User Privacy Specification Interfaces

In the state of the art, a lot of work was performed in the area of specifying privacy requirements in form of machine-understandable policies by experts. Even if the focus of our work is to enable non-experts to specify privacy requirements in natural lan-guage, the interface concepts for machine-understandable policies can be transferred to natural language interfaces for privacy policy specification.

PERMIS [13] is a generic RBAC-based (Role-Based Access Control) authorization infrastructure. PERMIS policies are created, for example, via a "Policy Wizard". This tool uses a step-by-step specification wizard as the policy specification paradigm. It asks supportive questions to guide the user through the specification process. KAoS [15] is a policy and domain service framework. It contains the KAoS Policy Administration Tool (KPAT) that is based on natural English sentences using hypertext templates. Policy templates are specified in an ontology and specified policies are automatically transformed into machine-readable equivalents. Johnson et al. [14] describe a method and a tool named SPARCLE for eliciting concrete security requirements of users with varying background knowledge. The tool allows the user to enter his security requirement in natural language or in a structured natural language-based format. SPARCLE can transform the structured format into machine-understandable policies. P3P (Platform for Privacy Preference Project) is a protocol that allows websites to declare their intended use of information they collect from users [18]. In addition, APPEL (A P3P Preference Exchange Language) was developed for users to describe collections of privacy preferences [19]. Fang and LeFevre [17] propose an active learning wizard that enables users to set their own privacy and security policies by making regular, brief decisions on whether or not to share a particular data item with an entity.

Besides the academic approaches, many domain specific policy authoring tools exist in practice. The Local Group Policy Editor of Windows systems (e.g., Windows 7) mainly targets system administrators and offers a variety of settings (e.g., firewall settings, password policies, startup/shutdown scripts) for Windows environments. Facebook allows its users to specify their privacy requirements in a very fine-grained manner. Even if studies revealed that users expected in some cases a different behavior from the specified privacy policies [16], they are in general empowered to specify them at all. Both tools, the Windows editor as well as the Facebook privacy settings, provide a lot of specification support, such as explanations or examples. They use template based specification and small wizards for specific security and privacy settings. All modern browsers contain privacy and security settings. Google Chrome (Version 64), Microsoft Edge (Version 41) and Mozilla Firefox (Version 52) allow their users to enable and disable pre-defined default privacy and security policies. The Microsoft Internet Explorer (Version 11) uses a security level approach for setting the coarse-grained security settings. If required, users can customize these security levels by selecting from pre-defined default options. For the privacy requirements in online accounts, Google has introduced a privacy check wizard that guides the user through multiple pages to configure the use of personal information by Google services and third parties.

2.2 Selected Specification Paradigms

We found that all specification paradigms from literature and practice differ in their configurability (how many decisions they request) and their guidance (how much help does the user receive during the specification). We rated all specification paradigms accordingly and selected paradigms (All Screens displayed to the subjects and further supplementary material such as sample solution and access to primary data can be found in [22]) with all four combinations of high and low configurability (C) and guidance (G):

1. Template instantiation (high-C, low-G): The user can instantiate desired privacy requirements by adjusting selection options in a template-based interface. The templates offer multiple decisions and thus allow a fine-grained specification of own privacy requirements. The user can choose the order of specification.
2. Default Policies (low-C, low-G): The user can chose from multiple predefined privacy policies per topic. The number of decisions in the specification is limited.
3. Wizard (high-C, high-G): The user can instantiate privacy requirements based on a template-based interface, which is split in several small steps. The user cannot decide on the specification order. The specification process is well guided in each step.
4. Security levels (low-C, high-G): The user can select a level of privacy that contains a predefined set of default privacy requirements without having customization possibilities per requirement.

3   The Different Types of Users

Each user has different characteristics, capabilities and resources. This leads us to the assumption that different paradigms are likely to fit differently well to a certain user. To explore the relationship between suitable specification paradigms and users, we first explored related work regarding user type models and then selected a model for clustering users according to relevant characteristics.

3.1   Related Work Regarding User Type Models

There are several ways to cluster users into categories that explain their character traits and behavior. Some clustering methods describe human traits and behavior in general, i.e., they are not bound to a particular situation or domain. Examples are the Big Five personality traits [6], Keirsey's Temperaments [7] and the Myers-Briggs Type Indicators [8]. Besides the generic clustering approaches, other work relates to the use of computers and the character traits relevant for security and privacy decisions. For example, Westin's [4] classification is based on users' privacy concerns. In most of his 30 privacy surveys, he clusters the users into three categories: Fundamentalist (high concern), Pragmatist (medium concern), and Unconcerned (low concern). Westin's approach is controversially discussed in the literature. For example, Urban and Hoofnagel [9] argue that Westin's work is neglecting the importance of knowledge or available information about privacy practices, domain specific business processes. Smith's approach "Concern for Information Privacy (CFIP)" [10] measures the privacy concern of a person as a numerical value based on a calculation on fifteen statements about privacy. The scenarios of CFIP are kept quite abstract and do not directly relate to online services that collect and process user data. Malhotra et al. improved and extended previous work (e.g., CFIP) in their approach called Internet Users' Information Privacy Concerns (IUIPC) [12]. They reflect the concerns of internet users about information privacy with a special focus on the individuals' perception of fairness in the context of data privacy. Morton's Information Seeking Preferences [11] are an approach to cluster users into five groups based on the ranking of 40 privacy related statements. The groups are: Information controllers, security concerned, benefit seekers, crowd followers and organizational assurance seekers. Considering the criticism on Westin's privacy indexes, Dupree proposed her privacy personas [5]. Those five personas can be differentiated on two attributes of the user: the user's knowledge about security and privacy as well as the user's motivation to spend effort to protect privacy and security. The personas also describe the handling of personal data in the internet age and the general need for security in the IT sector.

3.2 Selection of the User Type Model

When searching for the appropriate model, we found that all available models can be characterized by two properties: focus on IT security and privacy and focus on technical systems (see Fig. 1 left). In both cases, there are very special models developed for a specific subdomain or system as well as generic approaches. We chose the Dupree model [5] as a suitable middle way. This model mainly distinguishes users by their motivation and their knowledge to specify privacy requirements (see Fig. 1 right). Dupree has derived the five personas from personal interviews with 32 university related digital natives, who had an average age of 26.3 (SD = 5.9). The personas are:

- Marginally Concerned: Low knowledge and low motivation
- Amateur: Medium knowledge and medium motivation
- Technician: Medium knowledge and high motivation
- Lazy Expert: High knowledge and low motivation
- Fundamentalist: High knowledge and high motivation.

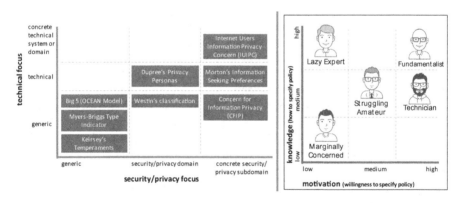

Fig. 1. Left: classification of different user type models | Right: Dupree' Persona Matrix

4 Experiment Design and Execution

4.1 Research Questions

The experiment objective was to identify which paradigms are suitable for a specific persona with regard to objective and perceived correctness. Each paradigm requires the user to make a certain number of decisions during the specification of privacy requirements. If the decision taken differs from the sample solution, we regard this deviation as a mistake. We consider a paradigm to be suitable if the ratio of mistakes to all decisions is low (high objective correctness). Moreover, we aimed at finding the best matching paradigm for a precise self-estimation with respect to the objective correctness (Can people estimate that they made mistakes?). We defined following research questions:

- RQ1: Which paradigm best suits a particular type of person (represented by a persona) in terms of objective correctness?
- RQ2: Which paradigm is best suited to a particular type of person (represented by a persona) in terms of correctly estimated perceived correctness (confidence regarding objective correctness)?

4.2   Scenario and Tasks

The scenario and the corresponding privacy requirements in the experiment were derived from a real project in the context of the digitization of rural areas using the RE method described in [21]. In this method, workshops with users and experts of the problem domain are conducted with selected State of the Art RE methods in order to elicit relevant templates of privacy requirements. In the project, village citizens have access to digital services such as an online marketplace with local merchants, a delivery service where citizens deliver goods from local merchants to other citizens (called BestellBar) and a digital village bulletin board. The participants should imagine that they use these novel, digital services of this project and that this has potential privacy impact to them as personalized data is used in those services. The participants had the task to adjust the privacy requirements of these services to given privacy requirements. The requirements were not their own but specified by the authors of this paper. The presetting of the privacy requirements was necessary so that all participants could use the specification interfaces in a comparable way. This enabled us to compare the measured mistakes made by the participants.

The requirements were described as part of the six tasks. One task was, for instance; "When I place an order in the BestellBar app, I do not under any circumstances want to receive advertising from other providers that refers to the ordered product. They may not use my data." The requirements did not match one-to-one with the wording in the specification interfaces, because a one-to-one match would cause that the participants compare the buzzwords of the task and the interfaces but not the semantic content.

The scenario description and the tasks were provided on a digital handout, which the participants were advised to print out. The scenario description was supported by a short video that introduces the novel, digital services for citizens of a village. Four specification interfaces were created according to the selected specification paradigms presented in Sect. 2.2. We refer to these interfaces as the four specification paradigms in the following. The participants had to complete the same six tasks for each specification paradigm. The introduction material is presented in the supplementary experiment material [22].

All implementations of the specification paradigms in this experiment use the same templates, which is the outcome from the used RE method [21]. The paradigms template instantiation and wizard let the participant instantiate concrete privacy requirements from the templates. The paradigms default policies and security levels provide a limited list of already instantiated privacy requirements from the templates to choose from. In case of the paradigm security levels, the user can chose from three different sets of privacy requirements. All tasks in the experiment can be solved with all four specification paradigm implementations.

During the experiment design we had to decide whether we should provide a perfect match with the tasks for the paradigm security levels. This means that one of the security levels solves all tasks of the scenario. Such a perfect match is unlikely in real life. However, the lack of a perfect solution could confuse the participants in the experiment letting them abort. In addition, a massive influence on the experiment results (correctness and satisfaction) was expected. Thus, we decided to have a perfect match because we did not want to compromise the proper execution of the experiment.

4.3   Procedures and Instruments

Our experiment was created as a publically available online experiment. In order to avoid misuse, a participant could only start the experiment once with a unique eight digit participant id. It was possible to interrupt the experiment and continue with the participant id in the same place. However, it was not possible to repeat already executed steps. The experiment was provided in German and English.

Our experiment was structured as follows. First of all, the participants had to agree to an informed consent and confirm that they are at least 18 years old. Thereafter, the participants had to answer demographic questions about age, gender and educational level as well as their relationship to the authors' institutions and their research topics. The answers were used to determine whether the participants' characteristics and capabilities have an impact on the results of the experiment. Then, a self-assessment followed about one's own expertise and motivation in the areas of IT security and protection of one's own privacy as well as experience in dealing with digital services. Afterwards, the participants were asked to select the persona out of the five offered personas that they think fits best to them. All five personas of Dupree were described on the basis of nine to twelve original character traits [5] formulated in the ego-perspective. The order of the personas displayed was randomly determined. Thereupon, the scenario including the concrete tasks (privacy requirements) was explained by video and handout. Next, the participants were instructed that on the following pages they should set all the privacy requirements for each of the four different specification paradigms: default policies, security levels, template instantiation and wizard. The order in which the specification paradigms were presented to the participants was randomly determined to minimize learning effects. After each specification paradigm, the participants were asked whether they thought they did mistakes, how they liked the current type of specification in the current scenario and how they would like it transferred to real life. After completing the four specifications, the participants were asked to rank the four specification types according to their preference of using them in real life. Finally, participants should determine how well they can identify with the scenario and the chosen persona. Screenshots showing all steps of the experiment can be found in the supplementary experiment material [22].

4.4 Execution

We acquired the participants by means of a non-binding invitation by e-mail in the circle of friends and acquaintances of the authors as well as in the authors' institution. The participants were asked to forward the non-binding invitation to other persons. We sent each interested person a specific invitation email with a handout attached. The handout contained instructions for starting and conducting the experiment, the individual participant id and the scenario description. We sent 120 personal invitation emails and deleted them directly after sending in order ensure the anonymity of the participants. The online experiment was available for 14 days. Participants were informed about the approximate duration of the experiment of 30–40 min, but had no time limit for completion.

4.5 Data Analysis

All statistical analyses were conducted with SPSS 19 and Microsoft Excel. First of all, the plausibility of the self-selection of personas was checked by analyzing whether the self-reported security knowledge matches the persona classification by Dupree (see [5]). Moreover, we analyzed how well participants identified with the selected persona.

To answer RQ1, the number of mistakes was analyzed. The different paradigms required different numbers of decisions: One decision in security levels, six decisions in default policies, 18 decisions in template instantiation and 18 decisions in wizard. This means that the pure number of mistakes is not directly comparable, but the ratio of incorrect decisions had to be compared. To evaluate the differences between the paradigms, Wilcoxon signed rank test were used. We also performed a Kruskal-Wallis (suitable for small sample sizes) test ($\alpha = 0.05$) to investigate whether the persona has an influence on the objective correctness. The fundamentalist were excluded from analysis because of their small number.

To answer RQ2, we investigated whether there is an influence of the persona on the perceived correctness or not. The perceived correctness was measured by asking the participants after the use of each paradigm whether they think that they solved all tasks in the paradigm correctly (zero mistakes). A Fisher's exact test, which is a test for small sample sizes, was performed for the results of each paradigm.

5 Results and Discussion

5.1 Participant Description

Out of 120 invitations sent, 61 persons finished the experiment with complete data sets. We did not find any indications that would have caused us to consider records as invalid. 43% of the participants are female. The participants' age ranges from 18 to 82 ($M = 40.54$; $SD = 14.37$). The majority of the participants (33 out of 61) hold a university degree as highest educational level, nine participants hold a doctoral degree, seven have an entrance qualification for higher education and eleven a secondary school leaving certificate as highest level of education. About half of the participants (54%) were related the authors' institution, 20 of them being scientific and eight non-scientific employees and five being students working with the authors' institution. 28 participants (46%) had no relation to the authors' institution. Table 1 shows the distribution of the personas chosen by the participants. The largest group with 34% of the participants is the persona amateur. The fundamentalists make up the smallest group with five percent. The ratio of the other personas varies between 18 and 23%.

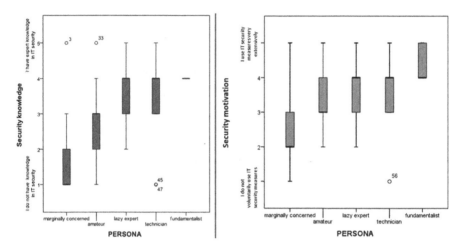

Fig. 2. Left: knowledge to persona mapping | Right: motivation to persona mapping

To verify the plausibility of the persona self-selection, we asked the participants to rate their IT security knowledge. The participants' security knowledge fits well to the chosen personas, except for the lazy experts (see Fig. 2 left side). Based on Dupree's categorization (see Fig. 1 right side), we expected the lazy experts to have higher self-estimated knowledge. The participants' security motivation fits to the model of Dupree as well (see Fig. 2 right side). Moreover, we asked the participants, how well the chosen persona matches them on a scale from 1 (Not very well, but it matched best out of the five options) to 5 (I can identify myself very well with the persona). The participants responded on average with a score of 3.75. Not a single person reported the value 1.

Table 1. Chosen personas

Persona	Number	Ratio	Persona	Number	Ratio
Marginally concerned	12	20%	Technician	14	23%
Amateur	21	34%	Fundamentalist	3	5%
Lazy expert	11	18%	Total	61	

5.2 Experiment Results

The results regarding the objective correctness are presented first. Thereafter, the results of the perceived correctness in relation to the objective correctness are shown.

Table 2. Participants with 100% objective correctness and mistakes made by personas

Persona	Number of participants with all paradigms correct/n per persona	% of participants per persona	Mistakes made in relation to decisions		Default Policies	Security Levels	Template Instantiation	Wizard
			Degrees of freedom	6	1	18	18
Marginally concerned	1/12	8.33%	Average mistakes	0.56	0.25	0.49	0.50
			Std. deviation	0.36	0.45	0.29	0.29
Amateur	4/21	19.05%	Average mistakes	0.12	0.05	0.12	0.12
			Std. deviation	0.22	0.22	0.16	0.14
Lazy expert	1/11	9.09%	Average mistakes	0.15	0.00	0.16	0.21
			Std. deviation	0.26	0.00	0.16	0.21
Technician	4/14	36.36%	Average mistakes	0.17	0.00	0.15	0.11
			Std. deviation	0.27	0.00	0.25	0.16
Fundamentalist	0/3	0%	Average mistakes	0.00	0.00	0.06	0.13
			Std. deviation	0.00	0.00	0.06	0.08
All participants	10/61	16.39%	Average mistakes	0.22	0.07	0.20	0.21
			Std. deviation	0.31	0.25	0.25	0.24

Objective Correctness. Different aspects were taken into account in the analysis of the objective correctness (see Table 2): First, we identified the number of the participants with perfect objective correctness. Secondly, the concrete number of mistakes in relation to the decisions per paradigm were analyzed. Fewest mistakes were made with security levels. Seven percent of participants chose the wrong security level. In the other three paradigms, which provided more decision options, about one in five decisions were taken incorrectly. Thus, for the whole population of the experiment there is no difference in objective correctness, except for a significant difference to the paradigm security levels (compared to default: $z = 3.83$, $p < 0.01$, template: 4.22, p < 0.01, wizard: 4.35, p < 0.01). Only 10 out of 61 participants made no mistakes, thus they achieved 100% objective correctness in all paradigms.

The persona selection has a significant effect on the mistakes made in the paradigms default policies ($\chi^2 = 13.88$, p < 0.01), template instantiation ($\chi^2 = 14.10$, p < 0.01), and wizard ($\chi^2 = 17.04$, p < 0.01), and also on the security levels ($\chi^2 = 7.99$, p < 0.05) but not that strong. The effect of the persona is likely given because of the significant difference of the marginally concerned to the other personas. For example, within the paradigm default policies, the amount of mistakes by the marginally concerned is significantly higher compared to the other personas (for each persona p < 0.05). The effect sizes for all paradigms are strong (d < 0.6; see details about the statistical results in the supplementary experiment material [22]).

Perceived Correctness in Relation to Objective Correctness. We asked the participants after each paradigm they used, whether they think that they solved all tasks correctly. The experiment results provide that the persona selection does not influence the perceived correctness in any paradigm (template: p = 0.96; default: p = 0.87; security level: p = 0.85; wizard: p = 0.62). This means that there is no difference in how optimistic or pessimistic the participants of the different personas are regarding these paradigms. In our experiment, we aimed at identifying which paradigm suits best for a correct self-estimation (perceived correctness) regarding the objective correctness. A self-estimation of a privacy requirements specification is rated as correct, if the participant did zero mistakes and was confident about the perfect solution or if the participant did at least one mistake and was confident that he did mistakes. Overall, 42 participants thought that they used all paradigms correctly, however, only eight of them made indeed no mistakes in all paradigms. Twelve persons reported mistakes in one paradigm and two persons even in all four paradigms. Thus, the perceived correctness is very high, regardless of the many mistakes that were made. Only four persons had a too pessimistic self-estimation. Table 3 shows the correct estimations per paradigm for all participants and for each persona. Overall, the self-estimation was best with the security levels (78.7%) and worst with the wizard (29.5%). We found that more decisions during specification led to worse self-estimation.

Table 3. Accuracy of perceived correctness (correct positive (P) and negative (N) estimations)

	Default policies		Security levels		Template instantiation		Wizard	
	P/N	%	P/N	%	P/N	%	P/N	%
Marginally concerned	2/1	25.0	8/1	75.0	1/2	25.0	1/0	8.3
Amateur	12/1	61.9	16/1	81.0	6/1	33.3	6/1	33.3
Lazy expert	7/2	81.8	8/0	72.7	2/1	27.3	1/2	27.3
Technician	8/1	64.3	12/0	85.7	6/2	57.1	6/1	50.0
Fundamentalist	3/0	100	2/0	66.7	1/0	33.3	0/0	0.0
All participants	32/5	60.7	46/2	78.7	16/6	36.1	14/4	29.5

Comparison of Results Regarding Personas. The **marginally concerned** made using the security levels paradigm least mistakes and achieved best perceived correctness compared to other paradigms (Average Mistakes (AM): 25%, see Table 2; Correct Estimations (CE): 75%, see Table 3)). In all other paradigms, this group of people made more mistakes. The **amateurs** also achieved best results with the security levels (AM: 5%; CE: 81%). For the other paradigms, the AM values are equal at 12%. Regarding the perceived correctness, participants assessed themselves rather good with the default policies (CE 61.9%). Amateurs did rather few mistakes with the paradigms template instantiation and wizard, but the self-assessment is worse than with other paradigms. The **technician** achieved as all other personas better results in the paradigms security levels (AM: 0%; CE: 86%) and default policies (AM: 17%; CE: 64%). However, the technicians achieved best values regarding the perceived correctness and rather low rates of mistakes for the paradigms template instantiation (AM: 15%; CE: 57%) and wizard (AM: 11%; CE: 50%). The **lazy experts** are described by Dupree as people with a high level of knowledge and low motivation in terms of security and privacy (see Fig. 1 right side). It is interesting to note that they performed worse than amateurs and technicians in many direct value comparisons. The values for the default policies (AM: 15%; CE: 81.8%) and security levels (AM: 0%; CE: 72.7%) are best. Since only three participants have chosen the persona **fundamentalist**, no conclusions can be made about this persona. Still, the results reflect the persona scheme of Dupree [5].

5.3   Threats to Validity

We did not control the participants during or after the experiment, which is a threat to internal validity. We cannot exclude the possibility that the participants talked about the experiment with other participants before their participation, nor that the participants could not find the necessary information or concentration to solve the tasks adequately. Distraction might increase the number of mistakes. However, we adequately instructed participants with a text handout, a scenario video and instructions in various steps in the experiment as we would have done in a controlled setting. We did not find any hint for an inadequate introduction (e.g., in the feedback at the end of the experiment). Thus, we assess this threat as low. A participant who could not identify with the provided privacy requirements well, maybe had lower motivation to take effort in correctly using the paradigms in the experiment. This may negatively affect the objective correctness and is a threat to internal validity.

The experiment tried to represent the use of privacy requirements in real life. In reality, participants would have their own individual requirements. However, we had to preset the privacy requirements in order to measure the correctness as the discrepancy between the participants' results and the sample solution. Thus, we cannot be sure whether the same correctness values would be achieved in the real world with own privacy requirements. This poses a threat to external validity. The paradigm security levels in combination with the given tasks does most likely not reflect the reality since the preset tasks matched perfectly to one of the security levels. This is rarely the case in real life and therefore limits the external validity to some extent. However, we decided to propose a perfect solution, as the lack of the perfect match may have influenced the measured correctness and irritated the participants, which would have been a threat to internal validity. Furthermore, the experiment was conducted in a scenario that represents a single use case for privacy requirements (mono-operation bias). Further experiments that confirm our results in different scenarios would increase the generalization of the results and therefore the external validity. The number of participants per persona is quite small, especially the number of fundamentalists (three persons). In addition, a large number of participants are academics. This does not reflect the overall population. Those aspects are threats to external validity.

The selection of the specification paradigms is based on our observations of the paradigms most commonly used in practice. We cannot rule out the possibility that there are other paradigms that could lead to better results in a comparable experiment. This implies a threat to conclusion validity with respect to our recommendations of best suitable specification paradigms. For the specification of privacy requirements the participants use concrete 'tools', which are implementations of the specification paradigms. This mixes findings on specification paradigms and corresponding tools. To minimize this threat to conclusion validity, usability experts supported us to make the 'tools' as unobtrusive as possible. We discuss the generalizability of the experiment results in the following section.

5.4   Discussion

We wanted to investigate the relation between the selected persona and specification paradigm used in relation to objective correctness (RQ1) and self-estimation regarding perceived correctness (RQ2) with our research questions.

With respect to RQ1, we identified that all personas did least mistakes with the specification paradigm security levels. The number of mistakes related to decisions differs only marginally between the other paradigms. However, the persona marginally concerned differs significantly from the others with respect to objective correctness as they did more mistakes. The cumulated mistakes are higher than expected by the authors. This raises the question about the difficulty of the tasks to be solved. It was possible to solve all tasks without mistakes, because 10 out of 61 participants achieved the perfect objective correctness (zero mistakes in total). No one explained that he did not understand the tasks or the scenario in free text comments at the end of the experiment.

Regarding RQ2, we found that the perceived correctness is related to the number of decisions of a paradigm. More freedom led to worse perceived correctness in our experiment. However, there is no significant difference in how personas perform regarding perceived correctness in these paradigms. We did not expect that only few participants (8 out of 61) estimated perceived correctness rightly. Most of the others overestimated themselves and only four underestimated their correctness. Overestimation could in practice frustrate a user of privacy settings, as the system is not acting as expected. This could reduce trust in the privacy settings interface and its providing company. The participants underestimating their achieved correctness might appreciate the correct specification and the effect by the system, but they also might be frustrated because they have the feeling of not having control over the system.

Our experiment relies on the personas developed by Dupree [5]. We decided to go for these personas since they were developed based on empirical data. The personas mainly differ regarding motivation and security knowledge but also include more valuable information (e.g. valuing convenience more than security). Moreover, they contain concrete security behaviors such as use of strong passwords. We assume that such concrete information ease the self-classification compared to a scale with short statements, which are prone to a subjective interpretation (i.e. expert knowledge might be interpreted differently). Our two questions in the experiment about security knowledge and motivation had the purpose to control whether the persona selection is reasonable. However, we do not consider these to questions as sufficient to replace the personas. In practice, it would be preferable to have a small selection questionnaire for the user to persona mapping. However, to the best of our knowledge, that does not exist.

In the study by Dupree [5], the number of fundamentalists was the smallest by far, such as in our experiment. More fundamentalists are needed to draw conclusions about an appropriate specification paradigm. The other personas were represented by 11, 12, 14, and 21 participants, respectively. The numbers seem small as well but were enough to properly apply statistical analyses with the chosen tests. Nevertheless, the experiment need to be repeated with more participants to improve the generalizability of the results.

Many participants are academics or related to an academic work environment (69% academics, 54% employees of the authors' institution, 93% german-speaking participants). Obviously, the group of participants does not reflect the overall population (e.g., 15% academics in Germany). We cannot rule out that this had an influence on the results and a negative impact their generalizability. It seems unlikely to us that the level of education has a direct impact, but indirect effects seem reasonable. The level of education is related to certain jobs and interests and by this to knowledge about IT-security. More precise questions have to be asked in future to properly investigate the relation of education to correctness. Questions could be 'is your job related to IT-security or privacy?' and 'do you spend time in your spare time to learn about privacy?'

6   Conclusion and Future Work

In this article, we have shown that appropriate specification interfaces can be assigned to users to promote the correct specification of privacy requirements and to give users confidence that they have made the right decisions. To this end, we have categorized the common types of specification interfaces used in practice as specification paradigms and have them used by different user types (personas) according to predefined tasks within a scenario. Through the results, we can recommend specification paradigm assignments to personas to achieve the highest possible objective and perceived correctness. In summary, we can clearly recommend the security levels for all personas. In addition, amateurs, lazy experts and technicians performed well with default policies. In case of necessity for fine-grained specifications, template instantiation and wizard can be effective enough for technicians. Due to the small number of fundamentalists, we cannot give recommendations for this persona.

The main focus of the overall experiment is to identify potential for increasing effectiveness, efficiency and satisfaction of privacy policy specification interfaces for users. This paper shows that effectiveness can be increased for personas by the selection of the right specification paradigm. We show in [20] that the specification paradigm also influences efficiency and satisfaction. In our results, effectiveness and efficiency of specification paradigms are aligned, satisfaction behaves contrary. People do not like "security levels" but perform efficiently and effectively with this paradigm. Vice versa, people like the paradigms "wizard" and "template instantiation", but are more ineffective and inefficient with them. This poses a dilemma for the provider that needs to select the appropriate specification paradigm for the privacy specification interfaces of the own software product. High effectiveness and efficiency may be desired by users, however the low satisfaction with the paradigm may hinder users to specify privacy requirements at all. Contrary, a satisfying tool that leads to incorrect privacy settings may limit the trust in the provider. Besides that also other obligations might be fulfilled, such as legal requirements or the necessity of the provider to collect data due to the business model of the software product. Thus, with current results we cannot give generic recommendations for the specification paradigms selection. Providers must carefully balance pros and cons before selecting a paradigm based on the personas which best reflect the users.

To confirm our results, we need to perform non-exact replications of our experiment including a larger sample of participants from all user types and additional scenarios. We need to find out whether optimizations in the implementations of the paradigms can positively influence the objective and perceived correctness. Therefore, we also need to explore the use of additional paradigms and discuss the current look and feel as well as the interaction process of the used paradigms.

Acknowledgements. The research presented in this paper is supported by the German Ministry of Education and Research projects "Nationales Referenzprojekt für IT-Sicherheit in der Industrie 4.0 (IUNO)" (grant number 16KIS0328) and "Transparente und selbstbestimmte Ausgestaltung der Datennutzung im Unternehmen (TrUSD)" (grant number 16KIS0898). The sole responsibility for the content of this paper lies with the authors.

References

1. European Commission: Special Eurobarometer 431 - Data Protection (2015). http://ec.europa.eu/commfrontoffice/publicopinion/archives/ebs/ebs_431_en.pdf
2. Symantec: State of Privacy Report 2015 (2015). https://www.symantec.com/content/en/us/about/presskits/b-state-of-privacy-report-2015.pdf
3. Rudolph, M., Feth, D., Polst, S.: Why users ignore privacy policies – a survey and intention model for explaining user privacy behavior. In: Kurosu, M. (ed.) HCI 2018. LNCS, vol. 10901, pp. 587–598. Springer, Cham (2018). https://doi.org/10.1007/978-3-319-91238-7_45
4. Kumaraguru, P., Cranor, L.: Privacy indexes: a survey of Westin's studies (2005). http://repository.cmu.edu/isr/856
5. Dupree, J.L., Devries, R., Berry, D.M., Lank, E.: Privacy personas: clustering users via attitudes and behaviors toward security practices. In: Conference on Human Factors in Computing Systems (2016)
6. Digman, J.M.: Personality structure: emergence of the five-factor model. Ann. Rev. Psychol. **41**, 417–440 (1990)

7. Keirsey, D.: Please Understand Me 2. Prometheus Nemesis Book Company, Carlsbad (1998)
8. Myers, I.B., McCaulley, M.H., Most, R.: Manual: A Guide to the Development and Use of the Myers-Briggs Type Indicator, vol. 1985. Consulting Psychologists Press, Palo Alto (1985)
9. Urban, J.M., Hoofnagle, C.J.: The privacy pragmatic as privacy vulnerable. In: Workshop on Privacy Personas and Segmentation, SOUPS, Menlo Park, CA, 9–11 July 2014
10. Smith, H.J., Milberg, S.J., Burke, S.J.: Information privacy: measuring individuals' concerns about organizational practices. MIS Q. **20**, 167–196 (1996)
11. Morton, A., Sasse, M.A.: Desperately seeking assurances: segmenting users by their information-seeking preferences. In: 2014 Twelfth Annual International Conference on Privacy, Security and Trust (PST), pp. 102–111 (2014)
12. Malhotra, N.K., Kim, S.S., Agarwal, J.: Internet users' information privacy concerns (IUIPC): the construct, the scale, and a causal model. Inf. Syst. Res. **15**(4), 336–355 (2004)
13. Information Systems Security Research Group. PERMIS, University of Kent. http://sec.cs.kent.ac.uk/permis/
14. Johnson, M., Karat, J., Karat, C.M., Grueneberg, K.: Usable policy template authoring for iterative policy refinement. In: IEEE International Symposium on Policies for Distributed Systems and Networks, POLICY, Fairfax, Virginia, USA (2010)
15. Uszok, A., et al.: KAoS policy and domain services: toward a description-logic approach to policy representation, deconfliction, and enforcement. In: IEEE 4th International Workshop on Policies for Distributed Systems and Networks, POLICY (2003)
16. Liu, Y., Gummadi, K.P., Krishnamurthy, B., Mislove, A.: Analyzing Facebook privacy settings: user expectations vs. reality. In: ACM Conference on Internet Measurement (2011)
17. Fang, L., LeFevre, K.: Privacy wizards for social networking sites. In: Proceedings of the 19th International Conference on World Wide Web. ACM, New York (2010)
18. Cranor, L.F.: P3P: making privacy policies more useful. IEEE Secur. Priv. **99**, 50–55 (2003)
19. Cranor, L., Langheinrich, M., Marchiori, M.: A P3P Preference Exchange Language 1.0 (APPEL1.0) (2002). https://www.w3.org/TR/P3P-preferences/
20. Rudolph, M., Polst, S.: Satisfying and efficient privacy settings. Mensch und Computer (2018)
21. Rudolph, M., Feth, D., Doerr, J., Spilker, J.: Requirements elicitation and derivation of security policy templates—an industrial case study. In: 24th International Requirements Engineering Conference (RE), Beijing, China, pp. 283–292 (2016)
22. Supplementary Experiment Material including extended Figures for this Paper. http://s.fhg.de/yU6

RE-SWOT: From User Feedback to Requirements via Competitor Analysis

Fabiano Dalpiaz[1]([⊠])(iD) and Micaela Parente[2]

[1] RE-Lab, Department of Information and Computing Sciences,
Utrecht University, Utrecht, The Netherlands
f.dalpiaz@uu.nl
[2] Scaura B.V., Amsterdam, The Netherlands
micaelagparente@gmail.com

Abstract. [**Context & Motivation**] App store reviews are a rich source for analysts to elicit requirements from user feedback, for they describe bugs to be fixed, requested features, and possible improvements. Product development teams need new techniques that help them make real-time decisions based on user feedback. [**Question/Problem**] Researchers have proposed natural language processing (NLP) techniques for extracting and organizing requirements-relevant knowledge from the reviews for one specific app. However, no attention has been paid to studying whether and how requirements can be identified from competing products. [**Principal ideas/results**] We propose RE-SWOT, a tool-supported method for eliciting requirements from app store reviews through competitor analysis. RE-SWOT combines NLP algorithms with information visualization techniques. We evaluate the usefulness of RE-SWOT with expert product managers from three mobile app companies. [**Contribution**] Our preliminary results show that competitor analysis is a promising path for research that has direct impact on the requirements engineering practice in modern app development companies.

Keywords: Requirements engineering · SWOT analysis ·
Natural language processing · Requirements analytics · CrowdRE

1   Introduction

User feedback is a precious resource for requirements elicitation [1,12,18]. When effectively managed, user involvement may be beneficial for project success [1]. On the contrary, ill-managed user involvement may be harmful, e.g, if excessive effort is required for processing the collected feedback.

Crowd-based Requirements Engineering (CrowdRE) is a recent trend in Requirements Engineering (RE) that studies semi-automated methods to gather and analyze information from a large number of users, ultimately resulting in validated user requirements [11]. Automation, which is a distinguishing feature of CrowdRE, reduces the effort required to cope with high volumes of feedback.

© Springer Nature Switzerland AG 2019
E. Knauss and M. Goedicke (Eds.): REFSQ 2019, LNCS 11412, pp. 55–70, 2019.
https://doi.org/10.1007/978-3-030-15538-4_4

Natural Language Processing (NLP) techniques have been employed in CrowdRE for summarizing and classifying user input into structured knowledge. Many of the existing approaches process user-generated reviews posted on app stores: Guzman and Maalej [12] automatically extract app features and the associated sentiment, Di Sorbo et al. [7] organize reviews according to their intention, and the AR-Miner tool [4] identifies and summarizes the most informative reviews.

Current CrowdRE approaches that analyze app store reviews focus on a single app. A gap exists in the use of competitor analysis to uncover requirements based on an explicit comparison of one app's reviews with those of competing apps. The only work we could identify that considers competitors (see Sect. 2) extracts and compares pairs of sentences for the same feature from multiple reviews [16].

In this paper, we propose RE-SWOT: a tool-supported method for eliciting requirements from user reviews through competitor analysis. The tool combines NLP automation with information visualization techniques, and belongs to the domain of requirements analytics [5]. Our approach is inspired by classic literature in management, as it adapts the Strength-Weakness-Opportunity-Threat (SWOT) analysis framework [14] to the field of RE. By presenting RE-SWOT, we make three contributions to the literature:

- An algorithm that extracts features from the reviews of a set of competing apps, and then generates a SWOT matrix on the basis of the sentiment that the users have expressed toward the identified features;
- An information visualization technique that plots the results of the algorithm in a chart, and helps analysts visually explore the competing apps with the aim of eliciting new requirements;
- A qualitative evaluation of the practical applicability of our approach. After demonstrating our implemented tool to three product managers of different apps, we collect their opinion through follow-up interviews.

Organization. Section 2 discusses background and related literature. Section 3 details the algorithm for extracting features and classifying them through the SWOT framework. Section 4 illustrates our information visualization tool. Section 5 reports on the evaluation, while Section 6 discusses our findings and presents future work.

2   Related Work

We present the necessary background for this paper in Sect. 2.1, and discuss related approaches in Sect. 2.2.

2.1   Background

Crowd-Based Requirements Engineering. The rise of social media platforms has significantly increased the volume of feedback from software users. As a response, the RE community has initiated a shift toward data-driven and user-centered prioritization, planning, and management of requirements [21].

One of the emerging initiatives is Crowd-based Requirements Engineering (CrowdRE), which is defined [11] as *"an umbrella term for automated or semi-automated approaches to gather and analyze information from a crowd to derive validated user requirements"*. In CrowdRE, the considered feedback comes from users who are not bond with the software company.

App Store Reviews in Requirements Elicitation. The reviews that are posted in app stores contain diverse types of feedback. Besides functional issues (e.g., "I used to love it, but I can't watch videos anymore!") and non-functional concerns (e.g., usability or performance), the users also comment on not-yet-implemented aspects by requesting improvements or new features [20].

Analyzing app store reviews can lead to a better understanding of how apps are actually used, fast detection of newly introduced bugs [22], and insights from a more diverse range of users [15]. Unfortunately, several challenges exist:

- *Volume:* to cope with the large quantity of reviews, CrowdRE proposes to use NLP tools [11]. However, requirements elicitation is a "fundamentally human activity" [3] and new tools are called upon to "bringing the human into the loop and promoting thinking about the results" [2].
- *Noise:* Chen *et al.* [4] found that only 35.1% of app reviews contain information that can directly help developers improve their apps. Thus, CrowdRE approaches need to use filtering and aggregation of content [4, 22, 23].
- *One-way communication:* app store reviews lack meta-data about users and app usage; moreover, the user-developer communication is unidirectional. As such, the development team cannot reach back the users and ask for clarifications and context information.
- *Conflicting opinions:* reviews often contain conflicting opinions [11, 15, 21, 28]. Classic negotiations mechanisms are inhibited by the unidirectional communication; as a result, prioritization approaches are necessary to weight issues and wishes according to their prevalence and impact [19].

In practice, app development companies depend on community managers [19] for reading and replying to user reviews, often facilitated by tools that provide average ratings, distribution of stars over time, automatic labeling of reviews, etc. However, such tools do not explicitly support the elicitation of new requirements.

Visual Requirements Analytics. Reddivari *et al.* [26] proposed a framework that characterizes the visual requirements analytics process. They argue that, when proposing a requirements visualization, one has to explicitly define many aspects: the user, the goal, the questions to be answered, how to preprocess data, and the visualization type. Furthermore, they explain how requirements analytics tools need to go beyond the mere visualization and rather focus on the *interaction* between analyst and visualization.

2.2 Related Literature: Mining Requirements from App Store Reviews

Opinion mining approaches are applicable to app store reviews, but extra challenges exist [10] due to (i) the fine-grained reviews that include comments not only on product features, but also specific parts of the user interface, or particular user-app interactions; and (ii) the short length of app store reviews (71 characters on average [10]). While most papers are still exploratory, some key steps of mining requirements from app store reviews are discussed in the following.

Preprocessing Reviews. This activity is necessary to reduce noise in the reviews. Typical techniques include stop word removal, stemming, and lemmatization. Unfortunately, none of them delivers perfect accuracy; for example, while removing common English words tends to improve classification accuracy [20], it can hide user intentions (e.g., "should" for a feature request, "but" for a bug). Similarly, lemmatization and stemming are alternative ways for standardizing words with similar meaning, but no clear winner exists [9,20]. Other preprocessing techniques include removing short reviews [7], matching synonyms, and filtering words having specific POS tags like nouns, adjectives, and verbs [20].

Classifying Review Content. The goal is to classify reviews according to a given taxonomy. Yang and Liang [31] distinguish between functional and non-functional requirements by searching for keywords that are typically associated with either category. Most techniques in the literature [7] focus on two aspects: (i) *user intention*: the user's goals when writing the review (e.g., reporting a bug vs. requesting a feature); and (ii) *review topic*: the entire app, its interface, or a specific feature. Maalej and Nabil [20] compare various algorithms for classifying review intention as "Bug report", "Feature request", "Rating", or "User experience". Panichella *et al.* [23] employ a different taxonomy: "Feature request", "Problem discovery", "Information seeking" or "Information giving", which is then used by the SURF tool [7] to classify reviews according to both intention and topics: app, GUI, pricing, security, etc.

Extracting Features. NLP techniques can automatically extract the features that a review refers to. Harman *et al.* [13] extract features from publicly available app descriptions from an app store. They rely on the informal patterns that developers use to illustrate the main features of an app, like bullet lists. Based on these patterns, groups of commonly occurring co-located words are employed to represent the feature. Guzman and Maalej [12] use word collocations appearing in at least 3 reviews in their fine-grained analysis. Gao *et al.* [9] identify "phrases" derived from bi-grams to prioritize issues for developers.

The SAFE framework [17] improves over previous methods, and it exhibits a precision of 70%, recall of 56% and F1-score of 62%. They do so by defining a list of POS patterns and sentence patterns that are frequently used to describe features, and then applying cosine similarity algorithms.

Summarizing Reviews. Algorithms in this category reduce the feedback volume. AR-Miner [4] summarizes reviews by displaying the ten most important topics (groups of features) found, ranked by an importance score called *Group-Score*. Guzman *et al.* [12] use a two-level summary that shows the frequency and sentiment per topic (groups of features) or per feature.

Competitor Analysis. Jin *et al.* [16] identify comparable sentences in different reviews. Through feature extraction, sentiment analysis, similarity functions and clustering, they compare the opinions on a topic by analyzing pairs of extracted sentences. The WisCom system [8] enables summarization at the review, app, and market level. These precursory approaches, however, do not provide a systematic method for eliciting requirements through competitor analysis.

3   The RE-SWOT Method

Our method for eliciting requirements from app store reviews is inspired by SWOT analysis, a prominent framework for strategic planning in organizations that gives an overview of how a product or business is positioned, *vis à vis* its external environment [14]. SWOT analysis identifies four types of factors:

- *Strengths:* internal factors that enhance performance. For example, the high loyalty of an organization's employees.
- *Weaknesses:* internal factors that diminish performance. For instance, reliance on too rigid business processes.
- *Opportunities:* external (i.e., outside the organization's reach) enhancers to performance that could be exploited. For example, economic growth.
- *Threats:* external factors that inhibit performance. For example, a large foreign firm joining the domestic market, which increases competition.

The crux of SWOT analysis is that, in order for an organization to improve its competitiveness, it has not only to maximize the internal strengths and minimize its own weaknesses, but also has to be aware and to react quickly and effectively to the changing context by exploiting opportunities and mitigating threats.

Table 1. The RE-SWOT matrix: SWOT analysis adapted to CrowdRE.

Feature performance	App with the feature	
	Reference app	*Competitor app*
Positive and above market average	**Strength:** keep and/or extend the feature	**Threat:** imitate the competitor's feature to survive
Negative and below market average	**Weakness:** fix bugs or improve on a feature's issues	**Opportunity:** launch new feature to exploit an existing gap

We draw a parallel between SWOT analysis and RE for a software product. Consider an app that is distributed through one or more app stores; the requirements for the next releases are expected to leverage its strengths, mitigate the app's weaknesses, exploit market gaps, and imitate the successful features of the competitors. Table 1 shows the RE-SWOT matrix that classifies a feature into one SWOT category by comparing a reference app with a competing app. The *reference app* belongs to the company that executes the RE-SWOT analysis.

The matrix builds on the notion of *feature performance*, a real number in the $[-1, +1]$ range that represents whether the feature implemented in a given app has a prevalently positive (>0) or negative (<0) appreciation in the reviews. The same feature may exhibit different performance when implemented in multiple apps. In RE-SWOT, feature performance is calculated automatically from user reviews, as described in Sect. 3.1.

We illustrate the RE-SWOT matrix with some examples. Consider a feature f_1, which is included in a reference app a_r; if the feature performance of f_1 as implemented in a_r is positive and also above the market average for that feature, then f_1 is a *strength* for app a_r. Consider f_2 instead, which is possessed by a competitor app a_c; if the feature performance of f_2 as implemented by a_c is negative and below market average, then f_2 represents an opportunity for a_r.

3.1   Step-by-Step Method Description

We detail the steps of our method (overview in Fig. 1), thus clarifying how the performance of a feature is calculated and how the RE-SWOT matrix is built.

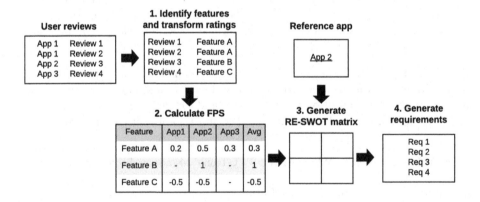

Fig. 1. The RE-SWOT method: an overview.

Step 1: Identify Features and Transform Ratings. App features are identified from the user reviews. To do so, we employ NLP techniques for feature identification, see Sect. 4.1 for the details. Furthermore, the original user ratings (a natural number between 1 and 5) are mapped to the $[-2, +2]$ integer scale in which three stars becomes the neutral score (0).

Step 2: Calculate FPS per Feature. Given a set of apps $A = \{a_1, a_2, \ldots, a_m\}$ and a set of features $F = \{f_1, f_2, \ldots, f_n\}$, we define the feature performance score (FPS) of app a_i in relation to feature f_j as per Eq. 1:

$$FPS_{i,j} = \frac{S_{i,j} \cdot V_{i,j}}{\sum_{k=1}^{m} |S_{k,j} \cdot V_{k,j}|} \tag{1}$$

– $S_{i,j}$ represents the user sentiment for feature f_j from app a_i: the sum of the transformed user ratings given to the reviews mentioning the feature, divided by the maximum possible sum. For instance, if a feature is mentioned in two 5-star reviews and one 2-star review, the feature sentiment score for that feature corresponds to $(2 + 2 - 1)/(2 + 2 + 2) = +0.5$.
– $V_{i,j}$ is the feature volume for feature f_j from app a_i: the number of user reviews from app a_i that mention feature f_j. Take an app with 2 reviews "App crashes when uploading photos; whenever I try to upload my photos, an error occurs" and "App is crashing a lot recently". The feature volume for *upload photos* is 1, for only the first review mentions that feature.

Step 3: Generate RE-SWOT Matrix. The FPS scores from Step 2 are used to generate the RE-SWOT matrix (illustrated earlier in Table 1). For each feature, the scores for each app are evaluated according to two criteria:

– *Positive/negative/neutral FPS.* A FPS is *positive* if Eq. 2 holds true, *negative* if Eq. 3 is true, and *neutral* when the FPS is within the range $(-\sigma, +\sigma)$. Based on the results of an exploratory study in which we applied our formulas to a few apps and their reviews, we pragmatically set σ to 0.1; in future work, more rigorous experimentation and tuning are necessary.

$$FPS_{i,j} \geq \sigma \tag{2}$$
$$FPS_{i,j} \leq -\sigma \tag{3}$$

– *Feature performance in the market.* We determine if a feature f_j is unique, above or below market average $(\overline{FPS_j})$. A FPS is *above average* if Eq. 4 holds true, *below average* if Eq. 5 applies. Moreover, a feature f_j is *unique* when only app a_i has reviews concerning f_j.

$$FPS_{i,j} - \overline{FPS_j} \geq \sigma \tag{4}$$
$$FPS_{i,j} - \overline{FPS_j} \leq -\sigma \tag{5}$$

Features from the competition with a positive FPS that is above the market averages are classified as *threats*. On the other hand, features with a negative FPS and below the market average represent *opportunities*. If the FPS refers to a feature of the reference app, it can be a *strength* (FPS is positive and above the market average) or a *weakness* (FPS is negative and below the market average). Feature that do not fit the aforementioned scenarios are not classified.

Table 2. The RE-SWOT matrix applied to photo editing apps.

Feature performance	App with the feature	
	Photo1	*Photo2 or Photo3*
Positive and above market average	**Strengths:** filters	**Threats:** edit photos, syncing (Photo2) save photos (Photo3)
Negative and below market average	**Weaknesses:** save photos	**Opportunities:** filters, save photos (Photo2) exporting (Photo3)

Step 4: Generate Requirements. In SWOT analysis, the TOWS framework [29] is used to identify strategies that can improve a company's competitiveness. In RE-SWOT, we adapt TOWS to identify the most suitable requirements for the app to excel in the market. With examples from the RE-SWOT matrix of Table 2, we illustrate the four types of requirements originating from TOWS:

– **SO requirements** aim at pursuing opportunities that fit well with the strengths. For example, feature *filters* should be boosted to exploit the opportunity that stems from the negative appreciation of filters in Photo2.
– **WO requirements** aim at overcoming weaknesses to pursue opportunities. For instance, the *save photos* weakness could be overcome by leveraging the opportunity given by the negative appreciation of that feature in Photo2.
– **ST requirements** aim at using strengths to reduce vulnerability to threats. No examples of this category exist in Table 2.
– **WT requirements** aim at minimizing weaknesses to make them less susceptible to threats. For example, Photo1 could imitate the implementation of the feature *save photos* in Photo3, which is currently a threat.

4   Prototype Tool

We implemented a tool that automatically creates an RE-SWOT matrix starting from a set of user reviews for the reference app and its competitors. The tool is built in R and Tableau Software and is available as an open source project[1].

The tool consists of two modules: (i) an *NLP module* implemented in R that creates the RE-SWOT matrix; and (ii) a *visualization module* for the analyst to interact with an RE-SWOT matrix, which is built using Tableau software. Both modules can be deployed through a Shiny web application.

4.1   NLP Module

First, the module pre-processes the user reviews through the following steps:

1. **Tokenization:** the reviews are split into sentences and words via *Udpipe*.

---

[1] https://github.com/RELabUU/RE-SWOT.

2. **To lowercase:** all tokens are converted to lowercase to make them uniform.
3. **Stopword removal:** common English words are removed using the stopword list of the *tm* package; moreover, additional words that are commonly found in reviews (e.g., the app name, "feature", "app") are filtered out.
4. **Noun, verb, and adjective extraction:** features are more likely to be described through nouns, verbs, and adjectives [12]. Thus, we used *Udpipe*'s POS tagging to select the tokens that meet those POS tags.
5. **Lemmatization:** we apply *Udpipe*'s lemmatizer to the tokens so that words such as "photos" and "photo" are reduced to the common term "photo".

In line with previous studies [12], we identify features through a collocation finding algorithm that identifies pairs of words (nouns, adjectives, verbs) that co-occur often in the reviews of each app. We exclude pairs that co-occur up to three times, and collocations that follow the patterns (adj, adj), (verb, adj), and (verb, verb), for our manual inspection revealed that they did not extract meaningful features. Hence, the considered collocation patterns are (noun, noun), (noun, adj), (noun, verb), (adj, noun), (adj, verb), and (verb, noun).

To further cope with the heterogeneous wording that users employ to refer to a same feature, we merge similar features (e.g., "photo edition" and "edit picture") by invoking the Cortical.IO service[2] to compute the cosine semantic similarity between all combinations of features. We merge feature labels with similarity score ≥ 0.60, and assign as label that having the highest frequency.

4.2 Visualization Module

This module is an Information Visualization approach for analysts to interact with the RE-SWOT matrix. We describe it via Pfitzner's framework *et al.* [25].

Data Factor. Three data objects are used: reviews, extracted features, and apps. Reviews have a date, a title, and a rating. A feature has a name, the related app, the FPS score, and the feature volume. An app can be classified as reference or competitor. Two relationship link the objects: (i) $mention(f, r)$ denotes that feature f is mentioned in review r, and (ii) $SWOT(f, a, c)$ denotes the class c (strength, weakness, opportunity, or threat) of feature f for app a.

Task Factor. This focuses on what actions the user can perform on the data and is described according to Shneiderman mantra's dimensions overview, zoom, filter, and detail-on-demand [27]. An overview of the tool is shown in Fig. 2.

Overview. The user can see a set of circles, each representing a feature. A feature's x-axis position represents the app where the feature was identified, and the y-axis position represents the feature's uniqueness. The size of the circle corresponds to the feature frequency in the reviews, and its color illustrates its SWOT classification from the perspective of the reference app.

---

[2] http://www.cortical.io/compare-text.html.

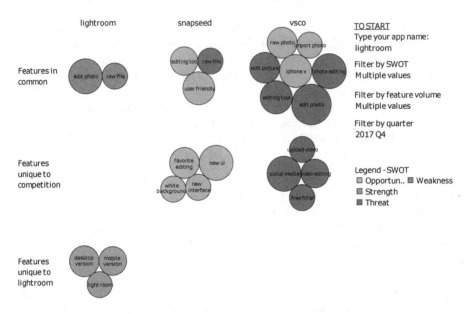

Fig. 2. The visualization of features in the RE-SWOT tool.

Zoom. The tool allows to zoom into a feature via a click, showing only the selected feature across all the apps with reviews mentioning that feature.

Filter. The tool allows to filter the visualized information in different ways:

1. By quarter. In Fig. 2, 2017 Q4 is shown;
2. By feature volume: *low* when the review volume is lower or equal to 1/6 of the range, *medium* if between 1/6 and 2/6 of the range, and *high* otherwise. In Fig. 2, only features with medium and high volume are shown;
3. By SWOT classification. In Fig. 2, features that are not assigned any of the four SWOT classes are omitted.

Details-on-Demand. If necessary, the analyst can request details about (i) a feature, through a tooltip that shown the distribution of user ratings and other information concerning the feature (Fig. 3); and (ii) a review, showing the entire sentence in which a feature is mentioned.

5   Evaluation

We performed a preliminary evaluation aimed to determine how practitioners find RE-SWOT supportive to requirements elicitation through competitor analysis. In particular, we conducted three semi-structured interviews with three product management members from different app developers.

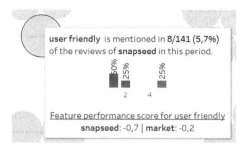

Fig. 3. Inspecting the details of a feature.

Interview Protocol. Due to logistic constraints, the interviews were conducted remotely via online meetings that allowed for screen sharing and recording. The interview protocol, fully described in the appendix of [24], included five parts:

1. *Introduction* (5 min): an explanation of the research and the interview goals.
2. *Contextual questions* (10 min) were made concerning the company, the interviewee's role, the product, and their current app review analysis practices.
3. *Demo* (10 min): the tool was showcased on a set of photo editing apps.
4. *Tool use* (20 min): the participant could interact freely with the tool prepared with reviews concerning the interviewee company's app and its competitors. In this phase, the researcher minimized interference, while think aloud was encouraged, and the participant was allowed to stop before the time expired.
5. *Follow-up questions* (15 min) on the participant's experience with the tool, pros and cons, missing features, and a comparison with the current practice.

Two participants were recruited through a post in the online community MindTheProduct, an international community for product management. One participant was recruited via convenience sampling. All participants represented companies with a mobile app on Google Play or iOS App Store, and could identify 2+ competing app. Both the reference app and the competitors needed to have 200+ reviews in English over the same period and distribution platform.

Case Descriptions. For confidentiality restrictions, we cannot disclose the identity of the companies. Pseudonymized data, including the periods from which we mined the reviews, is summarized in Table 3 and described below:

- *Case 1: dating apps.* We interviewed a senior business analyst, working for 2 years at a Canadian company whose service (*dat-ref*) has 150 million registered users; besides mobile apps for iOS, Android, and Windows Phone, *dat-ref* users can also use a website. As competitors, the interviewee suggested the market leader (*dat-c1*) and a fast-growing company (*dat-c2*).
- *Case 2: travel apps for tourists.* The reference app (*trv-ref*) supports the booking of activities and tickets, and is produced by a company with 400 employees distributed over three continents. We interviewed a senior product

manager with 6+ years of expertise in the field, who is responsible for the development roadmap. The competitors are an app for the Asian market (*trv-c1*) and the market leader (*trv-c2*).

– *Case 3: puzzle games.* The reference app (*pzl-ref*) has 135 puzzle types and is created by a small European company (6 employees). We interviewed the CEO of the company, who is a software engineer and has 9 years of experience in app development. The competitors *pzl-c1* and *pzl-c2* are similar apps suggested by the interviewee.

Table 3. Overview of the data collected for the three cases. The number of features refers to those that were *mined* by our tool.

Case 1: Dating apps May 2018			Case 2: Travel apps Dec 2016–May 2018			Case 3: Puzzle games Jan 2017–Jun 2018		
ID	Reviews	Features	ID	Reviews	Features	ID	Reviews	Features
dat-ref	3,220	280	trv-ref	253	9	pzl-ref	743	11
dat-c1	992	46	trv-c1	506	30	pzl-c1	2,105	72
dat-c2	802	66	trv-c2	375	14	pzl-c2	3,321	176

Results: Current Practice. All interviewees reported that they read the reviews for their app to some extent. The *dat-ref* interviewee reads all reviews approximately once per month to understand user perception and to identify areas for improvement. The reviews of *trv-ref* are automatically re-posted to the development team communication channel, giving everyone the opportunity to read them on a continuous basis. The CEO of *pzl-ref* reads the reviews occasionally through the Google Play Developers console, but found them only mildly useful for guiding product development. None of the interviewees has the habit of reading their competitors reviews, either due to time constraints (*dat-ref*) or because the option has never been considered (*trv-ref* and *pzl-ref*).

Positive Aspects and Insights. All participants referred to the visual and interactive aspect of RE-SWOT as the main positive feature of the tool. According to the *dat-ref* interviewee, "The tool is easy to learn and navigate", while the *trv-ref* interviewee described the experience as a "deep-dive analysis".

The *dat-ref* product manager highlighted other positive aspects: the possibility to zoom and see details can impact positively the communication between stakeholders, and the automated detection of phrases from the reviews is useful to work with a large volume of reviews. The same interviewee was surprised to discover that one of the competitors received fewer reviews than *dat-ref*.

The *trv-ref* interviewee stated to have become aware of a feature from the competitors that was previously unknown, and this—if time allows—may influence product development. It was also possible to see that one competitor was conducting a promotion because people are commenting on promo codes.

The CEO of *pzl-ref* said that the tool confirms that competitor apps adopt a similar business model, but found the insight generation limited, mostly due to the nature of reviews received by games, which are generic and not informative.

Improvements and Missing Features. Both the *dat-ref* and the *trv-ref* interviewees indicated the possibility to see trends over time as the most valuable improvement. While the *dat-ref* product manager found that the feature could make the tool directly usable in practice, the *trv-ref* interviewee would have liked to see the reviews for a custom period of time, instead of selecting one quarter.

The *trv-ref* participant observed some weaknesses in the feature extraction algorithm; despite our attempt to merge some features via lemmatization, there are still cases in which two word collocations are not merged automatically.

Concerning the SWOT classification, both the *trv-ref* and the *pzl-ref* participants found some opportunities to be inaccurate, for bugs in other apps do not necessarily represent an opportunity (*trv-ref*), and because some opportunities referred to features that are already implemented in the reference app (*pzl-ref*).

Finally, the *pzl-ref* interviewee suggested some usability improvements, including (i) a filter for the analyst to remove uninformative (e.g., short) reviews; and (ii) an automatically generated preview of the reviews mentioning a given feature, a sort of summarization.

Comparison to Current Practice. None of the participants currently read their competitors reviews; thus, the interviewees answered based on the way they read their own app's reviews. The *dat-ref* interviewee found the feature generation algorithm to be an improvement over their current practice. The *trv-ref* product manager thought that the visualization tool has the potential to deliver knowledge about the competitors. Finally, the *pzl-ref* interviewee referred us to the Google Play Console, which provides review highlights using similar techniques to RE-SWOT for feature extraction. However, according to the participant, analyzing reviews through RE-SWOT is more visual and interactive.

Factors Influencing Adoption. The *dat-ref* interviewee could see RE-SWOT being integrated into their workflow if more competitors could be handled (currently, it supports two competitors besides the reference app), and if trend analysis was included. As a drawback, the tool uses Tableau Software, which could make it unaffordable to some companies. Also the *trv-ref* participant thought they could adopt the tool, when a functionality was created to support the analysis of trends. On the other hand, the *pzl-ref* CEO found no real incentive to adopt the tool, unless a notification mechanism is put in place so that changes in sentiment are automatically pushed to the product management.

6   Discussion and Future Work

We have presented the RE-SWOT method for eliciting requirements for mobile apps based on competitor analysis through the automated processing of user reviews posted in app stores. RE-SWOT draws inspiration from strategic planning and classifies app features as strengths, weaknesses, opportunities, and threats.

RE-SWOT employs NLP algorithms to automatically extract features from the reviews and to classify the features according to the SWOT framework. The results are rendered in an interactive visualization that helps analysts explore their app's market and identify possible requirements for the next releases.

Main Findings. The *feature extraction* algorithm was evaluated positively by the *dat-ref* participant, while the other two interviewees found that the results include too many false positives. It is worth noting that the *dat-ref* receives 100 times the rate of reviews than the other reference apps; as such, we hypothesize that the algorithm is more effective for apps with a high review volume.

The *SWOT classification* was understood quite well by all interviewees. The most recurrent feedback was that not all strengths or weaknesses of the competitors represent actual threats or opportunities. Our to-be-expected conclusion is that the insights that RE-SWOT returns do not automatically result in new requirements for the reference app; human analytical skills are essential.

The *interactive visualization* of the tool was indicated as a positive factor by all interviewees. On the other hand, they indicated the need to include *change detection* techniques, either via trend analysis or through a notification system that informs analysts of significant changes in the sentiment toward a feature.

Validity Evaluation. We discuss the major threats to validity based on the distinction between internal, conclusion, construct, and external validity [30].

Internal Validity. All of our interviewees adopted practices in which competitor reviews were not considered. Therefore, the positive appreciation could be explained by the fact the interviewees had never analyzed competitor reviews. Moreover, the review volume differed greatly across apps, therefore resulting in a large variability in terms of the period we analyzed.

Conclusion Validity. The interviews were manually coded into observations, and therefore we may have inserted our own beliefs during this process. Moreover, the number of cases ($N = 3$) is insufficient to draw definitive conclusions.

Construct Validity. RE-SWOT has been evaluated as a whole rather than by its parts. Therefore, we cannot determine, for example, the extent to which the SWOT classification mechanism is effective, for the practitioners may have focused on other factors like the size of the circles (the volume).

External Validity. As observational case studies were applied, there is no population to sample from. Therefore, generalization is analytical rather than statistical. Moreover, the number of reviews for case 2 and case 3 are rather low to justify an automated approach; as such, the case of dating apps is probably the most representative of the intended audience.

Future Directions. Many improvements to RE-SWOT are possible. For feature extraction, we adapted Guzman and Maalej's technique [12], but we could experiment with the SAFE framework [17] or other recent algorithms. Also, the thresholds we used to determine the SWOT classes should be adjusted. Furthermore, as pointed out by the interviewees, trend analysis should be included for increasing the impact of the tool. The sentiment score calculation can be improved by looking at the text characteristics, instead of using only the number of stars assigned by the users. Inevitably, more empirical evaluation is necessary; in particular, we need to assess the effectiveness of the framework when used in the daily practice of requirements engineers and product managers.

In general, this work offers numerous opportunities for research that combines NLP and information visualization in RE; for another example of such synergy, see our work on terminological ambiguity [6]. In order for automated techniques to become useful for practitioners, the results of automation have to be turned into requirements analytics tools [26] that are built for use by human analysts.

References

1. Bano, M., Zowghi, D.: A systematic review on the relationship between user involvement and system success. Inf. Softw. Technol. **58**, 148–169 (2015)
2. Berry, D.: Natural language and requirements engineering–nu? In: International Workshop on Requirements Engineering (2001)
3. Bourque, P., Fairley, R.E.: Guide to the software engineering body of knowledge (SWEBOK (R)): version 3.0. IEEE Computer Society Press (2014)
4. Chen, N., Lin, J., Hoi, S.C.H., Xiao, X., Zhang, B.: AR-miner: mining informative reviews for developers from mobile app marketplace. In: Proceedings of ICSE, pp. 767–778 (2014)
5. Cooper Jr., J.R., Lee, S.W., Gandhi, R.A., Gotel, O.: Requirements engineering visualization: a survey on the state-of-the-art. Proceedings of REV, pp. 46–55 (2009)
6. Dalpiaz, F., van der Schalk, I., Brinkkemper, S., Aydemir, F.B., Lucassen, G.: Detecting terminological ambiguity in user stories: tool and experimentation. Inf. Softw. Technol. (2019). https://doi.org/10.1016/j.infsof.2018.12.007
7. Di Sorbo, A., et al.: What would users change in my app? Summarizing app reviews for recommending software changes. In: Proceedings of FSE, pp. 499–510 (2016)
8. Fu, B., Lin, J., Li, L., Faloutsos, C., Hong, J., Sadeh, N.: Why people hate your app: making sense of user feedback in a mobile app store. In: Proceedings of SIGKDD, pp. 1276–1284 (2013)
9. Gao, C., Wang, B., He, P., Zhu, J., Zhou, Y., Lyu, M.R.: PAID: prioritizing app issues for developers by tracking user reviews over versions. In: Proceedings of ISSRE, pp. 35–45 (2016)

10. Genc-Nayebi, N., Abran, A.: A systematic literature review: opinion mining studies from mobile app store user reviews. J. Syst. Softw. **125**, 207–219 (2017)
11. Groen, E.C., et al.: The crowd in requirements engineering: the landscape and challenges. IEEE Softw. **34**(2), 44–52 (2017)
12. Guzman, E., Maalej, W.: How do users like this feature? A fine grained sentiment analysis of app reviews. In: Proceedings of RE, pp. 153–162 (2014)
13. Harman, M., Jia, Y., Zhang, Y.: App store mining and analysis: MSR for app stores. In: Proceedings of MSR, pp. 108–111 (2012)
14. Hill, T., Westbrook, R.: SWOT analysis: it's time for a product recall. Long Range Plann. **30**(1), 46–52 (1997)
15. Hosseini, M., Phalp, K., Taylor, J., Ali, R.: Towards crowdsourcing for requirements engineering. In: Proceedings of REFSQ, pp. 82–87 (2014)
16. Jin, J., Ji, P., Gu, R.: Identifying comparative customer requirements from product online reviews for competitor analysis. Eng. Appl. Artif. Intell. **49**, 61–73 (2016)
17. Johann, T., Maalej, W.: Democratic mass participation of users in Requirements Engineering? In: Proceedings of RE, pp. 256–261 (2015)
18. Kabbedijk, J., Brinkkemper, S., Jansen, S., van der Veldt, B.: Customer involvement in requirements management: lessons from mass market software development. In: Proceedings of RE, pp. 281–286 (2009)
19. Keertipati, S., Savarimuthu, B.T.R., Licorish, S.A.: Approaches for prioritizing feature improvements extracted from app reviews. In: Proceedings of EASE, pp. 1–6 (2016)
20. Maalej, W., Nabil, H.: Bug report, feature request, or simply praise? On automatically classifying app reviews. In: Proceedings of RE, pp. 116–125 (2015)
21. Maalej, W., Nayebi, M., Johann, T., Ruhe, G.: Towards data-driven requirements engineering. IEEE Softw. **33**, 1–6 (2015)
22. Pagano, D., Maalej, W.: User feedback in the AppStore: an empirical study. In: Proceedings of RE, pp. 125–134 (2013)
23. Panichella, S., Di Sorbo, A., Guzman, E., Visaggio, C.A., Canfora, G., Gall, H.C.: How can I improve my app? Classifying user reviews for software maintenance and evolution. In: Proceedings of ICSME 2015, pp. 281–290 (2015)
24. Parente, M.G.: Using NLP and information visualization to analyze app reviews. Master's thesis, Utrecht University, the Netherlands (2018). https://dspace.library.uu.nl/handle/1874/368082
25. Pfitzner, D., Hobbs, V., Powers, D.: A unified taxonomic framework for information visualization. In: Proceedings of APVis (2003)
26. Reddivari, S., Rad, S., Bhowmik, T., Cain, N., Niu, N.: Visual requirements analytics: a framework and case study. Requir. Eng. **19**(3), 257–279 (2014)
27. Shneiderman, B.: The eyes have it: a task by data type taxonomy for information visualizations. In: Proceedings of VL/HCC, pp. 336–343 (1996)
28. Srivastava, P.K., Sharma, R.: Crowdsourcing to elicit requirements for MyERP application. In: Proceedings of CrowdRE, pp. 31–35 (2015)
29. Weihrich, H.: The TOWS matrix–a tool for situational analysis. Long Range Plan. **15**(2), 54–66 (1982)
30. Wohlin, C., Runeson, P., Höst, M., Ohlsson, M.C., Regnell, B., Wesslén, A.: Experimentation in Software Engineering. Springer, Heidelberg (2012). https://doi.org/10.1007/978-3-642-29044-2
31. Yang, H., Liang, P.: Identification and classification of requirements from app user reviews. In: Proceedings of SEKE, pp. 7–12 (2015)

Tracelink Quality

Increasing Precision of Automatically Generated Trace Links

Paul Hübner[(✉)] and Barbara Paech

Institute for Computer Science, Heidelberg University,
Im Neuenheimer Feld 205, 69120 Heidelberg, Germany
{huebner,paech}@informatik.uni-heidelberg.de

Abstract. **[Context and Motivation]** In order to use automatically created trace links during a project directly, the precision of the links is essential. Our interaction-based trace link creation approach (IL) utilizes the interactions of developers recorded in an integrated development environment (IDE) while working on a requirement. For this, developers need to indicate the requirement they are going to work on before coding. This approach worked well in an open-source project with developers who were interested in the interaction logs, but did not work well with students who were not particularly motivated to trigger the interaction recording. **[Question/problem]** Developers often create trace links themselves by providing issue identifiers (IDs) in commit messages. This causes little effort and does not require the awareness for interaction recording. However, as confirmed by recent research, typically only 60% of the commits are linked. In this paper, we study whether and how IL can be improved by a combination with links created by issue IDs in commit messages. **[Principal ideas/results]** We changed our approach so that interaction logs are associated with requirements based on the IDs in the commit-messages. Thus, developers do not need to manually associate requirements and interaction logs. We performed a new student study with this approach. **[Contribution]** In this new study, we show that with this new approach and link improvement techniques precision is above 90% and recall is almost 80%. We also show that for our data this is better than using commit-messages only and better than the often used information retrieval-based approaches.

Keywords: Traceability · Interaction · Requirement · Source code · Precision

1 Introduction

Existing trace link creation approaches are most often based on information retrieval (IR) and on structured requirements, such as use cases [3,5]. These approaches mostly focus on the optimization of recall [3]. In addition, their precision is bad which makes the approaches not applicable when directly using created links [5]. Therefore, a review of the created link candidates by an expert

© Springer Nature Switzerland AG 2019
E. Knauss and M. Goedicke (Eds.): REFSQ 2019, LNCS 11412, pp. 73–89, 2019.
https://doi.org/10.1007/978-3-030-15538-4_5

is necessary before their usage. In security-critical domains such as aeronautics and the automotive industry, complete link sets are required. These links are only created periodically, when needed for certification to justify the safe operation of a system [4]. Therefore, the additional effort to remove many false positive links is accepted.

Nowadays, many software companies use issue tracking systems (ITS) to specify their requirements [15]. For open source projects, the usage of an ITS is a crucial point and de facto standard [18]. In ITS, the requirements text is unstructured and requirement issues are mixed with other issues for e.g. bug tracking, task and test management [18]. Furthermore, for many development activities, it is helpful to consider the links between requirements and source code *during development*, e.g. in maintenance tasks, for program comprehension and re-engineering [7,16].

If these links are created continuously during the development, e.g. after each commit performed by a developer, they can be used continuously. In these cases, the big effort of handling false positives, and thus bad precision is not practicable. Therefore, a trace link creation approach for links between unstructured requirements and code with perfect precision and good recall is needed.

Our interaction-based trace link creation approach (*IL*) aims at continuous link creation and usage. *IL* relies on developers manually selecting the requirement in their IDE before they start to work on it. Then, interactions recorded in the IDE are assigned to this requirement and the code files touched during interactions assigned to this requirement are used to create trace links. The approach is implemented in a corresponding tool[1].

In an initial study [10] based on open source data, we could show that *IL* links can have perfect precision and good recall (i.e. at least above 80%), if the developers use the requirements selection systematically. Since the initial recall of *IL* for one of the data sets used in this study was below 80%, we also used *source code structure* to improve the recall. Source code structure denotes relations between source code files such as references. Basically, we added further links by following the references of already linked files.

In a second study [11] with students as developers, the developers did not perform the manual selection of the requirements systematically. This lead to the creation of wrong trace links by our *IL* approach (precision of 43.0%, recall of 73.7% and $f_{0.5}$-measure of 0.469). To countervail the creation of wrong links, we came up with *wrong link detection techniques*. On the one hand, we used techniques based on data of the recorded interaction (e.g. interaction duration and frequency). On the other hand, we used techniques based on the source code structure. With these wrong link detection techniques, we could improve the precision of *IL* to 68.2% ($f_{0.5}$-measure of 0.624) [11]. However, the precision improvement also resulted in a decline of the recall to 46.5%. This is still not satisfying. Thus, we looked for a way to remove the error-prone manual selection of the requirement by the developers.

---

[1] https://se.ifi.uni-heidelberg.de/il.html, tool and data download.

The usage of issue identifiers (IDs) to link commits to requirements and bug reports is a common convention in open source projects [2,18,23]. Developers often create trace links themselves by providing issue IDs in commit messages [22]. Trace links can be created by linking all files affected by a commit with the requirement specified by the issue ID in the commit message. This is little effort and does not require the awareness for interaction recording. However, as confirmed by recent research, typically only 60% of the commits are linked [23]. Therefore, our idea is to combine the ID-based linking with interaction recording. Instead of using manually selected requirements, the issue IDs from developers' commit messages are used. All code files touched in the interactions before the commit are associated to the requirement identified through the issue ID.

As the students of our second study also used requirement issue IDs in their commit messages, we first simulated the combination of issue ID and IL retrospectively with the data of our previous study (without using the wrong link detection techniques). This directly improved the precision from 43.0% to 56.6% without affecting the recall.

This encouraged us to improve our approach with consideration of IDs in the commits. This new approach is called IL_{Com}. We applied IL_{Com} in a new study with students. Without further wrong link detection techniques, IL_{Com} had a precision of 84.9% and a recall of 67.3% ($f_{0.5}$-measure of 0.807). We also applied our wrong link detection techniques [11] and recall improvements [10] and could finally achieve a precision of 90.0% and a recall of 79.0% ($f_{0.5}$-measure of 0.876). Only using the issue IDs and the list of changed files from commits for link creation similar as described by [23] together with our wrong link detection and recall improvement techniques resulted in a precision of 67.5% and recall of 44.3% ($f_{0.5}$-measure of 0.611). For IR-created links using latent semantic indexing (LSI) [6], also including our wrong link detection, precision was 36.9% and recall 55.7% ($f_{0.5}$-measure of 0.396). Thus, in our new study we show that IL_{Com} achieves very good precision and recall and that it is much better in both precision and recall than the standard techniques.

The remainder of the paper is structured as follows. Section 2 introduces basics for evaluation of automatically created trace links, the projects used for the evaluation, our basic IL approach and former study results. Section 3 illustrates the details of the IL_{Com} approach and its implementation. It also reports on our retrospective preliminary study. Section 4 outlines the experimental design of our new study. Section 5 presents and discusses the results of our new study. Section 6 discusses the threats to validity and Sect. 7 related work. Finally, Sect. 8 concludes the paper and gives an outlook on our further research.

2 Background

In this section we introduce basics of trace link evaluation, describe the used study projects, introduce our IL approach and report about IR based trace link creation and results of our former studies.

2.1 Trace Link Evaluation

In the following, we sketch the basics of trace link evaluation as already described in our paper [11]. To evaluate approaches for trace link creation [3,5], a gold standard which consists of the set of all correct trace links for a given set of artifacts is important. To create such a gold standard, it is necessary to manually check whether trace links exist for each pair of artifacts. Based on this gold standard, precision and recall can be computed.

Precision (P) is the amount of correct links (true positives, TP) within all links found by an approach. The latter is the sum of TP and incorrect links (false positive, FP). Recall (R) is the amount of TP links found by an approach within all existing correct links. The latter is the sum of TP and false negative (FN) links:

$$P = \frac{TP}{TP + FP} \qquad R = \frac{TP}{TP + FN} \qquad F_\beta = (1 + \beta^2) \cdot \frac{P \cdot R}{(\beta^2 \cdot P) + R}$$

F_β-scores combine the results for P and R in a single measurement to judge the accuracy of a trace link creation approach. As shown in the equation, for F_β above, β can be used to weight P in favor of R and vice versa. In contrast to other studies, our focus is to emphasize P, but still consider R. Therefore, we choose $F_{0.5}$ which weights P twice as much as R. In addition, we also calculate F_1-scores to compare our results with others. For approaches using structured [8] and unstructured [19] data for trace link creation good R values are between 70 and 79% and good P values are between 30 and 49%.

2.2 Evaluation Projects

In the following, we describe the three projects we used for the evaluation of our approach. The first project is Mylyn a open source project which we used in our first *IL* evaluation [10]. In the project a plug-in to manage development tasks directly within the IDE is developed. We used the public accessible project's requirements and interaction log data stored in an ITS and source code in the Git version control system to create our data sets. We created two data sets using excerpts of the Mylyn project data from the years 2007 and 2012. They are called M_{2007} and M_{2012} in the following. Details can be found in [10].

The other two projects are university student projects we created one data set for each project using interaction recording of our tools, requirements managed in an ITS and source code in a version control system. Since the first university student project finished in 2017 and the second in 2018 the data sets for these project are called S_{2017} and S_{2018} respectively. Both are Scrum-oriented working with a real world customer in sprints. The first of them lasted from October 2016 to March 2017. We used it in the evaluation of a first *IL* improvement [11]. The second project lasted from October 2017 to March 2018. We used this project's data set S_{2018} in the actual evaluation. The details of the second data set are explained in Sect. 4.2.

The aim of the S_{2017} *project* was to develop a system to store and manage all health care reports for a patient in a single data base. The customer was the IT department of the university hospital. The aim of the S_{2018} project was to develop an Android-based indoor navigation app for students in university buildings. Typical use cases for such an app are navigating to the room of a certain lecture or finding any other point of interest efficiently. The customer was a mobile development company. In both projects, an adviser from our chair was involved. Seven students participated in the S_{2017} project and six students in the S_{2018} project. The projects were split in a corresponding number of sprints. In each of these sprints, one of the students acted as Scrum master and thus was responsible for all organizational concerns such as planning the development during the sprint and communicating with the customer.

For all requirement management-related activities, in both projects a Scrum Jira[2] Project was used. This included the specification of requirements in the form of user stories and the bundling of the stories in epics. An example of a user story in the navigation app project is *Show point to point route* and the corresponding epic of this story is *routing*. To assign the implementation of user stories to developers, sub-task issues were used. A sub-task comprises partial work to implement a user story, e.g. *Show route info box*. For the implementation, the developers used Git as version control system and the Webstorm[3] version of intelliJ in the first and the Eclipse IDE with the Android software development kit (SDK) in the second project. For both IDEs we provided plugins implementing our interaction recording tools. For the usage of Git in the S_{2018} project, there was an explicit guideline to use a Jira Issue ID in any commit message to indicate the associated Jira Issue. Although not directly required, the developers used this convention in the S_{2017} project as well.

In the first S_{2017} project, the developers used JavaScript as programming language which was requested by the customer. Furthermore, the MongoDB[4] NOSQL database and the React[5] UI framework were used. In the S_{2018} project, the customer provided a proprietary Java SDK of their own for the general use case to develop Android mobile navigation apps. The developers needed two sprints to understand the complexity of the SDK and to set up everything in a way to work efficiently on the implementation of requirements. The programming language for the logic and data management part was Java and the UI was implemented in Android's own XML based language.

In both projects at the beginning of the first sprint, we supported the developers with the installation and initial configuration of our interaction log recording tools. We also gave a short introduction on the implemented interaction-recording mechanism and how to use the tools during the project.

In Sect. 2.4 we summarize the previous evaluations and compare them with information retrieval based link creation. In Sect. 3.3 we use the S_{2017} project to

---

[2] https://www.atlassian.com/software/jira.

[3] https://www.jetbrains.com/webstorm/.

[4] https://www.mongodb.com/.

[5] https://reactjs.org/.

test our assumption that using issue IDs in commit messages improves the precision. In Sect. 4 we use the S_{2018} project to evaluate our new approach IL_{Com}.

2.3   IL Approach Overview

Figure 1 shows the overview of our *IL* approach consisting of three steps. In the first step *Interaction Capturing*, interaction events in the IDE of a developer are captured and associated to a requirement. We implemented our approach as plug-in for the IntelliJ IDE. For this, we extended an existing activity tracker plug-in to also track the interactions with requirements. In addition, we used the *Task & Context* functionality of IntelliJ to associate interactions with requirements. The developers could connect IntelliJ to the Jira project and the developers had to select the specific Jira issue with the UI of the *Task & Context* functionality when working on a requirement. As a result, the interaction log contained activation and deactivation events for requirement issues. These activation and deactivation events were used to allocate all interactions between the activation and deactivation event for a specific requirement to this specific requirement. Since the developers also used sub-task issues and sub-tasks describe details for implementing the requirement, we combined the interactions recorded for requirements and for the corresponding sub-tasks.

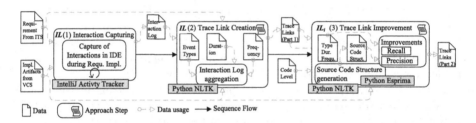

Fig. 1. *IL* Trace link creation overview: interaction capturing, trace link creation and improvement IL_i

In the second step *Trace Link Creation*, all interaction events captured for a requirement are used to generate trace links between the requirement and the source code files affected by the interactions. We did not consider files such as build configurations, project descriptions, readme files, meta-data descriptions, binaries etc. and files from 3rd parties such as libraries, as we focused on the code created by the developers. Interaction event-specific metadata like the event type (edit or select), the duration as the sum of all events' durations based on the interactions' time stamps for specific files and the frequency of how often an interaction occurred for a specific file were captured. The result of this second step is a list of trace links including the metadata aggregated from these interactions which is used as input for the third step *Trace Link Improvement*.

In this third step, precision is improved by removing potential wrong links using the interaction-specific metadata frequency, duration, and event type from the previous step. For frequency, duration, and event type, different settings are possible. Precision is also improved by using the source code structure, i.e. the references from one source code file to other source code files. In our P_{2017} study, we found that linking only source code files which are connected by source code structure with each other improves the precision significantly (*source code structure in story*) [11]. Finally, we also use the source code structure to improve the recall of *IL*. In this case, the source code structure of source code files which are already linked to a requirement is utilized. We add links by following the relations of the source code structure to other source code files up to a certain level [10].

In the following, we denote our *IL* approach as *IL* when applying the first two steps only and as IL_i when also applying the improvement techniques of the third step.

2.4 IR Based Link Creation and Previous Studies

To compare the results of our *IL* approach we also created links with information retrieval (*IR*). *IR* based link creation uses the textual content of documents and creates links based on textual similarity. Before document text content is processed by *IR* preprocessing of the textual content is performed. We performed all common *IR* preprocessing steps like stop word removal, punctuation, character removal, and stemming [1,3]. We also performed camel case identifier splitting (e.g. RouteInfoBox becomes Route Info Box), since camel case notation has been used in the source code [6]. In our studies we used the two most common *IR* techniques for trace link creation vector space model (VSM) and latent semantic indexing (LSI) [3,5,6]. The basic difference between these two *IR* techniques is that LSI can also consider synonyms of terms as similar whereas VSM only considers equal terms.

In the P_{2018} project the requirements were specified in German, but the source code files were in English. Thus we automatically translated the P_{2018} requirements using the googletrans Python library[6] before preprocessing and *IR* application. Since the user stories of both student projects P_{2017} and P_{2018} contained only short texts, the used threshold values for *IR* had to be set low. Source code structure-based precision and recall improvements (cf. Sect. 2.3) have also been applied to the *IR* (IR_i) and *IL* created trace links (IL_i).

Table 1 shows the results for *IR* and *IL* for our previous studies using the data sets explained in Sect. 2.2. When comparing the precision, recall and $f_{0.5}$-measures of IR_i and IL_i, IL_i clearly outperforms IR_i in all three data sets.

3 Commit Based Link Creation and IL$_{\text{Com}}$

In this section, we introduce our commit-based variant of *IL*, called IL_{Com}. We provide an overview of all trace link creation techniques used in our new study.

---

[6] https://pypi.org/project/googletrans/.

Table 1. Results for *IR* and *IL* in previous studies

Approach[a]		Data Set	Pre-cision	Re-call	$F_{0.5}$	$F_{1.0}$	#Links[b]					#Sto-ries	Src Files	
							CE	TP	FP	GS	FN		Used	GS
IL_i	Interaction link creation with improvement	M_{2007}	1.000	0.929	0.985	0.963	2565	2565	0	2761	196	50	627	627
		M_{2012}	1.000	0.800	0.952	0.889	1126	1126	0	1408	282	50	363	702
		P_{2017}	0.682	0.465	0.624	0.553	148	101	47	217	116	13	63	91
IR	Information retrieval link creation	M_{2007}	0.310	0.248	0.295	0.275	1058	328	730	1324	996	41	200	585
		M_{2012}	0.298	0.558	0.328	0.388	920	274	646	491	217	35	169	444
		P_{2017}	0.343	0.161	0.280	0.219	102	35	67	217	182	9	17	91
IR_i	Information retrieval link creation with improvement	M_{2007}	0.386	0.440	0.396	0.411	3143	1214	1929	2761	1547	41	308	627
		M_{2012}	0.283	0.557	0.314	0.376	2766	784	1982	1408	624	35	354	702
		P_{2017}	0.351	0.217	0.312	0.268	134	47	87	217	170	9	21	91

[a] *IR* settings for the data sets are denoted as <IR-*model(similarity threshold)*>: M_{2007} *LSI*(0.3), M_{2012} *LSI*(0.5), P_{2017} *LSI*(0.1)

[b] created (CE), true positive (TP) $\cong$ correct, false positive (FP) $\cong$ wrong, gold standard (GS), false negative (FN) $\cong$ not found

This also includes the creation of trace links by only using commit data [22]. We also present the results of a preliminary retrospective simulated application of IL_{Com} to the data set P_{2017}.

3.1 IL$_{Com}$

The difference between *IL* and IL_{Com} lies in the first interaction capturing step. IL_{Com} uses both recorded interactions and issue IDs in commit messages for link creation. In IL_{Com}, interactions are recorded until a developer performs a commit. If the commit message contains an issue ID, all recorded interactions are associated to this issue ID and the history of recorded interactions is cleared. If multiple issue IDs are contained in the commit message, the recorded interactions are associated to all issue IDs. If no issue ID is contained in the commit message, interaction recording continues until there is a commit with a commit message containing an issue ID. Clearly, this can impact precision and recall, as the commits without ID might be associated with another issue [9,13]. This will be discussed in Sect. 5.4. After the association of issue IDs with interactions has been obtained, link creation can be performed as described for *IL* in Sect. 2.3.

We implemented the interaction capturing for IL_{Com} for the P_{2018} project as plug-in for the Eclipse IDE. Our tool bundles all recorded interactions and uploads them to the Jira issue specified by the Jira issue ID in the commit message. The interaction events recorded by our tool comprise a time stamp, the type of interaction (select or edit), the part of the IDE in which the interaction occurred (e.g. editor, navigator, etc.), the file involved in the interaction, and a degree of interest (DOI) metric for the file. The DOI is a numerical value calculated for a file considering the number of interactions (frequency) and the type of interactions with the file, i.e. edit interactions are rated higher than select interactions [12].

3.2 Trace Link Creation Techniques

In the following we summarize the notations for the different link creation (IR, IL, $ComL$ and IL_{Com}) and improvement techniques (shown by subscript i):

IR denotes the approach for link creation by information retrieval and **IR_i** denotes that also source code structure based improvement techniques have been applied (cf. Sect. 2.4).

IL denotes the approach for link creation by using the recorded interactions and **IL_i** denotes that also interaction-specific metadata and source code structure based improvement techniques have been applied (cf. Sect. 2.3).

$ComL$ denotes the approach for link creation by using the issue IDs from commit messages and the files contained in the commits and **$ComL_i$** denotes that also source code structure based improvement techniques have been applied.

IL_{Com} denotes the approach for link creation by using the recorded interactions and the issue IDs from commit messages and **IL_{Com_i}** denotes that also interaction-specific metadata and source code structure based improvement techniques have been applied (cf. Sect. 3.1).

3.3 Retrospective Study

As described in the introduction, we analyzed the P_{2017} project data set regarding IDs in commit messages. We found that there were significantly more commits with issue IDs (per developer) than there were activation and deactivation events in the recorded interaction logs. For one developer, the processing of 18 requirements was recorded in the interaction logs, but there were 71 commits with requirement issue IDs for the same developer in Git. This does not directly indicate that the interaction log recording is wrong, since it is possible that a developer performed multiple commits for one requirement successively. However, after a random check of the time span of interaction recording for two requirements we found that there were commits with different issue IDs in this time span. This encouraged us to analyze the data further and thus simulate retrospectively the application of IL_{Com}.

Table 2. 2017 project results: precision and recall for created trace links

Approach		Pre-cision	Re-call	$F_{0.5}$	$F_{1.0}$	#Links					#Sto-ries	#Sub-tasks	Src Files	
						CE	TP	FP	GS	FN			Used	GS
IL	Interaction link creation	0.430	0.737	0.469	0.543	372	160	212	217	57	19	98	89	91
IL_i	With improvement	**0.669**	0.465	**0.615**	0.549	151	101	50	217	116	13	72	63	91
$ComL$	Commit link creation	0.620	0.465	0.581	0.532	163	101	62	217	116	19	98	78	91
$ComL_i$	With improvement	**0.659**	0.401	**0.584**	0.499	132	87	45	217	130	11	66	59	91
IL_{Com}	Inter. and commit link creation	0.566	0.733	0.593	0.639	281	159	122	217	58	19	98	86	91
IL_{Com_i}	With improvement	**0.736**	0.539	**0.686**	0.622	159	117	42	217	100	13	72	63	91

Table 2 shows the results for our retrospective study with the data from the data set P_{2017}. We created the trace links by the different approaches as described in the following. For *ComL*, we created links for all commits with requirement issue IDs in the commit message from the requirement referenced by the ID to all source code files of the commit. For IL_{Com}, we used the interactions recorded for *IL* and the commits with issue IDs. We ordered the Git commits with requirement issue IDs and the interaction log recording by time. All interaction log recordings between two commits with issue IDs are assigned to the issue from the second commit. Since there were also commits without issue ID which we just ignored in our evaluation, this kind of interaction log recordings to commit assignment is not perfect. If a developer just did not add an issue ID in a commit, interactions are assigned wrongly and precision is impaired. This simulates retrospectively the application of IL_{Com}.

Table 2 always shows the best achieved $f_{0.5}$-measure within all performed settings for an approach. Moreover, the overall best values for precision and $f_{0.5}$-measure are highlighted. IL_{Com_i} has a precision of 73.6%, a recall of 53.9% and a $f_{0.5}$-measure of 0.686 which outperforms the precision and recall of all other approaches. This confirmed our idea that *IL* can be combined with the use of issue IDs from commit messages.

4   Experiment Design

In this section, we describe the details of our new study starting with the research questions and the description of how we created the trace links and compared the results with our former studies in Sect. 4.1, followed by the description of the data sources in Sect. 4.2 and and the gold standard creation in Sect. 4.3.

4.1   Research Questions

The research questions we answer in our study are:

RQ$_1$: *What is the precision and recall of IL_{Com}- and IL_{Com_i}-created trace links?* Our hypothesis was that the initial precision of IL_{Com} improves, compared to our P_{2017} study, since there is no additional effort for requirement selection by developers. For IL_{Com_i} compared to IL_{Com}, we expected a further precision improvement.

RQ$_2$: *What is the precision and recall of ComL- and ComL$_i$-created trace links?* Our hypothesis was that precision and recall are worse than the precision of IL_{Com}- and IL_{Com_i}-created links respectively, as the latter uses more information (the interactions).

RQ$_3$: *What is the precision and recall of IR- and IR$_i$-created trace links?* Our hypothesis was that *IR* has a significantly worse precision and similar recall in comparison to IL_{Com}.

The overall goal of this new study is to evaluate, whether the interaction and commit based link creation by IL_{Com} improves the precision compared to the only interaction based link creation by *IL* (RQ$_1$). Moreover, we also would like to investigate whether recording and using interactions outperforms link creation, which relies on commit data only (RQ$_2$). Finally, we also compare the results of *IL$_{Com}$*-created links with *IR*, since *IR* serves as a baseline for automated link creation and for the comparison with our previous studies (RQ$_3$).

4.2 Data Sources

In our evaluation we used three different data sources which are described in the following.

Source Code in the Git Version Control System. The Git repository comprises 406 commits. 226 commits (55.67% of all commits) did contain a Jira issue ID which is a similar proportion as reported by others [22]. We excluded the same file types from the Git repository as for *IL* (cf. Sect. 2.3).

We used the first 395 commits in the Git Repository for link creation. The 395th commit is the commit for the finish of the project's last sprint. Commits after the 395th commit did not contain issue IDs and were performed to refactor the source code to the customer's needs after the final project presentation. The Git repository for the 395th commit contained 40 java and 26 xml files.

Requirements as Issues in Jira. After the project was finished, there were 23 story issues in the Jira project. However, three of the story issues did not specify requirements, but testing and project organization. Therefore, we removed these three stories from our evaluation. Furthermore, the processing status of 3 story issues was unresolved at the end of the project and in addition all sub-tasks of these 3 unresolved stories where unresolved as well. Therefore, we also removed these 3 stories and their interaction recordings from our evaluation and used only the 17 remaining stories and their 74 sub-tasks along with their interaction recordings.

Interaction Recordings. The interaction recordings for the 17 stories and 74 sub-tasks comprise 6471 interaction events separated in 205 commits. After removing interaction events whose files were out of scope as described previously (cf. Sect. 2.3), 4012 interaction events were left in the interaction recordings and used for link creation.

4.3 Gold Standard Creation

The gold standard creation was performed in March 2018 by the 6 developers of the project between the finish of the last sprint and the final presentation to the customer. The developers vetted link candidates between requirements and the source code files in the actual version (395th commit) in the projects Git repository.

The developers vetted the links based on their involvement in the sub-tasks of a requirement. If there were two developers with an equal amount of sub-tasks, both vetted the links and only the links vetted as correct by both were used in the gold standard. For each developer, a developer-specific interactive questionnaire spreadsheet with all link candidates to vet was generated. This contained for each requirement, all possible link candidates to all 66 source code files. The vetting resulted in 309 gold standard trace links, where each requirement and each code file was linked at least once.

5   Results

This section reports the results of our evaluations and answers the RQs.

Table 3. Results for IL_{Com} and IL_{Com_i} with different settings

Approach		Set-ting[a]	Pre-cision	Re-call	$F_{0.5}$	$F_{1.0}$	#Links					Src Files	
							CE	TP	FP	GS	FN	Used	GS
IL_{Com}	Default interaction link creation	none	0.849	0.673	0.807	0.751	245	208	37	309	101	58	66
IL_{Com_i}	Interaction type improvement	$T{:}e$	0.904	0.460	0.758	0.609	157	142	15	309	167	58	66
IL_{Com_i}	Interaction type improvement	$T{:}s$	0.829	0.282	0.597	0.420	105	87	18	309	222	37	66
IL_{Com_i}	Duration improvement	$D10$	0.885	0.521	0.776	0.656	182	161	21	309	148	52	66
IL_{Com_i}	Duration improvement	$D60$	0.901	0.411	0.727	0.564	141	127	14	309	182	50	66
IL_{Com_i}	Frequency improvement	$F2$	0.813	0.463	0.706	0.590	176	143	33	309	166	54	66
IL_{Com_i}	Frequency improvement	$F10$	0.850	0.311	0.631	0.455	113	96	17	309	213	40	66
IL_{Com_i}	Source code structure in story imp.	Sis	0.904	0.485	0.771	0.632	166	150	16	309	159	40	66
IL_{Com_i}	Selected improvement tech. setting	$T{:}e,s;$ $Sis;CS$	**0.900**	0.790	**0.876**	0.841	271	244	27	309	65	62	66

[a] $T{:}e|s = Type{:}edit|select$, $D10|D60 = dur. >= 10|60$ sec., $F2|10 = freq. >= 2|10$, $Sis = Source$ code structure in story, $CS = Source$ code structure

5.1   Answer to RQ1: Comparison of IL and IL$_{Com}$

Table 3 shows the results for IL_{Com} and for different settings for IL_{Com_i}. IL_{Com} has a precision of 84.9% and a recall of 67.3% and thus a $f_{0.5}$-measure of 0.807. Similar to our P_{2017} study, we evaluated different settings for our improvement techniques (cf. first column of Table 3) [11]. Initially, we investigated the different wrong link detection techniques in isolation and then combined different techniques to achieve the overall best precision improvement. On this best precision result, we also applied our source code structure-based recall improvement. The last row of Table 3 shows this best case of IL_{Com_i}. For this, the setting was to use the type select and edit (T:e,s), to restrict the source code files to be connected with each other by code structure in the story (Sis) and to use the code structure to improve recall (CS). In this best case, IL_{Com_i} has a precision of 90.0% and a recall of 79.0% and thus a $f_{0.5}$-measure of 0.876. Thus, IL_{Com_i} improves precision by 5.1%, recall by 22.7% and $f_{0.5}$-measure by 0.069 compared to IL_{Com}.

5.2   Answer to RQ2: Comparison of IL$_{Com}$ and ComL

Table 4 shows the results for $ComL$ and $ComL_i$ and for comparison also the previously reported results of IL_{Com}. $ComL$ has a precision of 66.8% and a recall of 41.7% and thus a $f_{0.5}$-measure of 0.597. For $ComL_i$, we first applied the *source code structure in story* precision improvement followed by *source code structure* recall improvement. $ComL_i$ has a precision of 67.5% and a recall of 44.3% and thus a $f_{0.5}$-measure of 0.611. In comparison to IL_{Com} and IL_{Com_i}, precision, recall, and $f_{0.5}$-measure are worse respectively.

Table 4. Results for $ComL$, $ComL_i$ and comparison with IL_{Com}

Approach[a]		Pre-cision	Re-call	$F_{0.5}$	$F_{1.0}$	#Links					Src Files	
						CE	TP	FP	GS	FN	Used	GS
IL_{Com}	Inter. and commit link creation	0.849	0.673	0.807	0.751	245	208	37	309	101	58	66
IL_{Com_i}	With improvement	0.900	0.790	0.876	0.841	271	244	27	309	65	62	66
$ComL$	Commit link creation	0.668	0.417	0.597	0.514	193	129	64	309	180	59	66
$ComL_i$	With improvement	0.675	0.443	0.611	0.535	203	137	66	309	172	61	66

[a] For the application of improvement techniques the best case is shown

5.3   Answer to RQ3: Comparison of IL$_{Com}$ and IR

Table 5 shows the results for IR and IR_i and for comparison also the previously reported results of IL_{Com} and IL_{Com_i}. IR has a precision of 33.5% and a recall of 49.2% and thus a $f_{0.5}$-measure of 0.358. For P_{2018}, IR_i has a precision of 36.9% and a recall of 55.7% and thus a $f_{0.5}$-measure of 0.396. IR_i improves precision by 3.4%, recall by 6.5% and $f_{0.5}$-measure by 0.038 compared to IR. In comparison to IL_i and IL_{Com_i}, precision, recall, and $f_{0.5}$-measure is worse respectively. For all data sets, IL_i outperforms IR_i. The IR results for our former projects are quite similar and similar to other studies as well [19].

Table 5. Results for IR, IR_i and comparison with IL_{Com} and IL_{Com_i}

Approach[a]		Pre-cision	Re-call	$F_{0.5}$	$F_{1.0}$	#Links					#Sto-ries	Src Files	
						CE	TP	FP	GS	FN		Used	GS
IL_{Com}	Inter. and commit link creation	0.849	0.673	0.807	0.751	245	208	37	309	101	17	58	66
IL_{Com_i}	With improvement	**0.900**	0.790	**0.876**	0.841	271	244	27	309	65	17	62	66
IR	Information retrieval link creation	0.335	0.492	0.358	0.398	454	152	302	309	157	16	60	66
IR_i	With improvement	0.369	0.557	0.396	0.444	466	172	294	309	137	16	64	66

[a] IR settings are denoted as <IR-*model(similarity threshold)*> : *VSM(0.2)*

5.4   Discussion

Precision and recall of IL_{Com} are better than IL. When looking at all studies we performed, it can be seen that IL and IL_{Com} outperform all other link creation approaches, i.e. IR- and commit-based link creation $ComL$ (cf. Table 1 in Sect. 2.4). The fact that IR link creation between unstructured requirements in ITS and source code is worse than in structured requirement cases is reported by others [3,8,19]. This is also confirmed by our three studies (cf. results for IR in Tables 1 and 5) and was one of our initial motivations for the development of IL.

There are several possible reasons for the worse behaviour of $ComL$ in comparison to IL_{Com}. It is interesting that the precision of $ComL$ is roughly 60% in the retrospective study and in the new study. That means the issue IDs given by the developers are only partly correct. This observation is similar to research within developers' commits behavior and the contents of commits [9,13]. These studies report about tangled changes, that is a commit often comprises multiple unrelated issues. Also, we observed that developers manually excluded files in one commit, which were correct in the gold standard and then included these files in a follow-up commit. A reason for this behavior could be a change of the requirement during the project time. Thus, the exclusion behavior was correct when the commit was performed, but was wrong for the final state of the requirement. The reasons for the worse recall of $ComL$ in comparison to IL_{Com} could be select interactions. Select interactions are not detected by commits. These missed files also affect the application of source code structure-based recall improvement.

The improvement techniques developed in our last studies also proved to be reasonable in this new study. Moreover, the improvement techniques also performed well for links created with IR and $ComL$. By applying our wrong link detection techniques, the precision is improved, independent of how the links were created. As wrong links detection techniques impair recall, we apply source code-structured based recall improvement. The improvement of recall by using the source code structure worked reasonable for IL in the last two studies and is outperformed in this new study. The application of recall improvement in this new study resulted in the best overall recall for the complete studies.

Altogether we showed that the creation of links with interaction and commit data by IL_{Com_i} achieves very good precision and recall. This confirms our assumption that the additional effort of manually selecting the requirement to work on caused the bad precision of IL in our previous P_{2017} study. We think that precision and recall can be even better, if developers directly use the created links during the projects, as in the Mylyn project. The use will likely motivate developers to use interaction logging and commit IDs carefully.

6   Threats to Validity

As described in our previous study [11] the internal validity is threatened as manual validation of trace links in the gold standard was performed by the students working as developers in a project context of our research group. However, this ensured that the experts created the gold standard. Also the evaluation of the links was performed after the project had already been finished so that there was no conflict of interest for the students to influence their grading.

When comparing the results achieved with our approach to *IR*, the setup of the *IR* algorithms is a crucial factor. Regarding preprocessing, we performed all common steps including the identifier splitting which is specific to our used data set. However, the low threshold values impair the results for the precision of *IR*. Therefore, further comparison of *IL* and *IR* in which higher threshold values are possible (e.g. with more structured issue descriptions) is necessary.

The external validity depends on the availability of interaction logs and respective tooling and usage of the tooling by developers. The generalizability based on one student project is clearly limited. Although explicitly requested, not all commits contained a Jira issue ID in the commit messages. This affects the resulting association of recorded interaction logs to requirement issues and thus the created trace links. However, the percentage of commits with issue IDs is similar as reported for other projects [22]. This indicates that the results of our evaluation might also apply for industry projects.

7 Related Work

In our previous papers [10,11], we already discussed related work on *IR*, interaction logging and the assessment of interaction recording quality which is shortly summarized in the following: The systematic literature review of Borg on *IR* trace link creation [3] gives an overview of *IR* usage and results. In [14], Konopka uses interaction logs to detect relations between code files and in [24], Soh showed with an observation study that observed interaction durations do not always correspond to recorded interaction durations.

In [20], Omoronyia published an approach in which interactions are used to visualize and navigate trace links. In a follow up paper [21] of the same authors, they also use interactions for trace link creation. They consider developer collaboration and rank interaction events. Their approach achieves a precision of 77% in the best case which is still not as good as our results for IL_{Com}.

In [22], Rath report about a data set *Ilm7* they created from seven open source projects for the purpose of evaluating traceability research. They used the issue IDs in commit messages to link issues to code files. They report that only 60% of the commits contain an issue ID.

In their follow-up work [23], they use the *Ilm7* data set to train different machine learning classifiers to countervail the problem of commits without issue IDs. To train their classifiers, they not only used the files and issue IDs from commits, but also textual similarity (*IR*) between different artifacts (i.e. the commit message text, the issue text, the source code text) and further data like developer-specific information. In their final experiment, they used the trained machine learning classifiers to identify the matching issues for commits without issues and achieved an averaged recall of 91.6% and precision of 17.3%. A direct comparison with *IR*-based link creation is missing. However, since these results are quite similar to what others have achieved with relying on *IR* [19] and ITS data only, it seems that the usage of *IR* to train machine learning classifiers results in the same low precision values as when relying on *IR* only. When directly comparing their results with the results achieved by IL_{Com} in this study (recall of 79.0% and precision of 90%), it is clear that for our research goal of precision optimization IL_{Com} is far superior.

8   Conclusion and Outlook

In this paper, we investigated the precision and recall of our interaction-based trace link creation approach IL_{Com}. In contrast to our previous studies, we changed the implementation of our interaction log recording tool. With the new implementation, we reduce the additional effort for developers to assign interaction log recordings to requirements and removed the need for interaction log recording awareness.

Our new approach and tool build on the common practice to specify issue IDs in commit messages. It uses these issue IDs from commit messages to assign interaction log recording to requirements. IL_{Com} has a precision of 90.0% and recall of 79.0% which outperforms the results of our previous P_{2017} study (precision of 68.2% and recall of 46.5%). Thus, precision is not perfect, but we think that this is a very good basis for continuous link creation and usage. Furthermore, the new approach is applicable also where developers are not particularly interested in interaction recording. We showed that our new approach outperforms *IR* and purely commit-based linking and is superior to current machine learning based approaches as well [23]. Clearly, it is interesting to confirm this with further studies and to study whether this also holds for more structured requirements where *IR* is typically used. Another important step for applicability in practice is to investigate the maintenance of links such as [17].

Acknowledgment. We thank the students of the projects for their effort.

References

1. Baeza-Yates, R., de Ribeiro, B.A.N.: Modern Information Retrieval, 2nd edn. Pearson Addison-Wesley, Boston (2011)
2. Bird, C., Rigby, P.C., Barr, E.T., Hamilton, D.J., Germán, D.M., Devanbu, P.T.: The promises and perils of mining git. In: MSR (2009)
3. Borg, M., Runeson, P., Ardö, A.: Recovering from a decade: a systematic mapping of information retrieval approaches to software traceability. ESE **19**(6), 1565–1616 (2013)
4. Briand, L., Falessi, D., Nejati, S., Sabetzadeh, M., Yue, T.: Traceability and SysML design slices to support safety inspections. ToSEM **23**(1), 9 (2014)
5. Cleland-Huang, J., Gotel, O.C.Z., Huffman Hayes, J., Mäder, P., Zisman, A.: Software traceability: trends and future directions. In: ICSE/FOSE. ACM (2014)
6. De Lucia, A., Fasano, F., Oliveto, R., Tortora, G.: Recovering traceability links in software artifact management systems using information retrieval methods. ToSEM **16**(4), 13 (2007)

7. Ebner, G., Kaindl, H.: Tracing all around in reengineering. IEEE Softw. **19**(3), 70–77 (2002)
8. Hayes, J., Dekhtyar, A., Sundaram, S.: Advancing candidate link generation for requirements tracing: the study of methods. TSE **32**(1), 4–19 (2006)
9. Herzig, K., Zeller, A.: The impact of tangled code changes. In: MSR. IEEE (2013)
10. Hübner, P., Paech, B.: Using interaction data for continuous creation of trace links between source code and requirements in issue tracking systems. In: Grünbacher, P., Perini, A. (eds.) REFSQ 2017. LNCS, vol. 10153, pp. 291–307. Springer, Cham (2017). https://doi.org/10.1007/978-3-319-54045-0_21
11. Hübner, P., Paech, B.: Evaluation of techniques to detect wrong interaction based trace links. In: Kamsties, E., Horkoff, J., Dalpiaz, F. (eds.) REFSQ 2018. LNCS, vol. 10753, pp. 75–91. Springer, Cham (2018). https://doi.org/10.1007/978-3-319-77243-1_5
12. Kersten, M., Murphy, G.C.: Using task context to improve programmer productivity. In: SIGSOFT/FSE. ACM (2006)
13. Kirinuki, H., Higo, Y., Hotta, K., Kusumoto, S.: Hey! Are you committing tangled changes? In: ICPC. ACM (2014)
14. Konopka, M., Navrat, P., Bielikova, M.: Poster: discovering code dependencies by harnessing developer's activity. In: ICSE. ACM (2015)
15. Maalej, W., Kurtanovic, Z., Felfernig, A.: What stakeholders need to know about requirements. In: EmpiRE. IEEE (2014)
16. Mäder, P., Egyed, A.: Do developers benefit from requirements traceability when evolving and maintaining a software system? Empir. SE **20**(2), 413–441 (2015)
17. Maro, S., Anjorin, A., Wohlrab, R., Steghöfer, J.: Traceability maintenance: factors and guidelines. In: ASE (2016)
18. Merten, T., Falisy, M., Hübner, P., Quirchmayr, T., Bürsner, S., Paech, B.: Software feature request detection in issue tracking systems. In: IEEE RE Conference (2016)
19. Merten, T., Krämer, D., Mager, B., Schell, P., Bürsner, S., Paech, B.: Do information retrieval algorithms for automated traceability perform effectively on issue tracking system data? In: Daneva, M., Pastor, O. (eds.) REFSQ 2016. LNCS, vol. 9619, pp. 45–62. Springer, Cham (2016). https://doi.org/10.1007/978-3-319-30282-9_4
20. Omoronyia, I., Sindre, G., Roper, M., Ferguson, J., Wood, M.: Use case to source code traceability: the developer navigation view point. In: IEEE RE Conference (2009)
21. Omoronyia, I., Sindre, G., Stalhane, T.: Exploring a Bayesian and linear approach to requirements traceability. IST **53**(8), 851–871 (2011)
22. Rath, M., Rempel, P., Mäder, P.: The IlmSeven dataset. In: RE Conference (2017)
23. Rath, M., Rendall, J., Guo, J.L.C., Cleland-Huang, J., Mäder, P.: Traceability in the wild: automatically augmenting incomplete trace links. In: ICSE (2018)
24. Soh, Z., Khomh, F., Guéhéneuc, Y.G., Antoniol, G.: Noise in Mylyn interaction traces and its impact on developers and recommendation systems. ESE **23**(2), 645–692 (2018)

Impact of Gamification on Trace Link Vetting: A Controlled Experiment

Salome Maro[1]([⊠]) [iD], Emil Sundklev[1], Carl-Oscar Persson[1],
Grischa Liebel[2]([⊠]) [iD], and Jan-Philipp Steghöfer[1] [iD]

[1] Software Engineering Division, Chalmers | University of Gothenburg,
Gothenburg, Sweden
{salome.maro,emil.sundklev,carl-oscar.persson,jan-philipp.steghofer}@gu.se
[2] School of Computer Science, Reykjavik University, Reykjavik, Iceland
grischal@ru.is

Abstract. [**Context**] Automatically generated trace links must be vetted by human analysts before use. The task of vetting trace links is considered boring due to its repetitive nature and tools that are not engaging to the analyst. Therefore, a lack of developer engagement can hamper the successful implementation of a traceability strategy in an organisation. [**Objective**] In this study, we examine whether two gamification features, levels and badges, have a positive effect on human analysts' engagement and ultimately on the quality of vetted trace links. [**Method**] We have conducted a controlled experiment with 24 participants that vetted trace link candidates and recorded their speed, correctness, enjoyment, and perceived usability of the tool. [**Results**] The results indicate that there was no significant difference between the speed, correctness, and perceived usability of the control and the experiment group. However, gamification features significantly increased the users' perceived enjoyment. Levels and badges were perceived positively by the majority of the participants while some pitfalls and improvements were pointed out. [**Conclusion**] Our study indicates the need for further research as the results raise several questions, in particular w.r.t. what analyst behaviour gamification incentivises, and the impact of gamification on long-term enjoyment.

Keywords: Software engineering · Gamification · Traceability · Traceability management

1 Introduction

Traceability is important in the software industry as it aids both developers and managers in maintaining the relationships between software artefacts such as requirements, design, code, and documentation. Traceability is also required by certain safety standards, such as ISO 26262, or to obtain certification for organisational maturity, e.g., when using Capability Maturity Model Integration (CMMI). Creating and maintaining trace links is cumbersome when the systems

© Springer Nature Switzerland AG 2019
E. Knauss and M. Goedicke (Eds.): REFSQ 2019, LNCS 11412, pp. 90–105, 2019.
https://doi.org/10.1007/978-3-030-15538-4_6

involved are large and contain a large number of artefacts. To reduce the effort of creating and maintaining trace links, information retrieval approaches [2] such as machine learning [5] have been proposed to automatically generate trace links. However, since automated approaches produce a relatively high number of candidates that are not valid links, a human analyst needs to vet candidates before they become actual trace links. This task of vetting trace links is perceived as boring by many analysts [27].

Previous studies, e.g., Kong et al. [23] and Dekhtyar et al. [10], investigate how analysts vet trace links and how this process can be improved. However, none of these studies have investigated how to make the vetting process more engaging and enjoyable to the human analyst.

When attempting to engage users, gamification has shown to have a positive motivational effect [15,16,32]. Additionally, gamification has been shown to reduce the rate of failure and assists in the learning process in some areas [4]. Specifically for traceability, Parizi [31] showed that gamification concepts improve the task of creating trace links between code and tests during software development. She also points out that gamification elements could be useful for other human-centered tracing activities, such as vetting automatically generated trace links.

To address the lack of studies about the impact and potential benefit of applying gamification to traceability task, we investigate the effects of gamification on vetting automatically generated trace links. Specifically, we investigate the effect of two gamification features – levels and badges. Concretely, we aim to answer the following research question:

RQ: What is the impact of gamification on the task of vetting automatically generated trace links?

To answer these questions, we conducted a controlled experiment in which we asked 24 participants to vet automatically generated trace links. Twelve participants used the traceability management tool Eclipse Capra [26] without modifications, while the remaining twelve participants used the same tool extended with gamification elements. We investigated the impact of gamification on the total number of links vetted, the accuracy of vetted links, on the motivation of the vetting task, and on the perceived usability of the tool.

Our results show no significant difference between the two groups with regards to the final precision and recall of the vetted links, total number of vetted links and usability of the tool. However, the results show that gamification elements have the potential to increase enjoyment and motivate the users for such a task.

The remainder of this paper is structured as follows: In Sect. 2, we discuss the background as well as similar studies on trace link vetting and gamification in software engineering. We then describe our methodology in Sect. 3 and our results in Sect. 4. Section 5 provides answers to our research questions before we conclude the paper in Sect. 6.

2   Background and Related Work

This section discusses the background of our work and related studies. We discuss trace link vetting and the use of gamification elements in software engineering.

2.1   Vetting Automatically Generated Links

Automatically generated trace links are flawed and need a human analyst to vet them for correctness and completeness. Hayes et al. [18,19] discovered that the human analyst can make the generated set of trace links worse. Since then, several studies have been conducted to better understand and to improve the process of vetting trace links. In a controlled experiment, Cuddeback et al. [6] showed that human analysts decreased the quality of a high-quality set of initial trace links, while they increased the quality if it was initially low. In other experiments, Cuddeback et al. [7] and Kong et al. [24] confirm these findings.

To understand different strategies used by human analysts in vetting links, Kong et al. [23] studied logs from a link-vetting experiment and identified strategies such as "accept-focused", where the analyst only accepted links, and "first good link", where the analyst focused on finding the first good link. Additionally, Hayes et al. [17] conducted a simulation study on the different vetting strategies to understand which strategy was the most effective. The authors show that analysts have the best performance when they examine a list of top candidate links that has been pruned based on some heuristics to remove low ranked links, and if the tool takes the analyst's feedback into consideration to modify the list of candidate links dynamically.

Dekhtyar et al. [10] conducted an experiment to understand how factors such as the development experience, and tracing experience of the analyst affect their performance when vetting trace links. The authors showed that development experience, tracing experience, effort used to search for missing links, and how prepared the analyst felt had no significant influence on the performance. However, they also show that the self-reported effort used on validating trace links had a significant effect on the performance: analysts that spent a lot of time validating links ended up reducing recall by rejecting correct links.

While these existing studies investigate the performance of the human analyst, there exist to our knowledge no studies dedicated to improve the trace link vetting process by making it more engaging.

2.2   Gamification in Software Engineering

Several studies have investigated how to incorporate gamification elements in software engineering tasks for the purpose of increasing engagement and motivation of people performing different tasks. Pedreira et al. [32] published a systematic mapping study that shows the distribution of gamification studies in software engineering. The authors show that most studies focus on the software implementation task (coding), followed by project management and process support, while only few studies targeted requirements engineering and software testing.

Since the publication of this mapping study, more studies have been published in the area of requirements engineering, e.g., in requirements elicitation [8,25] and requirements prioritization [21,22].

Additionally, there exist a number of studies on a meta-level, focusing on how gamification can best be introduced in software engineering. These studies, for example Kappen and Nacke [20], Morschheuser et al. [30] and Garcia et al. [14] define guidelines and frameworks to guide software engineers on how to effectively gamify software engineering activities. Our research method is in line with these frameworks that suggest analyzing the activity to be gamified, implement the gamification features, and evaluate the impact of the features.

We are aware of only one study that targets traceability and is therefore related to our study. Parizi [31] investigated the impact of gamification when tracing between code and tests. The authors conducted an experiment showing that use of gamification elements, namely case points, feedback, reputation, avatars, progress and quests, improved both precision and recall of the recovered set of manually created trace links. The gamification elements encouraged the developers to create more links. In this paper, we study a different phenomenon where gamification elements are applied to encourage the human analyst to vet trace links based on candidates created automatically.

3   Research Method

In order to answer our research question, we conducted a controlled experiment [34], comparing vetting of automatically generated trace links with and without gamification.

3.1   Experiment Design

We used a simple one-factor experiment design with two treatments [34], namely the use of the traceability software without gamification and the use of the same software with gamification. We refer to the subjects using the software without gamification as our *control group*, while the subjects using the gamified software are in the *experiment group*. The dependent variables are the overall number of vetted trace links (*vetted*), the fraction of correctly vetted trace links (*vettedCor*), the self-reported motivation throughout the experiment (*motivation*), and the impact of gamification on the perceived usability (*usability*). The variables *vetted* and *vettedCor* can furthermore be divided into accepted and rejected trace links, i.e., *accepted*, *rejected*, *acceptedCor*, and *rejectedCor*. We derive the following null hypotheses and corresponding alternative hypotheses:

- $H0_{vetted}$: There is no significant difference in *vetted* between the control group and the experiment group.
- $H1_{vetted}$: There is a significant difference in *vetted* between the control group and the experiment group.
- $H0_{vettedCor}$: There is no significant difference in *vettedCor* between the control group and the experiment group.

- $H1_{vettedCor}$: There is a significant difference in *vettedCor* between the control group and the experiment group.
- $H0_{motivation}$: There is no significant difference in *motivation* between the control group and the experiment group.
- $H1_{motivation}$: There is a significant difference in *motivation* between the control group and the experiment group.
- $H0_{usability}$: There is no significant difference in the perceived *usability* between the control group and the experiment group.
- $H1_{usability}$: There is a significant difference in the perceived *usability* between the control group and the experiment group.

To decide what kind of gamification elements to implement, we sent out a survey to 14 subjects that had participated in a previous study using trace link vetting with Eclipse Capra, reported in [27]. For each candidate gamification element, we asked the subjects a number of questions pertaining to the potential enjoyment and distraction caused by the element. We received 11 responses to our survey. The results and implementation of the gamification elements are described in Sect. 4.

We used MedFleet as an instrument, a drone fleet coordination system which contains requirements and fault descriptions as well as source code. A manually created set of trace links served as a ground truth to which we could compare the vetting results. We generated trace link candidates using Vector Space Model with Term Frequency – Inverse Document Frequency (TFIDF), a technique that is commonly used to generate links between textual artifacts [33].

During the experiment, we asked participants to work through a list of candidate trace links between any of the three artefact types. For each link, participants had to decide whether the two linked artefacts indeed have a relation to each other. If yes, the candidate link should be *accepted*, if not, then it should be *rejected*. To support this process, Eclipse Capra offers the ability to open and view the artifacts the candidate link refers to, including the source code files. Prior to the experiment, we handed out a written document describing all relevant features of Eclipse Capra. For the experiment group, this description also contained an explanation of the gamification elements.

Data Collection and Analysis. The participant sample for this experiment consisted of 24 students with an academic software engineering background. We assigned the participants randomly into balanced experiment and control groups. While all subjects were students, some had experience as software developers. Only eight of the students, four in the control group and four in the experiment group, had experience with traceability. Additionally, all students had some experience with using Eclipse. The use of student subjects in experimentation has been debated heavily and controversially [13]. As this is an initial study, we believe that the use of student subjects is favourable over practitioners due to the higher homogeneity in their knowledge and thus higher internal validity [13].

After the introduction to Eclipse Capra, participants had 45 min to complete their task. Using the features of Eclipse Capra freely, we encouraged participants to accept and reject as many candidate links as they could, while taking the time they needed for decision making. Participants were allowed to ask questions regarding the operation of Eclipse Capra and the gamified system during the entire experiment.

We instrumented Eclipse Capra to monitor participant activity, namely accept and reject events, as well as opening events of artifact files. Additionally, we collected data through a pre-experiment questionnaire (collecting demographic data) and a post-experiment questionnaire (collecting perceptions about gamification and system usability scale (SUS) [3] scores). All survey instruments as well as the instructions are available online [28].

3.2 Validity Threats

There are several potential threats to validity in this study.

To avoid survey questions being misinterpreted by participants, we ran each questionnaire through several internal review rounds, identifying and improving potentially ambiguous questions.

Domain knowledge about the MedFleet system can affect the correctness of trace links per participant. While none of the participants had any prior knowledge of MedFleet, and therefore an advantage in domain knowledge, this lack of domain knowledge could also threaten the external validity of the study. We accepted this potential threat in favour of having a higher internal validity due to the homogeneity of the student population.

Individual differences between participants could pose another threat to validity, as we did not use a crossover design. Since we only had a single software system with all the required artefacts (requirements, source code, faults, and traces between them), we had to accept this potential threat.

Given that gamification features were added to Eclipse Capra, there is a potential threat that these modifications affected the usability of the system and, hence, confounded the results. Additionally, the specific implementation of the features could have an effect on the results. To assess this, we collected usability information in the post-experiment survey as discussed in Sect. 4.

As for all empirical studies, there is a trade-off between internal and external validity [13]. We opted for a higher internal validity, e.g., by choosing student subjects. This naturally limits the generalisability of our results. For this initial work, we believe that this restriction is acceptable, but at the same time encourage replications with a more diverse sample of participants.

4   Results

We first explain the two gamification features we chose to test in our experiment—levels and badges. We then describe the results of our experiments, including answers from the questionnaires as well as the analysis of vetting accuracy.

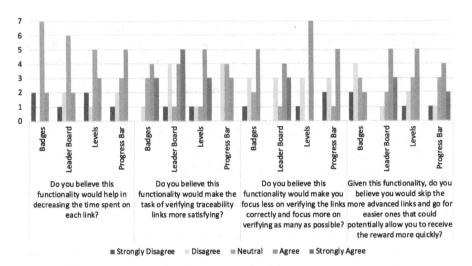

Fig. 1. Pilot survey results showing aggregated responses for the gamification features.

Gamification Features. We used the responses from the pilot survey (cf. Sect. 3) to decide on the gamification features to be implemented and tested in the experiment. Out of the four suggested gamification features, we selected *levels* and *badges* as the most viable options. As can be seen in Fig. 1, the results of the pilot survey were very mixed across the different features. While the *progress bar* received the most positive results in terms of potential decrease of the time spent on each link, some commentators also pointed out that a progress bar that does not fill up quickly, e.g., because of the large number of links to vet, can be discouraging. In addition, there were participants that felt that they would optimise towards vetting as many links as possible and potentially skip difficult ones. *Leader boards*, on the other hand, received high scores in the ranking for how satisfying they would make the task, while also showing a high spread. However, there are indications from the free text comments that leader boards can be perceived as too competitive, even though findings from the literature show that competitiveness might have positive effects on performance [11]. In addition, there were respondents who strongly agreed that they would again favour number of links over vetting more complicated ones. For both *badges* and *levels*, no indications could be found that they would decrease the time spent on each link, but both have good values for increase in satisfaction. While there are indications that levels would shift focus to vetting as many links as possible, there is no strong indication that users would skip more complicated links.

Both implemented features are shown in Fig. 2. The current *level* of the user is shown within the green star next to the total points accumulated and how much progress is left until the next level is reached. This is different from the progress bar suggested as a feature since it does not measure progress of the overall vetting task, but still provides feedback on the progress towards the next level. The levelling system awards 10 points for accepting or rejecting a candidate link. The next level is reached after 100 points have been collected.

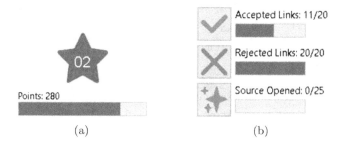

(a)   (b)

Fig. 2. The level and badges as shown in the modified version of Eclipse Capra.

We integrated three different *badges*: one is awarded after accepting 20 links, one after rejecting 20 links, and one after opening 25 source code files. The figure shows an icon for each badge, how many links have been accepted or rejected, how many source code files have been opened, and how much progress has been made for each badge. When the requirements of a badge are fulfilled, the logo turns green as can be seen on the "rejected links" badge.

Experience with and Understanding of Experiment System. The post-experiment part of the survey contained some questions common for both groups. Two questions aimed at understanding previous experience with systems similar to the one used in the experiment and the confidence that participants felt in working with the system. The answers to these questions allowed us to gauge if any of the groups had an advantage over the other due to previous experience or a vastly higher confidence in working with the system. The responses in Table 1 show, however, that no significant differences exist. Only two of the participants, both in the experiment group, had prior experience in similar systems and confidence levels for understanding the system are very similar.

Participant Enjoyment and Motivation. To understand the impact of the gamification features on the enjoyment of the participants and on their motivation to complete the vetting task, all participants were asked explicitly about these aspects in the post-experiment questionnaire. As can be seen in Fig. 3, the experiment group shows a tendency towards finding the vetting process more enjoyable and feeling more motivated to complete the task. The Mann-Whitney u-test on the responses shows that the results are statistically significant ($p \approx 0.040$), thus corroborating $H0_{motivation}$. This result shows that adding gamification features is beneficial to the enjoyment of vetting the links and to the motivation of completing the task.

Table 1. Experience with systems similar to the experiment system and confidence of understanding the experiment system.

		Control group	Experiment group
Experience with systems similar to MedFleet	Yes	0	2
	No	12	10
Confidence of understanding the MedFleet system	Strongly disagree	0	0
	Disagree	2	2
	Neutral	3	6
	Agree	6	3
	Strongly agree	1	1

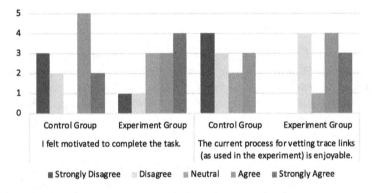

Fig. 3. Results of the post-experiment survey showing aggregated responses for enjoyment of the task and motivation to complete the task.

System Usability Scale. In order to compare the usability of the gamified and the regular versions of Eclipse Capra, we used the System Usability Scale (SUS) [3]. It contains a total of ten statements which are answered on a five-point Likert scale. From the responses, we also computed the overall SUS score. For this purpose, we deducted 1 from the score for each positively-worded statement (statements 1, 3, 5, 7, and 9) and deducted the score of each negatively worded statement (statements 2, 4, 6, 8, 10) from 5. The resulting scores were multiplied by 2.5 and added up to achieve a range from 0 to 100. The results are shown in Table 2.

According to Bangor et al. [1], SUS scores between 0 and 25 are considered *worst imaginable*, scores between 26 and 38 are considered to be *poor*, scores between 38 and 52 are considered to be *OK*, scores between 52 and 73 are considered to be *good*, scores between 73 and 85 are considered to be *excellent* and finally scores between 85 and 100 are considered the *best imaginable*. Therefore, the scores provided both by the control group and the experiment group are in the *good* range with a slight advantage for the gamified version.

Table 2. SUS for the control group and the experiment group. For each question, the average values in the groups are depicted, with standard deviation in brackets.

		Control group	Experiment group
Q1	I think that I would like to use this system frequently	2.25 (1.55)	3.00 (1.05)
Q2	I found the system unnecessarily complex	2.33 (1.37)	2.08 (1.08)
Q3	I thought the system was easy to use	3.83 (0.94)	4.17 (0.58)
Q4	I think that I would need the support of a technical person to be able to use this system	1.92 (1.08)	2.25 (1.22)
Q5	I found the various functions in the system were well integrated	3.66 (0.89)	3.75 (0.86)
Q6	I thought there was too much inconsistency in the system	1.75 (0.75)	1.92 (1.08)
Q7	*I would imagine that most people would learn to use this system very quickly*	4.08 (1.16)	4.08 (1.00)
Q8	I found the system very cumbersome to use	2.25 (1.60)	2.17 (0.94)
Q9	I felt very confident using the system	3.00 (0.95)	3.50 (1.68)
Q10	I needed to learn a lot of things before I could get going with this system	2.00 (1.21)	2.25 (1.14)
SUS score		66.56	69.58

The results from a Mann-Whitney u-test on the average score from both groups showed to be insignificant ($p \approx 0.904$). The SUS-scores show that the usability of Eclipse Capra is *good* with and without extension with level and badge features. We can thus reject $H1_{usability}$ and conclude that there is no significant difference in usability.

Attitude Towards Levels and Badges. To gauge the attitudes of the participants towards the gamification features, we asked both groups different questions about their perceptions. While the experiment group was asked about how they rated their experience, the control group was given a brief demonstration of the gamification features after they completed their task and were then asked about how these features might have influenced their experience. We were also interested in gauging whether the participants thought that there was an impact on the vetting process or on their individual performance. All questions were answered on a five-point Likert scale. The attitudes of the experiment group are shown in Table 3 and the attitudes of the control group in Table 4.

The averages in the tables show no major difference between the levels and badges features. The majority of the participants understood the features, but it was considered easier to understand the badges which is overall the biggest dif-

Table 3. Attitude of the experiment group towards the levels and badges feature

	Levels	Badges
I had no issue understanding the levels/badges	3.4 (1.31)	4.2 (1.11)
The levels/badges made the task of vetting trace links satisfying	3.6 (0.90)	3.8 (0.94)
The levels/badges helped decrease the time spent on each link	3.2 (0.94)	2.9 (0.90)
The levels/badges made me focus more on verifying as many links as possible instead of verifying each link correctly	3.1 (1.17)	3.1 (1.38)
I felt that the levels/badges contributed towards being motivated to complete the task	3.4 (1.08)	3.5 (1.24)
Overall, the levels/badges feature was a good addition to the traceability tool	3.9 (0.67)	3.8 (0.94)

ference between the two features. The control group on average thought that the levels feature would make them focus less on correctness and more on verifying as many links as possible, at least compared to the badges feature.

Table 4. Attitude of the control group towards the levels and badges feature

	Levels	Badges
Levels/badges make the task of verifying trace links more satisfying	3.4 (1.24)	3.6 (1.62)
Levels/badges help in decreasing the time spent on each link	2.75 (1.49)	2.7 (1.16)
Levels/badges make me focus less on verifying the links correctly and more on verifying as many as possible	3.4 (1.38)	2.8 (1.22)
Levels/badges would make me skip the more advanced links and go for easier ones in order to "level up"/receive more badges faster	3.4 (1.24)	3.2 (1.53)

Vetting Task Results. This section presents the results from the vetting task that all the participants undertook. The results from both groups can be seen side-by-side in Table 5. On average, participants in the experiment group vetted 130 links, while participants in the control group vetted 160. The average rate of correctly accepted links for the experiment group was 16.54% and 17.19% for

Table 5. Results of the vetting task for the control group and the experiment group.

	True positive	False positive	Total positive	Rate	True negatives	False negatives	Total negatives	Rate	Precision	Recall
Control group										
Avg.	9	66.92	75.92	17.19%	77.58	5.75	83.33	92.14%	0.17	0.62
Stdev.	2.26	43.79	43.33		57.83	3.28	60.25		0.14	0.19
Experiment group										
Avg.	9.67	60	69.67	16.54%	56	4.67	60.67	92.15%	0.17	0.67
Stdev.	2.71	30.84	31.92		21.34	2.46	22.23		0.08	0.18

the control group. The average rate of correctly rejected links for the experiment group was 92.14% and 92.15% for the control group. This is reflected in the measures for precision and recall that show a low precision of 0.17 for both groups, but a recall of 0.62 and 0.67, respectively. This indicates that detecting correct links was harder compared to rejecting wrong links that were obvious to spot. Standard deviations for the total number of links as well as for precision are relatively high, indicating that there was a relatively large spread in the rate of true positives amongst all selected positives. Indeed, the control group, e.g., ranged between a correctness of 7.7% and 52%.

We tested our null hypotheses $H0_{vetted}$ and $H0_{vettedCor}$ with a Mann-Whitney u-test, yielding p-values of $p \approx 0.542$ and $p \approx 0.912$, respectively. Therefore, we can not reject the null hypotheses and can not detect a statistically significant difference in either the number of vetted links or the correctness of vetting decisions between the experiment group and the control group.

5   Discussion

In this section we discuss the implications of the results and how they relate to our research question. To recap, our research question is: *What is the impact of gamification on the task of vetting automatically generated trace links?*

Our results show that, on one hand, there is no significant difference in the total amount of links vetted and also in the accuracy of the vetted links between the experiment and the control group. From the survey carried out to elicit which gamification features are suitable, there were indications that gamification might lead to participants vetting more links but reduce accuracy. However, our results show that this is not the case. We would like to emphasise that this is not a negative result. In contrary, the results mean that the newly added gamification elements did not lead to participants rushing the vetting task in favour of reaching higher levels or winning badges. Indeed, it was difficult for participants to know which accuracy they attained since there was no feedback as to whether the links accepted or rejected were correct. For the future, we consider alternative means of rewarding correctness, such as rewarding taking extra time to analyse an artefact in detail. Another alternative proposed by an experiment participant is to allow the participant to see the vetting decisions of other users before making their own. Decisions of other users would allow the current user to get an idea of what others thought was correct, but is by no means guaranteed to be correct. Since reward options are limited if correctness can not be checked automatically, the usefulness of gamification for trace link vetting can be restricted. Agreement with other users might be used as a stand-in, but might lead to skewed results when users are incentivised to agree with others.

The design of the badges and the associated reward system could have an influence on the precision achieved by the participants. In our case, participants felt the need to accept approximately as many links as they rejected since both actions were associated with the reward of badges. The low number of correct links among the link candidates might have contributed to the low correctness rate of accepted links. To better understand this factor, more research is needed with different types of badge designs and reward systems.

The results show that the experiment group found the vetting task to be more enjoyable and motivating than the control group. Many studies on gamification consider how and if a gamified implementation has had an impact on intrinsic and extrinsic motivation (see, e.g., [12,16,29]). Intrinsic motivation can be described as being motivated to perform a task because one enjoys doing it, while extrinsic motivation can be described as completing a task because of the incentive one gets after completing it [9]. When attempting to motivate people, it is considered best practice to aim at increasing intrinsic motivation, since being motivated to do something because of enjoyment is more sought after than being motivated by extrinsic rewards [9]. In our case, since participants of the experiment group reported that they enjoyed the task and felt more motivated to perform it, but did not increase the number of links or their accuracy, there is an indication that the participants had more intrinsic than extrinsic motivation. However, we cannot conclude that this is the case and further research is needed to investigate this motivational aspect by, e.g., letting participants choose if they want to perform the vetting task or not and observing their performance over time.

Our findings are also inconclusive w.r.t. the long-term effects of gamification. Since participants were only exposed to the gamification features for one session, we can conclude that within this session, enjoyment and motivation was increased, but can not state that these positive effects would be present over a longer period of time and a number of consecutive sessions. There is a chance that participants get used to the features and their level of enjoyment and their motivation decreases over time. This can be counteracted with a reward system and gamification features that keep users engaged continuously, e.g., with specific rewards for higher levels. Our experiment is only an initial step and more research is required to understand the long-term motivational aspects in more detail.

6 Conclusion

In this paper, we investigated the impact of gamification on trace link vetting. We identified suitable gamification features based on existing studies and a survey, and implemented levels and badges in the traceability management tool Eclipse Capra. To test the impact of these features, we conducted a controlled experiment with 24 student participants, comparing the use of Eclipse Capra with and without gamification features. Specifically, we investigated the impact of having levels and badges on the correctness and the number of vetted links, as well as the perceived motivation of the participants and the usability of the tool.

The results show that our implementation of levels and badge features had no significant effect on the correctness and amount of vetted links. However, the participants found the gamified system to be more enjoyable. Furthermore, participants did not identify differences in the usability of the gamified and the non-gamified system. The results of our initial survey also showed a difference in participants' preferences toward competitive gamification elements (e.g., leader boards) compared to non-competitive elements (e.g., levels).

For future work, we see a number of possibilities. First, it is essential to study the long-term effects of gamification on enjoyment or motivation, and how to keep subjects engaged over longer periods of time. Our experiment only serves as an initial indication that gamification indeed increases motivation in the short term, while it remains to be studied whether this effect wears off over time. Second, we see the need to replicate our study in an industrial setting with professional developers. Since the experiment setup requires a ground truth of which traces are correct and which ones are not, this is a challenging task. Finally, there is a need to study how a more advanced implementation of levels and badges affect the vetting task since in this study we only test our specific implementation.

References

1. Bangor, A., Kortum, P., Miller, J.: Determining what individual SUS scores mean: adding an adjective rating scale. J. Usability Stud. **4**(3), 114–123 (2009)
2. Borg, M., Runeson, P., Ardö, A.: Recovering from a decade: a systematic mapping of information retrieval approaches to software traceability. Empir. Softw. Eng. (ESE) **19**(6), 1565–1616 (2014)
3. Brooke, J., et al.: SUS-a quick and dirty usability scale. Usability Eval. Ind. **189**(194), 4–7 (1996)
4. Charles, D., Charles, T., McNeill, M., Bustard, D., Black, M.: Game-based feedback for educational multi-user virtual environments. Br. J. Educ. Technol. **42**(4), 638–654 (2011)
5. Cleland-Huang, J., Czauderna, A., Gibiec, M., Emenecker, J.: A machine learning approach for tracing regulatory codes to product specific requirements. In: 32nd ACM/IEEE International Conference on Software Engineering ICSE 2010, pp. 155–164 (2010)
6. Cuddeback, D., Dekhtyar, A., Hayes, J.: Automated requirements traceability: the study of human analysts. In: RE 2010, pp. 231–240. IEEE (2010)
7. Cuddeback, D., Dekhtyar, A., Hayes, J.H., Holden, J., Kong, W.K.: Towards overcoming human analyst fallibility in the requirements tracing process. In: ICSE 2011, pp. 860–863. ACM (2011)

8. Dalpiaz, F., Snijders, R., Brinkkemper, S., Hosseini, M., Shahri, A., Ali, R.: Engaging the crowd of stakeholders in requirements engineering via gamification. In: Stieglitz, S., Lattemann, C., Robra-Bissantz, S., Zarnekow, R., Brockmann, T. (eds.) Gamification. PI, pp. 123–135. Springer, Cham (2017). https://doi.org/10.1007/978-3-319-45557-0_9

9. Deci, E.L., Koestner, R., Ryan, R.M.: A meta-analytic review of experiments examining the effects of extrinsic rewards on intrinsic motivation. Psychol. Bull. **125**(6), 627 (1999)

10. Dekhtyar, A., Dekhtyar, O., Holden, J., Hayes, J.H., Cuddeback, D., Kong, W.K.: On human analyst performance in assisted requirements tracing: statistical analysis. In: RE 2011, pp. 111–120. IEEE (2011)

11. Dubois, D.J., Tamburrelli, G.: Understanding gamification mechanisms for software development. In: FSE 2013, pp. 659–662. ACM (2013)

12. Eickhoff, C., Harris, C.G., de Vries, A.P., Srinivasan, P.: Quality through flow and immersion: gamifying crowdsourced relevance assessments. In: Proceedings of the 35th International ACM SIGIR Conference on Research and Development in Information Retrieval, pp. 871–880. ACM (2012)

13. Falessi, D., Juristo, N., Wohlin, C., Turhan, B., Münch, J., Jedlitschka, A., Oivo, M.: Empirical software engineering experts on the use of students and professionals in experiments. Empir. Softw. Eng. **23**(1), 452–489 (2018)

14. García, F., Pedreira, O., Piattini, M., Cerdeira-Pena, A., Penabad, M.: A framework for gamification in software engineering. J. Syst. Softw. **132**, 21–40 (2017)

15. Hamari, J., Koivisto, J., Sarsa, H.: Does gamification work? – A literature review of empirical studies on gamification. In: 47th Hawaii International Conference on System Sciences (HICSS), pp. 3025–3034. IEEE (2014)

16. Hanus, M.D., Fox, J.: Assessing the effects of gamification in the classroom: a longitudinal study on intrinsic motivation, social comparison, satisfaction, effort, and academic performance. Comput. Educ. **80**, 152–161 (2015)

17. Hayes, J.H., Dekhtyar, A., Larsen, J., Guéhéneuc, Y.G.: Effective use of analysts' effort in automated tracing. Requir. Eng. **23**(1), 119–143 (2018)

18. Hayes, J.H., Dekhtyar, A., Osborne, J.: Improving requirements tracing via information retrieval. In: RE 2003, pp. 138–147. IEEE (2003)

19. Hayes, J.H., Dekhtyar, A., Sundaram, S.: Text mining for software engineering: how analyst feedback impacts final results. In: ACM SIGSOFT Software Engineering Notes, vol. 30, pp. 1–5. ACM (2005)

20. Kappen, D.L., Nacke, L.E.: The kaleidoscope of effective gamification: deconstructing gamification in business applications. In: Proceedings of the 1st International Conference on Gameful Design, Research, and Applications, pp. 119–122. ACM (2013)

21. Kifetew, F.M., et al.: Gamifying collaborative prioritization: does pointsification work? In: RE 2017, pp. 322–331. IEEE (2017)

22. Kolpondinos, M.Z.H., Glinz, M.: Behind points and levels–the influence of gamification algorithms on requirements prioritization. In: RE 2017, pp. 332–341. IEEE (2017)

23. Kong, W.K., Hayes, J.H., Dekhtyar, A., Dekhtyar, O.: Process improvement for traceability: a study of human fallibility. In: RE 2012, pp. 31–40. IEEE (2012)

24. Kong, W.K., Huffman Hayes, J., Dekhtyar, A., Holden, J.: How do we trace requirements: an initial study of analyst behavior in trace validation tasks. In: Proceedings of the 4th International Workshop on Cooperative and Human Aspects of Software Engineering, pp. 32–39. ACM (2011)

25. Lombriser, P., Dalpiaz, F., Lucassen, G., Brinkkemper, S.: Gamified requirements engineering: model and experimentation. In: Daneva, M., Pastor, O. (eds.) REFSQ 2016. LNCS, vol. 9619, pp. 171–187. Springer, Cham (2016). https://doi.org/10.1007/978-3-319-30282-9_12

26. Maro, S., Steghöfer, J.P.: Capra: a configurable and extendable traceability management tool. In: RE 2016, pp. 407–408. IEEE (2016)

27. Maro, S., Steghöfer, J.P., Huffman Hayes, J., Cleland-Huang, J., Staron, M.: Vetting automatically generated trace links: what information is useful to human analysts? In: RE 2018, pp. 52–63. IEEE (2018)

28. Maro, S., Sundklev, E., Persson, C.O., Liebel, G., Steghöfer, J.P.: Impact of gamification on trace link vetting: a controlled experiment, January 2019. https://doi.org/10.5281/zenodo.2540646. Dataset

29. Mekler, E.D., Brühlmann, F., Opwis, K., Tuch, A.N.: Do points, levels and leaderboards harm intrinsic motivation?: an empirical analysis of common gamification elements. In: Proceedings of the 1st International Conference on Gameful Design, Research, and Applications. pp. 66–73. ACM (2013)

30. Morschheuser, B., Hamari, J., Werder, K., Abe, J.: How to gamify? A method for designing gamification (2017)

31. Parizi, R.M.: On the gamification of human-centric traceability tasks in software testing and coding. In: Software Engineering Research, Management and Applications (SERA), pp. 193–200. IEEE (2016)

32. Pedreira, O., García, F., Brisaboa, N., Piattini, M.: Gamification in software engineering-a systematic mapping. Inf. Softw. Technol. **57**, 157–168 (2015)

33. Schütze, H., Manning, C.D., Raghavan, P.: Introduction to Information Retrieval, vol. 39. Cambridge University Press, Cambridge (2008)

34. Wohlin, C., Runeson, P., Höst, M., Ohlsson, M.C., Regnell, B., Wesslén, A.: Experimentation in Software Engineering. Springer, Heidelberg (2012). https://doi.org/10.1007/978-3-642-29044-2

Requirements Management (Research Previews)

Refinement of User Stories into Backlog Items: Linguistic Structure and Action Verbs
Research Preview

Laurens Müter[1]([✉]), Tejaswini Deoskar[2]([✉]), Max Mathijssen[1]([✉]),
Sjaak Brinkkemper[1]([✉]), and Fabiano Dalpiaz[1]([✉])

[1] RE-Lab, Department of Information and Computing Sciences, Utrecht University,
Utrecht, The Netherlands
{L.H.F.Muter,M.Mathijssen,S.Brinkkemper,F.Dalpiaz}@uu.nl
[2] Department of Languages, Literature, and Communication,
Utrecht Institute of Linguistics, Utrecht University, Utrecht, The Netherlands
T.Deoskar@uu.nl

Abstract. **[Context and motivation]** In agile system development methods, product backlog items (or tasks) play a prominent role in the refinement process of software requirements. Tasks are typically defined manually to operationalize how to implement a user story; tasks formulation often exhibits low quality, perhaps due to the tedious nature of decomposing user stories into tasks. **[Question/Problem]** We investigate the process through which user stories are refined into tasks. **[Principal ideas/results]** We study a large collection of backlog items (N = 1,593), expressed as user stories and sprint tasks, looking for linguistic patterns that characterize the required feature of the user story requirement. Through a linguistic analysis of sentence structures and action verbs (the main verb in the sentence that indicates the task), we discover patterns of labeling refinements, and explore new ways for refinement process improvement. **[Contribution]** By identifying a set of 7 elementary action verbs and a template for task labels, we make first steps towards comprehending the refinement of user stories to backlog items.

Keywords: Requirements engineering · User stories · Backlog items · Natural language processing · Sprint tasks

1 Introduction

User stories (USs) have made their way into the development process of companies [1] and their adoption is evolving to higher levels [1,2]. USs are the starting point for specifying software that is developed, according to the agile development paradigm, through a series of sprints. The USs are distributed to the development teams that refine the USs into a number of (usually 3 to 6) so-called

© Springer Nature Switzerland AG 2019
E. Knauss and M. Goedicke (Eds.): REFSQ 2019, LNCS 11412, pp. 109–116, 2019.
https://doi.org/10.1007/978-3-030-15538-4_7

backlog items (but also called tasks) to break down a US into specific executable tasks for developers to carry out during the sprints.

Software specifications have been thoroughly studied from the viewpoint of their linguistic structure. Researchers have proposed approaches for finding ambiguity [3,4] and other types of defects [5] in natural language requirements, for generating conceptual models [6,7], and much more [8].

Previous work has conducted linguistic analyses of USs and defined guidelines for writing a *good* specification in agile development [1,9]. The template structure of a US "As a [Role] I want to [Action], so that [Benefit]" is often misused and many real-world USs are poorly written requirements [10]. However, there is no study on the requirements-related artifacts that stem from USs in agile development and Scrum, i.e., backlog items or *tasks*.

Table 1. Example US that has been refined into 3 tasks

US: As a webshop visitor I want to add shipping addresses so that I can send presents to my friends	
Task-1	Create ShippingAddresses records for visitors
Task-2	Update validity check for Addresses
Task-3	Add data-item for LastShippingAddress to visitor

Table 1 shows the refinement of a US into three tasks. By reading the table, one can see that tasks are the bridge between user-centered requirements (USs) and development artifacts like code and test cases. It is not surprising that the tasks are the basic constituents of sprint backlogs, i.e., they define what functionality will be included in the next release of the product.

The contribution of this paper is a linguistic analysis of a large industrial product backlog that includes 195 USs and 1,593 tasks. We study the linguistic structure of the task labels as well as the main verb that indicates what actions the developers are expected to carry out. Based on the analysis, we distill guidelines for writing tasks in a clear and consistent way.

After describing our research approach in Sect. 2, we present our linguistic analysis of the sentence structure (Sect. 3) and of the main verb in a task (Sect. 4). Finally, we present conclusions and outline future directions.

2   Research Approach

We considered a large product backlog provided to us by a multinational software development company, located in the Netherlands, and having circa fifty employees. The company's main product is a web-based platform to manage contract and tender processes of companies in the procurement industry.

The initial data consisted of 2,702 backlog items, each labeled as Epic, Feature, Task, or Bug. In this paper, we focus on the tasks (1,593, 59.04%). Each backlog item has an attribute that defines the development status in the product development: New (6.49%), To Do (3.74%), Approved (1.41%), Committed (1.33%), In Progress (1.26%), Done (85.29%), Removed (0.48%).

Our linguistic analysis started with running the Stanford Part-of-Speech (POS) tagger to determine the structure of the task labels; for example, "Define (VB) box (NN) type (NN) actions (NNS) and (CC) implement (VB) them (PRP). (.)"[1] indicates that "define" is a verb, "box" is a singular noun, "actions" is a plural noun, "and" is a conjunction, and so on.

We experienced that the POS tagger accuracy was not perfect, presumably because task labels are hardly written as grammatically correct sentences. Two major problems we encountered were words that can be tagged as either verbs or nouns (e.g., "update") and spelling mistakes (e.g., "crate" instead of "create").

We then looked at the first-occurring verb in each task label, trying to identify recurring patterns. After tagging the unique verbs, we employed classes of VerbNet to cluster the identified verbs in families of related verbs.

Finally, we extracted regular expression patterns that fit most of the tasks and that can be used as a recommended template for task label writers.

3   Linguistic Structure of Task Labels

The goal of this analysis is to identify the most common linguistic structures in the sentences that represent tasks labels. Because of the vast number of existing POS tags, we grouped the tags as shown in Table 2. For example, verbs tagged with different tenses (present/past) are grouped into the *verb* category.

Table 2. Grouping of POS tags employed in analysis

Group tag	POS tags	Occurrence	%	Unique first words
verb	VB, VBD, VBG, VBP, VBZ	1,173	73.63	70
noun	NN, NNS, NNP, NNPS	322	20.21	65
adjective	JJ, JJR, JJS	27	1.69	13
adverb	RB, RBR, RBS	27	1.69	4
pronoun	PRP, PRP$	7	0.44	2
other		37	2.32	11
Total		1,593	100	165

Despite the grouping, the Stanford POS tagger identified 968 different linguistic structures that represent the 1,593 tasks, thereby showing the various ways task labels are formulated by developers.

---

[1] The individual tags refer to the Penn Treebank tagset [11].

Table 3. The ten most frequent structures of task labels

Structure	Freq.	%	Example
VB, NN(S), NN	130	8.17	Create tender-settings component
VB, NN(S), NN, NN(S)	67	4.18	Create messages DB tables
NN, NN(S), NN(S)	25	1.57	Admin licenses breadcrumbs
VB, NN(S), IN, NN	21	1.32	Add filters for KO
VB, NN, NN(S), NN(S), NN	20	1.26	Implement TenderPlan actions business logic
VB, JJ, NN(S), NN	18	1.13	Create disqualified offers card
VB, NN	27	1.67	Create TenderProcessDefinitionLevelRule
VB, NN(S), IN, NN, NN	15	0.94	Bind rules per section item
VB, NN, NN, IN, NN, NN(S)	13	0.82	Create SQL Script for AcceptedById items
NN, NN(S)	10	0.62	Update actions

POS taggers are trained with long newswire text and not with short, sketched sentences like task labels, so to further improve the accuracy we performed a manual amendment of some tags (especially verb instead of noun). The ten most frequent structures are shown in Table 3. In the table, we use the following abbreviations: NN = noun, VB = verb, IN = conjunction, and JJ = adjective. The most frequent pattern is a verb followed by two nouns, for example: "Create tender-settings component" (VB, NN, NN). Several variations exist that add an adjective or a conjunction to the sequence of nouns. In the top-10 list, only two structures start with a noun, which usually indicates the architectural location of the task. Task labels starting with a noun will be analyzed in future work.

Given the variations in sentence structures as presented in Table 3, we distill a template that we propose as a guideline for writing task labels. The extended Baccus-Naur form (EBNF) grammar for the template (shown below) states that a task is expressed by a verb, followed by one or more `follow` elements, each being either a noun, a conjunction, an adjective, a "to", or a cardinal number.

```
task = verb, follow, {follow};
follow = noun | conjunction | adjective | "to" | cardinal number;
```

The pattern matches 42.4% of the tasks in the dataset (676 out of 1,593). Further research will reveal more detailed patterns in the label set in order to develop guidelines for task refinement.

4   On the Choice of an Action Verb

Task labels describe an *action* for the developer to carry out in order to implement part of a software function, or to improve existing code. We have first

Table 4. Most frequent action verbs that occur in a task label

Rank	Action verb	Frequency
1	Create	578
2	Modify	125
3	Add	85
4	Implement	79
5	Change	27
6	Extend	19
7	Set	18
8	Check	16
9	Load	14
10	Remove	13
11	Bind	11
12	Update	11
13	Move	10
14	Show	10
15	Delete	9
16	Get	9
17	Redesign	9
18	Setup	8
19	Fix	8
20	Review	8

analyzed the first *action verb* that occurs in a task label. To do so, we employed the Stanford POS tagger and extracted the action verbs from our 1,593 task labels. This resulted in 56 different verbs, which became 81 after some manual pre-processing of spelling errors and noun-verb conversion. The 20 most frequently occurring action verbs are shown in Table 4.

The most frequent action verb is *create*, which amounts to about one third of the entire task set. This figure is a strong indicator of the feature creep phenomenon [12]. On the other hand, a very related verb such as *delete* occurs only in 1.5%. However, while analyzing the results, we observed that quasi-synonyms exist; for instance, the *remove* verb is a synonym of *delete*.

The observed relatedness of some verbs and the quasi-synonyms motivate to obtain a smaller set of action verbs for use in task descriptions. We resorted to VerbNet [13], a taxonomy of verbs that groups similar verbs in so-called *verb classes*. For example, the class *create* (CREATE-26.4) includes alternative terms, besides the namesake verb, the similar verbs *coin*, *fabricate*, *construct*, etc. We identified verb classes in VerbNet that could act as containers for multiple verbs; moreover, we performed some adjustments to cope with the domain-specific

Table 5. Families of action verbs in task labels

Family	Members of the verb-family
Create	Code, create, define, design, implement, insert, make
Update	Add, adjust, change, edit, extend, fix, improve, insert, renew, replace, refactor, redesign
Merge	Bind, export, insert, integrate, invite, link, list, offer
Delete	Delete, remove
Validate	Check, evaluate, research, test, verify
Control	Accept, allow, apply, bind, cancel, check, configure, control, determine
Investigate	Inquire, investigate, research, search

Table 6. Elementary action verbs for task labeling

Verb	Explanation	Example
Create	Add new features	Create new tender property
Update	Change existing functionality	Update all permissions screens
Merge	Combine existing functionalities	Integrate localization in datetime picker
Delete	Remove existing functionalities	Delete offer stored procedure
Validate	Test existing functionalities	Evaluate inserted event
Control	Manage existing functionality	Control of access to box content
Investigate	Study potential functionality	Research angular 2.0 validation and refactoring components

jargon of software development. The analysis of our dataset resulted in the seven families of action verbs listed in (Tables 5 and 6).

Our analysis of the data set leads us to distill the following recommendations regarding the use of elementary action verbs in task labels:

- Each task should start with an action verb.
- The family-verb defines the nature of the development action to be performed with the code.
- The starting action verb should be in the imperative mood.
- When a suitable member-verb exists in Table 5, that verb should be used.

When re-analyzing our data set using our guidelines, we found many well formed task labels but also several poorly defined lables. A poorly defined task would be "Box breadcrumb component", which could be rewritten as "Create box breadcrumb component". On the other hand, "Update validity check for Addresses" from Table 1 is a well defined task, for "update" is listed in Table 5.

5 Conclusions and Directions

Our linguistic analysis of a large industrial product backlog resulted in preliminary guidelines for writing backlog items/tasks in a consistent manner, which also offers possibilities for the development of tools that assist analysts in the authoring of high-quality task descriptions.

Tasks play a key role in agile development, for they bridge the problem space (the requirements) and the solution space (the architecture and the code). The tasks refine the product requirements expressed as USs. A poorly formulated task is likely to lead to issues in the developed code and sprint velocity.

This research-in-progress paper simply paves the way for future work in the field. First and foremost, we have used a single dataset in our analysis. The guidelines are likely to need some amplification, and their impact on software development needs to be evaluated *in vivo*. In the long run, we hope this research will bring insights and theories to the "wild" world of agile development.

References

1. Lucassen, G., Dalpiaz, F., Werf, J.M.E.M., Brinkkemper, S.: The use and effectiveness of user stories in practice. In: Daneva, M., Pastor, O. (eds.) REFSQ 2016. LNCS, vol. 9619, pp. 205–222. Springer, Cham (2016). https://doi.org/10.1007/978-3-319-30282-9_14
2. Kassab, M.: The changing landscape of requirements engineering practices over the past decade. In: Proceedings of EmpiRE, pp. 1–8 (2015)
3. Berry, D.M., Kamsties, E., Krieger, M.M.: From contract drafting to software specification: linguistic sources of ambiguity. Technical report, School of Computer Science, University of Waterloo, Canada (2001)
4. Bano, M.: Addressing the challenges of requirements ambiguity: a review of empirical literature. In: Proceedings of EmpiRE, pp. 21–24 (2015)
5. Rosadini, B., et al.: Using NLP to detect requirements defects: an industrial experience in the railway domain. In: Proceedings of REFSQ, pp. 344–360 (2017)
6. Lucassen, G., Robeer, M., Dalpiaz, F., van der Werf, J.M.E.M., Brinkkemper, S.: Extracting conceptual models from user stories with visual narrator. Requir. Eng. **22**(3), 339–358 (2017)
7. Yue, T., Briand, L.C., Labiche, Y.: A systematic review of transformation approaches between user requirements and analysis models. Requir. Eng. **16**(2), 75–99 (2011)
8. Bakar, N.H., Kasirun, Z.M., Salleh, N.: Feature extraction approaches from natural language requirements for reuse in software product lines: a systematic literature review. J. Syst. Softw. **106**, 132–149 (2015)
9. Wautelet, Y., Heng, S., Kolp, M., Mirbel, I.: Unifying and extending user story models. In: Jark, M., et al. (eds.) CAiSE 2014. LNCS, vol. 8484, pp. 211–225. Springer, Cham (2014). https://doi.org/10.1007/978-3-319-07881-6_15

10. Lucassen, G., Dalpiaz, F., van der Werf, J.M.E.M., Brinkkemper, S.: Improving agile requirements: the quality user story framework and tool. Requir. Eng. **21**(3), 383–403 (2016)
11. Marcus, M.P., Marcinkiewicz, M.A., Santorini, B.: Building a large annotated corpus of English: the Penn treebank. Comput. Linguist. **19**(2), 313–330 (1993)
12. Jones, C.: Strategies for managing requirements creep. Computer **29**(6), 92–94 (1996)
13. Schuler, K.K.: VerbNet: a broad-coverage, comprehensive verb Lexicon. Ph.D. thesis, Philadelphia, PA, USA (2005). AAI3179808

Requirements Engineering for Innovative Software Ecosystems: A Research Preview

Karina Villela[1(✉)], Shashank Kedlaya[1,2], and Joerg Doerr[1]

[1] Fraunhofer IESE, Kaiserslautern, Germany
{karina.villela,joerg.doerr}@iese.fraunhofer.de
[2] TU Kaiserslautern, Kaiserslautern, Germany
skedlaya@rhrk.uni-kl.de

Abstract. [Context and motivation] In order to stay competitive in the Digital Transformation era, many organizations are engaging in innovative software ecosystems (SES). However, there is a lack of specific methods for tackling SES engineering challenges. [Question/problem] This paper presents a Requirements Engineering (RE) decision framework and a process for guiding key SES partners in the process of shaping their SES. [Principal ideas/results] Both the framework and the process build upon the results of a literature review and interviews with practitioners, and have undergone a preliminary qualitative evaluation. [Contribution] The systematic approach for shaping SES together with an explicit and clear definition of its application context will enable practitioners and researchers to apply it and/or translate it to other application contexts.

Keywords: Innovative digital solutions · Software ecosystems ·
Requirements Engineering · Software product management ·
Software platform management

1 Introduction

Digital transformation means "the profound and accelerating transformation of business activities, processes, competencies, and models aimed at fully leveraging the changes and opportunities of digital technologies and their impact across society in a strategic and prioritized way" [3]. The digital solutions in this scenario are inherently innovative, even disruptive. On the other hand, they integrate several complex and interdependent systems spanning multiple, interconnected application domains and provided by different organizations.

The paradigm of Software Ecosystems (SES) [5] can offer an answer to the challenge of developing the aforementioned digital solutions. However, Manikas's longitudinal literature study [9] concluded that there is a lack of specific theories, methods and tools for tackling SES problems. He argues that a big part of the problem derives from the fact that the notion of SES is very wide and arguably complex. Therefore, one of his recommendations is to focus more on research contributions to the field and explicitly characterize their context of application.

© Springer Nature Switzerland AG 2019
E. Knauss and M. Goedicke (Eds.): REFSQ 2019, LNCS 11412, pp. 117–123, 2019.
https://doi.org/10.1007/978-3-030-15538-4_8

In addition, Manikas's study [9] allows the conclusion that Requirements Engineering (RE) for Software Ecosystems (RE4SES) has been under-investigated.

Our organization has actively participated in several projects aimed at shaping innovative digital solutions based on SES (e.g., [11]). In these projects, the characteristic initial situation was the decision by some companies to combine their strengths in an SES in order to offer solutions that go far beyond their current and individual portfolio of solutions, towards the digital transformation of their business. This situation calls for a top-down approach, which means progressing from the definition of an overall SES concept towards innovative, typically more disruptive services, applications, and technical infrastructure. A bottom-up approach, i.e., gradually evolving the existing portfolio of solutions into a cohesive SES, would not achieve the desired level of innovation. Despite being typically applied in green field, top-down approaches to software engineering can also be applied in brown field. In this case, existing assets are incorporated if they fit the new SES concept. In this paper, we propose an RE decision framework and a process that build upon, but go beyond, our creativity workshops [12]. The goal is to provide holistic guidance to requirements engineers on how to contribute to the shaping of innovative SES as part of the SES leadership team [2].

Following Manikas's characterization scheme [9], our contribution is applicable to ecosystems whose orchestration is *not an anarchy*, whose means of value creation are *proprietary or hybrid*, and whose common technology can vary. Considering Bosch's category dimension and the spectrum between directed and undirected opening-up approaches [1], our contribution targets *applications* where the opening-up approach tends to be *directed*. We did not use Bosch's [1] platform dimension because ecosystems aiming at digital transformation frequently span all categories in this dimension.

The remainder of this paper is structured as follows: Sect. 2 presents our research method together with the findings from the literature and interviews with practitioners. Section 3 describes our RE decision framework and a process that sketches the dynamics among the decisions. In Sect. 4, we discuss the results of an initial qualitative evaluation of our contribution and present our future work.

2   Research Method and Main Findings

Our research has followed the five steps of the Design Science Research Cycle (DSRC) [15]: (1) awareness of the problem, (2) suggestion, (3) development, (4) evaluation and (5) conclusion. This research preview reports on the results from the first design cycle.

In the first step, we searched the literature for RE4SES challenges from the scientific perspective and performed individual, semi-structured 1-h interviews with ten practitioners from our organization in order to capture the practitioners' perspective. These practitioners reported on the RE challenges experienced in seven different projects regarding the conception and/or development of innovative SES. For the literature survey, we used the search string "Software Ecosystems" and ("Requirements" or "Requirements Engineering") in SpringerLink, ScienceDirect, IEEE Xplore, and ACM Digital Library. In the second step, we collected from the literature the currently available RE4SES approaches. Based on the knowledge acquired in steps (1) and (2), we designed an RE decision framework and a process, which will be described in Sect. 3. The evaluation step was performed by collecting feedback from eight practitioners (a subset of the previously interviewed ten practitioners, due to availability) in individual 1-h interviews, where the produced artifacts were explained to the interviewees, who were then asked to openly comment on their structure and contents and propose improvements.

Using a clustering approach over the literature survey's results, we extracted the following areas of challenges (introduced with an abbreviation for later reference):

- Requirements negotiation (*ReqNeg*) due to the interplay with several partners who must align their own interests and schedules and negotiate alternative solutions [10];
- Software integration (*SoftInt*) due to release planning cycles not being properly synchronized and product versions being launched at different points in time [17];
- Governance (*Gov*) due to the need to define clear responsibilities, make business strategy explicit, and determine the level of knowledge sharing [17];
- Support for the emergent requirements flow (*EmergFlow*) [7,14,17] due to the need to contextualize those requirements, map them to specific subsystems, and communicate them to the stakeholders [7].

The practitioners mentioned all these challenges and others: the uncertainty involved in the shaping of the ecosystem (*Unc*), as there is no one delivering concrete ecosystem requirements; the need to deal with several domains as well as with technical, legal, and business aspects simultaneously (*DomAsp*); the challenge of separating the requirements to be fulfilled by the platform (the common infrastructure in all our projects so far) and by the services and applications that will build on it (*PlatServ*); support for the on-boarding of new ecosystem partners (*OnB*), which requires the usage of prototypes and convincing capabilities; and change management (*CM*), due the need to deal with the inherent uncertainty and the on-boarding of partners.

As for the currently available RE4SES approaches, there are some approaches for dealing with specific challenges and activities [4,8,14,16]. However, there is still no guidance for requirements engineers on how to contribute to the top-down shaping of SES. As expected in competence/maturity models, Jansen et al. [6] present a wide range of capabilities, but at a very high level of abstraction. Santos and Werner [13] provide a set of concrete activities, but focus on the opening of existing platforms and on monitoring and management activities.

3   Decision Framework and Process for RE4SES

The proposed decision framework is composed of the following decision points:

Actors: organizations that interact or are expected to interact directly or indirectly with each other as part of the SES. Existing relationships such as trade relationships and collaborations are also of interest.

Business Strategy: flows that implement the ecosystem business, such as the flow of data, the flow of goods, and the flow of money.

Services/Applications: software services and applications that are required to implement the business strategy or influence it. Their identification is necessary to clarify which contributions are needed from the SES partners.

Openness Strategy: the degree of openness for the SES. This has two dimensions: (1) the ecosystem's openness for new partners, which can be tuned by entry conditions and facilities for the integration of contributions; and (2) openness of data, knowledge, artifacts and communication for the SES partners, which can be defined through IP rules, licensing policies, and collaboration principles.

Technical Infrastructure: requirements for the SES's common technological infrastructure at operation time and at development time, which are defined in alignment with the decisions about the openness strategy. This decision point also includes the identification of relevant data sources and the definition of user feedback mechanisms.

The decision points *Actors, Business Strategy* and *Service/Applications* were mainly derived from our workshop approach for the initial design of SES [12]; in addition, relationships among actors are addressed in [7,16]; the need to define clear responsibilities and make the business strategy explicit is mentioned in [7,17]; and Valença et al. refer to the identification of strategic features aimed at composing an SES roadmap [17]. The decision point *Openness Strategy* was motivated by [7] and [4]. The decision point *Technical Infrastructure* was also inspired by [7], where a technical infrastructure is made available to support decisions regarding openness, and by several references reporting the need to provide user feedback mechanisms [7,14,17].

For the application of the proposed decision framework, we envision the dynamics depicted in Fig. 1, which presents an iterative process that can be repeated until the SES concept is clear enough for the realization of its first version. According to Naab et al. [11], the first versions should cover a small subset of the SES focused on priority goals and on what needs to be solved in the short term, with the goal being to learn from the on-boarding of partners and the initial operation.

Preliminary Definition of SES Concept: Activities for defining the SES concept include the identification of actors and different end-user roles, the definition of the overall business strategy, the definition of software services and applications for composing the SES, and a preliminary discussion of openness alternatives. This also encompasses the indication by key SES partners of their intended contribution to the SES.

Elaboration of SES Enablers: Both the openness strategy and the technical infrastructure are key aspects for making the SES attractive to its current and

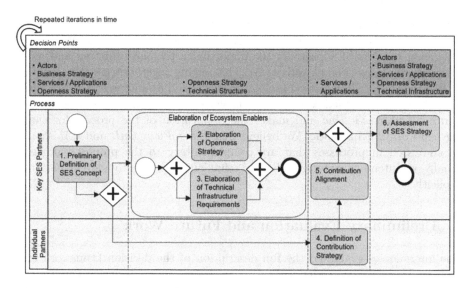

Fig. 1. Process for guiding the performance of RE4SES (BPMN 2.0)

potential partners. As the technical infrastructure goes beyond providing technical support to the openness strategy, the elaboration of the openness strategy and of the technical infrastructure requirements can start in parallel. The open software enterprise model [4] can help key SES partners in choosing the degree of openness for their SES.

Definition of the Contribution Strategy: Activities performed by each SES partner individually to determine their contribution to the SES. Linåker and Regnell [8] provide guidance on how to perform these activities. A contribution roadmap should indicate the features included in each contribution release as well as estimated release dates.

Alignment of Contribution Strategies: Activities to support the alignment of the contributions proposed by the SES partners, resulting in a joint SES roadmap. This potentially involves negotiation and may result in refinements of the overall SES concept and/or individual contributions. Knowing the power-dependence relations described in [16] is crucial for understanding power disputes and finding satisfactory solutions.

Assessment of SES Strategy: After making so many decisions and aligning individual contributions in a joint SES roadmap, it is time to assess the overall SES strategy in terms of the value it brings to all involved actors and end-users, consistency among all the decisions made, and the uncertainties and risks to be addressed and monitored from this time on.

The consideration of business, technical, and legal aspects [11] (*DomAsp*) is a concern that crosscuts all activities of the proposed process. The need to align the interests and contributions of the key SES partners [17] (derived from *ReqNeg* and *SoftInt*) is exactly the reason for: (1) having the key SES partners define the preliminary SES concept jointly (Fig. 1, Activity 1); (2) allowing the partners to define their contribution strategy separately (Fig. 1, Activity 4); and (3) giving the key SES partners the opportunity to jointly discuss and align their contributions (Fig. 1, Activity 5). This setting together with the activities in *Elaboration SES Enablers* (Fig. 1, Activities 2 and 3) addresses *Gov*. In addition, the aforementioned setting together with the possibility of having several iterations addresses *Unc* and makes the application of the process for shaping real-world SES realistic. We believe that *EmergFlow*, *OnB* and *CM* should be addressed in processes that are complementary to the proposed process. Finally, we intend to investigate how to refine our approach to address *PlatServ* explicitly.

4   Preliminary Evaluation and Future Work

The interviewees evaluated the full description of the decision framework and process. The evaluation was qualitative and open, with interviewees indicating the aspects that they particularly liked or disliked, and aspects that they missed. In some cases, they asked for information to be added to the description of the decision points. The critical improvement suggestions included making the SES platform more evident in the decision points and/or process, and addressing change management and the on-boarding activities. These improvement suggestions are exactly related to the practitioners' challenges that we believe should be addressed by complementary processes (*OnB* and *CM*) or that we want to address in future work (*PlatServ*).

The next step of this research will be to perform a thorough analysis of the evaluation interviews and thereby conclude the first design cycle. In the second design cycle, we will make the necessary adaptations to our contribution based on the received feedback. In addition, we will suggest notations for capturing decisions and propose the structure of the process artifacts. Regarding the evaluation in the second design cycle, we plan to carry out an industrial case study. In the long term, more case studies and other types of empirical studies should be performed in order to provide evidence of the suitability of the proposed approach and support its evolution.

Acknowledgement. This work was done in the context of the project Smart MaaS funded by the German Federal Ministry for Economic Affairs and Energy (grant number 01MD18014B).

References

1. Bosch, J.: From software product lines to software ecosystems. In: SPLC, pp. 111–119. Carnegie Mellon University (2009)
2. Hess, S., Knodel, J., Naab, M., Trapp, M.: Engineering roles for constructing ecosystems. In: ECSAW. ACM (2016). Article 24

3. i-SCOOP: Digitization, digitalization and digital transformation: the differences (2017). https://www.i-scoop.eu/digitization-digitalization-digital-transformation-disruption/. Accessed 22 Oct 2017
4. Jansen, S., Brinkkemper, S., et al.: Shades of gray: opening up a software producing organization with the open software enterprise model. J. Syst. Softw. **85**(7), 1495–1510 (2012)
5. Jansen, S., Finkelstein, A., Brinkkemper, S.: A sense of community: a research agenda for software ecosystems. In: ICSE, pp. 187–190. IEEE (2009)
6. Jansen, S., Peeters, S., Brinkkemper, S.: Software ecosystems: from software product management to software platform management. In: IW-LCSP@ICSOB, pp. 5–18 (2013)
7. Knauss, E., Yussuf, A., et al.: Continuous clarification and emergent requirements flows in open-commercial software ecosystems. RE J. **23**(1), 97–117 (2018)
8. Linåker, J., Regnell, B.: A contribution management framework for firms engaged in open source software ecosystems - a research preview. In: Grünbacher, P., Perini, A. (eds.) REFSQ 2017. LNCS, vol. 10153, pp. 50–57. Springer, Cham (2017). https://doi.org/10.1007/978-3-319-54045-0_4
9. Manikas, K.: Revisiting software ecosystems research: a longitudinal literature study. J. Syst. Softw. **117**, 84–103 (2016)
10. Manikas, K., Hansen, K.M.: Software ecosystems-a systematic literature review. J. Syst. Softw. **86**(5), 1294–1306 (2013)
11. Naab, M., Rost, D., Knodel, J.: Architecting a software-based ecosystem for the automotive aftermarket: an experience report. In: ICSA. IEEE (2018)
12. Nass, C., Trapp, M., Villela, K.: Tangible design for software ecosystem with Playmobil®. In: NordiCHI, pp. 856–861. ACM (2018)
13. Santos, R., Werner, C.: ReuseECOS: an approach to support global software development through software ecosystems. In: ICGSEW, pp. 60–65. IEEE (2012)
14. Schneider, K., Meyer, S., Peters, M., Schliephacke, F., Mörschbach, J., Aguirre, L.: Feedback in context: supporting the evolution of IT-ecosystems. In: Ali Babar, M., Vierimaa, M., Oivo, M. (eds.) PROFES 2010. LNCS, vol. 6156, pp. 191–205. Springer, Heidelberg (2010). https://doi.org/10.1007/978-3-642-13792-1_16
15. Takeda, H., Veerkamp, P., Yoshikawa, H.: Modeling design process. AI Mag. **11**(4), 37 (1990)
16. Valença, G., Alves, C.: A theory of power in emerging software ecosystems formed by small-to-medium enterprises. J. Syst. Softw. **134**, 76–104 (2017)
17. Valença, G., Alves, C., et al.: Competition and collaboration in requirements engineering: a case study of an emerging software ecosystem. In: RE Conference, pp. 384–393. IEEE (2014)

Assessment of the Quality of Safety Cases: A Research Preview

Jose Luis de la Vara[1(✉)], Gabriel Jiménez[1], Roy Mendieta[2], and Eugenio Parra[1]

[1] Departamento de Informática, Universidad Carlos III de Madrid, Leganes, Spain
jvara@inf.uc3m.es,
{gabriel.jimenez,eparra}@kr.inf.uc3m.es
[2] The REUSE Company, Leganes, Spain
roy.mendieta@reusecompany.com

Abstract. **[Context and motivation]** Safety-critical systems in application domains such as aerospace, automotive, healthcare, and railway are subject to assurance processes to provide confidence that the systems do not pose undue risks to people, property, or the environment. The development of safety cases is usually part of these processes to justify that a system satisfies its safety requirements and thus is dependable. **[Question/problem]** Although safety cases have been used in industry for over two decades, their management still requires improvement. Important weaknesses have been identified and means to assess the quality of safety cases are limited. **[Principal ideas/results]** This paper presents a research preview on the assessment of the quality of safety cases. We explain how the area should develop and present our preliminary work towards enabling the assessment with Verification Studio, an industrial tool for system artefact quality analysis. **[Contribution]** The insights provided allow researchers and practitioners to gain an understanding of why safety case quality requires further investigation, what aspects must be considered, and how quality assessment could be performed in practice.

Keywords: Safety case · Quality · Quality assessment · System assurance · Safety-critical system · Verification Studio

1 Introduction

Safety-critical systems are those whose failure can harm people, property, or the environment [17], e.g. systems in aerospace, automotive, healthcare, and railway. These systems are subject to rigorous, systematic, and planned assurance processes to provide confidence that the systems satisfy given requirements. These requirements can be system requirements (i.e. about the properties of a system, including safety requirements) or be indicated in standards with which a system must comply. Among the artefacts to manage for systems assurance, safety cases are arguably the main ones.

A safety case is a structured argument, supported by a body of evidence, that provides a compelling, comprehensible and valid case that a system is safe for a given

E. Knauss and M. Goedicke (Eds.): REFSQ 2019, LNCS 11412, pp. 124–131, 2019.
https://doi.org/10.1007/978-3-030-15538-4_9

application in a given environment [16]. Safety cases have been used in industry for over two decades, first in application domains such as defence and energy and more recently in domains such as automotive and healthcare. Many researchers have worked on the specification and management of structured safety cases [17], e.g. with GSN (Goal Structuring Notation). The notion of safety case has also evolved towards the more general concept of assurance case, to justify system dependability, and other specific cases such as security case. Although the term safety case is not used in some applications domains and standards, the concept of artefact to justify system safety and dependability exists in all safety-critical contexts.

Despite the importance and wide use of safety cases, certain aspects of their development require improvement to ensure that the quality of a safety case is sufficient and thus system safety has been acceptably justified. Among the authors that have studied safety case quality, Nancy Leveson is one of the most well-known experts that has doubted the quality and effectiveness of safety cases. For example, she argues that confirmation bias can easily appear in a safety case and has reviewed issues in past safety cases such as obscure language and compliance-only exercises [12]. Greenwell et al. [8] found several types of fallacies in the arguments of existing safety cases, e.g. using wrong reasons, drawing wrong conclusions, and omission of key evidence.

Even researchers and practitioners that strongly support the use of safety cases have acknowledged the risk of developing low-quality safety cases. Kelly [10] has referred to issues such as the "apologetic safety case", the document-centric view, the approximation to the truth, the prescriptive safety case, and the illusion of pictures, and Bloomfield and Bishop [3] argue that improvements are needed in safety case structure and confidence. In a seminal paper on software safety certification [9], Hatcliff et al. refer to the weakness that there are many possible forms of an assurance case, some good and some bad, and to the lack of guidance to produce effective assurance cases, among other issues. Langari and Maibaum [11] review challenges for safety cases, including size and complexity, readability, checking soundness, and checking completeness, and Wassyng et al. [22] discuss weaknesses about argumentation.

Recent studies about the state of the practice [5, 18] report that practitioners face challenges to effectively create and structure safety cases, that tool support for safety cases is basic, and that safety case evolution does not seem to be properly addressed. How safety case quality is managed, including its evolution, can be improved.

In summary, and as further discussed below, the current practices and tools to ensure and assess the quality of safety cases seem to be insufficient and further research is needed. We are working towards filling the gaps in the state of the art, and in this paper we present a research preview about (1) the main needs to take into account for effective assessment of the quality of safety cases in practice, and (2) our current results on the development of a solution to assess safety case quality with Verification Studio [21], an industrial tool for system artefact quality analysis. We have been able to successfully use Verification Studio to analyse the quality of safety cases specified with ASCE (Assurance and Safety Case Environment) [1]. The quality analysis is partial and several important aspects have not been addressed yet, but the results represent a promising initial step towards the assessment of the quality of safety cases in industry.

This paper distinguishes from prior work by focusing on how the quality of safety cases should be assessed and proposing a solution linked to quality analysis in practice. The insights provided can help industry and academia gain a better understanding of what factors can influence safety case quality, why the topic requires further research, what aspects should be considered, and how quality assessment could be performed.

The rest of the paper is organised as follows. Section 2 introduces the main needs for assessing the quality of safety cases. Section 3 presents our current results and Sect. 4 our next steps. Finally, Sect. 5 summarises our conclusions.

2 Needs for Assessing the Quality of Safety Cases

This section presents the six main needs that, in our opinion, must be addressed to enable the effective assessment of the quality of safety case in practice.

(1) **The information about safety case quality is scattered.** There exists guidance about the quality properties that a safety case should have; e.g. the GSN standard [7] presents errors to avoid. However, this information is in many different sources [20]: standards, research literature, tool documentation... It is necessary to create a unifying framework for safety case quality and that the framework gathers information from different sources, harmonising the guidance from different application domains.

(2) **Quality metrics for safety cases are limited.** As a follow-up need, it is not clear how safety case quality could be objectively and suitably measured. Some metrics can be found in the literature, e.g. the number of unsupported claims, but the metrics (1) have not been developed in the scope of a sound quality framework and (2) usually deal with simple attributes. Most of the tool support for measurement of safety case quality further corresponds to research prototypes [14]. More mature tools, e.g. AdvoCATE [6], provide very limited and narrow sets of metrics. In addition, most metrics defined for safety-related assessments (e.g. [4]) do not apply to the specific quality needs of safety cases, but the metrics should be adapted or re-defined. Once the framework from the previous need is developed, metrics and measurement procedures must be defined and implemented to be able to quantitatively asses the quality of safety cases.

(3) **Safety case quality goes beyond safety case structure and syntax.** Most work on safety case quality has focused on structural and syntactical aspects [20], e.g. the language used to specify a claim or how to assess the confidence in a claim. However, safety case quality is also based on e.g. the semantics of the elements and how well the argumentation is formed. These aspects indeed relate to some of the main criticisms that safety cases have received. It is necessary to pay further attention to them.

(4) **Safety cases are most often managed as textual documents.** This is arguably the need that has been most widely disregarded by the research community. Prior work has focused on analysing graphical structured safety cases [17], but the reality in industry is that safety cases are most often managed as textual documents. These documents might include graphical arguments created with e.g. GSN, but the diagrams would correspond to only a part of the safety case document. It is necessary to think of how the textual descriptions could be analysed to assess the quality.

(5) **Safety case quality depends on the quality of many other system artefacts.** Safety cases relate to other artefact types [5], e.g. safety analysis results and V&V results. Hundreds of references to other artefacts can be found in the safety case of a complex system, and the quality of the safety case depends on these artefacts. The relationship with other artefacts and their influence must be characterised from a quality perspective, also considering that the influence might vary among artefact types.

(6) **Safety case quality evolves.** It is strongly recommended that safety cases are created incrementally [10], evolving from a preliminary version at e.g. system analysis phase to an interim version during implementation and an operational one when system development finishes. A safety case should also be maintained during system operation and can be impacted by changes in other artefacts [5]. It is necessary that the approaches to assess the quality of safety cases consider that a safety case evolves during a system's lifecycle and that what the quality of a safety case is can vary between different phases.

3 Current Results

We have already started to work to enable our vision for the assessment of the quality of safety cases. We have first dealt with technological aspects, setting the scope of how a tool-based solution could effectively support the assessment of safety case quality in practice. We have performed little work on the quality framework and the quality metrics related to the first two needs presented above. This requires a deep investigation, including systematic reviews of the literature that take both academic publications and other sources such as safety standards into account.

Figure 1 presents an overview of our current solution. It is based on the integration of two commercial tools: ASCE [1] and Verification Studio [21]. ASCE supports the specification of structured safety cases with e.g. the GSN notation. It is arguably the main tool in industry for this purpose [5, 18]. Verification Studio supports the analysis of the quality of different system artefact types and in different formats, such as textual requirements, logical system models with UML or SysML, or physical system models with Modelica or Simulink. The analysis is based on metrics for which measurement procedures are specified and for which quality levels are defined, i.e. the quality will be assessed as high or low depending on a metric's measurement result and thresholds. The quality is analysed according to the information in a System Knowledge Repository, which is a domain representation with an ontology.

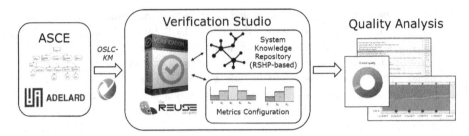

Fig. 1. Solution overview

The use of Verification Studio is suitable because it fits the needs presented above:

- Verification Studio provides default metrics to analyse artefact quality, mainly according to an ontology. The users can also define their own metrics and specify measurement procedures (need 2).
- Verification Studio supports semantics-based analyses of artefact quality, as well as analyses based on syntactical aspects and on artefact structure (need 3).
- The RSHP language [13] is used as the main basis for artefact representation in Verification Studio. It supports universal information representation via the different elements of an artefact, their relationships, and their semantics. Artefacts in different formats (text, models, etc.) can be represented with RSHP, including safety cases specified as diagrams or as documents (need 4).
- Verification Studio supports the centralised analysis and management of the quality of different artefact types, and it is part of tool suite that also supports the management of the traceability between system artefacts (need 5).
- A recent feature of Verification Studio supports the analysis of the evolution of the quality of an artefact [19], including the use of different metrics at different moments of the lifecycle of an artefact to assess its quality (need 6).

For integration of ASCE and Verification Studio, we exploit the OSLC-KM technology [2], which provides generic means for tool interoperability. The technology allows us to transform ASCE files into data that Verification Studio can manage, i.e. data in the RSHP format. We have performed similar RSHP-targeted integrations in the past (e.g. for SysML [15]).

Once the information about an ASCE diagram (claims, arguments, evidence, etc.) has been imported into Verification Studio, we can analyse the quality of the safety case. To show that this is a feasible approach, we have first analysed the quality of structured safety cases available in the literature (e.g. [10]) with a set of default metrics that Verification Studio provides to evaluate artefact correctness. The metrics selected consider the precision, concision, non-ambiguity, singularity, completeness, quantifiers, and quantification in the text of an element. For instance, the number of vague adverbs and adjectives, the use of "and/or", the presence of domain terms, the text length, and the possible subjectivity of the sentences are considered for quality assessment. We have used a default ontology with English terms but a specialised one could have been employed, i.e. with case-specific concepts. Further details about how the quality analyses have been performed are not provided due to page limitations.

Figure 2 presents a summary of the quality analysis results for a specific safety case. The report includes a quantitative score of the individual elements of the safety case (e.g. claims) and a qualitative evaluation with stars to show whether the quality is low, medium, or high. A pie chart shows an overview.

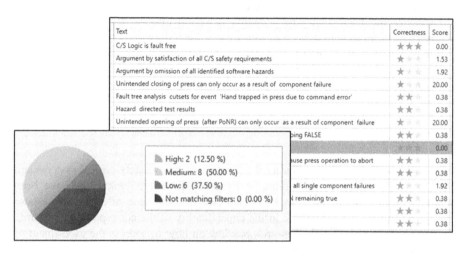

Text	Correctness	Score
C/S Logic is fault free	★ ★ ★	0.00
Argument by satisfaction of all C/S safety requirements	★	1.53
Argument by omission of all identified software hazards	★	1.92
Unintended closing of press can only occur as a result of component failure	★	20.00
Fault tree analysis cutsets for event 'Hand trapped in press due to command error'	★ ★	0.38
Hazard directed test results	★ ★	0.38
Unintended opening of press (after PoNR) can only occur as a result of component failure	★	20.00
...ing FALSE	★ ★	0.38
		0.00
...use press operation to abort	★ ★	0.38
	★ ★	0.38
...all single component failures	★	1.92
...N remaining true	★ ★	0.38
	★ ★	0.38
	★ ★	0.38

High: 2 (12.50 %)
Medium: 8 (50.00 %)
Low: 6 (37.50 %)
Not matching filters: 0 (0.00 %)

Fig. 2. Example of quality analysis results summary

4 Next Steps

In the previous sections we have presented the needs that we envision for effective assessment of the quality of safety cases and the results that we have obtained so far. In this section we present our next steps to realise our vision. Five main steps can be distinguished to complete the underlying research process.

(1) **Review of the current guidance for safety case quality.** The goal of this step is to gather information about the practices that are used or should be used to ensure safety case quality. Different sources will be used, namely research literature, safety standards, and practitioners. For the latter, surveys and case studies could be conducted.

(2) **Specification of a quality framework for safety cases.** This step aims at providing a framework based on which safety case quality can be assessed. The framework, which will address all the needs introduced in Sect. 2, will aggregate and synthesise the information collected in the previous step and will consist of different properties that could be analysed, metrics to characterise the properties, and measurement procedures for the metrics.

(3) **Validation of the framework.** This step will confirm that the framework is suitable by comparing it against industrial practices. For example, a wide range of practitioners could be asked about the framework to identify possible missing aspects.

(4) **Implementation of the framework.** This step refers to the enactment of the validated quality framework via tool support. The tool could correspond to a tailored usage of Verification Studio, but since the quality framework will be generic and tool-independent, it could be implemented with other tools (e.g. AdvoCATE extension).

(5) **Validation of the implementation of the framework.** The last step will evaluate whether the framework and its implementation effectively assess safety case quality. In addition to using past safety cases, we will try to perform the validation in running projects. The safety cases will be both structured ones and documents, and we will use publicly available safety cases and safety cases provided by our industry network.

5 Conclusion

Safety cases must be managed during the lifecycle of many safety-critical systems and the quality of the safety cases must be ensured. However, weaknesses have been identified in the current practices for safety case development, affecting safety case quality and in turn the confidence in the dependability of the corresponding systems.

This paper has presented a research preview on how to address the assessment of the quality of safety cases. This includes dealing with needs such as that the information about safety case quality is scattered, quality metrics for safety cases are limited, quality goes beyond safety case structure, safety cases are most often managed as textual documents, safety case quality depends on the quality of many other system artefacts, and safety case quality evolves. If these needs are not fulfilled, it is difficult that the quality of safety cases can be effectively assessed in practice.

As a first step to meet the needs, we have developed a preliminary solution to link safety case specification and system artefact quality analysis. It integrates ASCE (Assurance and Safety Case Environment) and Verification Studio. The solution has allowed us to assess the quality of safety cases with a set of default metrics that Verification Studio provides and to show that the further development with Verification Studio of means for assessment of safety case quality can be a feasible approach.

We will work on meeting the needs discussed and on tool support in the future, taking the next steps presented.

Acknowledgments. The research leading to this paper has received funding from the AMASS project (H2020-ECSEL ID 692474; Spain's MINECO ref. PCIN-2015-262). We also thank REFSQ reviewers for their valuable comments to improve the paper.

References

1. Adelard: ASCE Software. https://www.adelard.com/asce/. Accessed 26 Sept 2018
2. Alvarez-Rodriguez, J.M., et al.: Enabling system artefact exchange and selection through a linked data layer. J. Univ. Comput. Sci. **24**(11), 1536–1560 (2018)

3. Bloomfield, R., Bishop, P.: Safety and assurance cases: past, present and possible future - an adelard perspective. In: SCSS (2010)
4. Cruickshank, K.J., et al.: A validation metrics framework for safety-critical software-intensive systems. In: SoSE (2009)
5. de la Vara, J.L., et al.: An industrial survey on safety evidence change impact analysis practice. IEEE Trans. Softw. Eng. **42**(12), 1095–1117 (2016)
6. Denney, E., Pai, G.: Tool support for assurance case development. Autom. Soft. Eng. **25**, 435–499 (2018)
7. Goal Structuring Notation: GSN Community Standard Version 1 (2011)
8. Greenwell, W.S., et al.: A taxonomy of fallacies in system safety arguments. In: ISSC (2006)
9. Hatcliff, J., et al.: Certifiably safe software-dependent systems. In: FOSE (2014)
10. Kelly, T.: Safety cases. In: Handbook of Safety Principles. Wiley, Hoboken (2018)
11. Langari, Z., Maibaum, T.: Safety cases: a review of challenges. In: ASSURE (2013)
12. Leveson, N.: The Use of Safety Cases in Certification and Regulation. MIT (2011)
13. Llorens, J., Morato, J., Genova, G.: RSHP: an information representation model based on relationships. In: Damiani, E., Madravio, M., Jain, L.C. (eds.) Soft Computing in Software Engineering. STUDFUZZ, vol. 159, pp. 221–253. Springer, Heidelberg (2004). https://doi.org/10.1007/978-3-540-44405-3_8
14. Maksimov, M., et al.: Two decades of assurance case tools: a survey. In: ASSURE (2018)
15. Mendieta, R., et al.: Towards Effective SysML Model Reuse. In: MODELSWARD (2017)
16. MoD: Defence Standard 00-56 Issue 4 (2007)
17. Nair, S., et al.: An extended systematic literature review on provision of evidence for safety certification. Inform. Softw. Tech. **56**(7), 689–717 (2014)
18. Nair, S., et al.: Evidence management for compliance of critical systems with safety standards: a survey on the state of practice. Inform. Softw. Tech. **60**, 1–15 (2015)
19. Parra, E., et al.: Analysis of requirements quality evolution. In: ICSE (2018)
20. Rinehart, D.J., et al.: Current Practices in Constructing and Evaluating Assurance Cases With Applications to Aviation. NASA (2015)
21. The REUSE Company: Verification Studio. https://www.reusecompany.com/verification-studio. Accessed 26 Sep 2018
22. Wassyng, A., Maibaum, T., Lawford, M., Bherer, H.: Software certification: is there a case against safety cases? In: Calinescu, R., Jackson, E. (eds.) Monterey Workshop 2010. LNCS, vol. 6662, pp. 206–227. Springer, Heidelberg (2011). https://doi.org/10.1007/978-3-642-21292-5_12

From Vision to Specification

Refining Vision Videos

Kurt Schneider[1]([envelope]), Melanie Busch[1], Oliver Karras[1],
Maximilian Schrapel[2], and Michael Rohs[2]

[1] Software Engineering Group, Leibniz Universität Hannover,
Welfengarten 1, 30167 Hannover, Germany
{kurt.schneider,melanie.busch,
oliver.karras}@inf.uni-hannover.de
[2] Human-Computer Interaction Group, Leibniz Universität Hannover,
Welfengarten 1, 30167 Hannover, Germany
{maximilian.schrapel,
michael.rohs}@hci.uni-hannover.de

Abstract. **[Context and motivation]** Complex software-based systems involve
several stakeholders, their activities and interactions with the system. Vision
videos are used during the early phases of a project to complement textual
representations. They visualize previously abstract visions of the product and its
use. By creating, elaborating, and discussing vision videos, stakeholders and
developers gain an improved shared understanding of how those abstract visions
could translate into concrete scenarios and requirements to which individuals can
relate. **[Question/problem]** In this paper, we investigate two aspects of refining
vision videos: (1) Refining the vision by providing alternative answers to previously open issues about the system to be built. (2) A refined understanding of
the camera perspective in vision videos. The impact of using a subjective (or
"ego") perspective is compared to the usual third-person perspective.
[Methodology] We use shopping in rural areas as a real-world application
domain for refining vision videos. Both aspects of refining vision videos were
investigated in an experiment with 20 participants. **[Contribution]** Subjects
made a significant number of additional contributions when they had received not
only video or text but also both – even with very short text and short video clips.
Subjective video elements were rated as positive. However, there was no significant preference for either subjective or non-subjective videos in general.

Keywords: Vision · Video · Refinement · Camera-perspective · Experiment

1 Introduction: Shared Understanding and Vision Videos in RE

When a complex technical or socio-technical system is being conceived, overall visions
are developed before software requirements can be specified. In development processes
like the V-model (www.iabg.de), *system* requirements and *system* design precede
software requirements. Changes in business processes, complex interactions, or societal
change call for stakeholder participation and discourse. However, it is often difficult to
convey the concepts and visions to diverse stakeholders [10]. Due to the large number

© Springer Nature Switzerland AG 2019
E. Knauss and M. Goedicke (Eds.): REFSQ 2019, LNCS 11412, pp. 135–150, 2019.
https://doi.org/10.1007/978-3-030-15538-4_10

of available options, building software prototypes for all of them is impossible. Details of their scope and impact are initially unclear.

One of the main challenges in requirements engineering (RE) is to create a shared understanding of the future system among developers and different stakeholder groups [14]. Minutes of stakeholder meetings are usually limited to only one facet of various points of view and a shared vision [12]. Several researchers [8, 11, 19] proposed applying videos in RE due to their communication richness and effectiveness [4]. For example, Brill et al. [6] demonstrate the benefits of using ad-hoc videos compared to textual use cases in order to clarify requirements with stakeholders.

In RE, videos of human-computer interaction were used to document system context [15], product vision [6, 23], or scenarios [22, 28, 29]. They were used as input to a requirements workshop [7], for analyzing usability [22], or for complementing speci-fications [8, 20]. Fricker et al. [12] proposed to record stakeholder meetings on video as a source of authentic requirements. Many approaches use videos but do not report details about how to produce them [6, 8, 18, 28]. This lack of guidance could be a reason why videos are not yet an established RE documentation practice [17, 21]. In the process of eliciting, refining, and validating requirements with video, we investigated two aspects that may contribute to the benefit of videos: (1) Refining visions by presenting alter-natives and (2) refining the camera perspective for better emotional involvement. Refining vision videos can empower elicitation and validation. Creighton et al. [8] proposed a high-tech approach to videos in RE. We follow a different line of research.

Affordable Video Approach: While high-end marketing videos obviously help to convince people, we target *affordable videos* that assist in elicitation and validation of requirements and visions. Hence, creating and refining videos should be affordable with respect to effort, time, and resources. We envision a video-based approach for ambitious requirements engineers in ordinary software development teams.

This paper is structured as follows: Sect. 2 introduces the example application as a background. In Sect. 3, we describe the concepts of vision videos in RE and of refining them in particular. Related work is presented in Sect. 4, before we outline the exper-iment design (Sect. 5) and report about results (Sect. 6). Discussion and threats to validity (Sect. 7) lead to the conclusion (Sect. 8).

2 Application Example: Shopping in Rural Areas

According to Schneider et al. [25, p. 1], "spatial planning problems are characterized by large and heterogeneous groups of stakeholders, such as municipalities, companies, interest groups, women and men, young people and children". Challenges in spatial planning include shrinking population in rural areas. Mobility options are discussed, and shopping opportunities are related to mobility: How can inhabitants of villages and peripheral areas get access to medical services; how can they buy food and daily supplies if grocery stores close down, and public transportation is missing?

Traditionally, neighborhood help or a grocery bus initiative will be discussed in meetings with citizens. Scheduling and conducting those meetings is difficult and usually reaches only a small portion of citizens and stakeholders. Possibilities to participate are initially high and decrease as more and more aspects are decided. According to the "Paradox of Participation", however, interest in participation tends to be low in the beginning and only rises when there is little left to decide. Therefore, it is desirable to enable and motivate stakeholders to start participating early.

CrowdRE stands for technical approaches to support participation of crowds (of stakeholders, citizens, etc.) in requirements engineering. In [25], we proposed to extend the approach beyond RE towards participating in public discourse. The example application chosen for this paper is a sub-aspect of mobility in rural areas. Shopping without shops seems to call for some kind of ordering online and requires an adequate way of delivering the ordered goods. All variants of ordering and delivery require internet access and sophisticated coordination, which must be provided by software. Long before software can be specified, however, stakeholders should get to see the vision and the variants associated with different proposals.

Shopping in rural areas is a real-world application domain of growing importance. This topic has caught public attention and is discussed in newspapers [1]. Findings from the experiment, therefore, apply to the rural context – and may be applicable to other domains with similar challenges. This is, however, beyond the scope of this paper.

3   Concepts to Improve the Use of Vision Videos

As outlined above, vision videos are a good representation for communicating what is proposed, and how it would feel to use it. Following our *Affordable Video Approach*, we intend to solicit feedback, questions, and even objections by affordable self-made video clips in order to start effective discourse early.

Refinement Process: Stakeholders should be able to participate in the process of comparing alternatives, selecting, and refining options. As refinement progresses, the discussion with all its proposals and questions and rationale will change its nature: From imagining a vision over defining system alternatives to finally narrowing down on software requirements. Requirements are derived by refining visions.

Emotion: Emotional reactions need to be taken seriously. For example, one variant of delivery is frequently discussed in the media: A parcel service deposits parcels in the trunk of their recipients. This asynchronous delivery to a personal space sounds attractive to many. However, when they see how someone opens a trunk with personal items in it, their emotional reaction is sometimes less positive. Video is always concrete. A video confronts stakeholders with possible scenarios that should be considered. Similar to other prototypes, validation of assumptions and elicitation of unexpected reactions merge when watching vision videos.

Definition and Investigated Scenarios: The experiment assumes there is a discussion on shopping in a rural area, as described above. At this point, "some kind of internet delivery" is proposed.

> **Definition:** By the term **"vision video refinement"**, we refer to the process of replacing gaps, abstract, or vague parts of a vision video by more concrete or detailed video clips (i.e. short parts of the video).

This definition of vision video refinement expands into three scenarios:

1. **Open Question:** As long as no proposal has been elaborated, vision videos can show the problem; stakeholders are then asked for their suggestions.
2. **Closed Choice:** Discussion moderators or requirements engineers identify a small number of pre-selected options. They create vision videos to visualize those options in an affordable way. Those videos are distributed and shown to stakeholders, asking them for feedback, such as advantages and disadvantages, newly arising questions, concerns, decisions with rationale.
3. **Refined Video:** After all open questions have been addressed, selected refinements are embedded in the overall video. Gaps and vague parts have been replaced by selected video clips. The resulting refined vision video can be distributed, shown at town hall meetings, or further refined in social media discussions.

The experiment below covers scenarios (1) and (2): Preparing open questions, and selecting from different variants. Scenario (3) was not included in this experiment since it follows the same pattern on the next refinement level. We decided to show all alternatives (A-B-C and 1-2-3) in one video, one after the other (see Fig. 2). Vision videos should not be longer than a few minutes.

3.1   Camera Perspectives

Emotional involvement and stimulation of empathy are considered strengths of video [17]. When stakeholders can literally see what an intended solution would mean for them, they are enabled to judge alternative proposals and to participate effectively in the decision-making process. Stakeholder groups face different challenges and may

Fig. 1. Examples of subjective (top) and corresponding third-person perspective (bottom) from the experiment videos. Variant IDs are displayed temporarily (e.g. "Variante A").

hold different values. Stakeholder should be represented adequately in a video to improve empathy, e.g. by *actors* of their age group and by *subjects* of an experiment. Inspired by research in the HCI community [2, 13], subjective camera perspective may also emphasize identification of stakeholders with actors while watching a video. We illustrate and define core terms for the remainder of this paper (Fig. 1).

Definition: Subjective Camera Perspective
In the subjective (also "first-person" or "ego") perspective, a video shows the scene from the perspective of a particular actor. Video seems to be recorded through the eyes of that actor. Audio reflects what the actor hears in that situation.
Definition: Third-Person Perspective
The situation and scenario is being recorded from an outside point of view. Camera and microphone do not appear (or pretend to be) close to eyes and ears of an actor.

---

4   Related Work

Vision Videos for RE: A vision is a positive imagination of the future. It can refer to the capabilities, features, or quality aspects of a part of reality that does not yet exist, but can be imagined. Video is the format in which the vision (content) is presented. Thus, a vision video of a software-based system typically shows a problem, an envisioned solution, and its impact, pretending the solution already exists.

According to this definition, the work by Brill et al. [6] investigated a situation in which one group of subjects created a textual use case specification while a second group prepared a vision video during the same short period of time. Complementary advantages were found. While there was intentional time pressure and inexpensive equipment used in this case, Creighton et al. [8] produced high-end vision videos in cooperation with Siemens and overlaid them visually with UML diagrams. Xu et al. [27] followed this line of research by starting with videos (pixels) and then replacing parts of them with operational software prototypes (bytes). This work demonstrated that visions could successfully be fed into software development activities. In our own work, Karras and Schneider [21] propose developing a quality model for videos that can be used by requirements engineers to produce "good-enough" vision videos. Today, smartphone cameras are of sufficient quality to produce useful vision videos [21]. Practitioners need only a few hints to produce technically sufficient and effective vision videos for eliciting requirements. Pham et al. [23] explored ways of arranging short videos on a custom-made video editor that associated the clips and their arrangement with semantic annotations. Vision videos have been created to promote a societal vision, as in the work of Darby et al. [9] on design fiction: A vision video shows a consultation session of a nurse with a patient. The visionary aspect is a tool that is able to read and interpret body sensors. This tool does not yet exist, but the video pretends it does. The video serves as a visual prototype of the software, its use and context long before even detailed specifications are known. Brill et al. [6] had used videos for the same purpose in our research group. This paper addresses the capability of videos for a discussion process of refinement and discourse rather than for promotional purposes.

Camera Perspective: Galinsky et al. [13, p. 110] show how perspective-taking, i.e. "the process of imagining the world from another's vantage point or imagining oneself in another's shoes," decreases stereotyping of others and facilitates social coordination. Aitamurto et al. [2] suspect that the sense of presence may be positively correlated with emotional engagement, empathy, and attitude change as viewers embed themselves in the perspectives of others. The authors suspect that view switching may support taking different perspectives and lead to a better understanding of the perspectives of the different characters, e.g. if the video is filmed in first-person view. Akkil and Isokoski [3] visualized the actor's gaze point in an egocentric video and show that this improves the viewers' awareness of the actor's emotions. Kallinen et al. [16] compared first- and third-person perspectives in computer games and found higher presence for first-person perspective. The concept of *embodiment* in VR refers to the users' experience that the virtual body is perceived as their own. It has been shown that first-person VR environments can create this illusion [26]. This paper analyzes the impact of the subjective perspective in vision videos to refine guidelines for making good vision videos.

5 Experiment Design

We used the Goal-Question-Metric Paradigm [5] to formulate goals, hypotheses, questions, and metrics of the experiment.

5.1 Goals of Refining Vision Videos

We want to apply vision videos for stimulating discussions on open questions.

Main Improvement Goals: (1) We want to support the process of making choices by refining a vision into more detailed and concrete scenarios. (2) As a separate measurement goal, we want to explore the impact of a subjective camera perspective.

Goal 1 can be rephrased into GQM format: (**Purpose**) Analyze and compare (**Quality Aspect**) number of (new) contributions (**Object**) in feedback (**Perspective**) from young adults. Various combinations of text and video are compared, as specified below.

Research Questions: In particular, we are interested in the benefit of providing a second medium. With respect to the GQM goal statement, we investigate whether new contributions can be raised ("stimulated") by video and text, respectively. The camera perspective is directly related to Goal 2 above.

RQ1: Can adding videos stimulate discussion better than text alone?
RQ2: Can adding text stimulate discussions better than video alone?
RQ3: Does a subjective camera perspective in refined vision videos help to empathize with the actor representing a stakeholder?

5.2   Video Set-Up and Experiment Procedure

The chosen study design leads to a simple and uniform process of conducting subject sessions. We describe here how the procedure unfolds, and explain our rationale with respect to answering the research questions while considering threats to validity.

Approach to Refining a Vision Video: In a live or online discussion on rural shopping, discussions led to identifying ordering and delivery as two crucial open issues. Each subject chooses one refinement A-B-C for ordering, and one refinement 1-2-3 for delivery. Offered options were: (A) Ordering by taking a picture, (B) using a Dash Button, and (C) a self-ordering sensitive box. Delivery was offered (1) through neighbor-pickup, (2) drones, and (3) deposit in the trunk of a parked car. We used individual sessions for each subject. They saw the videos and texts on a laptop. On the side, they completed the paper questionnaire. Q1 to Q8 are the feedback "object" of Goal 1.

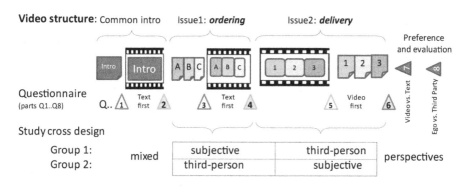

Fig. 2. Video structure and experiment design, with Questionnaire parts Q1..Q8

In the experiment, we followed the procedure depicted in Fig. 2. We provided a scenario of buying groceries with two open issues (halt points): (Issue 1) "How can groceries be ordered?" and (2) "How are they delivered?" Subjects completed a questionnaire with eight parts Q1...Q8: Triangles in Fig. 2 indicate what parts of the questionnaire were answered when. For example, Q1 asks for ideas for rural shopping after reading the intro text. Q2 was completed after an introductory video was shown.

There are **two groups of subjects** in the experiment (Fig. 2). Group 1 saw *subjective style videos first* (for ordering), and then third person videos (delivery). Group 2 *started with third-person videos* (ordering), and then saw subjective videos for delivery. This cross design is supposed to mitigate learning effects while at the same time exposing every subject to both camera perspectives. It is important to note that *the presented alternatives (refinements A-B-C and 1-2-3)* of ordering and delivery *must be shown in the same order to all subjects:* They are part of the stimulus that must be kept unchanged in order to produce comparable results.

5.3   Hypotheses

In the first block of hypotheses, we investigate subjective aspects of the research questions which are devoted *preference*. The second block of hypotheses investigates the *performance* in terms of the number of contributions. In particular, we investigate the following alternative hypotheses which represent our assumptions. Null hypotheses are reported in the result section (Sect. 6) together with the results they refer to.

Preference: What do Subjects Like?
Preference is measured by directly asking subjects about their opinion. In the experiment, such a rating is collected after several steps of the experiment.

$H1_1$: Subjects prefer obtaining a video in addition to a text to getting only the text.
$H2_1$: Subjects prefer obtaining a text in addition to a video to getting only the video.
$H3_1$: There is a difference between the Group 1 and Group 2 in how much they like the subjective perspective.
$H4_1$: Subjects' preference differs between the subjective or third-person perspective.

Performance: Added Contributions to RE and Shared Understanding
Performance is measured by counting contributions (GQM "quality aspect"). In the context of RE, *we consider new ideas, new questions, requirements, and rationale as "contributions" for improving shared understanding*. We did not count meaningless and repetitive contributions. The quality of contributions was not rated or evaluated. In this context, the term *"idea"* refers to a contribution about a new form of ordering or delivery.

When information is first represented as text and then a video is added, the benefit of that video is measured in terms of the number of new ideas and new contributions (see above) compared to the ideas respectively the contributions made after seeing only text before. In the inverse case, a video is presented first, and then a text is added:

$H5_1$: Providing a video in addition to a text leads to new solution ideas.
$H6_1$: Providing a video in addition to a text leads to new contributions.
$H7_1$: Providing a text in addition to a video leads to new contributions.

Emotional Effect of the Camera Perspective: Which of the Two Perspectives has a Greater Emotional Potential?
Emotional effect of the camera perspective is measured by directly asking subjects about their opinion. In the experiment, such a rating is collected after subjects saw both types of videos, i.e. in subjective and in third-person perspective.

$H8_1$: There is a difference in the subjects' perceived emotional involvement of between Group 1 and Group 2.

5.4   Selection of Actors, Subjects, and the Affordable Video Approach

There are obviously various age groups of stakeholders affected: Seniors with limited mobility, but also young people on the verge of leaving the village. Seniors and young adults will probably react differently to variants, and they will evaluate them from a different perspective. This important fact is obvious in videos. For this experiment, we focused on the group of young residents. A young actor in a room with modern furniture and big-screen TV has more appeal for empathy to young experiment subjects than a senior in a traditional living room – and vice versa. We collected data (ratings, evaluations, and contributions) from 20 subjects, aged between 20 and 33 years ($M = 25.2$ years). Seven were women, 13 men. We randomly asked members of the intended age group to participate, e.g. during an Open-Door day at the university. Nineteen of them use online shopping, but only eight of them had bought articles of daily use online.

According to our *Affordable Video Approach*, all video clips together were recorded within 3:15 h of a single day. They were cut using ordinary video editing software within another half day. Video equipment consisted of a standard video camera (300 €) with Rode microphone (330 €) attached, since we found comprehensible audio important in earlier work [25]. Subjective video clips were recorded using a mobile phone camera mounted on a Gimbal (180 €) for the subjective video parts. Mobile phone cameras also would have been sufficient. All four lay actors and video personnel were members of the research group with no advanced video background or training.

The texts for introduction, ordering, and delivery variants are typically read by subjects in silence (32 s for intro, 29 s ordering, and 35 s delivery). Subjective videos on ordering run for 60 s (all three variants together), and 68 s in normal camera perspective. Delivery is more complex and includes interaction beyond the (first person) actor. Delivery variants run for a total of 155 s (subjective) and 150 s (third-person).

6 Experiment Results

For evaluating the alternative hypotheses in 5.3, we state corresponding null hypotheses. We provide additional descriptive analysis of ratings, evaluations, and subject opinions as boxplots. Results are clustered in the same three above-mentioned categories: Preference, performance, and emotional effect of the camera perspective.

Preference

> $H1_0$: Subjects' preference does not differ between obtaining a video in addition to a text and getting only the text.

Subjects had first received a text describing the ordering options and then an additional video illustrating the same ordering options. After watching the video, we asked whether they preferred having the video in addition to the text, or only the text (see Fig. 2, Q4). According to a chi-square test of independence ($\chi^2 = 1.05, p = .3$), there is no difference between the two groups. Thus, we could aggregate the data for analysis. Since we had nominal data, we performed a chi-square goodness-of-fit test with a significance level $\alpha = .05$. Corresponding to $H1_0$, one would expect a 0.5/0.5 distribution of the stakeholders' preference. We found significant deviation from the hypothetical distribution ($\chi^2 = 12.8, p = .0003$). We can reject $H1_0$ and accept $H1_1$. *Subjects prefer obtaining a video in addition to text rather than having only the text.*

$H2_0$: Subjects' preference does not differ between obtaining a text in addition to a video and getting only the video.

Subjects had first received a video illustrating the delivery options and then an additional text describing the same delivery options. After reading the text, we asked whether they preferred having the text in addition to the video, or only the video (see Fig. 2, Q6). We performed a chi-square test of independence ($\chi^2 = 1.25, p = .26$), which indicates no difference between the two groups. Since there is no difference between the groups, we aggregated the nominal data. We found a significant deviation from this distribution ($\chi^2 = 7.2, p = .007$). Thus, we can reject $H2_0$ and conclude: *Subjects prefer obtaining a text in addition to a video rather than having only the video.*

$H3_0$: There is no difference between Group 1 and Group 2 in how much they like the subjective perspective.

At the end of the experiment, the subjects assessed the statement: "I liked the ego-perspective." on a Likert-scale from 0 (totally disagree) to 5 (totally agree) (see Fig. 2, Q8). According to Kolmogorv-Smirnov ($K = .19, p = .07$) and Shapiro-Wilk tests ($W = .9, p = .05$), the data is normally distributed. Next, we performed a Mann-Whitney U test. The test indicated that the rating of Group 1 ($Mdn = 4$) for the subjective perspective was significantly higher than for Group 2 ($Mdn = 2.5$), $Z = 2.35, p = .02$. Thus, we can reject $H3_0$. *There is a difference between Group 1 and Group 2 in how much they like the subjective perspective.*

$H4_0$: Subjects consider both subjective and third-person perspectives equally good.

We asked subjects if they preferred subjective or third-person perspective (see Fig. 2, Q8). According to the chi-square independence test ($\chi^2 = 1.14, p = .56$), there is no difference between the two groups and we can aggregate the nominal data. We applied a chi-square goodness-of-fit test ($\alpha = .05$). According to the $H4_0$, there would be a .5/.5 distribution. We found no significant deviation from the hypothesized distribution ($\chi^2 = 1.125, p = .29$). We cannot reject H4$_0$. *There is no significant difference between the subjects' preference for one of the two perspectives.*

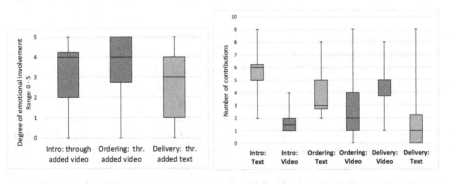

Fig. 3. Emotional involvement at Q2, Q4, Q6; No. of contributions at Q1/2; Q3/4; Q5/6

We asked how emotionally involved subjects were after seeing the second medium (video after text/text after video). Figure 3 (left) shows the high ratings on a 0 to 5 Likert scale. In all three cases (introduction, ordering, delivery) the emotional involvement was higher after receiving the second medium. All videos received very high ratings ($Mdn = 4$); the stimulated emotional involvement. With text, values are a little lower.

Performance

The performance is measured in number of contributions after text or videos were provided. Figure 3 (right) shows the three parts: introduction, ordering, and delivery. Boxplots on the left of each pair show the number of contributions made after the first element was provided; the right-hand boxplots show additional contributions solicited after the *second* element was provided. Light boxes stand for text, darker ones for video.

$H5_0$: Providing a video in addition to a text does not lead to new solution ideas.

Subjects had first received text and were asked to write down solution ideas (see Fig. 2, Q1). After participants had received the video, we asked if they had any additional solution ideas (see Fig. 2, Q2). According to Kolmogorov-Smirnov ($K = .34, p < .001$) and Shapiro-Wilk ($W = .81, p = .001$) tests, the number of solution ideas are not normally distributed. We investigated whether the two groups differ from each other by using Mann-Whitney U test: $Z = .53, p = .60$. Since we did not find a difference between the two groups, we aggregated the data and performed the non-parametric one-sample Wilcoxon Signed-Rank test. The test showed a significant number of additional, not yet mentioned, solution ideas by the stakeholders ($Z = -3.62, p < .001$). $H5_0$ is rejected: *Providing a video in addition to text leads to new solution ideas.*

$H6_0$: Providing a video in addition to a text does not lead to new contributions.

After the subjects read the text of the ordering options we asked them to select one option and to write down their rationale, requirements, and questions (Fig. 2, Q3). Afterwards the participants received a video of the ordering options and we asked them for further requirements-related contributions (Fig. 2, Q4). We investigated the collected number of contributions for normal distribution with Kolmogorov-Smirnov test and Shapiro-Wilk test. Both tests indicated that the data is not normally distributed ($K = .21, p = .02, W = .89, p = .02$). There is no difference between the groups by means of a Mann-Whitney U test: $Z = .91, p = .36$. We analyzed all data together by using the one-sample Wilcoxon Signed-Rank test. This test yields a significant difference, i.e. a significant number of new contributions ($Z = -3.62, p = .0002$). $H6_0$ is rejected: *Providing a video in addition to a text leads to new contributions.*

$H7_0$: Providing a text in addition to a video does not lead to new contributions.

For the delivery options, subjects saw the video first and we asked them to select one option. Based on their choice, we asked them to write down their rationale, requirements, and questions (Fig. 2, Q5). Then they read the text describing the delivery options and we asked them for further requirements-related contributions

(Fig. 2, Q6). The statistical analysis follows the same procedure: The Kolmogorov-Smirnov test ($K = .27, p < .001$) and Shapiro-Wilk test ($W = .74, p < .001$) showed that the data is not normally distributed. There was no difference between the groups in a Mann-Whitney U test: $Z = .76, p = .45$. We analyzed all data together by using the non-parametric one-sample Wilcoxon Signed-Rank. The test yields a significant number of additional contributions after the subjects read the text ($Z = -3.06$, $p = .001$). $H7_0$ is rejected. *Providing a text in addition to a video leads to new contributions.*

Emotional Effect of the Camera Perspective

$H8_0$: There is no difference in the subjects' perceived emotional involvement between Group 1 and Group 2.

Subjects first received the text of the variants and then the video. Afterwards, we asked subjects to indicate their emotional involvement by assessing the statement "I was more emotionally involved in the problem due to the video." on a Likert-scale from 0 (totally disagree) to 5 (totally agree) (see Fig. 2, Q4). While the Kolmogorov-Smirnov test ($K = .20, p = .07$) indicated that the data is normally distributed, the Shapiro-Wilk test found the data to be not normally distributed ($W = .88, p = .03$). Due to this discrepancy, we used a non-parametric Mann-Whitney U test. It showed no difference between the group that watched a subjective video ($Mdn = 4$) and the group that watched a third-person video ($Mdn = 3$), $Z = .44, p = .66$. We cannot reject $H8_0$ and conclude: *There seems to be no difference between Group1 and Group 2 in the perceived emotional involvement of subjects.*

Evaluations and Subject Opinions

Finally, we asked subjects in Q7 for more detailed feedback (Fig. 4) after all texts and videos had been presented.

(a) Text important for choosing a variant
(b) Video important for choosing a vari-ant
(c) I liked the videos
(d) Videos provide important information
(e) Videos convey atmosphere
(f) Video quality was sufficient
(g) Videos were obsolete

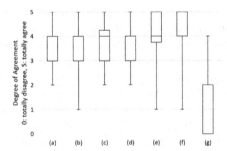

Fig. 4. Subjects' detailed evaluation results. (g) means: "videos were **not** obsolete"

As Fig. 4 indicates, both text (a) and video (b) were considered important for making decisions about the refinement variants. Most subjects liked the videos (c). Most subjects also found videos provided important information (d). The ratings for "video conveys atmosphere" (e) were even higher, but there were also a few low ratings. In (f), a large majority considered video quality sufficient, despite the

Affordable Video Approach. Most disagreed with "videos were obsolete" (g) - not an obvious result, given the short runtime of all videos and the fact that there were also texts available.

7 Interpretation and Discussion

We investigated whether adding videos to previously available texts would solicit additional contributions for discourse. In Q6, we also measured the inverse situation: Adding text to previously shown videos. In real decision situations about rural areas, most stake holders would read brief texts (in the newspaper [1], or online) before they decide to watch a short video about it. The results confirm the usefulness of enriching early discussions about visions and requirements with both text and video. Preference and evaluation were very positive, and a number of statistically significant results confirm that adding either video or text (to the other) stimulated more contributions.

7.1 Threats to Validity

The experiment design presented in Sect. 5 is rather sophisticated. It reflects the complexity of evaluating the role of vision videos in refining visions towards requirements. The real-world application domain is of substantial complexity. Hence, a number of specific threats to validity must be considered.

Internal Validity: *Causality.* Possible influences on the outcome are numerous, due to the high complexity. For the experiment, we used texts and videos that were created independently. Neither did one build on the other, nor was there a competition to outperform each other. The mission was to explain the introduction and refinement options concisely and self-sufficiently. Some subjects might have felt pressed to provide more contributions when they were shown an extra video or text. However, we checked whether those new contributions were original or repetitive and counted only new ones. There were several cases in which a question did not solicit any additional responses.

External Validity: *Can results be generalized?* Despite the above-mentioned precautions, our findings cannot be generalized directly to every kind of text and every type of video. Texts and videos can be useful or difficult to understand and annoying - intentionally or by accident. There are so many types and styles of video (and text) that one should take even our significant findings with a grain of salt.

Construct Validity: *Adequate concepts?* As explained in Sect. 5, we counted new questions, new reasons to choose or reject a variant as *contributions* to the discourse as RE contributions. In the area of RE, a good question can be valuable [14] for clarifying visions and requirements. The results and findings should be read with this definition in mind. Conceptualizations of "contribution" that deviate substantially from this definition may not be covered by our experiment. The treatments in our experiment was adding a second medium (video/text). We analyzed the effect of getting that treatment by comparing contributions before and after receiving the second medium.

Conclusion Validity: *Adequate conclusions?* The positive impact of adding video or text could be a case of "paraphrasing", presenting a situation from different angles. It is possible and likely that adding other media could have had similar effects. We wanted to investigate whether low-effort video with its own advantages was also qualified as a useful second medium. *Our results confirm the benefit of taking the extra effort of providing a second medium.* Please note that providing "both video and text at a time" may seem a similar and attractive option, but poses yet another threat to validity: Its impact will depend highly on how the media are presented: if and in which order subjects look at them. This aspect was beyond the scope of our study.

Deciding about rural shopping is an integral part of much wider concerns. There are so many parameters and influence factors that cannot – and should not – be controlled in order not to distort the phenomenon of interest. We decided to study the very basic mechanisms of refining a vague vision of shopping into several variants by video. The technical choice of a camera perspective is related. Those mechanisms are the basis for more complex interactions of vision and requirements communication and clarification.

8   Conclusions

We had expected to stimulate additional questions and ideas by showing videos – where usually only a few short texts would be provided. However, we did not expect the number of additional contributions stimulated by the videos (Fig. 3), and the very positive evaluation of videos in hindsight (Fig. 4). In the introduction to the experiment, exactly the same text was provided to *read* – and then to *hear* in the video. Nevertheless, almost all subjects recommended showing the video in addition to the text in the future. We had included the inverse direction (text after video) in the study as a matter of curiosity. Given the less than 10-line texts and 20-s video clips describing an ordering refinement, we had not expected performance and preference indicators to be as clear as they were: *Provide both media.*

Subjective camera perspective seemed to be a matter of taste. There was no significant performance advantage over third-person videos, nor was the empathy rating higher. Some subjects preferred subjective over third-person perspective – and vice versa. According to Runeson et al. [24], case studies are appropriate for investigating phenomena that require complex subsets of reality to occur. Based on this established baseline of experimental insights, we plan to triangulate our findings in case studies.

Acknowledgement. This work was supported by the Deutsche Forschungsgemeinschaft (DFG) under Grant No.: 289386339, project ViViReq. (2017–2019).

References

1. Hannoversche Allgemeine Zeitung: Federal mail will sell bread. In rural areas, shopping gets increasing difficult - now, the postman could sell groceries on the doorstep (original in German) (2018). 15 Sept 2018
2. Aitamurto, T., Zhou, S., Sakshuwong, S., Saldivar, J., Sadeghi, Y., Tran, A.: Sense of presence, attitude change, perspective-taking and usability in first-person split-sphere 360° video. In: Proceedings of the 2018 CHI Conference on Human Factors in Computing Systems (2018)

3. Akkil, D., Isokoski, P.: Gaze augmentation in egocentric video improves awareness of intention. In: Proceedings of the 2016 CHI Conference on Human Factors in Computing Systems (2016)
4. Ambler, S.: Agile Modeling. Wiley, Hoboken (2002)
5. Basili, V.R., Caldiera, G., Rombach, H.D.: The goal question metric approach. In: Encyclopedia of Software Engineering, Wiley (1994)
6. Brill, O., Schneider, K., Knauss, E.: Videos vs. use cases: can videos capture more requirements under time pressure? In: Wieringa, R., Persson, A. (eds.) REFSQ 2010. LNCS, vol. 6182, pp. 30–44. Springer, Heidelberg (2010). https://doi.org/10.1007/978-3-642-14192-8_5
7. Broll, G., Hussmann, H., Rukzio, E., Wimmer, R.: Using video clips to support requirements elicitation in focus groups – an experience report. In: SE 2007 Workshop on Multimedia Requirements Engineering (2007)
8. Creighton, O., Ott, M., Bruegge, B.: Software cinema – video-based requirements engineering. In: 14th IEEE International Requirements Engineering Conference (2006)
9. Darby, A., Tsekleves, E., Sawyer, P.: Speculative requirements: design fiction and RE. In: 26th IEEE International Requirements Engineering Conference (2018)
10. Dutoit, A.H., McCall, R., Mistrík, I., Paech, B.: Rationale Management in Software Engineering. Springer, Heidelberg (2007). https://doi.org/10.1007/978-3-540-30998-7
11. Feeney, W.: Documenting software using video. In: IEEE Computer Society Workshop on Software Engineering Technology Transfer (1983)
12. Fricker, S.A., Schneider, K., Fotrousi, F., Thuemmler, C.: Workshop videos for requirements communication. Requir. Eng. 21(4), 521–552 (2016)
13. Galinsky, A.D., Ku, G., Wang, C.S.: Perspective-taking and self-other overlap: fostering social bonds and facilitating social coordination. Group Process. Intergroup Relat. 8(2), 109–124 (2005)
14. Glinz, M., Fricker, S.A.: On shared understanding in software engineering: an essay. Comput. Sci.-Res. Dev. 30, 363–376 (2014)
15. Jirotka, M., Luff, P.: Supporting requirements with video-based analysis. IEEE Softw. 23, 42–44 (2006)
16. Kallinen, K., Salminen, M., Ravaja, N., Kedzior, R., Sääksjärvi, M.: Presence and emotion in computer game players during 1st person vs. 3rd person playing view: evidence from self-report, eye-tracking, and facial muscle activity data. In: 10th Annual International Workshop on Presence (2007)
17. Karras, O.: Software professionals' attitudes towards video as a medium in requirements engineering. In: Product-Focused Software Process Improvement (2018)
18. Karras, O., Hamadeh, A., Schneider, K.: Enriching requirements specifications with videos – the use of videos to support requirements communication. In: Softwaretechnik-Trends, vol. 38, no. 1 (2017)
19. Karras, O., Kiesling, S., Schneider, K.: Supporting requirements elicitation by tool-supported video analysis. In: 24th IEEE International Requirements Engineering Conference (2016)
20. Karras, O., Klünder, J., Schneider, S.: Enrichment of requirements specifications with videos – enhancing the comprehensibility of textual requirements. Zenodo (2016)
21. Karras, O., Schneider, K.: Software professionals are not directors: what constitutes a good video? In: 2018 1st International Workshop on Learning from other Disciplines for Requirements Engineering (D4RE) (2018)
22. Karras, O., Unger-Windeler, C., Glauer, L., Schneider, K.: Video as a by-product of digital prototyping: capturing the dynamic aspect of interaction. In: 25th IEEE International Requirements Engineering Conference Workshops (2017)

23. Pham, R., Meyer, S., Kitzmann, I., Schneider, K.: Interactive multimedia storyboard for facilitating stakeholder interaction: supporting continuous improvement in IT-ecosystems. In: 8th International Conference on the Quality of Information and Communications Technology (2012)

24. Runeson, P., Host, M., Rainer, A., Regnell, B.: Case Study Research in Software Engineering: Guidelines and Examples. Wiley, Hoboken (2012)

25. Schneider, K., Karras, O., Finger, A., Zibell, B.: Reframing societal discourse as requirements negotiation: vision statement. In: 25th IEEE International Requirements Engineering Conference Workshops (2017)

26. Schultze, U.: Embodiment and presence in virtual worlds: a review. JIT **25**(4), 434–449 (2010)

27. Xu, H., Creighton, O., Boulila, N., Bruegge, B.: From pixels to bytes: evolutionary scenario based design with video. In: Proceedings of the ACM SIGSOFT 20th International Symposium on the Foundations of Software Engineering (2012)

28. Zachos, K., Maiden, N.: ART-SCENE: enhancing scenario walkthroughs with multi-media scenarios. In: 12th IEEE International Requirements Engineering Conference (2004)

29. Zachos, K., Maiden, N., Tosar, A.: Rich-media scenarios for discovering requirements. IEEE Softw. **22**(5), 89–97 (2005)

A Lightweight Multilevel Markup Language for Connecting Software Requirements and Simulations

Florian Pudlitz$^{(\boxtimes)}$ (ID), Andreas Vogelsang$^{(\boxtimes)}$ (ID), and Florian Brokhausen$^{(\boxtimes)}$

Technische Universität Berlin, Berlin, Germany
{florian.pudlitz,andreas.vogelsang}@tu-berlin.de,
florian.brokhausen@campus.tu-berlin.de

Abstract. [**Context**] Simulation is a powerful tool to validate specified requirements especially for complex systems that constantly monitor and react to characteristics of their environment. The simulators for such systems are complex themselves as they simulate multiple actors with multiple interacting functions in a number of different scenarios. To validate requirements in such simulations, the requirements must be related to the simulation runs. [**Problem**] In practice, engineers are reluctant to state their requirements in terms of structured languages or models that would allow for a straightforward relation of requirements to simulation runs. Instead, the requirements are expressed as unstructured natural language text that is hard to assess in a set of complex simulation runs. Therefore, the feedback loop between requirements and simulation is very long or non-existent at all. [**Principal idea**] We aim to close the gap between requirements specifications and simulation by proposing a lightweight markup language for requirements. Our markup language provides a set of annotations on different levels that can be applied to natural language requirements. The annotations are mapped to simulation events. As a result, meaningful information from a set of simulation runs is shown directly in the requirements specification. [**Contribution**] Instead of forcing the engineer to write requirements in a specific way just for the purpose of relating them to a simulator, the markup language allows annotating the already specified requirements up to a level that is interesting for the engineer. We evaluate our approach by analyzing 8 original requirements of an automotive system in a set of 100 simulation runs.

Keywords: Markup language · Requirements modeling · Simulation · Test evaluation

1 Introduction

In many areas, software systems are becoming increasingly complex through the use of open systems, highly automated or networked devices. The complexity

© Springer Nature Switzerland AG 2019
E. Knauss and M. Goedicke (Eds.): REFSQ 2019, LNCS 11412, pp. 151–166, 2019.
https://doi.org/10.1007/978-3-030-15538-4_11

leads to an increasing number of requirements, which are often expressed in natural language [9]. To master the complexity of development and test management, simulation is increasingly being used to anticipate system behavior in complex environments. Simulation has several advantages over classic testing. Tests only pass or fail, but there is little information about the contextual situation. Additionally, simulations are more flexible towards covering variations in context behavior.

However, in current practice and especially in large companies, simulation and requirements activities are often not aligned. Simulation scenarios are not derived from requirements but handcrafted by specialized simulation engineers based on their own understanding of the problem domain. On the other hand, the results of simulation runs are not fed back to the level of requirements, which means that a requirements engineer does not benefit from the insights gained by running the simulation. This misalignment has several reasons. First, requirements engineering and simulation is often conducted in different departments. Second, simulators are complex systems that need to be configured by simulation experts. That makes it hard for requirements engineers to use simulators. Third, requirements and simulations are on different levels of abstraction which makes it hard to connect events generated by the simulation to requirements, especially, when they are written in natural language. As a result, the simulation scenarios are often unrealistic and do not ensure that all requirements are covered.

Modeling can help closing this gap between requirements and simulation. However, if the necessary models are too formal, requirements engineers fear the effort to model the requirements. Therefore, we propose a lightweight modeling approach that allows engineers to annotate their natural language requirements instead of expressing them as models. Based on these annotations, the respective part of a requirement can be linked to a simulation event. By analyzing logs of simulation runs for the linked simulation events, we can feed back information about system execution to the level of the annotations and thereby to the level of requirements. The available annotations build a markup language. A distinct feature of our markup language is that it contains annotations on different levels of detail. An engineer can decide how detailed he or she wants to annotate a requirement. The more detailed a requirement is annotated, the more information can be retrieved from a simulation run.

In this paper, we present the general idea of our approach, the details of the markup language, and an evaluation on a Cornering Light System. Our approach provides a minimal invasive way to connect (existing) requirements with simulation. Thereby, requirements engineers can profit from insights gained by simulation much faster and without having to invest in extensive modeling efforts. The requirements engineer gets feedback whether the requirements are covered by the current selection of simulation scenarios and whether there are misconceptions in the requirements that are uncovered by the simulation (e.g. false assumptions).

2   Background and Related Work

Testing and Simulation: Software Testing is the verification that a software product provides the expected behavior, as specified in its requirements. The conventional development and testing process for complex systems is based on the V-model, which structures the development process into phases of decomposition of the system elements and their subsequent integration. Each requirement being specified on a certain level of abstraction is reflected by a test case on the same level which determines whether the requirement has been implemented correctly. The increasing complexity of the systems, the many possible test cases, and the uncertainty about the system's context challenge this conventional testing process. Therefore, the use of simulations is becoming more and more popular.

Simulation is the imitation of the operation of a real-world process or system [1]. The act of simulating something first requires that a model is developed; this model incorporates the key characteristics, behavior, and functions of the selected physical or abstract system or process. A simulator is a program that is able to run a simulation. Each simulation run is one execution of the simulation.

When simulation is used in a systems development process, the model usually consists of a submodel that describes the system-under-development (SuD) and one or several submodels that describe the operational environment of the SuD. The simulation represents the operation of the SuD within its operational context over time.

A simulation scenario defines the initial characteristics and preliminaries of a simulation run and spans a certain amount of time. The scenario defines the global parameters of the operational context model. The model of the SuD is not affected by the definition of the simulation scenario. Therefore, a simulation scenario can be compared to a test case in a conventional testing processes. The expectation is that the SuD performs according to its desired behavior in a set of representative simulation scenarios.

Requirements and Test Alignment: Alignment of requirements and test cases is a well-established field of research and several solutions exist. Barmi et al. [2] found that most studies of the subject were on model-based testing including a variety of formal methods for describing requirements with models or languages. In model based testing, informal requirements of the system are the base for developing a test model which is a behavioral model of the system. This test model is used to automatically generate test cases. One problem in this area is that the generated tests from the model cannot be executed directly against an implementation under test because they are on different levels of abstraction. Additionally, the formal representation of requirements often results in difficulties both in requiring special competence to produce [10], but also for non-specialist (e.g. business people) in understanding the requirements. The generation of test cases directly from the requirements implicitly links the two without any need for manually creating (or maintaining) traces [3]. However, depending on the level of abstraction of the model and the generated test cases, the value of the traces might vary. For example, for use cases and system test cases, the tracing was reported as being more natural in comparison to using state machines [5]. Errors in the models are an additional issue to consider when applying model-based testing [5].

Lightweight Requirements Modeling: The use of constrained natural language is an approach to create requirements models while keeping the appearance of natural language. Several authors propose different sets of sentence patterns that should be used to formulate requirements [4,8]. Besides the advantage that requirements are uniformly formulated, the requirements patterns enrich parts of the requirement with information about the semantics. This information can be used to extract information from the requirements. Lucassen et al., for example, use the structure of user stories to automatically derive conceptual models of the domain [7]. With our approach, we try to combine the strength of lightweight requirements annotations with the potential to be enriched with behavioral information collected in simulations.

End-to-End Tooling: A comparable approach to validate requirements within a testing and simulation environment in an end-to-end fashion is presented by the tool Stimulus by software company Argosim[1]. Stimulus lets the user define formalized requirements and enrich the system under development with state machines and block diagrams to include behavioral and architectural information, respectively. With the help of a build-in test suite, signals from the environment on which the systems depends and reacts can be simulated. The system behavior within these simulations is evaluated with regards to its constraints specified by the requirements and violations are detected. The main features include the detection of contradicting and missing requirements.

This tooling approach however exhibits some major differences to the methodology proposed in this paper. First and foremost, the form in which requirements are drafted in Stimulus is in a highly formalized manner from which this approach is to be differentiated. While there are many efforts within the research community to explicitly formalize requirements to improve on their validation possibilities [2], this markup language aims to provide the requirements engineer with a means to intuitively annotate natural language requirements in order to unfold the implicitly contained information in a way it can be used for validation purposes within a simulation. Secondly, the testing capability provided by Stimulus depends on the user to define inputs to the system and assign a range of values to them for test execution. This step however shall be automated with the proposed approach. From the data provided by the markups, a scenario for the simulation environment will be constructed, which evaluates the underlying constraints.

3   Approach

Our approach is schematically displayed in Fig. 1. The starting point is a document of requirements formulated in natural language containing software

---

[1] www.argosim.com.

specifications. The present requirements are written without pattern or other grammatical restrictions. With elements of our markup language the engineer marks key phrases. These are matched with signals of the simulation and system, which is called a mapping. The simulation is created automatically and the resulting scenario contains configurations of the simulation environment influenced by the selections made in the requirements. Simulation results are output as log files, which in connection with the mapping results, are fed back to the original requirements document. In addition to log data from traffic simulations, it is also possible to use real driver log data. In this way, real log data can be matched with natural language requirements. The simulation results or real data are displayed directly in the originally analyzed phrases.

In contrast to state of the art procedures, there is no necessity for translation into executable languages. Therefore, the entire scope of simulation options of the natural language requirements remains without any translation loss. Another improvement of today's standards lies in the testability of software at any state of development. First behaviors of the software can be simulated with simple markings early in the development process. Especially new assistance systems or functions such as autonomous driving are very complex and can only be tested with complex simulations. The test engineers therefore need a lightweight approach to evaluate requirements without formal translation.

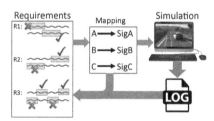

Fig. 1. Schematic representation of a requirements specification linked to a simulation with influencing intermediate steps

3.1 Markup Language

For marking software functions and environment conditions, we developed a lightweight multilevel markup language to connect requirements specifications and simulation runs. We developed our markup language to meet four demands.

First, a lightweight, intuitive approach for marking objects in natural language software requirements.

Second, a possibility to observe single objects as well as complex relations between elements in the simulation without a formal translation.

Third, an extraction of important simulation environment properties that must occur in the simulation.

Fourth, a possibility to evaluate software behavior already during the development process.

The resulting language consists of elements, which are assigned to phrases in the natural language requirements documents with defined content characteristics. This part of the process is performed by an engineer and is the starting point for the automated evaluation by the tool. Each element is assigned to one of four levels, which define the level of detail of the evaluation.

Elements: Elements are the basic component of our markup language. Available elements and their description are shown in Table 1. It also shows, how the elements are strictly associated with different levels of detail. The correct understanding of the elements by the engineer is crucial, since the manually performed labeling effects the type of automated simulation evaluation.

Levels: Figure 2 shows the four levels with the associated elements. The properties as well as the limits of the levels are explained in the following.

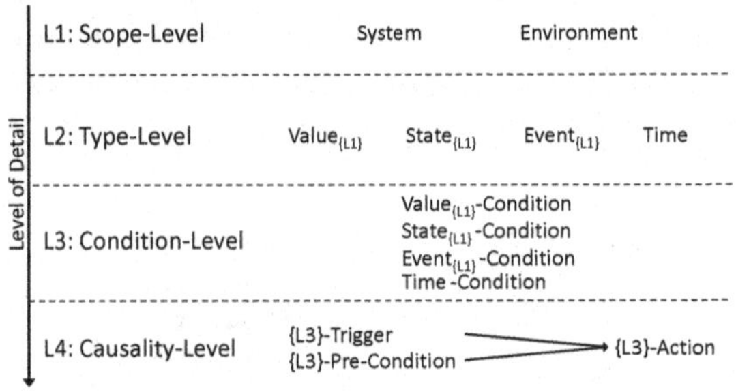

Fig. 2. Overview of levels and elements

The *Scope-Level* is used to differentiate between information on the system and on the simulation environment. As a result, the appearance of the objects in the simulation is displayed. However, no further information is available.

The *Type-Level* distinguishes the phrase of Level 1 into different types of text phrases depending on the behavior in the system. The different Level 2-types influence the type of evaluation and are the basis for the definition of conditions in Level 3.

The *Condition-Level* connects a type of Level 2 with a specific value via comparison operators to create condition statements. However, the formulated conditions have no connection among each other.

The *Causality-Level* establishes a relationship between the conditions of Level 3 and creates causal relationships. This requires detailed knowledge of the system and the necessary work process performed by the user is time consuming. The result however is an in-depth evaluation.

Table 1. Overview of all elements

Level	Element	Description
1	System	Describes all information concerning the system, including any property perceptible from the outside as well as internal information. Result: link to signal available or not available
	Environment	Describes information on the simulation environment (e.g., weather) and simulation properties (e.g., simulation duration), and checks fulfillment of scenarios before a simulation run. Result: link to signal available or not available
2	Value$_{\{L1\}}$	Characterized by a value-continuous range and linked to system or environment. Result: progression over simulation time
	State$_{\{L1\}}$	Describes objects with multiple possible, but exclusive states (e.g., door - open/closed). Result: all appearing states
	Event$_{\{L1\}}$	Once or sporadically occurring object, often associated with signals. Result: number of appearances and average intermediate time
	Time	Concrete time specifications; automatically linked to simulation time. Result: not presented
3	Value$_{\{L1\}}$-Condition	Values of Level 2 linked by $<; \leq; =; >; \geq; \neq$ with a number or parameter. Result: duration of the fulfilled condition
	State$_{\{L1\}}$-Condition	States of Level 2 linked by $=$ or $\neq$ with a possible state. Result: frequency, and duration in percent of the fulfilled condition
	Event$_{\{L1\}}$-Condition	Event from Level 2 with the values 1 or 0 for appearance and non-appearance. Result: number of appearances and average intermediate time
	Time-Condition	Time statements from Level 2 linked by $<; \leq; =; >; \geq$ or by natural language expressions such as "longer," "shorter," or "within"; must be linked to other conditions as an extension of other Level 3 conditions. Result: not presented
4	{L3}-Trigger	Level 3 statements linked by AND, OR; if condition is fulfilled, {L3}-Action is triggered. Result: number of appearances
	{L3}-Pre-Condition	Level 3 statements linked by AND, OR; pre-condition must be fulfilled in order to start a {L3}-Action. Result: number of appearances in total and as pre-condition with percentage
	{L3}-Action	Level 3 statements linked together; following a {L3}-Trigger or {L3}-Pre-Condition. Result: number of appearance

3.2   Marking Requirements

There are two main motivations to use this approach: to find information needed in order to choose a suitable simulation scenario; and to check or monitor functionalities of a software component in different states of development. Our markup language facilitates the highlighting of necessary information and the observation in the simulation with an adaptable level of detail.

Figure 3 shows three example requirements [CL-1, CL2, CL-3] of a Cornering Light in a car, which is automatically switched on when turning. The dynamic and static cornering light function improves illumination of the road ahead when cornering.

Requirement Specification: Cornering Light	
ID	**Object Text**
CL-1 L1/L2	At v < vMaxInd, the <u>indicator</u> has priority over _{States} the <u>steering wheel angle</u> (e.g., <u>roundabout</u>) _{Values} _{Environment}
CL-2 L2	<u>Cornering light</u> is activated according to the active _{States} indicator
CL-3 L2	<u>Cornering light</u> is deactivated at <u>v > vMax</u> _{States} _{Values}

Fig. 3. Example of requirements of a Cornering Light System with initial marks of elements on Level 1 and 2

CL-1 contains Level 1 (Environment) and Level 2 (State$_S$ and Value$_S$) markings. If the aim is to ensure the presence of a roundabout in the simulation, this element will be marked with "Environment". The "State" mark for the indicator represents all occurring states. To observe the angle of the steering wheel and to evaluate the simulation duration, the choice of Level 2 mark "Value" is necessary.

CL-2 and CL-3 contain only Level 2 (State$_S$) markings. The subscript S stands for system; the subscript E describes an element of the simulation environment. Concerning objects of the environment, their occurrence is checked before runtime of the simulation scenario.

Figure 4 shows the identical requirements with an unchanged CL-1, but continually edited Level 2 objects in CL-2 and CL-3. By linking these objects to a newly marked condition, a Level 3 statement was created. A special feature is the link of a time condition in order to extend another condition. A time condition can exclusively be linked to other conditions.

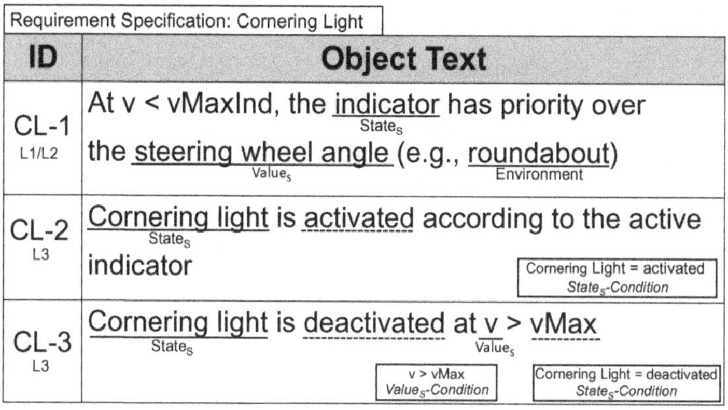

ID	Object Text
	Requirement Specification: Cornering Light
CL-1 L1/L2	At v < vMaxInd, the <u>indicator</u> (State$_s$) has priority over the <u>steering wheel angle</u> (Value$_s$) (e.g., <u>roundabout</u>) (Environment)
CL-2 L3	<u>Cornering light</u> (State$_s$) is <u>activated</u> according to the active indicator [Cornering Light = activated / State$_s$-Condition]
CL-3 L3	<u>Cornering light</u> (State$_s$) is <u>deactivated</u> at <u>v > vMax</u> (Value$_s$) [v > vMax / Value$_s$-Condition] [Cornering Light = deactivated / State$_s$-Condition]

Fig. 4. Example of Requirements of a Cornering Light System with adopted marks with increasing complexity on Level 1, 2 and 3

In Fig. 5, which is again showing the identical requirements, the Level 3 elements in CL-3 are brought into a relationship with each other by manually selecting them. By this causal relationship, Level 4 is reached.

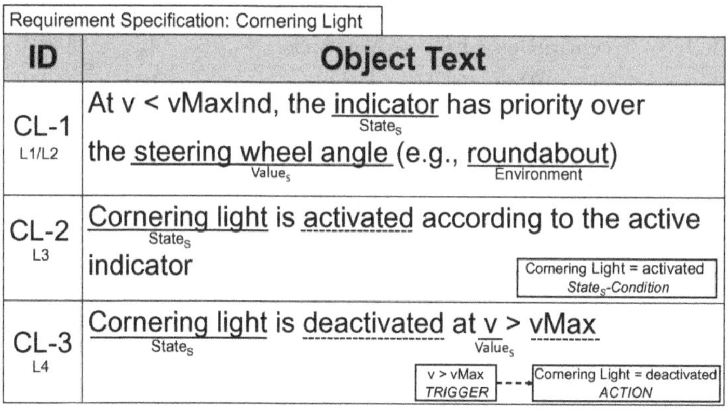

ID	Object Text
	Requirement Specification: Cornering Light
CL-1 L1/L2	At v < vMaxInd, the <u>indicator</u> (State$_s$) has priority over the <u>steering wheel angle</u> (Value$_s$) (e.g., <u>roundabout</u>) (Environment)
CL-2 L3	<u>Cornering light</u> (State$_s$) is <u>activated</u> according to the active indicator [Cornering Light = activated / State$_s$-Condition]
CL-3 L4	<u>Cornering light</u> (State$_s$) is <u>deactivated</u> at <u>v > vMax</u> (Value$_s$) [v > vMax / TRIGGER] --- [Cornering Light = deactivated / ACTION]

Fig. 5. Example of requirements of a Cornering Light System with complex marks on Level 1, 2, 3 and 4

Figure 5 displays the result of the development process performed by the engineer, in this example with appearance of all four levels. With these marked requirements, simulations can now be carried out and evaluated in different depth of detail.

Table 2. Mapping from natural language expressions to signal names

signals	roundabout	→	<RB_Stat>
	vehicle speed	→	<V_vehicle>
	steering wheel angle	→	<Angle>
	Cornering light	→	<CL_Left_Stat> <CL_Right_Stat>
	indicator	→	<Indicator_Left_Stat> <Indicator_Right_Stat>
constants	vMax	→	55
	vMaxInd	→	30

Table 3. Excerpt of a log file

Vehicle id	Source	Target	Signal	Value	Time
veh_1	centralBox	ECU	V_vehicle	40	88.010
veh_1	indicator	ECU	Indicator_Left_Stat	0	88.020
veh_1	cl	ECU	CL_Left_Stat	0	88.030
veh_1	centralBox	ECU	Angle	0	88.040
veh_1	centralBox	ECU	V_vehicle	25	89.010
veh_1	indicator	ECU	Indicator_Left_Stat	1	89.020
veh_1	cl	ECU	CL_Left_Stat	1	89.030
veh_1	centralBox	ECU	V_vehicle	20	90.010
veh_1	centralBox	ECU	Angle	10	90.040
veh_1	centralBox	ECU	V_vehicle	20	91.010
veh_1	centralBox	ECU	Angle	90	91.040
veh_1	centralBox	ECU	V_vehicle	25	92.010
veh_1	centralBox	ECU	Angle	10	92.040
veh_1	centralBox	ECU	V_vehicle	40	93.010
veh_1	indicator	ECU	Indicator_Left_Stat	0	93.020
veh_1	cl	ECU	CL_Left_Stat	0	93.030
veh_1	centralBox	ECU	Angle	0	93.040

3.3 Simulation Execution and Representation

Before the start of the simulation, the marked text passages are mapped to signal names, like shown in Table 2. The signal names may be internal signals of the system or signals of the simulation environment. However, mapping is not always feasible if the matching signal does not exist in the simulation. This might indicate that the choice of scenario is not suitable or that the state of development is still too early. Nonetheless, it is still possible to start the simulation and just validate a subset of the system requirements. Further, the markups from the text and the signals from the simulation are not necessarily a one-to-one but can also be established as a one-to-many mapping. The expressions "Cornering Light" and "indicator" in Table 2 demonstrate such a mapping. When tested in a simulation run, either of the two mapped signals can produce validation results for the annotated requirement since both should exhibit the same behavior according to their shared specification. After the preparation of the requirements document, the simulation can now be started. An excerpt of a possible resulting log file after running the simulation with CL-1, CL-2 and CL-3 is shown in Table 3.

The log data provided shows that the indicator is turned on at simulation time 89.020. The vehicle speed being 25 km/h fulfills the condition for the cornering light to be turned on, which the simulation log shows occurred at time 89.030. The values of the vehicle speed and steering angle then indicate that the vehicle made a turn. After the successful turn the indicator is turned off at time 93.020, which leads to the disabling of the cornering light. The table does not show the values of the indicator and the cornering light for simulation time 90 through 92, since no changes occurred during that time; with the indicator activated and the velocity under 30 km/h, the cornering light keeps being activated as intended.

This example of a small selection of requirements in a simple simulation scenario emphasizes the possible dimensions of a log file based on a whole requirements document with a comprehensive simulation. The extent also increases with the simulation duration.

An essential feedback mechanism is the presentation of the results in the original requirements document, depending on the chosen elements in the requirements and the analysis of the log data. Figure 6 shows the presentation of the evaluation results based on the simulation run in the presented example.

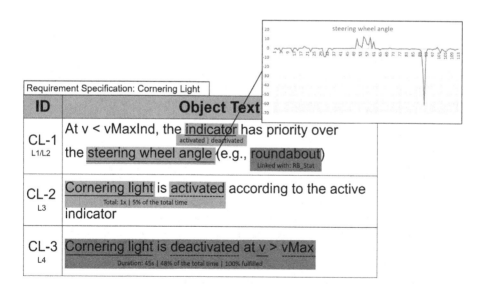

Fig. 6. Resulting marks of a simulation evaluation

In CL-1, the environment phrasing "roundabout" is mapped to the signal "RB_Stat". The element "indicator" belongs to Level 2, therefore all occurring states can be displayed. In contrast, "steering wheel angle" is a value and an element of Level 2 and therefor it can be displayed graphically over the entire simulation time. If the steering wheel is turned to the left, the value is negative, so right turns are positive. Values below 20° are lane changes. Large peaks between 45 and 90° show the process of turning off.

In Cl-2, two conditions belonging to Level 3 are displayed. Depending on the selected condition, the according number of appearances is output. Additional information on $State_{\{L1\}}$-$Condition$ is the percentage of fulfillment over the simulation duration. For $Event_{\{L1\}}$-$Condition$, information about average occurrence is available. The possibility of linking these conditions by $Time$-$Conditions$ is not displayed; however the latter can not be used alone.

In CL-3, a $Trigger$ and a dependent $Action$ as elements of Level 4 are shown. Regarding the $Trigger$, information on total appearance is available. Further $Action$-related information is the number of appearances. In combination with the excerpt of the log file, the tool can confirm the causality of CL-3 and consequentially the given requirement as fulfilled.

The given example illustrates the influence of the specification degree on possible evaluation options. For basic analysis or early system development stages, lower and less time-consuming evaluation levels are suitable. However the tool also includes more complex options of evaluation. Though increasing complexity requires an increasing effort, evaluation and validation of entire requirements is possible.

4   Experiment

The approach was used in the automotive context to perform an experiment. Two aspects were examined: practicality of the language and identification of errors in its implementation. The following paragraph describes the structure, and execution. After that, results of the experiment as well as a summary of the advantages and disadvantages are subject of discussion.

4.1   Experimental Design

Object of the experiment are natural language requirements of Daimler AG. The used specifications describe the Intelligent Light System. Overall, the specification contains 3464 requirements and is divided into various subsystems. Among other things, it includes cross light, motorway light and cornering light. The requirements of the cornering light system used in Sect. 3 is extended by four further requirements and implemented in a separate vehicle function. All used requirements are part of an export of a DOORS database. They are written in natural language without limitation to patterns, or other structural or grammatical constraints. To carry out the marking process, the requirements are managed in a self-developed tool. The test engineer chooses a selection of marks according to the desired levels of results. In the presented experiment, the engineer marks a total of 13 text passages on all 4 levels, consisting of two markings on Level 1 and 2, five markings on Level 3 and four on Level 4.

Next step is linking the marked text passages to the signals of the simulation. This supports the creation of a scenario, which itself is the starting point for the simulation framework VSimRTI [11]. This framework links different simulators together and enables the virtual modeling of complex systems. Major simulator is the tool SUMO [6] developed by DLR, used for traffic simulation. VSimRTI makes it possible to equip SUMO vehicles with additional self-developed functions. An excerpt of an OpenStreetMap of Berlin is used for a realistic road network and traffic light settings. Inclusion of all environment properties from Level 1 is checked before the start of the simulation run. The simulation run is performed 100 times with varying driving routes and an average of 53 vehicles involved. Each run is taking 163 s.

The vehicle function essentially consists of three parts: two cornering lights (left and right), and a central control unit. All components in the vehicle communicate via a virtual data bus, which is a modeled CAN communication. Each message sent and received via the bus is also written to a log file. This log file contains the time stamp, sender and recipient of the message. In addition, for each simulation step, vehicle data such as the steering angle, vehicle speed and status of the indicators are included in the log data. Following the simulation, the log data of all 100 vehicles is loaded by the developed tool. Evaluating these log data with the signal mapping from the initial step is closing the loop.

4.2   Results and Discussion

The tool reads the log data and provides the results, depending on the marks and the selected levels, in three categories: requirement fulfilled in green and not fulfilled in red (available for Level 1 and 4); and information available in blue (available for Level 2 and 3).

Figure 7 shows the presentation of the results in the original requirements for this experiment. Level 1, 2 and 3, as part of CL-1, CL-2 and CL-4, show the evaluation of word groups. One colored markup is displaying the results over the 100 simulation runs. Level 4 displays the evaluation of a causal connection between two items. For example in CL-3, $v > vMax$ was marked as trigger for the action *Cornering light* is *deactivated*. Since the requirement is fulfilled over the entire simulation time, it is colored green.

Even more complex are the requirements CL-5, CL-6 and CL-7, which also include Level 4 evaluations. Here, the triggers and actions have been marked and linked with each other across several requirements. The triggers *indicator is deactivated* (CL-5), $v < vMax$ (CL-5) and *curve radius* $>$ *angleOff* (CL-6) belong to the action *Cornering light is deactivated* in CL-6. A third Level 4 causality is also made up of the triggers from CL-5. In addition, the trigger *curve radius* $<$ *angleOff* (CL-7) is connected with all three triggers of CL-5 and the action *Cornering light is activated* in CL-7. The results are displayed in the requirement with the included action.

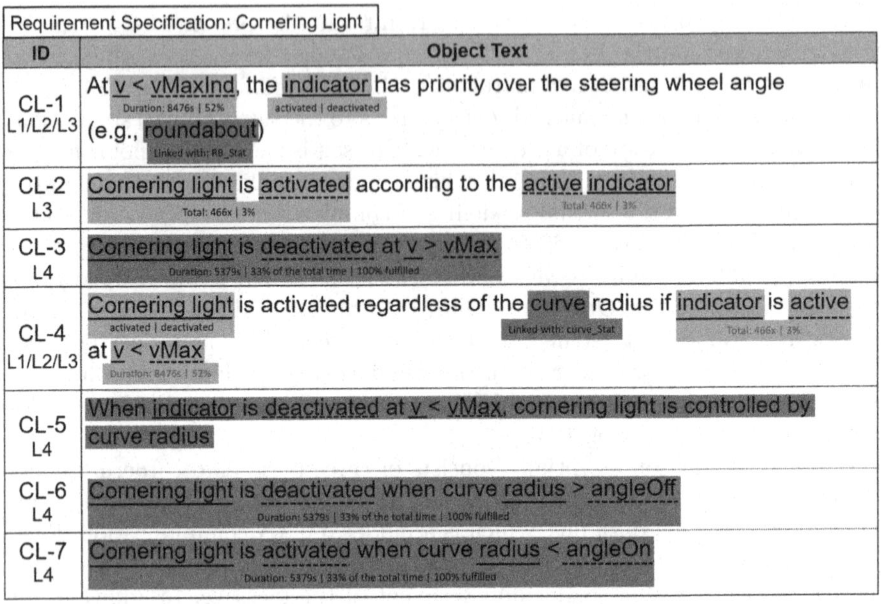
Requirement Specification: Cornering Light
ID
Object Text
CL-1 L1/L2/L3
At v < vMaxInd, the indicator has priority over the steering wheel angle (e.g., roundabout)
Duration: 8476s | 52%
activated | deactivated
Linked with: RB_Stat
CL-2 L3
Cornering light is activated according to the active indicator
Total: 466x | 3%
Total: 466x | 3%
CL-3 L4
Cornering light is deactivated at v > vMax
Duration: 5379s | 33% of the total time | 100% fulfilled
CL-4 L1/L2/L3
Cornering light is activated regardless of the curve radius if indicator is active at v < vMax
activated | deactivated
Linked with: curve_Stat
Total: 466x | 3%
Duration: 8476s | 52%
CL-5 L4
When indicator is deactivated at v < vMax, cornering light is controlled by curve radius
CL-6 L4
Cornering light is deactivated when curve radius > angleOff
Duration: 5379s | 33% of the total time | 100% fulfilled
CL-7 L4
Cornering light is activated when curve radius < angleOn
Duration: 5379s | 33% of the total time | 100% fulfilled

Fig. 7. Resulting marks of a simulation evaluation (Color figure online)

The major issue concerning all development approaches is the discrepancy between natural language requirements specifications and functionality of the software. The approach presented here bridges the gap between requirements on the one hand and simulative testing on the other. Particularly complex systems can be studied by the lightweight method at each stage of development. The mapping process is currently done manually and is time consuming for large software systems. However, if the presented approach is used parallel to the development, the mapping can also be maintained in parallel. New systems can build on previous mappings. Nevertheless, more research will be needed in an automated mapping process. Another challenge are changing software design decisions during the development process, which are not immediately updated in the original requirements documents. At present, this is performed at a later time, where some of the simulation and testing has already taken place. In our approach, the updates still have to be performed manually. However, the software engineer is motivated to perform the changes right away, so that the requirements documents always stay current and discrepancies during testing are prevented.

As the experiment shows, the evaluation can partly be sophisticated. This, however, is due to the complex requirements, which today are manually fragmented for testing. Our approach makes structuring and testing of conditions over multiple requirements possible.

5 Conclusion and Outlook

Complex software systems are based on ever larger requirement documents. Increasingly, these systems are being tested in simulations. State of the art is the translation of natural language requirements into executable models. Nowadays, the original requirements documents rarely influence the simulations and simulation results are usually not fed back to the specifications. Our lightweight multilevel markup language combines natural language requirements with simulations. Depending on the development stage, software functions can be monitored or complex requirements can be tested. The degree of detail of the evaluation can be determined by the tester. In our approach, there is no necessity for translating original requirements documents. Our experiment with 100 simulation runs of a Cornering Light System, the processing procedure, and the evaluation report illustrates its usability and emphasizes the relevance to large and complex requirements documents.

In future, we plan further steps for automation. One possible approach can be the manual signal mapping automated through the use of machine learning. Another improvement might be automated identification of Level 2 states with natural language processing methods, which are subject of recent research. Due to the rapid increase of model-based development, markups in UML diagrams are also a focus of research.

References

1. Banks, J., Carson, J.S., Nelson, B.L., Nicol, D.M.: Discrete-Event System Simulation. Prentice Hall, Upper Saddle River (2000)
2. Barmi, Z.A., Ebrahimi, A.H., Feldt, R.: Alignment of requirements specification and testing: a systematic mapping study. In: IEEE International Conference on Software Testing, Verification and Validation Workshops (2011). https://doi.org/10.1109/ICSTW.2011.58
3. Bjarnason, E., et al.: Challenges and practices in aligning requirements with verification and validation: a case study of six companies. Empir. Softw. Eng. **19**(6) (2014). https://doi.org/10.1007/s10664-013-9263-y
4. Eckhardt, J., Vogelsang, A., Femmer, H., Mager, P.: Challenging incompleteness of performance requirements by sentence patterns. In: IEEE International Requirements Engineering Conference (RE) (2016)
5. Hasling, B., Goetz, H., Beetz, K.: Model based testing of system requirements using UML use case models. In: International Conference on Software Testing, Verification, and Validation (2008). https://doi.org/10.1109/ICST.2008.9
6. Krajzewicz, D., Bonert, M., Wagner, P.: The open source traffic simulation package SUMO, June 2006
7. Lucassen, G., Robeer, M., Dalpiaz, F., van der Werf, J.M.E.M., Brinkkemper, S.: Extracting conceptual models from user stories with visual narrator. Requir. Eng. **22**(3) (2017). https://doi.org/10.1007/s00766-017-0270-1
8. Mavin, A., Wilkinson, P., Harwood, A., Novak, M.: Easy approach to requirements syntax (EARs). In: 2009 17th IEEE International Requirements Engineering Conference, pp. 317–322 (2009). https://doi.org/10.1109/RE.2009.9

9. Luisa, M., Mariangela, F., Pierluigi, N.I.: Market research for requirements analysis using linguistic tools. Requir. Eng. **9**(2), 151 (2004)
10. Nebut, C., Fleurey, F., Traon, Y.L., Jezequel, J.M.: Automatic test generation: a use case driven approach. IEEE Trans. Softw. Eng. **32**(3) (2006). https://doi.org/10.1109/TSE.2006.22
11. Schünemann, B.: V2X simulation runtime infrastructure VSimRTI: an assessment tool to design smart traffic management systems. Comput. Netw. **55**(14), 3189–3198 (2011)

Automated Analysis (Research Previews)

Supporting Feature Model Evolution by Lifting Code-Level Dependencies: A Research Preview

Daniel Hinterreiter[1]([✉]), Kevin Feichtinger[1], Lukas Linsbauer[1], Herbert Prähofer[2], and Paul Grünbacher[1]

[1] Institute Software Systems Engineering,
Christian Doppler Laboratory MEVSS, Johannes Kepler University, Linz, Austria
{daniel.hinterreiter,kevin.feichtinger,lukas.linsbauer,
paul.grunbacher}@jku.at
[2] Institute System Software,
Christian Doppler Laboratory MEVSS, Johannes Kepler University, Linz, Austria
herbert.prahofer@jku.at

Abstract. [**Context and Motivation**] Organizations pursuing software product line engineering often use feature models to define the commonalities and variability of software-intensive systems. Frequently, requirements-level features are mapped to development artifacts to ensure traceability and to facilitate the automated generation of downstream artifacts. [**Question/Problem**] Due to the continuous evolution of product lines and the complexity of the artifact dependencies, it is challenging to keep feature models consistent with their underlying implementation. [**Principal Ideas/Results**] In this paper, we outline an approach combining feature-to-artifact mappings and artifact dependency analysis to inform domain engineers about possible inconsistencies. In particular, our approach uses static code analysis and a variation control system to lift complex code-level dependencies to feature models. [**Contributions**] We demonstrate the feasibility of our approach using a Pick-and-Place Unit system and outline our further research plans.

Keywords: Product lines · Variation control system · Static analysis

1 Introduction

Feature models are widely used in software product lines and feature-oriented development approaches to define the commonalities and variability of software-intensive systems [1]. Frequently, features are defined for different spaces and at different levels [2,13]: problem space features generally refer to systems' specifications and are defined during domain analysis and requirements engineering; solution space features refer to the concrete implementation of systems created during development. Many techniques exist in software product lines and requirements engineering for mapping features to their implementation [1,2,5,7,16].

© Springer Nature Switzerland AG 2019
E. Knauss and M. Goedicke (Eds.): REFSQ 2019, LNCS 11412, pp. 169–175, 2019.
https://doi.org/10.1007/978-3-030-15538-4_12

Such mappings are also the basis for deriving products in a feature-based configuration process to compose valid product variants automatically.

Real-world product lines evolve continuously and engineers thus need to extend and adapt feature models to reflect the changes. However, engineers require deep knowledge about the domain and the implementation to avoid inconsistencies between a feature model and its implementation [4,16]. Ensuring consistency is challenging due to the complexity of both feature-to-artifact mappings and implementation-level artifact dependencies. Checking and resolving inconsistencies is particularly important when adding or changing features during product line evolution [3].

We report our ongoing research towards an approach for lifting code-level dependencies to the level of features, thus facilitating the detection and resolution of inconsistencies. Our research is part of a project on developing a platform for distributed and feature-based clone-and-own engineering [8]. Specifically, our approach integrates feature modelling, feature-to-artifact mappings [10], and static analysis [6] (Sects. 2 and 3). It uses a revision-aware feature model [14] to track the evolution of feature models and their feature-to-artifact mappings. It further relies on static analysis for determining code dependencies. We present the results of a preliminary evaluation we conducted using the Pick-and-Place-Unit case study (Sect. 4) and provide an outlook on future research (Sect. 5).

2   Approach

Figure 1 provides an overview of our approach:

(1) The bottom layer represents the different solution space *artifacts* such as source code, models, or documents. The artifacts are managed in a tree structure. The nodes of the tree represent elements of artifacts, e.g., individual code statements or paragraphs in a document.

(2a) The approach relies on *feature-to-artifact mappings*, i.e., each artifact element needs to know to which feature it belongs. We assume that these mappings are automatically created using a variation control system (VCS) [10,15]. A VCS creates and manages mappings between artifacts and their corresponding features during development and enables the composition of different product variants using feature-based configuration. For instance, Linsbauer et al. describe how feature-to-artifact mappings are determined and kept up-to-date in the VCS ECCO [11,12]: as soon as a developer commits a new product revision or variant ECCO analyzes the changes in the features and artifacts, which then allows to incrementally add and refine the mappings.

(2b) Our approach further allows computing the complex dependencies between implementation artifacts in the *artifact dependency graph* (ADG). We realize the ADG as a system dependence graph (SDG) [9] globally representing the control-flow and data-flow dependencies in a system.

(3) As explained, our aim is to lift implementation-level dependencies to the level of features, which can then be proposed to a modeller in the *feature model* as suggestions to evolve the model. Thus, our approach combines the information

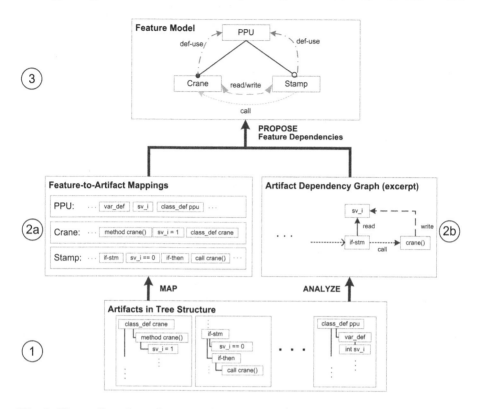

Fig. 1. The artifact dependency graph and feature-to-artifact mappings allow proposing feature dependencies in the feature model.

from the feature-to-artifact mappings and the dependency graph. In particular, we use the artifact mappings to collect the corresponding subset of ADG nodes, which are then the starting point for traversing the dependency graph to find potential dependencies to other features. During this step, we check if we can find an artifact mapped to another feature. If so, we suggest a relation between two features to the modeller.

We distinguish between two levels of feature relations (cf. Table 1): *Dependencies* are relations required to correctly compose products. For instance, in case of a def-use dependency, i.e., one feature uses a variable or procedure declared in the implementation of another feature, a *requires* constraint must exist at the level of features to ensure that the automatically composed product compiles successfully. *Interactions* indicate weaker relations between features. This is the case, for instance, if two features write to the same variable or if one feature writes and the other reads that variable. If such interactions are not considered in the feature model, the product may still be composed, but harmful interactions may occur during execution, e.g., if two optional features write to the same output variable. This could be avoided by modeling the two optional features as alternative features.

3   Implementation

We implemented the approach by integrating a feature modeling environment with a VCS and tools for analyzing artifact dependencies. We demonstrate the feasibility of our approach by using static code analysis techniques to lift complex code dependencies.

Specifically, we adopt the VCS ECCO [11] as part of developing our feature-oriented platform. While existing VCS are mostly bound to specific artifact types [10], ECCO can be extended with plug-ins to support different domain-specific implementation languages and artifact types, as long as they can be represented in a tree structure. For example, our prototype supports source code of textual and visual languages of the IEC 61131-3 standard, Java source code, as well as configuration files for describing mappings of software variables to hardware endpoints. ECCO then creates and maintains feature-to-artifact mappings by computing differences in features and artifacts of products [12]. We do not assume initial feature-to-artifact mappings, as they can be re-created by replaying the evolution history of a system, which we showed in our preliminary evaluation. We use a system dependency graph (SDG) [6] to analyze different

Table 1. Dependencies and interactions derived from a system dependency graph.

	Type	Description
Deps	call	A feature calls a function or method of a second feature
	def-use	A feature defines a variable or constant used by a second feature
Interactions	call-call	Two features call the same function or method of a third feature
	write-write	Two features write to a data object defined by a third feature
	write-read	A feature uses data written by a second feature, while a third feature defines the data object
	read-read	Two features read a data object defined by a third feature

Table 2. Dependencies and interactions discovered for different versions of the PPU.

	PPU_v3	PPU_v4	PPU_v5
def-use	3	4	5
call	0	0	0
call-call	2	4	4
read-read	0	6	6
write-read	1	19	22
write-write	4	34	58

types of code-level dependencies (cf. Table 1) and then lift them to the level of feature models by utilizing the feature-to-artifact mappings of the VCS.

4   Preliminary Evaluation

For the evaluation of our approach we re-played the evolution history of the Pick-and-Place Unit (PPU) product line [17], thereby automatically computing the feature-to-artifact mappings using ECCO. We then analyzed feature dependencies and interactions for different PPU versions to demonstrate the feasibility of our approach. The PPU is a well-known example of a manufacturing system for transporting and sorting different work pieces. A developer of our lab (not an author of this paper) implemented different revisions and variants of the PPU using an IEC-61131-3 compliant programming language for the control part and Java for the visualization part of the system [8].

For instance, the basic version of the PPU comprises the features *Stack*, *Crane*, and *Ramp*, while the additional features *Stamp* and *Sorter* were later added to the system. As explained above, a feature model would typically become inconsistent with its implementation after such code-level changes. To show the usefulness of our support for lifting dependencies we computed the number of different types of code-level dependencies and interactions for different versions of the PPU (cf. Table 2).

We manually inspected the code with the developer of the PPU system to confirm the validity of the computed dependencies and interactions. For instance, the newly found dependencies between versions of the PPU are directly related to the addition of new features. In PPU_v3 the feature *StackCylinder* uses the variable di_machineStarted to check if the machine is currently running. In PPU_v4 feature a *Crane* is introduced, which also uses this variable to check the state of the machine, thus leading to a new def-use dependency. Thus, a *requires* constraint between the features *StackCylinder* and *Crane* could be suggested to the developer. PPU_v5 introduced the feature *Ramp*, leading to interactions with the feature *Crane*. Both features read and write the variable state_crane_cur resulting in write-read and write-write interactions showing the close relationship between these features. Although no direct constraints can be derived from such interactions, they provide highly valuable hints to developers during evolution.

Overall, the preliminary evaluation with the PPU developer confirmed most of the found dependencies and interactions.

5   Conclusion and Research Outlook

We proposed an approach that uses feature-to-artifact mappings and an artifact dependency graph to lift artifact-level dependencies to feature models. To demonstrate usefulness and feasibility of our approach we presented the number of dependencies and interactions computed for different versions and variants of the PPU case study system.

In the short term we will use the information about artifact dependencies and interactions to analyze the coupling and cohesion of features, thus supporting engineers deciding about merging or splitting features during product line evolution. This will be particularly challenging in our context of distributed feature-oriented platform evolution [8]. We will extend our dependency analysis to other types of artifacts. Our long-term plan is to evaluate our approach using large-scale product lines from our industry partner based on our earlier case studies on program analysis of industrial automation systems [6].

Acknowledgements. The financial support by the Austrian Federal Ministry for Digital and Economic Affairs, the National Foundation for Research, Technology and Development, and KEBA AG, Austria is gratefully acknowledged.

References

1. Apel, S., Batory, D., Kästner, C., Saake, G.: Feature-Oriented Software Product Lines: Concepts and Implementation. Springer, Heidelberg (2013). https://doi.org/10.1007/978-3-642-37521-7
2. Berger, T., et al.: What is a feature? A qualitative study of features in industrial software product lines. In: Proceedings of the 19th SPLC, pp. 16–25 (2015)
3. Bürdek, J., Kehrer, T., Lochau, M., Reuling, D., Kelter, U., Schürr, A.: Reasoning about product-line evolution using complex feature model differences. Autom. Softw. Eng. **23**(4), 687–733 (2016)
4. Dintzner, N., van Deursen, A., Pinzger, M.: FEVER: an approach to analyze feature-oriented changes and artefact co-evolution in highly configurable systems. Empir. Softw. Eng. **23**(2), 905–952 (2018)
5. Egyed, A., Graf, F., Grünbacher, P.: Effort and quality of recovering requirements-to-code traces: two exploratory experiments. In: Proceedings of the 18th IEEE International Requirements Engineering Conference, Sydney, Australia, pp. 221–230 (2010)
6. Grimmer, A., Angerer, F., Prähofer, H., Grünbacher, P.: Supporting program analysis for non-mainstream languages: experiences and lessons learned. In: Proceedings of the 23rd SANER Conference, pp. 460–469 (2016)
7. Hajri, I., Goknil, A., Briand, L.C., Stephany, T.: Change impact analysis for evolving configuration decisions in product line use case models. J. Syst. Softw. **139**, 211–237 (2018)
8. Hinterreiter, D.: Feature-oriented evolution of automation software systems in industrial software ecosystems. In: 23rd IEEE International Conference on Emerging Technologies and Factory Automation, Torino, Italy, September 2018
9. Horwitz, S., Reps, T., Binkley, D.: Interprocedural slicing using dependence graphs. SIGPLAN Not. **23**(7), 35–46 (1988)
10. Linsbauer, L., Berger, T., Grünbacher, P.: A classification of variation control systems. In: Proceedings of the 16th ACM SIGPLAN International Conference on Generative Programming: Concepts and Experiences, GPCE 2017, pp. 49–62. ACM (2017)
11. Linsbauer, L., Egyed, A., Lopez-Herrejon, R.E.: A variability-aware configuration management and revision control platform. In: Proceedings of the 38th International Conference on Software Engineering (Companion), pp. 803–806 (2016)

12. Linsbauer, L., Lopez-Herrejon, R.E., Egyed, A.: Variability extraction and modeling for product variants. Softw. Syst. Model. **16**(4), 1179–1199 (2017)
13. Rabiser, D., et al.: Multi-purpose, multi-level feature modeling of large-scale industrial software systems. Softw. Syst. Model. **17**, 913–938 (2018)
14. Seidl, C., Schaefer, I., Aßmann, U.: Capturing variability in space and time with hyper feature models. In: Proceedings of the 8th International Workshop on Variability Modelling of Software-Intensive Systems, VaMoS 2014, pp. 6:1–6:8 (2013)
15. Stănciulescu, S., Berger, T., Walkingshaw, E., Wąsowski, A.: Concepts, operations, and feasibility of a projection-based variation control system. In: Proceedings of IEEE ICSME, pp. 323–333 (2016)
16. Vierhauser, M., Grünbacher, P., Egyed, A., Rabiser, R., Heider, W.: Flexible and scalable consistency checking on product line variability models. In: Proceedings of the IEEE/ACM International Conference on Automated Software Engineering, pp. 63–72 (2010)
17. Vogel-Heuser, B., Legat, C., Folmer, J., Feldmann, S.: Researching evolution in industrial plant automation: scenarios and documentation of the pick and place unit. Technische Universität München, Technical report (2014)

Identifying Requirements in Requests for Proposal: A Research Preview

Andreas Falkner[1], Cristina Palomares[2], Xavier Franch[2(✉)],
Gottfried Schenner[1], Pablo Aznar[2], and Alexander Schoerghuber[1]

[1] Siemens AG Österreich, Vienna, Austria
{andreas.a.falkner,gottfried.schenner,
alexander.schoerghuber}@siemens.com
[2] Universitat Politècnica de Catalunya (UPC), Barcelona, Spain
{cpalomares,franch,paznar}@essi.upc.edu

Abstract. **[Context & motivation]** Bidding processes are a usual requirement elicitation instrument for large IT or infrastructure projects. An organization or agency issues a Request for Proposal (RFP) and interested companies may submit compliant offers. **[Problem]** Such RFPs comprise natural language documents of several hundreds of pages with requirements of various kinds mixed with other information. The analysis of that huge amount of information is very time consuming and cumbersome because bidding companies should not disregard any requirement stated in the RFP. **[Principal ideas/results]** This research preview paper presents a first version of a classification component, OpenReq Classification Service (ORCS), which extracts requirements from RFP documents while discarding irrelevant text. ORCS is based on the use of Naïve Bayes classifiers. We have trained ORCS with 6 RFPs and then tested the component with 4 other RFPs, all of them from the railway safety domain. **[Contribution]** ORCS paves the way to improved productivity by reducing the manual effort needed to identify requirements from natural language RFPs.

Keywords: Requirements elicitation · Requirements identification ·
Request for Proposal · Bidding process · Classification

1 Introduction

In a bidding process, an organization or public agency aims at procuring a technological solution by specifying the requirements in a document called Request for Proposal (RFP), which is written in natural language and can be several hundred pages long. Based on this, companies present their bids that need to be compliant to the RFP. Last, the requesting organization agency will select one of these bids (or a combination of them) for developing the solution.

In spite of their technical nature, RFPs tend to mix text describing the requirements with other text that is merely informative ("prose") and thus is not relevant to the bidding company for compliance evaluation. This characteristic forces the bidder to invest resources to identify the real requirements, with the subsequent impact over productivity.

© Springer Nature Switzerland AG 2019
E. Knauss and M. Goedicke (Eds.): REFSQ 2019, LNCS 11412, pp. 176–182, 2019.
https://doi.org/10.1007/978-3-030-15538-4_13

The goal of this paper is to present the first results on the use of a software component, ORCS (OpenReq Classification Service), aimed at extracting requirements from an RFP in an efficient and effective way. In this context, by "effective" we mean a technique that does not miss any requirement (100% recall) and as a second priority, filters as much prose as possible. As stated by Berry [1], there are different notions of effectiveness, and the one above is justified because missing a requirement could damage the organization bid.

The paper is organized as follows. A typical bidding process for large infrastructure projects is introduced in Sect. 2. Section 3 presents the functionalities and internal structure of ORCS, and Sect. 4 shows the results of the preliminary evaluation of ORCS with real data (from Siemens). Finally, the paper is concluded in Sect. 5.

2 Bidding Processes for Large Infrastructure Projects

When an infrastructure provider such as Siemens decides to participate in a bid for a large infrastructure project, several of its departments and stakeholders (project management, finances, system development, etc.) must work together to find a good solution to cover all requirements. Requirements are usually organized and edited using a commercial RE tool such as IBM DOORS or POLARION REQUIREMENTS.

In a typical scenario, a bid project for the RFP is created within the company at the start of the process. A project team is set up with the bid project manager, the requirements manager, and the relevant stakeholders necessary for assessing the RFP. In the initial phase, the main workload is carried by the requirements manager. In the requirements capturing phase, the requirements manager is responsible for screening the RFP and for identifying all relevant and referenced external documents (e.g. international standards). The documents are then imported into the requirements management (RM) tool. The next step for the requirements manager is to analyse the imported documents and distinguish between merely informative text sections and text which specifies relevant requirements. This task is done for every entry in the RM tool. As there can be thousands of entries to be processed by the requirements manager, this is an important issue for improving the requirements management process. Consecutively, the identified requirements are assigned to the relevant stakeholder(s) which are responsible to evaluate them according to different criteria such as risk, compliance, etc. At the end of the bid project, a list of compliance is compiled, which contains a statement about the compliance of the bid, i.e. if and under what restrictions an offer can be submitted.

One of the potential bottlenecks of the process described above is the classification of the requirements as it is currently manually done by the requirements manager. In the following we describe how to speed up this process.

3 Identifying Requirements with ORCS

ORCS is part of a larger recommendation system, OpenReq [2]. ORCS' goal is to recommend a value to a requirement property that is binary (i.e., there are no more than two values available for that property). ORCS tackles that task by providing an API for a binary classifier. In the context of this paper, the property is *isReq*, and it represents whether a piece of text is a real requirement or prose (not relevant for the RE process). In other contexts, property could be requirement fields such as *component* (part of a system to which the requirement is talking about) or *priority*.

Among all the different possibilities, we decided that ORCS would be implemented as a supervised machine learning classifier [3]. Considering that we want to discover the "correct" label of a text and that we have a labelled dataset from previous projects, unsupervised learning techniques, which are useful for discovering how the data in the model is structured, do not suit properly [3].

From all the available supervised machine learning algorithms for classification, we are using Naïve Bayes (NB) [4]. NB is a probabilistic classifier based on applying the Bayes' theorem with strong (naive) independence assumptions between the features. NB is a good algorithm for working with text classification since, when dealing with text, it is very common to treat each unique word as a feature, and since the vocabulary in RFP comprises many thousands of words, this makes for a large number of features. The relative simplicity of the algorithm and the independent features assumption makes NB a strong performer for classifying texts [4]. Consequently, NB needs less training time (and therefore it is more scalable). In addition, NB needs less data for training than other supervised algorithms (such as Random Forest), which makes it good for classifying requirements in companies that do not have available hundred-thousands of requirements.

We built ORCS upon a component that already provides a NB classifier implementation, Mahout[1]. It offers the basics for different machine learning tasks (e.g., classification and clustering). Mahout currently has two NB implementations. The first is standard Multinomial NB. The second is an implementation of Transformed Weight-normalized Complement NB as introduced in [5], which extends the Multinomial NB that performs particularly well on datasets with skewed classes (which is the case in RFP, where most of the texts are real requirements; just a few pieces of text are non-relevant).

However, as most of the available implementations of classification algorithms, installing, configuring and using it is not an easy process, since deep knowledge of Mahout and how it works is needed (e.g., set up of environment paths, synchronization of the calls made, etc.). Therefore, we added specific code on top of Mahout to ease its integration and use by a final user.

Figure 1 shows the microservice-based internal architecture of ORCS. ORCS allows to *Train (MS1)* a machine learning model with specific data (this data is basically a list of pairs *<text, property value>*) and stores - using the *Data Manager (MS5)* - the training in a database (using as key the name of the requirement property and the

---

[1] https://mahout.apache.org/.

name of the organization). Thus, when the recommendation for the value of a requirement property is necessary, the user just calls the *Classify (MS3)* microservice passing the piece of text that needs the recommendation, the name of the requirement property and the name of the organization. Then, the data manager takes care of setting up the corresponding machine learning model in the core of Mahout and returning the recommendation. In addition, there are microservices to *Update (MS2)* a machine learning model when new data (again tuples of the kind *<text, property value>*) is available and also to *Test (MS4)* the classifier with a *k*-fold cross-validation passing the same kind of tuples as in the last microservice and the number of tests to *k*. As ORCS is part of OpenReq, all the data exchanged by the microservices is based on the ontology presented in [6].

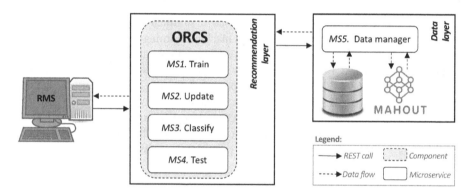

Fig. 1. ORCS' internal architecture

4   Preliminary Evaluation

For the evaluation of the requirements classifier, ten completed bid projects (RFPs) were made available by the Viennese Siemens Mobility department. In total, they comprised 28,200 requirement candidates, all of which had been classified by business experts as either a real requirement (DEF) or a merely informative comment (Prose). An example of a requirement is "A balise group shall consist of between one and eight balises", while an example of Prose is "The purpose of this document is to specify the unified European Train Control System (ETCS) from a technical point of view". The requirements' ID, text, and classification were extracted from the RM tool used at the department and stored in 10 JSON files, one for each project. Six of these projects were randomly chosen as training data set, including cross-validation, and disclosed to the UPC team. These six projects were used by UPC to run a first evaluation of ORCS using a 10-fold cross-validation test (Subsect. 4.1). The remaining four projects were kept secret and only used once for the final evaluation run by Siemens (reported in Sect. 4.2).

In both evaluations we use standard metrics for binary classification considering DEF (i.e., classification of a candidate as a real requirement) as the positive case: recall (true positive rate, number of correct positive results divided by the number of all relevant sample) and specificity (true negative rate, i.e., number of correct negative results divided by the number of all relevant sample). Recall is most important for the business experts because they want to avoid that some requirement is not detected as such, thus not being checked for compliance during the bid process which may lead to (potentially high) non-compliance costs (a business risk that must be avoided). Specificity is also important because unnecessary efforts arise if many comments are wrongly classified as DEF: experts are invited to check compliance for them although this is not necessary. We refrained from combining those two into a single metric (such as accuracy or F2-metric) in order to give the stakeholders (business experts) the chance to weight the two against each other.

4.1 Evaluation Results During Training and Validation

For first testing the results of ORCS, we used a stratified 10-fold cross-validation, which is a well-known technique to evaluate machine learning models. In this case, we used as sample 6 projects which contained 17,556 requirement candidates. From these candidates, 15,870 (90.4%) requirements were classified as DEF by experts. This means that only 1686 (9.6%) were of type Prose. In the case of ORCS, having unbalanced class labels is not a problem (as explained in Sect. 3).

Table 1 shows the results of calling the ORCS' Test microservice with $k = 10$ and this specific sample. As can be seen in Table 1, average recall is 85.06% and average specificity is 72.04%, showing a good start point for the classifier.

Table 1. 10-fold cross-validation results

	Test 1	Test 2	Test 3	Test 4	Test 5	Test 6	Test 7	Test 8	Test 9	Test 10	Total/Avge
# reqs	1734	1742	1689	1801	1788	1697	1792	1788	1719	1806	17556
TP	1335	1346	1280	1391	1372	1284	1389	1394	1327	1382	13500
FP	33	43	47	41	50	64	48	45	46	55	472
TN	133	110	127	131	119	124	129	118	101	122	1214
FN	233	243	235	238	247	225	226	231	245	247	2370
Recall	85.14%	84.71%	84.49%	85.39%	84.74%	85.09%	86.01%	85.78%	84.41%	84.84%	**85.06%**
Specificity	80.12%	71.90%	72.99%	76.16%	70.41%	65.96%	72.88%	72.39%	68.71%	68.93%	**72.04%**

4.2 Evaluation Results on Non-disclosed Test Data

The 4 projects used as test data set comprise 10,700 requirement candidates, 7,300 of which were classified as real requirements by experts. As the resulting prevalence (i.e., occurrence of DEF in the whole set of requirement candidates) of 69% is considerably lower than the prevalence of 84% in the training data set, we investigated and found out that the prevalence in a subset of three projects is 83% (based on micro-averaging [7]) whereas the fourth project shows a prevalence of only 16%. We consider this an outlier which was caused by the fact that the experts rated whole sections of the RFP as Prose because they contained information out of the scope of the bid project (e.g., because their contents were covered by another company in a bidding consortium). Such constellations cannot be covered easily by text-only classification and we still need to find a way how to deal with them properly.

First results are shown in Table 2. The classifier performs badly on the outlier (Eval 4), with only 21% specificity. However, the micro-average of the rest of the test data has a quite similar performance as the micro-average of the training data (nearly the same recall, specificity smaller by several percentage points). This indicates that the classifier is not overfitted to the training data as long as the prevalence of the test data is similar to the training data.

Table 2. Evaluation results

	Train 1	Train 2	Train 3	Train 4	Train 5	Train 6	*Train avg*	Eval 1	Eval 2	Eval 3	Eval 4	*Eval avg*
# reqs	1525	8123	1854	1382	853	3819	17556	1000	6510	841	2300	*8351*
TP	1112	6234	1390	1056	663	2832	13287	785	4645	675	343	*6105*
FP	59	170	29	51	8	115	432	11	375	13	1520	*399*
TN	257	1073	290	191	99	500	2410	110	784	93	401	*860*
FN	97	646	145	84	83	372	896	94	706	60	36	*987*
Recall	91.98%	90.61%	90.55%	92.63%	88.87%	88.39%	90.30%	89.31%	86.81%	91.84%	90.50%	*87.65%*
Specificity	81.33%	86.32%	90.91%	78.93%	92.52%	81.30%	84.80%	90.91%	67.40%	87.74%	20.87%	*71.21%*

5 Conclusions

In this paper, we present an approach of how identifying requirements in RFP in the setup of Siemens by using ORCS, a component that provides an API for machine learning classification based on NB. In addition, we present preliminary results of testing this component in Siemens. Although the results are good, they need to be improved, especially the recall of component (and therefore the number of false negatives), since we want to avoid that a real requirement is not detected as such, because in that case it would not be evaluated during the bid process, which may lead to non-compliance costs if the bid is won. To achieve this, we aim to improve ORCS in different aspects: NLP preprocessing (mainly stop words removal and lemmatization) and the incorporation of context in the classification process (e.g., the location of the text in the RFP so that we can more precisely differentiate between relevant and irrelevant information).

References

1. Berry, D.M.: Evaluation of tools for hairy requirements and software engineering tasks. In: REW 2017 (2017)
2. Palomares, C., Franch, X., Fucci, D.: Personal recommendations in requirements engineering: the OpenReq approach. In: Kamsties, E., Horkoff, J., Dalpiaz, F. (eds.) REFSQ 2018. LNCS, vol. 10753, pp. 297–304. Springer, Cham (2018). https://doi.org/10.1007/978-3-319-77243-1_19
3. Shalev, S., Ben, S.: Understanding Machine Learning. Cambridge University Press, Cambridge (2014)
4. Brink, H., et al.: Real-World Machine Learning. Manning Publications, New York (2016)

5. Rennie, J., et al.: Tackling the poor assumptions of Naive Bayes text classifiers. In: ICML 2003 (2003)
6. Quer, C., et al.: Reconciling practice and rigour in ontology-based heterogeneous information systems construction. In: Buchmann, R.A., Karagiannis, D., Kirikova, M. (eds.) PoEM 2018. LNBIP, vol. 335, pp. 205–220. Springer, Cham (2018). https://doi.org/10.1007/978-3-030-02302-7_13
7. Yang, Y.: An evaluation of statistical approaches to text categorization. J. Inf. Retrieval 1, 69–90 (1999)

Finding and Analyzing App Reviews Related to Specific Features: A Research Preview

Jacek Dąbrowski[1,2]([⊠]) ⓘ, Emmanuel Letier[1] ⓘ, Anna Perini[2] ⓘ,
and Angelo Susi[2] ⓘ

[1] University College London, London, UK
{j.dabrowski,e.letier}@cs.ucl.ac.uk
[2] Fondazione Bruno Kessler, Trento, Italy
{dabrowski,perini,susi}@fbk.eu

Abstract. [**Context and motivation**] App reviews can be a rich source of information for requirements engineers. Recently, many approaches have been proposed to classify app reviews as bug reports, feature requests, or to elicit requirements. [**Question/problem**] None of these approaches, however, allow requirements engineers to search for users' opinions about specific features of interest. Retrieving reviews on specific features would help requirements engineers during requirements elicitation and prioritization activities involving these features. [**Principal idea/results**] This paper presents a research preview on our tool-supported method for taking requirements engineering decisions about specific features. The tool will allow one to (i) find reviews that talk about a specific feature, (ii) identify bug reports, change requests and users' sentiment about this feature, and (iii) visualize and compare users' feedback for different features in an analytic dashboard. [**Contributions**] Our contribution is threefold: (i) we identify a new problem to address, i.e. searching for users' opinions on a specific feature, (ii) we provide a research preview on an analytics tool addressing the problem, and finally (iii) we discuss preliminary results on the searching component of the tool.

Keywords: Mining users reviews · Feedback analytics tool · Software quality · Requirement engineering

1 Introduction

Developing app reviews analytics tools is an active field of research aimed at extracting useful information from the large amount of user reviews found in app stores [12]. Analytics tools exploit data mining and analysis techniques to address different software engineering problems, including requirements engineering problems. Approaches have been proposed for inferring topics referred by reviews [14], for analyzing users' sentiments [5], and for classifying reviews

© Springer Nature Switzerland AG 2019
E. Knauss and M. Goedicke (Eds.): REFSQ 2019, LNCS 11412, pp. 183–189, 2019.
https://doi.org/10.1007/978-3-030-15538-4_14

as either bug reports, requests for new features [9], or discussion about non-functional properties [10,12].

However, these approaches do not allow software professionals to search for users' opinions on specific features of interest. Software professional interviewed about feedback analytics tools indicate two missing features they would like to see supported in future analytics tools: the ability to group and quantify app reviews to support requirements prioritization, and the ability to associate app reviews to work items in project management and issue tracking systems [8].

Our objective is to develop automated techniques to satisfy these requests. We present an automated tool that given a short feature description (e.g. *add reservations* for a Google Trip app), finds app reviews that refer to such feature and report historical trends about users sentiments, bug reports and enhancement requests related to this feature. Knowing what users' say about a specific feature is important to understand their needs [2,13]. It may support engineers to monitor users' satisfaction on a feature and its "health condition" over time [10]. This can also help to sketch a roadmap for next release, including decisions on which features should be changed first to improve the app performance [15].

The following questions guide the development and evaluation of our tool:

RQ1. What natural language and data analysis techniques can be used to develop our tool?
RQ2. What is the effectiveness of different techniques in searching for users' opinions on a feature?
RQ3. How useful do requirements engineers find the tool?

This research preview paper motivates our research through an example, outlines our envisioned technical solution, presents preliminary results for our app reviews search engine, relates our approach to previous work, and discuss our future research plans.

2   Motivating Scenarios

Google Trip app is an app that helps its users to organize trips and manage travel-oriented documents. The app is being used by more than 27,275 users and received over 8,500 reviews on Google Play Store. These reviews concern existing or desired functionalities, reported bugs and other aspects related to quality in-use. We use this app in our initial experiment in Sect. 4.

Suppose the issue tracking system for this app contains requests for introducing new features and improving existing features (for example *add the ability to create day plans, improve the ability to add a hotel reservation,* etc.) and the project manager has to decide which requests to implement first. Finding users reviews mentioning each of these features would allow the project managers to quickly compare how often each request appears in app reviews, for how long each request has been made, and whether the frequency of each request is increasing or decreasing. This information will provide concrete evidence of the relative importance of each request from the users' perspective. Such information is not sufficient by itself to prioritize change request because the perspective of other stakeholders must also be taken into account, but it can provide useful evidence-based data to partly inform such decisions.

Suppose now that a requirements engineer and the development team have been tasked to define and implement detailed requirements for one of these feature requests. Finding users reviews that refer to the feature will allow them to quickly identify what users have been saying about the feature. This cheap elicitation technique might be sufficient in itself or it might be the starting point for additional more expensive elicitation activities involving interviews, surveys, prototyping, or observations.

3   An Approach for Analyzing Users' Feedback on Feature

Figure 1 outlines our approach for finding and analysing users' reviews related to specific features. The main component of our tool is the searching component that takes as input a query that describes a feature (e.g. *add reservations*) and retrieves a set of users reviews that mention that feature. An example of review retrieved for the feature query *add reservations* is *Please, improve adding reservations as it crashes and obstructs the booking process.* Sentiment analysis and classification techniques are then used to classify the retrieved reviews as expressing either positive, neutral or negative sentiments and as reporting a bug or asking for an enhancement. The results of the search for different feature queries are then presented on a dashboard.

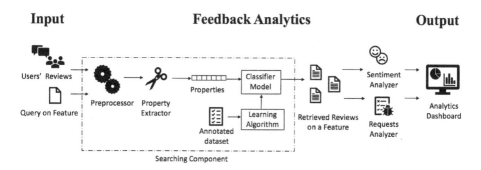

Fig. 1. Overview of our tool-based approach for finding and analysing users' opinions on a specific feature

We are exploring the following techniques to develop our tool:

Searching Component. We propose *machine-learned relevance* method to support searching for users' feedback on a feature [11]. The method exploits supervised machine learning (ML) techniques to classify reviews to be relevant or non-relevant to a query. Figure 1 illustrates details of searching component to be used for the method. The preprocessor performs standard text normalization steps of query and reviews to refine them from noisy information. The property extractor determines textual properties of filtered query and reviews, then convey them to the classifier as basis for selecting reviews to be returned. To produce a classification model, the learning algorithm is firstly provided with a training dataset including exemplary reviews annotated with respect to test queries.

Sentiment Analyzer. Two candidate techniques could be used to analyze sentiment of users' reviews: ML and lexicon-based [6]. ML techniques treat sentiment identification as binary or multiclass classification problem. The lexicon-based methods calculate the sentiment score of a word or sentence using lexicon provided with list of positive and negative words. These methods assume that the opinion of text is determined as the sum of the sentiment score of each word. Further, we propose to analyze sentiment on the aspect-level as it allows one to determine the sentiment within a segment of text for a mentioned feature, rather than for the text as a whole [6].

Users' Requests Analyzer. We aim to use one of existing data-driven methods to classify users' request as bug report or feature request. These methods exploit supervised classification techniques such as Naive Bayes, Support Vector Machine or Logistic Regression, and proved their effectiveness for classifying users' request into requirement-related information [4].

4   Preliminary Results

To evaluate the feasibility of searching for users' opinions on a feature we conducted a preliminary experiment. We collected 200 reviews for Google Trip app and the app description from Play Store. We manually extracted feature-related phrases from the description using Part Of Speech patterns and annotated the reviews with respect to these phrases [7]. We then built a prototype of the searching component using NLTK library and Weka tool. We trained algorithms with text properties such as query-term proximity, covered query term number, cosine similarity measure and Boolean matching [11]. We evaluated our prototype using 10-fold cross-validation and obtained precision of 0.360, recall of 0.257 and F1 score of 0.300. We observed that for queries formed by two keywords (e.g. *add reservation*) and term proximity less of than three words, the approach achieve precision at the level of 0.88. Furthermore, we observed that reviews discussing a queried feature by their synonyms are not retrieved. This problem could be addressed by query expansion or word embedding techniques.

Further, we concluded that some queries (e.g. *search for attractions*) express a functional topic aggregating several real features (e.g. *search for place* or *search for restaurant*) rather than a single feature. We plan to investigate whether we could use technique for ontology inference based on app description and reviews and extend our approach by concept similarity measure.

5 Related Work

Previous work focused on inferring features in app reviews rather than finding features that talk about specific features [1,5,7]. Guzman and Maalej proposed an approach for analyzing sentiments of reviews where prospective app features are identified. The approach identifies features as frequently co-occurring keywords and extract them from users' reviews. Extracted features are associated with sentiment and then grouped using topic modelling. The authors extended the work by classifying reviews associated with extracted features into categories related to usability and user experience [1]. Similarly, Johann et al. proposed an approach for extracting app features from users' reviews and app description based on linguistic rules [7]. The approach enables comparing lists of extracted app features to identify mismatch between extracted app features from reviews and app description.

These approaches identify phrases corresponding to app features and extract them from users reviews. They are evaluated against their ability to identify whether extracted phrases from reviews are really features. In contrast, our approach aims to support software professionals to search for users' feedback on specific features of their interest. Therefore, we plan to assess our tool's ability to retrieve users' feedback on a queried feature.

Other works provide tool-based approaches to support feedback analysis [3, 16,17]. The PAID approach groups frequently co-occurring keywords extracted from users' reviews and visualize them as topics by theme river [3]. The main objective of the tool is to visualize changes in topics in different versions of the app. MARK is a keyword-based tool for a semi-automated review analysis [16]. It enables one to automatically extract keywords from raw user reviews and rank them using their associations with negative sentiment. The tool provides a summary of the most relevant reviews related to the keywords and visualizes the trend of keyword occurrence. Similarly, PUMA extracts phrases from reviews which are associate with negative sentiment and visualize how sentiments evolve over a specific time period [17].

We envision our tool will use sentiment and trend analysis techniques similar to these used by previous app store analysis tools, but will perform a more fine-grained analysis on the subsets of reviews retrieved by our searching component.

6 Conclusion

In this research preview, we have presented a problem of searching for users' opinions on a specific feature. We demonstrated the problem and its relevance to support requirement engineering decisions by motivating scenarios. We proposed our tool-based approach to address the problem and analyze retrieved reviews in terms of their sentiments and users' requests. We presented preliminary results on the feasibility of the approach and technical challenges that need to be addressed.

As future work, we plan to implement remaining components of the tool and experiment with different techniques to elaborate our approach. In particular, we aim to investigate unsupervised techniques to support searching for opinionated features and analyzing associated sentiments expressed in user reviews. We plan to user and extend available datasets to evaluate our work [16]. We will select apps from different domains and app stores to investigate the generality of our approach. Further, we will use software professionals to (i) identify candidate features from app descriptions to form test queries, and to (ii) annotate users' feedback with respect to expressed users' request, opinionated feature and associated sentiment.

Finally, we will evaluate the usefulness of our tool in practice by observing and interviewing prospective users.

References

1. Bakiu, E., Guzman, E.: Which feature is unusable? Detecting usability and user experience issues from user reviews. In: 2017 IEEE 25th International Requirements Engineering Conference Workshops (REW), pp. 182–187, September 2017
2. Begel, A., Zimmermann, T.: Analyze this! 145 questions for data scientists in software engineering. In: Proceedings of the 36th International Conference on Software Engineering, ICSE 2014, New York, NY, USA, pp. 12–23. ACM (2014)
3. Gao, C., Wang, B., He, P., Zhu, J., Zhou, Y., Lyu, M.R.: PAID: prioritizing app issues for developers by tracking user reviews over versions. In: 2015 IEEE 26th International Symposium on Software Reliability Engineering (ISSRE), pp. 35–45, November 2015
4. Guzman, E., El-Haliby, M., Bruegge, B.: Ensemble methods for app review classification: an approach for software evolution (n). In: 2015 30th IEEE/ACM International Conference on Automated Software Engineering (ASE), pp. 771–776, November 2015
5. Guzman, E., Maalej, W.: How do users like this feature? A fine grained sentiment analysis of app reviews. In: 2014 IEEE 22nd International Requirements Engineering Conference (RE), pp. 153–162, August 2014
6. Hemmatian, F., Sohrabi, M.K.: A survey on classification techniques for opinion mining and sentiment analysis. Artif. Intell. Rev. (2017)
7. Johann, T., Stanik, C., Alizadeh M.B., Maalej, W.: SAFE: a simple approach for feature extraction from app descriptions and app reviews. In: 25th IEEE International Requirements Engineering Conference, RE 2017, Lisbon, Portugal, 4–8 Sept 2017, pp. 21–30 (2017)
8. Maalej, W., Kurtanović, Z., Nabil, H., Stanik, C.: On the automatic classification of app reviews. Requirements Eng. **21**(3), 311–331 (2016)
9. Maalej, W., Nabil, H.: Bug report, feature request, or simply praise? On automatically classifying app reviews. In: 2015 IEEE 23rd International Requirements Engineering Conference (RE), pp. 116–125, August 2015
10. Maalej, W., Nayebi, M., Johann, T., Ruhe, G.: Toward data-driven requirements engineering. IEEE Softw. **33**(1), 48–54 (2016)
11. Manning, C.D., Raghavan, P., Schütze, H.: Introduction to Information Retrieval. Cambridge University Press, New York (2008)
12. Martin, W., Sarro, F., Jia, Y., Zhang, Y., Harman, M.: A survey of app store analysis for software engineering. IEEE Trans. Softw. Eng. **43**(9), 817–847 (2017)

13. Morales-Ramirez, I., Muñante, D., Kifetew, F., Perini, A., Susi, A., Siena, A.: Exploiting user feedback in tool-supported multi-criteria requirements prioritization. In: 2017 IEEE 25th International Requirements Engineering Conference (RE), pp. 424–429, September 2017
14. Di Sorbo, A., Panichella, S., Alexandru, C.V., Visaggio, C.A., Canfora, G.: SURF: summarizer of user reviews feedback. In: 2017 IEEE/ACM 39th International Conference on Software Engineering Companion (ICSE-C), pp. 55–58, May 2017
15. Traynor, D.: How to make product improvements, August 2018. https://www.intercom.com/blog/ways-to-improve-a-product/
16. Vu, P.M., Nguyen, T.T., Pham, H.V., Nguyen, T.T.: Mining user opinions in mobile app reviews: a keyword-based approach (t). In: 2015 30th IEEE/ACM International Conference on Automated Software Engineering (ASE), pp. 749–759, November 2015
17. Vu, P.M., Pham, H.V., Nguyen, T.T., Nguyen, T.T.: Phrase-based extraction of user opinions in mobile app reviews. In: 2016 31st IEEE/ACM International Conference on Automated Software Engineering (ASE), pp. 726–731, September 2016

Requirements Monitoring

Supporting the Selection of Constraints for Requirements Monitoring from Automatically Mined Constraint Candidates

Thomas Krismayer[✉], Peter Kronberger, Rick Rabiser, and Paul Grünbacher

Christian Doppler Laboratory MEVSS, Institute for Software Systems Engineering,
Johannes Kepler University Linz, Linz, Austria
thomas.krismayer@jku.at

Abstract. [**Context and Motivation**] Existing approaches, e.g., in the areas of specification mining and process mining, allow to automatically identify requirements-level system properties, that can then be used for verifying or monitoring systems. For instance, specifications, invariants, or constraints can be mined by analyzing source code or system logs. [**Question/Problem**] However, the usefulness of mining approaches is currently limited by (i) the typically high number of mined properties and (ii) the often high number of false positives that are mined from complex systems. [**Principal Ideas/Results**] In this paper, we present an approach that supports domain experts in selecting constraints for requirements monitoring by grouping, filtering, and ranking constraint candidates mined from event logs. [**Contributions**] Our tool-supported approach is flexible and extensible and allows users to experiment with different thresholds, configurations, and ranking algorithms to ease the selection of useful constraints. We demonstrate the usefulness and scalability of our approach by applying it to constraints mined from event logs of two complex real-world systems: a plant automation system and a cyber-physical system controlling unmanned aerial vehicles.

Keywords: Requirements monitoring · Specification mining · Constraint selection

1 Introduction

Requirements monitoring approaches [14,17] have been successfully used to continuously check the adherence of systems to their specification during operation. However, such approaches rely on manually specifying requirements-level system properties, which is a challenging problem for complex and continuously evolving systems.

Researchers from different areas have thus proposed approaches to automatically or semi-automatically extract such properties, e.g., in the form of constraints, invariants or validity rules, by analyzing source code or outputs of

© Springer Nature Switzerland AG 2019
E. Knauss and M. Goedicke (Eds.): REFSQ 2019, LNCS 11412, pp. 193–208, 2019.
https://doi.org/10.1007/978-3-030-15538-4_15

software systems. Automatic extraction of system properties does not preclude manual definition, but can also be used to find additional properties that human experts did not think of. In the field of specification mining [9] static approaches use the source code of a program to detect invariants [15,20], while dynamic mining approaches analyze the output of the program, e.g., log statements, to derive specifications [5,8]. Approaches in the area of process mining [11,16] automatically generate models of existing processes, e.g., in the form of Petri nets, by analyzing (event) logs. In our own research we have developed a 5-step approach [6,7] for mining different types of constraints from event logs recorded in systems of systems to support requirements monitoring.

The usefulness of mining approaches, however, is typically challenged by the high number of mined properties and the high number of false positives. Constraints are only considered for monitoring if they describe something that can occur at runtime and are deemed as relevant by a domain expert. Users thus need to review many constraint candidates to select the ones that really need to be monitored.

In our earlier work on constraint mining [6,7] we presented a mining algorithm that also included preliminary support for ranking and filtering. During experiments with this approach on real-world systems we found that more advanced filtering and ranking techniques are required and we also received the feedback that similar constraints should be presented together. In this paper, we therefore present a significantly improved and extended approach to support domain experts by filtering, grouping, and ranking constraint candidates mined for requirements monitoring. We also present a tool supporting all stages of the mining process. It allows users to experiment with different parameters, configurations, and algorithms, to eventually select constraints for monitoring. We demonstrate the usefulness and scalability of our approach by applying it to constraints mined from event logs of two real-world systems – a plant automation software system [13] and a cyber-physical system controlling unmanned aerial vehicles (i.e., drones) [1] – and by collecting feedback from domain experts of these systems.

2   Running Example

We use the Dronology system by Cleland-Huang et al. [1] as a running example to illustrate key concepts of our approach. Dronology controls a group of drones and ensures that the drones operate as expected during their missions. The full behavior of complex software-intensive systems such as Dronology emerges during operation only, when the involved systems interact with each other and with their environment. Dronology thus relies on a runtime monitoring system that continuously checks important events for the involved drones. Our requirements monitoring approach [19], for instance, supports *temporal constraints* checking the occurrence, timing and order of events; *value constraints* checking the correctness of data related with events; and *hybrid constraints* combining the former two.

For instance, when a new drone connects to Dronology, a `handshake` event is sent containing the coordinates. Dronology then allows to assign routes to the connected drones, which are executed one after the other. During these flights each drone sends events to the ground station reflecting the progress on the assigned route. The events `startRoute` and `endRoute` represent the start and end of the execution of a route. A `waypoint` event is sent when the drone reaches one of the defined points of the current route. `startRoute`–`waypoint`–`endRoute` thus constitute a typical event sequence type (pattern) in Dronology. Additionally, a drone sends `state` events – approximately once per second – to report its position, speed, attitude, battery status, flight mode, etc.

We describe three examples of requirements (R1–R3) that are related with these events and can be expressed and formalized as constraints (cf. #1, #4, and #7 shown in Fig. 1):

R1. Drones have to complete the routes they are assigned in a given time. This can be defined as a temporal constraint (#1) checking that after the `startRoute` event occurred, the events `waypoint` and `endRoute` occur within 5 min.

R2. While a drone is flying on a route, its altitude has to be within a certain range to prevent it from crashing. The value constraint #4, for instance, checks if the flying altitude of the drone is between 5 and 30 m.

R3. When a new drone connects to the system, it has to be on the ground to wait for commands. The hybrid constraint #7 therefore checks after a `handshake` event, if the `status` reported in the next `state` event is STANDBY.

Temporal, value, and hybrid constraints all define an explicit trigger event type and one or multiple conditions. During requirements monitoring the conditions are evaluated as soon as an event of the trigger event type occurs [13].

3   Background: Our Constraint Mining Approach

In our own research we developed a 5-step approach [6,7] for mining different types of constraints for requirements monitoring by analyzing events and event data recorded from systems of systems. The final step of our approach also provided preliminary support for filtering and ranking. This paper presents more advanced algorithms for filtering, ranking, and grouping as well as tool support for the mining process. Here we briefly introduce the constraint mining approach, which is the basis for our approach presented in Sect. 4.

Step 0: Creating a Uniform Event Representation. In this preparatory step, the input event logs are parsed to an event object structure to make our approach independent of the type and format of the inputs. Our approach is not limited to simple logs with events having just a name (description) and a timestamp. Instead, events can contain additional data elements storing information such as sensor values, status information, or settings characterizing process execution (cf. the data elements described in R2 and R3). This information can often also be used to infer the type and provenance of events (i.e., their "scope" [18]). For instance, each drone is represented as a separate scope.

Step 1: Detecting Event Sequences. Our mining approach first detects event sequence types within the event log. Analyzing such sequences already allows to mine temporal constraints on event occurrence, order, and timing. First, sequence detection is performed for each scope independently. Our algorithm extracts sequence fragments, i.e., frequently co-occurring pairs of events between any two event types from this scope. For this purpose, we analyze the ratio of each pair of event types A and B by checking for each two consecutive events of type A (A_n and A_{n+1}), whether an event of type B occurred in between. We then calculate the ratio of co-occurrences for all pairs of events from the same scope. If this ratio exceeds a configurable threshold, A–B is considered a sequence fragment. In our running example both startRoute–waypoint and startRoute–endRoute form a sequence fragment. The sequence fragments are then combined such that the average time of the resulting sequence is minimal. Constraint #1 shown in Fig. 1 is an example of a constraint that could be mined in the first step.

Our algorithm then searches for events from other scopes that can be fit into the already extracted sequences. In addition to event sequence types containing multiple event types occurring in a given order, we also create event sequence types for individual events.

After detecting the event sequence types, we extract the individual event sequence instances (i.e., events that together match the event sequence type pattern) from the recorded event log. Additionally, we compute the time between the first and the last event of each sequence instance to estimate the maximum time for the temporal constraint that is generated from the respective event sequence type. We also remove outliers, i.e., event sequence instances that take significantly longer than the majority of the instances.

Step 2: Creating Feature Vectors. For each extracted event sequence instance our approach then generates a feature vector containing all event data elements and their values from the respective events in the sequence instance. During the mapping of sequence instances to feature vectors our algorithm aims to find data elements that contain the same value in all event sequences. These values can be assumed to remain unchanged for further runs and are thus extracted as value constraint candidates. We extract constant data element values that do not belong to the trigger event as candidates for both value constraints and hybrid constraints. The reason is that the event might also occur independently from this sequence, possibly with different data element values. An example for a hybrid constraint mined in step 2 is constraint #7 shown in Fig. 1.

Step 3: Analyzing Feature Vectors. We next analyze the distribution of non-constant values in the feature vectors. For numeric event data elements we extract an interval that contains all observed values. For example, the data element loc.z in waypoint–events, which contains the height of the drone, contains only values between 5 and 30. We can therefore extract constraint #4 shown in Fig. 1. Additionally, our algorithm detects multiple data elements – potentially from different events – that have the same value in each feature vector, e.g., an identifier. We can therefore create a constraint candidate checking that these data elements have the same value for all future logs.

We also extract all event data elements that have a constant value for a majority of all sequences. The threshold for the extraction, i.e., the percentage of sequences that can have a different value, is set to the threshold ϵ for constraints to be kept during filtering (cf. Sect. 4). If the data element does not belong to the first event of the sequence, the constraint is mined both as a value constraint and a hybrid constraint referring to the first event of the sequence, as also done for constant values in Step 2.

4   Filtering, Grouping, and Ranking Constraint Candidates

For complex software systems our constraint mining approach potentially detects a large number of constraint candidates. While many candidates can be removed from the list automatically, e.g., by removing duplicates, the selection of constraint candidates cannot be fully automated and will always rely on domain knowledge. Our constraint mining approach outlined in Fig. 1 thus provides filtering, grouping, and ranking strategies to support end users in selecting the relevant constraints from the candidates.

4.1   Constraint Filtering

The aim of the first step is to reduce the overall number of constraint candidates that are presented to the end user. For this purpose, we implemented different automatic and semi-automatic filters. Our tool implementation additionally provides an API allowing to add additional filtering algorithms (cf. Sect. 4.4).

Automatic Constraint Filtering. We provide two different automatic strategies to get rid of irrelevant constraint candidates: (i) filtering constraints that violate frequently; and (ii) finding highly similar constraints to keep just the most relevant candidate.

The first automatic filter drops frequently violating constraints, which typically indicate exceptions and problems. Such constraints are rarely selected by users. Our algorithm filters all constraints, which exceed a defined error rate ϵ for the complete input event log. A too high error rate would overly reduce the number of candidates, while a too low error rate would keep too many false positives. In our experiments we set ϵ to one third, which worked well for our datasets. Using this error rate, for example, the sixth constraint candidate in Fig. 1, which is only fulfilled for 40% of all state events in the event log, would be removed from the list. This constraint has been extracted during step 2 for the sequence handshake–state (cf. Sect. 3), but cannot be generalized to all state-events.

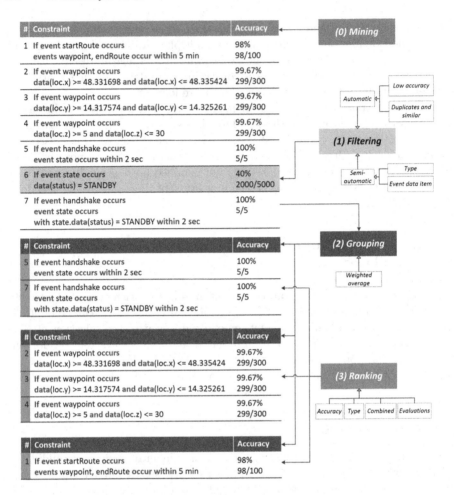

Fig. 1. Our approach for filtering, grouping, and ranking constraint candidates. The constraints are defined in a domain-specific language (DSL) described in [13].

The second automatic filter removes redundant constraint candidates before presenting them to the user. Specifically, our algorithm detects and filters duplicate constraints and constraints that refer to the same event data element. Duplicates are created, e.g., if a constraint for an event data element is found for a sequence and for the individual event (cf. Steps 2 and 3 in Sect. 3). Multiple different constraints can be found for the same event data element because our algorithm mines both value constraints checking constants and intervals, and hybrid constraints checking, e.g., a certain value across a sequence of events. Our automatic filtering algorithm thus decides which constraints to keep and which to discard based on (i) the constraint type—thereby keeping more general constraints as well as (ii) based on the percentage of sequences for which it evaluates to true—thus keeping constraints with higher accuracy. For instance, value constraints that can be evaluated for every event are preferred over hybrid constraints that can only be evaluated after a specific other event. In case of doubt, e.g., if the accuracy of a hybrid constraints is only slightly higher than the accuracy of a value constraint, we keep both and let the user decide.

Semi-automatic Constraint Filtering. In addition to the (configurable) automatic filtering, we also allow to filter constraint candidates matching user-defined rules. For instance, a user may decide to only consider temporal constraints or to filter constraints referring to certain fields that should be ignored. So far, we have implemented two different semi-automatic constraint filters: one based on the constraint type and the other based on the names of event data fields appearing in the constraint. The event data fields are stored in JSON format in our approach, which allows the second filter to target also groups of event data fields besides specific data fields. For example, it is possible to filter all constraints on drone location information by filtering for event data items with "location" as one of their JSON path parts. This filter would, for instance, remove constraints #2, #3, and #4 shown in Fig. 1, if desired by the user.

4.2   Constraint Grouping

The remaining constraint candidates can automatically be arranged into groups of similar constraints. Grouping is intended to streamline the selection or rejection of similar constraints. Correctly grouped constraint candidates allow a user, for example, to easily reject all constraint candidates related to a wrongly detected sequence or an irrelevant event type.

The similarities between all pairs of constraint candidates are calculated based on several weighted parts: the trigger event type, the constraint type, the event sequence, the event data item names, and the event data item values. The similarity between two constraint candidates is computed as the weighted average of these parts. From these similarities the groups are formed such that the similarity between any two constraint candidates in the group is above a configurable threshold.

For example, constraints #5 and #7 in Fig. 1 have the same trigger event type (`handshake`) and event sequence (`handshake – state`), but different constraint types: constraint #7 is a hybrid constraint that refers to data item `status`, while constraint #5 is a sequence constraint that does not check any data item. Constraint #2, #3, and #4 also have the same trigger event type and event sequence, but additionally have the same constraint type (value constraint). While they all refer to a location-related event data item, the exact name and values of the event data items are different.

Grouping the constraints from Fig. 1 by only using the trigger event, i.e., setting all other weight factors to 0, thus results in the groups [1], [2, 3, 4], and [5, 7]. Please note that constraint candidate #6 is already removed during filtering and thus not part of any group.

4.3   Constraint Ranking

Before presenting the remaining constraint candidates to the user, they are ranked to show the ones on top that are more likely to be accepted. For this purpose, our approach offers four ranking algorithms based on accuracy, constraint type, and combinations of them. New algorithms can be added using our API as described in Sect. 4.4.

Ranking Based on Accuracy. For this strategy, the rank is primarily based on the ratio between the number of times a given constraint evaluates to true and the total number of evaluations for this constraint within the complete event log. If the computed accuracy is equal for two constraint candidates, they are ranked based on the absolute number of event sequences for which the constraint evaluates to true. Candidates with higher accuracy receive a better rank.

Ranking Based on Constraint Type. Since temporal constraints represent the behavior of the software system to be monitored they are more likely to be included than the often very specific data checks. This algorithm therefore ranks temporal constraint candidates highest, followed by hybrid constraints, and then value constraints.

Combined Ranking. The third algorithm combines the first two ranking algorithms, i.e., it ranks the constraint candidates based on the average rank calculated from the rankings based on accuracy and type.

Ranking Based on Evaluations. The final ranking algorithm combines the accuracy and the relative number of positive evaluations (i.e., constraints evaluating to true) on the input dataset. The latter is the fraction of the number of positive evaluations for the given constraint candidate and the highest number of positive evaluations for any of the candidates in the list. If grouping is used, our approach ranks the groups rather than the individual constraints. This is done by ranking the constraint candidates from each group individually and then ranking the groups based on the highest ranked constraint candidate of each group.

4.4   Tool Support

We have implemented our filtering, grouping, and ranking algorithms in Java and provide an API that allows configuring all thresholds and factors influencing the calculations. New filtering or ranking algorithms or grouping factors can easily be added by implementing an interface.

We have also implemented a wizard-based interface (cf. Fig. 2) supporting end users in the mining process. This tool allows users to select the event logs to be analyzed, to (optionally) configure all stages of the mining process, and to review the constraint candidates for selection. In the tool, users can experiment with the different ranking and grouping algorithms and search in the list of candidates. They can also make minor adaptations to constraint candidates, e.g., to change the value or operator used in a value constraint. It is possible

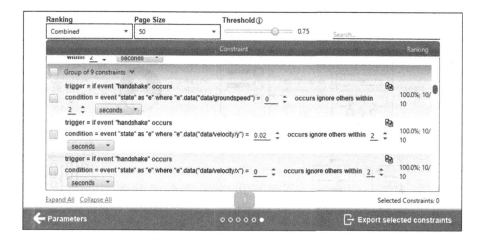

Fig. 2. End-user tool support for selecting constraints.

to select individual constraints or whole groups of constraints, which are then exported to text files that can be imported in a monitoring tool, e.g., our own monitoring tool REMINDS [19].

5   Evaluation

Our research method is shown in Fig. 3. We mined constraints from two datasets recorded from two different systems. The first dataset includes events monitored from an industrial plant automation system of our industry partner Primetals Technologies [13]. The second dataset contains events from a cyber-physical system controlling small unmanned aerial vehicles using the Dronology framework [1], already briefly explained when introducing our running example. We presented a list containing all the constraint candidates mined by our approach to a domain expert of each of these systems to select the constraints useful for monitoring. Additionally, we asked them to provide qualitative feedback and, in a follow-up step, to group the constraint candidates. Specifically, we investigated the following two research questions:

RQ1: How useful are the presented filtering, grouping, and ranking algorithms? We asked the domain experts to rate the mined constraints using the options *yes* ("I would select this mined constraint to be monitored at runtime for my system"), *yes, with minor changes* ("I would select this constraint after minor changes, e.g., of certain parameters or operators defined in the constraint"), and *no* ("I would not select this constraint"). For our experiments we treat all constraints rated with *yes* or *yes with minor changes* as relevant and all candidates rated with *no* as not relevant. We also rate constraints marked with *yes with minor changes* as useful, because these minor changes can easily be made when selecting useful constraints in our tool (cf. Sect. 4.4). For RQ1, we checked how many of the useful constraints, i.e., rated with *yes* or *yes with minor changes*,

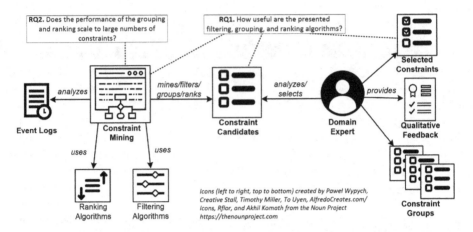

Fig. 3. Our research method.

were within the first ten, respectively, first twenty entries of the ranked list. To experiment with our different ranking algorithms, we ranked the lists differently, using the strategies described in Sect. 4.3. To compare the effectiveness of our ranking algorithms we report the precision (PR), recall (RE), and F_1 scores for the first ten and the first twenty entries of the ranked list for our datasets.

$$PR = \frac{\text{selected relevant}}{\text{selected}} \quad RE = \frac{\text{selected relevant}}{\text{relevant}} \quad F_1 = 2 * \frac{PR * RE}{PR + RE}$$

To evaluate the grouping algorithm we additionally asked the domain experts to manually group the complete list of constraint candidates. We then applied our grouping algorithm and compared how well they matched the grouping preferred by the experts. We again report the precision, recall, and F_1 scores.

RQ2: Does the performance of the grouping and ranking scale to larger numbers of constraints? We measured the execution time of our grouping and ranking approach for different, randomly generated constraint sets of different size. These experiments were performed on a computer equipped with an Intel® Core™ i7-6700 processor and 16 GB RAM, with 8 GB of memory given to the evaluation runs.

5.1   Datasets

For the first dataset engineers at Primetals Technologies used REMINDS [19] to record a 24-hour event log from an automation system running in a metallurgical plant in China during production. Specifically, the events were recorded from the Quality Control System (QCS) that collects and analyses data from different processes within a metallurgical plant. The dataset contains a total of 18,239 events with 35 different event types from four different scopes. Our constraint mining approach found 34 constraints of which 14 (41%) were regarded as useful by the domain expert [6]. One of the reasons for rating constraints as not useful were sequences of randomly co-occurring events. Similarly, several constraints checking the equality of event data items from different events were rated as not useful.

The second dataset contains events from the Dronology system [1]. To create our dataset, we used two pre-defined scenarios, in which five drones performed a total of 105 flights in the simulator. The Dronology simulator allows to experiment with drones using exactly the same control software system, but not the actual hardware. The scenarios were designed together with a domain expert. In the first scenario, two drones are used to deliver items from a central warehouse to one of ten different customer locations and return back to the warehouse. In the second scenario, three drones perform random aerial maneuvers at a flight field. Both scenarios are executed at the same time with the same type of drones. The Dronology dataset contains a total of 15,200 events with five different event types from five different scopes (i.e., the five different drones). For this dataset 50 constraints were mined of which 27 (54%) were rated as useful [6]. The constraints rated as not useful were, e.g., checking events that usually occur after each other, but are not actually connected. We also found two constraints that resulted from event data items, that were set to wrong values by the simulator and are therefore not useful for actual monitoring.

We cannot publish the QCS dataset due to non-disclosure agreements. The Dronology dataset is available at http://mevss.jku.at/?attachment_id=3056.

5.2   Filtering and Ranking

To address our first research question, we conducted experiments to compare the four ranking approaches, i.e., accuracy, type, combined, and evaluations (cf. Sect. 4.3), based on what constraint candidates the domain expert regarded as useful.

The QCS dataset also includes a total of eleven constraint candidates regarded as useful by the domain expert, but too similar to other useful constraints in the candidate list. For the ranking we therefore only considered the highest-ranked constraint candidate of each of these groups of similar candidates as relevant. All subsequent candidates were regarded as not relevant. We also excluded seven constraint candidates from the Dronology dataset, that could neither be classified as relevant nor as not relevant by the domain expert.

The results for both, the QCS and Dronology datasets can be seen in Table 1. When using only the ten highest-ranked list entries, the type-based and the combined ranking strategy gain a much higher F_1 measure for the QCS datasets, while the accuracy-based and evaluations-based strategies reach a higher F_1 score for the Dronology dataset. One reason for the lower values is that ten selected constraint candidates are just too few (especially compared to the 27 useful constraints of the Dronology dataset) – leading to low recall values.

Table 1. Precision, recall, and F_1 scores of different ranking algorithms (RQ1).

Data	Algorithm	PR_{10}	RE_{10}	$F_{1;10}$	PR_{20}	RE_{20}	$F_{1;20}$
QCS	Acc.	0.2	0.143	0.167	0.45	0.643	0.529
	Type	0.7	0.5	0.583	0.55	0.786	0.647
	Comb.	0.7	0.5	0.583	0.5	0.714	0.588
	Eval.	0.4	0.286	0.333	0.45	0.643	0.529
Dronology	Acc.	0.8	0.296	0.432	0.65	0.481	0.553
	Type	0.4	0.148	0.216	0.5	0.37	0.425
	Comb.	0.5	0.185	0.27	0.7	0.519	0.596
	Eval.	0.8	0.296	0.432	0.75	0.556	0.638

Consequently, the F_1 measure for all algorithms increases for both datasets on the 20 top-ranked candidates compared to the top ten. For the 20 highest-ranked constraint candidates the F_1 measure is highest for the evaluations-based strategy for the Dronology set. For the QCS all strategies gain relatively high results, with the type-based strategy performing best.

We conclude that the ranking algorithms can indeed support the user in selecting constraints. Specifically, presenting the top 20 constraint candidates led to high results for both datasets. Reviewing 20 constraint candidates also is a realistic task for a user according to our domain experts. For the two datasets different algorithms perform best, which further hints that allowing the user to choose the ranking strategy, just like we support with our tool (cf. Sect. 4.4), can be very helpful.

5.3 Grouping

To evaluate the grouping algorithm we asked each domain expert to manually group all constraint candidates mined from the respective dataset. We initially grouped the constraint candidates based only on the trigger event type to aid the experts in their task. This can be achieved by setting all weight factors (cf. Sect. 4.2) other than the trigger event factor to zero.

The domain expert from Primetals Technology deemed the default grouping based solely on the trigger event most useful. For the 34 mined constraints this approach resulted in eleven groups with one to seven constraints per group.

For the Dronology dataset the domain expert grouped the constraints based on a more complex rule set. This was necessary, because this dataset contained fewer event types and grouping based on only the trigger event would have led to large groups with up to 19 quite diverse constraint candidates. The expert grouped the constraint candidates first based on the trigger event type and then split these groups further depending on the constraint type and the event data elements. Following this strategy we set the weight for the trigger event in the similarity calculation to three, the weight for the constraint type to two, and the weight for the event data item to one. Using the default grouping threshold of

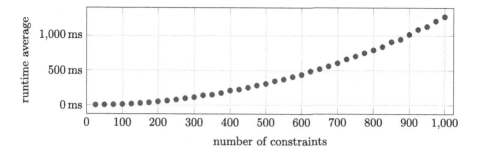

Fig. 4. Average runtime of grouping and ranking (RQ2).

0.75, this resulted a F_1 measure of 0.75 – with precision 0.612 and recall 0.968. This demonstrates the feasibility of our grouping algorithm. Based on our API, more specific grouping algorithms, e.g., better fitting the Dronology case, can easily be added.

5.4 Performance of Grouping and Ranking

To assess the performance and scalability of our grouping and ranking algorithms, we generated random sets of constraints for which we compared the average runtime of the grouping and ranking. Specifically, we created sets with 25 to 1,000 constraints – in steps of 25 constraints. The constraints were randomly distributed on sequence, value, and hybrid constraints (with equal probability) and all the event and field names were chosen randomly from ten different names.

For each of the sets we used our grouping and ranking approach and recorded their runtime. To ensure that all parts for the similarity calculation are used, we set all factors for the weighted average to one. For the ranking we used the combined ranking approach, which has the highest runtime, as it computes and combines both the type-based and accuracy-based ranking.

We repeated this process ten times to balance out variations in the runtime. To reduce the influence of the warm-up time of the Java VM, we included an additional run at the beginning, that was not considered for the calculations. We report the average runtime in Fig. 4.

The grouping algorithm calculates the similarity between all pairs of constraints, i.e., n^2 similarity scores for n constraints. As a result a quadratic increase in runtime had to be expected. The average runtime for the grouping and ranking of 1,000 constraints is 1,276 ms. In our experiments we mined 34 and 50 constraints for the QCS and the Dronology datasets; for this number of constraints the ranking and grouping takes on average only 3 ms.

5.5 Threats to Validity

A threat to the validity of our results is that we rely on feedback from domain experts from the systems we investigated. However, each domain expert is the main developer of the respective system and thus most appropriate for assessing our filtering, ranking, and grouping algorithms. We thus think that our evaluation is suitable to demonstrate the usefulness of our approach.

One additional threat for our experiments is that we only used two different systems – too few to make claims on the generalizability of our approach. The two examples we used, however, are very different from each other and both are complex, real world systems.

Regarding the performance evaluation of our grouping and ranking algorithms, a quadratic complexity might seem problematic. However, it still took only about one second to rank and group 1,000 constraints, which means that the performance is more than sufficient for practical purposes and for allowing an interactive use of the tool. Also, users would not want to look through a list of 1,000+ constraints in practice anyway.

6   Related Work

There is a large body of work on algorithms for sorting [2] and clustering [21] data. Especially with the advent of big data and the related field of data analytics, filtering, grouping, clustering, and ranking data has become ever-more challenging and important [4]. Our goal was not to re-invent the wheel, but to apply existing algorithms to our use cases in requirements monitoring. Here we describe existing research that also investigated this issue.

For instance, many existing specification mining approaches include some form of ranking or filtering, mostly filtering constraints with a low rank. Narayan et al. [12] use an accuracy-based ranking component and remove all mined constraints with an accuracy below a threshold, which is set close to 100%. The approach by Weimer and Necula [20] detects pairs of method calls that have to occur together (e.g., opening and closing a session) to find wrong usage within error-handling source code. This very specific use case also forces them to use multiple filters to, e.g., filter constraints that are never violated during error handling. Finally, they rank the remaining constraints based on their accuracy in non-error-handling source. While we also support ranking constraints based on accuracy, we provide additional filtering, ranking, and grouping algorithms.

The approaches by Lo and Maoz [10] and Lemieux et al. [8] both include filtering based on user-defined thresholds for accuracy ('confidence') and number of evaluations ('support'). We also present ranking strategies that include both of these numbers, but additionally combine them with other information such as constraint types.

The Daikon system [3] supports filtering very similar constraints (i.e., invariants referring to the same field with slightly different values) and invariants mined between incompatible abstract types. Our automatic filtering approach also includes filtering of similar constraints, but additionally detects similar constraints with different constraint types.

To the best of our knowledge there exists no approach or tool that also groups the mined constraints. Also, existing approaches typically do not focus on presenting mined constraints to domain experts and support them in the selection process.

7   Conclusions

We have presented a tool-supported approach that allows domain experts to filter, rank, group, and select constraints mined from event logs to support requirements monitoring at runtime. The approach is flexible and extensible, i.e., existing algorithms can be combined and configured in different ways and additional algorithms can easily be added. Our evaluation demonstrates that our existing algorithms are useful and scale for constraints mined from event logs of two complex real-world systems – a plant automation software system and a cyber-physical system controlling unmanned aerial vehicles. We also recently presented our tool to several potential users of our industry partner during a workshop and received very positive feedback. In the future we plan to apply our approach to further systems and perform a user evaluation with our tool. We also plan to investigate the possibility to use machine learning techniques to automatically detect the settings for ranking, filtering, and grouping algorithms.

Acknowledgments. The financial support by the Austrian Federal Ministry for Digital and Economic Affairs, the National Foundation for Research, Technology and Development, and Primetals Technologies is gratefully acknowledged.

References

1. Cleland-Huang, J., Vierhauser, M., Bayley, S.: Dronology: an incubator for cyber-physical systems research. In: Proceedings of the 40th International Conference on Software Engineering: New Ideas and Emerging Results, pp. 109–112. ACM (2018)
2. Cormen, T.H., Leiserson, C.E., Rivest, R.L., Stein, C.: Introduction to Algorithms. MIT Press, Cambridge (2009)
3. Ernst, M., et al.: The Daikon system for dynamic detection of likely invariants. Sci. Comput. Program. **69**(1), 35–45 (2007)
4. Fahad, A., et al.: A survey of clustering algorithms for big data: taxonomy and empirical analysis. IEEE Trans. Emerg. Top. Comput. **2**(3), 267–279 (2014)
5. Gabel, M., Su, Z.: Javert: fully automatic mining of general temporal properties from dynamic traces. In: Proceedings of the 16th ACM SIGSOFT International Symposium on Foundations of Software Engineering, pp. 339–349. ACM (2008)
6. Krismayer, T.: Automatic mining of constraints for monitoring systems of systems. In: Proceedings of the 33rd ACM/IEEE International Conference on Automated Software Engineering, pp. 924–927. ACM (2018)
7. Krismayer, T., Rabiser, R., Grünbacher, P.: Mining constraints for event-based monitoring in systems of systems. In: Proceedings of the 32nd IEEE/ACM International Conference on Automated Software Engineering, pp. 826–831. IEEE (2017)
8. Lemieux, C., Park, D., Beschastnikh, I.: General LTL specification mining (T). In: Proceedings of the 30th IEEE/ACM International Conference on Automated Software Engineering, pp. 81–92. IEEE (2015)

9. Lo, D., Khoo, S.C., Han, J., Liu, C.: Mining Software Specifications: Methodologies and Applications. CRC Press, Boca Raton (2011)

10. Lo, D., Maoz, S.: Scenario-based and value-based specification mining: better together. Autom. Softw. Eng. **19**(4), 423–458 (2012)

11. Maita, A.R.C., et al.: A systematic mapping study of process mining. Enterp. Inf. Syst. **12**(5), 505–549 (2018)

12. Narayan, A., Cutulenco, G., Joshi, Y., Fischmeister, S.: Mining timed regular specifications from system traces. ACM Trans. Embed. Comput. Syst. **17**(2), 46:1–46:21 (2018)

13. Rabiser, R., Thanhofer-Pilisch, J., Vierhauser, M., Grünbacher, P., Egyed, A.: Developing and evolving a DSL-based approach for runtime monitoring of systems of systems. Autom. Softw. Eng. **25**(4), 875–915 (2018)

14. Robinson, W.: A requirements monitoring framework for enterprise systems. Requirements Eng. **11**(1), 17–41 (2006)

15. Shoham, S., Yahav, E., Fink, S.J., Pistoia, M.: Static specification mining using automata-based abstractions. IEEE Trans. Softw. Eng. **34**(5), 651–666 (2008)

16. van der Aalst, W., et al.: Process mining manifesto. In: Daniel, F., Barkaoui, K., Dustdar, S. (eds.) BPM 2011. LNBIP, vol. 99, pp. 169–194. Springer, Heidelberg (2012)

17. Vierhauser, M., Rabiser, R., Grünbacher, P.: Requirements monitoring frameworks: a systematic review. Inf. Softw. Technol. **80**(December), 89–109 (2016)

18. Vierhauser, M., Rabiser, R., Grünbacher, P., Aumayr, B.: A requirements monitoring model for systems of systems. In: Proceedings of the 23rd IEEE International Requirements Engineering Conference, pp. 96–105. IEEE (2015)

19. Vierhauser, M., Rabiser, R., Grünbacher, P., Seyerlehner, K., Wallner, S., Zeisel, H.: ReMinds: a flexible runtime monitoring framework for systems of systems. J. Syst. Softw. **112**, 123–136 (2016)

20. Weimer, W., Necula, G.C.: Mining temporal specifications for error detection. In: Halbwachs, N., Zuck, L.D. (eds.) TACAS 2005. LNCS, vol. 3440, pp. 461–476. Springer, Heidelberg (2005)

21. Xu, R., Wunsch, D.: Survey of clustering algorithms. IEEE Trans. Neural Netw. **16**(3), 645–678 (2005)

Combining Monitoring and Autonomous Feedback Requests to Elicit Actionable Knowledge of System Use

Dustin Wüest[1]([✉]), Farnaz Fotrousi[2], and Samuel Fricker[1,2]

[1] Institute for Interactive Technologies,
FHNW University of Applied Sciences and Arts Northwestern Switzerland,
Windisch, Switzerland
{dustin.wueest,samuel.fricker}@fhnw.ch
[2] Software Engineering Research Laboratory (SERL-Sweden),
Blekinge Institute of Technology, Karlskrona, Sweden
{farnaz.fotrousi,samuel.fricker}@bth.se

Abstract. [**Context and motivation**] To validate developers' ideas of what users might want and to understand user needs, it has been proposed to collect and combine system monitoring with user feedback. [**Question/problem**] So far, the monitoring data and feedback have been collected passively, hoping for the users to get active when problems emerge. This approach leaves unexplored opportunities for system improvement when users are also passive or do not know that they are invited to offer feedback. [**Principal ideas/results**] In this paper, we show how we have used goal monitors to identify interesting situations of system use and let a system autonomously elicit user feedback in these situations. We have used a monitor to detect interesting situations in the use of a system and issued automated requests for user feedback to interpret the monitoring observations from the users' perspectives. [**Contribution**] The paper describes the implementation of our approach in a Smart City system and reports our results and experiences. It shows that combining system monitoring with proactive, autonomous feedback collection was useful and surfaced knowledge of system use that was relevant for system maintenance and evolution. The results were helpful for the city to adapt and improve the Smart City application and to maintain their internet-of-things deployment of sensors.

Keywords: Requirements monitoring · User feedback ·
Requirements elicitation · Smart city

1 Introduction

Software maintenance and evolution constitute a large part of the work of software engineers [1]. From a requirements engineering perspective, one of the goals is to gather user feedback about released software to identify user needs that can be translated into requirements for future releases [2]. Various efforts have been spent to monitor system use, elicit user feedback, and analyse the obtained data [3]. Common methods for gathering feedback are hotlines, email, contact forms, and ticket systems,

© Springer Nature Switzerland AG 2019
E. Knauss and M. Goedicke (Eds.): REFSQ 2019, LNCS 11412, pp. 209–225, 2019.
https://doi.org/10.1007/978-3-030-15538-4_16

feedback forms embedded in software, and user feedback mechanisms of app stores [2]. This data has been mined and analysed with the aim of extracting requirements [4].

In the context of a European-Asian innovation project, Wise-IoT (www.wise-iot.eu), we have implemented a FAME-like approach of system monitoring and feedback forms [5]. We aimed at understanding the problems of the developed prototype systems and identify opportunities to evolve them to increase value creation and quality-of-experience. The monitoring data turned out to be difficult to interpret, and the user feedback requests were disturbing for users [6] or lacked enough information about the context to which the feedback applied.

These challenges encouraged us to extend the FAME approach by combining system monitoring and user feedback with autonomously generated proactive requests for user feedback. We monitored the fulfilment of end-user goals with data gathered from internet-of-things (IoT) devices to detect whether users are in an interesting situation, such as having achieved a goal or having deviated from the pathway towards the goal. With this approach, we could issue requests for user feedback in a targeted way, making the feedback requests relevant for the concerned users and reducing our dependency on luck for useful feedback to be received.

In this paper, we present our approach of combining system monitoring with autonomously triggered user feedback and report on its evaluation in a Smart City application for parking management. The main research question for the evaluation was: *Do the combination of system monitoring and autonomously triggered user feedback provide added value to system evolution?* We were interested to see whether autonomous triggering of feedback requests allows eliciting requirements that would not have been identified by just using a passive monitoring and feedback collection approach.

The remainder of the paper is structured as follows. Section 2 gives an overview of related work and background. Section 3 presents the approach. Section 4 describes the evaluation. Section 5 presents the obtained monitoring and feedback data and answers the research question. Section 6 discusses the results. Section 7 concludes.

2   Combined Data Gathering for System Evolution

User requirements are changing, which is the primary driver for evolving a software system. Planning the system's evolution needs knowledge of when and what requirements have changed and how to enhance the system. The knowledge can be acquired by frequent observation or monitoring of how the system is used [7] and checking whether it meets the users' requirements [8].

Sometimes, engineers have assumptions of how a system should be evolved and take the proactive approach of implementing and validating a prototype that exposes the change to users at runtime [9]. These innovation experiments generate insight for testing the assumption and deciding whether the change should be sustained or abandoned [10]. Lean Start-up is an example of the innovation experiment method designed for small companies [11] and also adopted in large companies [12]. Critical for the success of innovation experiments is again the monitoring of the system use, e.g. to check the use of the innovation, and the collection of user feedback, e.g. to check whether the innovation generates value for users.

Monitoring the system use allows requirements engineers to determine whether and to what degree the implemented system is meeting its requirements at runtime [13]. The insertion of code or sensors into a running system allows the developers to continuously check the system health, observe users, record their activities and study the system's behaviour [14]. Such monitoring enables requirements engineers to detect requirements violations, e.g. system failures, and react fast to evolve the system [15]. Furthermore, observing the user activities, such as a sequence of feature usage, duration, and other contexts, enables requirements engineers to understand the user needs better [3]. However, such monitoring data alone might not directly show whether users are satisfied, what exactly users require, and what the details of the requirements are.

Feedback given by users is another source of information to understand user needs how satisfied the users are with the system [16]. Several feedback tools have been designed to collect such information with user feedback. These tools are either offered standalone or are embedded into the system [17, 18]. The feedback tools trigger feedback forms either by a user's request, e.g. pressing the feedback button, or by a system request, e.g. by an automatic pop-up window [19]. Such feedback forms enable users to communicate bug reports, feature requests, and praise [20]. The feedback may be collected as a simple combination of free text, selected categories, ratings, and screenshots with annotations [21, 22]. Regardless of the dialogue design, several studies describe challenges of analysing and interpreting user feedback, especially when information about the context is missing that the feedback applies to [2, 23].

Monitoring and user feedback collection at runtime together supports the communication of user needs while capturing information about the context. Seyff et al. proposed to connect user feedback with features of the user interface [17]. Fotrousi et al. proposed to correlate the users' Quality of Experience and with the system's Quality of Service [24]. Oriol et al. proposed a generic framework for combining the collection of feedback and monitoring data [5].

So far, the combination of monitoring and feedback has been validated with passively collected user feedback. While relevant insights could be generated, the passive approach limited developers in targeting feedback collection on interesting situations of system usage and generated the risk of collecting irrelevant or even fake feedback [25]. To avoid this problem, we rely on proactive, autonomous requests for user feedback when an interesting situation in the use of a system is detected.

3 Proactive, Autonomous Gathering of User Feedback

3.1 Control Loop

Our approach of eliciting and using monitoring and feedback data is based on the control loop for self-adaptive systems proposed by Cheng et al. [26]. The control loop allows collecting data, analysing that data with the help of rules or models of expected system usage, deciding how to act by interpreting these insights, and acting according to these decisions. A self-adaptive system fully automates this loop by examining, introspecting, and modifying itself at runtime. An evolving system keeps the engineers in the loop, allowing them to understand the system's achievements, problems, and needs for evolution.

Our approach can be used to build a control loop for a system to be evolved or maintained. The system may be a functional prototype or an operational system. The control loop spans the system runtime, the technical environment in which the system runs, the users of the system, and the engineers doing the development and maintenance.

The control loop is parametrised with the endpoints and model of the data that is to be collected for analysis and may include data from the system, e.g. generated by IoT sensors, data about the users, e.g. user preferences, and data generated as a result of user-system interaction, e.g. click-trails. The data parametrisation includes the definition of the questionnaires for collecting user feedback.

Another type of parametrisation concerns the analysis that is used to detect the interesting situations in which a proactive, autonomous request should be issued to a user for collecting feedback from that user. A there are many potential ways of defining the interestingness of such a situation, we have opted for a flexible plug-in approach. The currently developed plug-in assumes that a user tries to achieve a goal with a journey that can be expressed by a sequence of subgoals that the user will achieve while pursuing the goal.

We have defined interestingness of a situation with respect to the user's fulfilment of the goal and adherence to the journey: (a) the goal has been achieved and (b) the user has deviated from the following subgoal, or the goal if no subgoals remain, he was expected to achieve. We have implemented the goal monitoring based on the concepts suggested by Qian et al. [27]. This interpretation of interestingness allows asking the user to judge his satisfaction with the proposed goal and journey and offering rationales for the judgment and, if relevant, the deviations.

The start of journeys, the achievement of goals, and deviations from the journeys are offered to the engineer as a stream of insights. The insights are presented as structured and semantically annotated data that include collected supporting data and user feedback and are used by the engineer for further analysis and decision-making about system evolution and maintenance. The engineer may analyse the recently generated insights, for example as part of his continuous or daily system monitoring practice. The engineer may also decide to aggregate or correlate insights based on attributes of the data included in the included data.

The last step of the control loop, the evolution and maintenance of a system, is under the control of the engineer. Maintenance may be initiated if the insights indicate that something is wrong with the deployed system and needs fixing. Evolution may be initiated if important user needs or other opportunities for value creation are discovered and prioritised according to standard roadmapping and release planning activities [1].

3.2   Implementation

For implementing the feedback loop, we have developed a component, called SAR, that may be integrated into a software system and deployed for supporting the evolution of that system. SAR can be connected to streams of data from sensors and system monitors, thus supporting *data collection*. SAR can be instrumented with plugins with models of expected system use and rules for detecting fulfilment of usage goals or deviations from pathways towards achieving these goals, thus supporting *data analysis*. To support the interpretation of the analysis results, SAR can be instrumented with questionnaires to be triggered to obtain user feedback, thus completing data collection. SAR, finally, offers an insights stream that an engineer may subscribe, thus enabling the engineer to *decide how to act*. The engineer may then act with maintenance of the system and its components or by evolving the system as part of system development.

Figure 1 shows the integration of SAR into a system. The component may be integrated into a system that is to be maintained and evolved. SAR assumes the presence of a front-end application that offers a user interface for interacting with the users, a system back-end that offers system-specific data, and engineering tools for maintaining and evolving the system. In the current implementation, SAR offers libraries helping application developers to connect the front-end with SAR and expects a standard back-end interface, the Orion Context Broker (fiware-orion.readthedocs.io). It offers also an Orion interface that allows connecting engineering tools to the insights stream.

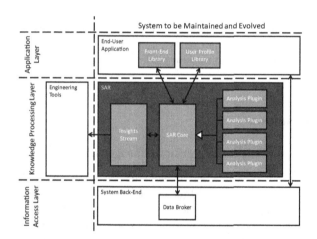

Fig. 1. Integration architecture (coloured: SAR, white: context into which SAR is integrated). (Color figure online)

The top layer is the *Application Layer*. It contains the end-user application and two front-end libraries that we developed to simplify the integration of the SAR component, taking care of all communication to the recommender via a RESTful API. The front-end library is an adaptation of the user feedback framework from the Supersede project (www.supersede.eu).

The bottom layer is the *Information Access Layer*. It contains third-party systems and services that provide IoT data to the recommender system and the end-user applications. The layer can also include third-party services, depending on the specific use case, e.g. a street map provider, or a routing framework. In the current implementation, SAR assumes that data is provided by a broker implementing the NGSI Open RESTful API (https://forge.fiware.org/plugins/mediawiki/wiki/fiware/index.php/FI-WARE_NGSI-9_Open_RESTful_API_Specification).

The middle layer is the *Knowledge Processing Layer*. It contains the parts of SAR that collect and process data to generate knowledge. SAR consists of multiple modules. Each module is a web service, some of them used as plug-ins with rules or models of expected system usage and functionality for analysing the collected data.

An essential plugin is the *System and Adherence Monitor*. It handles anonymous user sessions and monitors adherence to the recommendations provided to the user. It collects and combines user feedback with monitoring information and forwards the results to the insights stream.

The *Insights Stream* implements a publish-subscribe pattern to publish insights. An engineer may subscribe to the stream for obtaining monitoring data that is of interest, including measurements of the system behaviour, context, and usage and feedback of the users regarding their preferences, intentions, observations, and opinions. The stream is structured so that the engineer understands the relationships between the monitoring data and the user feedback. The tools used by the engineer to listen to the stream may be as simple as a logger that collects the insights in a format that may be inspected by an engineer. They may be as complex as a big data analytics tool that feeds packages of issues to development backlog management tools such as Atlassian Jira. Analysing the insights stream helps engineers to capture the users' needs and problems, which in turn can lead to short cycle times for improving and evolving the system.

4 Initial Evaluation

4.1 Smart City Application for Parking Management

We have evaluated our proactive, autonomous gathering of user feedback in a smart city prototype application for Android smartphones, called *Rich Parking*. The University of Cantabria (UC) had developed the application for the City of Santander in Spain. The application made use of thousands of IoT traffic and parking sensors that were deployed in the city of Santander and helped users find free parking spots within the city when they are travelling by car. Figure 2a shows a screenshot.

The application used a recommender system to generate recommendations of an unoccupied parking and a pathway to the recommended parking for end-users. The parking spot sensors provided data about the spots' current states (free/occupied) and allowed the app to display the free spots. Some of the streets contained sensors to measure traffic load and allowed the app to recommend routes that avoided traffic jams. Each recommendation consisted of a free parking spot and a fast route to the spot.

The UC team integrated our user feedback mechanism into their Android application using the front-end and user profiles libraries. We offered the SAR core as a service that we connected with the Smart City data broker from Santander using the NGSI API. For the UC team maintaining the Android application and for the Santander

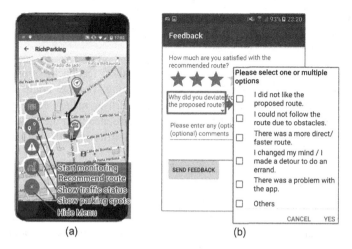

Fig. 2. Screenshots of (a) the Rich Parking application and (b) a feedback form.

team maintaining the Smart City infrastructure, we offered access to the Insights Stream using an own instance of the same NGSI API.

4.2 Parametrisation of the Control Loop

We parametrized the control loop to reveal issues with the Rich Parking application (e.g., usability problems, missing functionality), the parking and pathway recommender system (e.g., bad recommendations, slow performance), the behavior of the physical IoT devices (e.g., sensors delivering wrong values), and third-party software systems (e.g., outdated street map data).

To detect interesting situations, our system mapped the recommendation to a goal tree and monitored the user's adherence to the recommendation. The parking spot was the main goal, and each street segment of the route was a subgoal. When the users' GPS location matched with a street segment, the corresponding subgoal was set to *fulfilled*. Previous subgoals that were not already marked as *fulfilled* got marked as *skipped*. We specified the interesting situations as being those when subgoals were skipped, the user achieved the main goal, or abandoned it. In these situations, our goal monitor issued a feedback request tailored to the situation.

Based on the situation, the recommender system selected the feedback to be gathered from the user. One of the following three feedback forms was then displayed:

- Type 1, the user deviated from at least 50% of the pathway: the feedback form asked about the user's satisfaction with the recommended route (star rating) and the reasons for the deviation (multiple choice and free text answer). See Fig. 2b.
- Type 2, the user adhered to the pathway but selected a parking spot other than the recommended one: the feedback form asked about the user's satisfaction with the chosen spot (star rating) and the reasons for not taking the recommended parking spot (multiple choice and free text answer).

– Type 3, the users took the recommended spot: the form asked about the user's satisfaction with the recommended route and parking spot (star ratings) and offered to comment with a free text answer.

For the users' safety, we displayed the optional short feedback forms to the user only at the end of a session when the user stopped driving. The user could then rate her experience and provide reasons for the rating. If the user mainly followed the recommended route, the form asked about the user's experience with the parking spot she took. Otherwise, the form asked about the user's experience with the route and the reason for the deviation.

For providing anonymity and control of the data collection to the end-user, only sessions were tracked and only with a random ID. The user could decide to start the monitoring and whether she agreed to send her GPS data during the monitoring regularly. The session ended when the user parked the car or cancelled the monitoring.

All events, such as the creation of a session, the start and stop of the monitoring, the user feedback, and the monitoring result of each location comparison, got augmented with a timestamp and written into the insights stream. The structure of the insights stream used the session objects as the top-level entities. This structuring allowed combining the user feedback with the events that happen in the respective session. For example, when a user provides feedback about a route recommendation, we could compare the feedback with the actual route taken by that user.

4.3   Evaluation Setup and Method

The UC team initiated a pilot study to evaluate the Rich Parking application in Santander. In this context, we performed the first evaluation of our concept of combining system monitoring with autonomously triggered user feedback. Public meetings for citizens of Santander interested in IoT were held. The UC team informed the citizens about the evolution of Santander as a smart city and gave an overview of the most relevant projects, including Wise-IoT. The Rich Parking application was presented, and citizens could volunteer for the pilot study, given the prerequisite that they have an Android phone and a car. There was no reward for participants who agreed to test the application. The citizens who volunteered did so because of intrinsic motivation to help the city's evolution as a smart city. The pilot study lasted three months, from the end of February to the end of May 2018.

During the test phase of the pilot study, we were running a logger that listened to the insights stream and wrote the data from the stream into log files, one file per day. Once per month, manually analysed the log files and shared the main findings with the developers of the Rich Parking application.

Since we wanted to know whether the insights stream, i.e. the combination of system monitoring and proactively, autonomously gathered user feedback, could provide added value to system evolution, we were not merely observing during the three-month test phase but applied action research principles. The Spanish developers evolved the Rich Parking software and maintained the IoT-based smart city system. The application and its recommender system received two minor updates during the test phase.

When the test phase ended, we analysed the insights stream data. One goal of the insights stream was to support system evolution by helping engineers discover potential problems, user needs, and new requirements. Therefore, the stream should help to provide answers to engineering questions, such as: how satisfied are the users with the system? What are the issues that generate user churn? Table 1 shows the full list of questions.

Table 1. Summarised answers to the engineering questions for system evolution.

Engineer	Questions answered by analysing the insights stream
Application developer	**How satisfied are the users with the app and the information it offers?** Mediocre ratings for recommended routes and proposed parking spots **What are the issues that generate user churn?** Parking spots got occupied before the user arrives. Sensors showed free spots, but there was not enough space to park the car. Construction work blocked streets and parking spots **What are the preferences (likes, dislikes) of users?** Feedback in the insights stream shows what parking spots and routes received very good or bad ratings **What segments of the street map are incorrect?** Street segments with construction work not correctly marked as blocked **What Point-of-Interest information is incorrect?** Spaces between cars too small to park. Sensors between cars. Blocked spaces due to construction work
Smart city system engineer	**What is the users' trust rating in the IoT entities?** Mediocre ratings for the parking spots **What are the users' reasons for the trust ratings in the IoT entities?** Parking spots occupied, or not enough space to park the car **How credible are context information offered by the IoT entities?** The sensors worked fine but needed to see the size of the available spaces and see objects that are not placed directly on top of them

5 Results

5.1 Collected Data

41 citizens had registered and took part in the pilot study. A total of 303 sessions were created with recommendations for a route and parking spot. In 68 out of the 303 cases, users have started the session monitoring after receiving a recommendation. In 26 out of the 68 monitoring sessions, users allowed the mobile app to send their GPS positions to the system, enabling the system's adherence monitoring functionality. In ten out of these sessions (38.5%), the users have adhered to the recommended route (i.e., less than 50% of the user coordinates sent during the session were farther away from the recommended route than eight meters).

In 16 out of the 26 adherence-monitoring-enabled sessions, users submitted a feedback form. Seven of these forms were of type 1 concerning route deviations, five of type 2 concerning a parking spot deviation, and four of type 3 concerning a fulfilled recommendation.

We could not track users over multiple sessions due to the session-based privacy mechanism. We counted individual sessions instead. The users allowed the mobile app to send their GPS data in 38.2% of all monitoring sessions (26 out of 68). We considered this to be a good amount because some of the 68 monitoring sessions may have been started for testing the app functionality and not to go somewhere.

From the 26 sessions with user GPS data, we received 16 submitted feedback forms. This figure means that 61.5% of users who were presented with a feedback form decided to fill it out and submit it. If we consider all the sessions in which the monitoring has started, the ratio is 68/16 = 23.5%. Again, some of the sessions may have been started for testing the app functionality. We consider the 23.5% feedback ratio to be high in comparison to other feedback approaches or uses of surveys to collect feedback. The reason for this result could be that we kept the forms small and simple and that they were presented to the users in situations and with content that was relevant to them.

5.2   Data Analysis

The average user satisfaction rating of the parking spots was 2.125 and of the recommended routes was 2.071 out of 5 stars. We analysed the automatically collected user feedbacks for reasons why the scores were not higher and coded the free-text answers. Table 2 shows the resulting categories and number of answers in each category.

Table 2. Categorised user feedback from the free-text answers.

User feedback	Number of answers
The parking spot was occupied	6
There was a more direct or faster route	5
The parking spot was too small or the sensor in a bad location	5
The route or parking spot was blocked by construction work	2
The app was too slow or stalled	2
Found a free parking spot before arriving at the proposed one	1

To put the above feedback into context, we visualised the monitoring data on a map and added the feedback according to the GPS data of the users. Figure 3 shows the parking spots rated by the users, together with their feedback. It also shows one of the recommended routes and the corresponding route taken by the user.

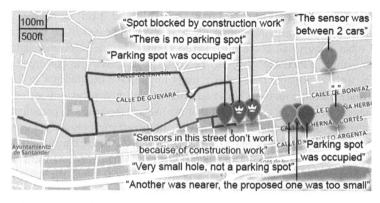

Fig. 3. Parking spot feedback (red: negative, red with crown: discussed in the text, green: positive). Blue line: a route recommended to a user. Violet line: route taken by that user. (Color figure online)

Despite the few user feedbacks received by the system, important issues could be identified with the analysis of the correlated monitoring and feedback data.

One feedback mentioned a blocked parking spot due to construction work and another a non-existent spot. When looking at the map, these two spots were close to each other (white crown markers). Also, a recommendation was leading to another spot nearby on the same street, and the user gave the feedback that the sensors on that street did not work because of construction work. The construction work in that street was an issue that was unveiled by combining user feedback and monitoring data.

The second group of red markers shows an accumulation of parking spots that were either occupied or too small. However, because of the few data points, we could not say whether this was a feature specific to that location, or whether this was a more general problem with the parking spots in the city. For example, one of the positively rated spots also received negative feedback (stating that the sensor was between two cars, which means that it was not possible to park there). But the green markers were both located in less crowded areas of the city, where the chance of finding a free spot was higher (whether it was the recommended one or another one close by).

Further, one user stated that no parking spot was available at the recommended location. However, the user's GPS data showed that the user never was in that location but went somewhere else instead. This observation is an example of how monitoring data can be used to verify the validity of user feedback. It seems that there was a different issue instead, e.g. the user may not have been able to read the map correctly.

5.3   Generated Insights

The analysis surfaced findings with a significant effect on the maintenance and evolution of the smart city system and the Rich Parking application.

Construction Work. Increasing construction work blocked streets and parking spots during the test phase. The recommender used an external street routing framework that was not updated with the construction work information in a timely fashion. Therefore, the recommender sometimes proposed routes with blocked street segments. The effect of increasing construction work during the trial phase appeared to be larger than the effects of other factors that could have led to improved route recommendations over time. 38.5% route adherence seems to be quite good, given the construction work problem as well as possible cases where users might have decided not to follow the proposed route for other reasons. However, this insight must be taken with care due to the low number of sessions and the fact that the users were aware of participating in a test, which could have biased them to follow the proposed routes eagerly. Furthermore, construction work could also have had a negative effect on the parking spot ratings. If a user gave a bad rating to a parking spot because it was lying inside a construction zone and thus not reachable, there was still a chance that next time, the system would propose one of the parking spots that are close to the badly rated spot and that are still located within the (same) construction zone.

Parking Sensors and Fluctuation in Parking Spot Availabilities. The system proposed parking spots to users that were unoccupied at the time when the user requested a recommendation. During high traffic, there was a good chance that another vehicle would park on the proposed spot before the user arrives. As a result, users may have experienced occupied spots and gave bad ratings. Vehicles were sometimes inaccurately placed on the parking sensors, in the worst case in the middle of two parking spots, and did not trigger the parking sensors. The insight implied that upgrading the hardware or updating the software is needed. An improvement to the software could be to let the recommender prioritise regions with large numbers of free parking spots or to introduce a reservation system. These issues pointed out by the insights stream could not be solved during the pilot phase. However, they provided developers with facts to think of how to improve the system.

Ratio Between User Ratings and Available Parking Spots. While we received nine user ratings about parking spots, the city of Santander contained hundreds of spots. The coverage of the city's parking spaces is relatively low. Broader use of the Smart City-generated IoT data is needed to generate insights for the totality of the city.

6   Discussion

6.1   Revisiting the Research Question

Our research question was: *do the combination of system monitoring and autonomously triggered user feedback provide added value to system evolution?* The initial evaluation of the proposed approach shows that we can answer our research question positively. The insights generated by the system have exposed important issues to the Rich Parking application and Smart City system engineers. The successful exposition and detection of these issues have set the control loop for system evolution in motion, which allows developers to come up with improved solutions [26].

The insights generated by combing monitoring data and autonomously gathered user feedback helped to answer the initially posed engineering questions, as Table 1 briefly summarizes. The insights could inform system evolution with advice for new features and how to enhance existing features: better parking sensors that can sense cars or obstacles that are not placed exactly on top of the sensors, a solution that takes into account the amount of fluctuation in the available parking spots, and a better synchronization of the routing framework with the real-world situation, maybe by connecting the system to the city's database with information about construction work or otherwise blocked streets. Also, knowing the context, which the user feedback applies to, allows adjusting the recommender to prefer less centrally located spots, or regions in which the density of free parking spots is higher. This modification could increase the probability for the user to find a free spot. These findings show the valuable outcome of combining monitoring data and autonomously gathered user feedback, which is also aligned with the research by Oriol et al. [5].

The combined analysis of monitoring and feedback data also allowed to identify two invalid user feedbacks: users who gave feedback about parking spots they never visited. Without the monitoring data, it would not have been possible to distinguish between valid and invalid feedback. This result shows that our proposed approach may be used to reduce the risk of collecting irrelevant or even fake feedback [25].

These findings were possible even though we had to make some compromises because of data privacy and because few users participated in the pilot and generated just a small number of feedbacks. User privacy implied that we were not allowed to identify or track users over multiple sessions. We had to introduce a random ID for each session and could only perform evaluations on a per-session rather than a per-user basis. The compromises, however, underline the effectiveness of proactive, autonomous gathering of user feedback for generating significant insights that can be translated into system maintenance and evolution actions.

Our approach targets the collection of user feedback on interesting situations of system use by basing the feedback requests on monitoring the fulfilment of user goal. This technique reduces the disturbance of users that is due to the feedback requests, but still requires feedback. In the presented use case, such disturbance could lead to accidents and, in the worst case, liability of the vendor for such an accident. We had chosen to avoid dangerous disturbance and ask users for feedback when they were in a safe situation after the experience. This delayed request for feedback may have been reducing the ability of the users to remember important details of the experience and produced ambiguity for understanding the context the feedback applies to. The insights generated about the monitored applications and systems may still be considered relevant. Earlier research showed that the disturbances have negligible impacts on the satisfaction level of the users with systems [6].

6.2 Discussion of the Results

One could argue that the issues found are to some extent obvious and that the same conclusions could be reached by "thinking hard" about the application. In retrospective, such sense-making is relatively easy. Identifying and expressing such issues in advance is difficult [28] and one of the reasons why requirements engineering is non-trivial. Our evaluation has shown an example of field testing of a prototype application and has shown that proactive, autonomous gathering of user feedback may be effective.

More lightweight approaches, such as questionnaires, may be used as an alternative or complement to elicit requirements [29]. With our approach, real system may be observed in use in the real environment and by real users. This gives the advantage that elicited input such as a feedback may be connected to a specific context, such as a physical location, time, or situation, where a system needs modification. Alternative elicitation approaches, such as surveys, would be too short in time, disturb many users, and would not allow understanding the contexts to which the users' feedbacks pertain.

In addition to being used during prototype development, our approach also has the advantage of being useful for a situation where a deployed system is evolved or maintained. With very little effort and cost, our approach allows continuously monitoring a system and warn support engineers for failures that result from the slow decay of the system that is being used often in situations where the context is changing. The availability of a development kit, outlined in Sect. 3.2, limits the effort of setting up the monitoring and feedback mechanism.

In comparison to bespoke methods, our approach also has the benefit that physical presence of an analyst or engineer is not required. It thus offers support and scales well in situations where the system is being deployed and used over geographical space. That has been the case for the Smart City application, where it would have been impractical to put a person on the side of the users.

The presented full automation of data collection, analysis, and streaming of insights may offer benefits beyond system maintenance and evolution. For example, the approach may be used by a system to self-adapt. Integration of the insights stream into a recommender system would allow the system to use the user feedback, ratings, and context data from the stream to improve future recommendations by automatically enhancing or discounting recommendation options. If some entities contained in the recommendations (such as points of interest) receive many bad user ratings, the recommender system may avoid recommendations with these entities in the future.

6.3   Threats to Validity

Conclusion Validity. We conducted a qualitative evaluation and did not focus on statistical significance, which can be seen as a threat. The number of logged sessions with GPS data was relatively small. However, the insights stream proved its usefulness by pointing out possibilities for system improvement which are valid for the involved group of users. The findings are in accordance with feedback given in the final survey conducted by the pilot partners.

Internal Validity. Due to the participant selection method, the participants had an interest in IoT that is above average. The participants could have been motivated to send GPS data or feedback just because they knew that they were part of a study. There is the possibility that the participants were friendlier than the average user. However, looking at the feedback ratings, we saw that they were not hesitant to give one-star ratings when they encountered a problem with a recommendation.

Construct Validity. The pilot has focused on the data collection and analysis steps of Chen's control loop. The short duration of the pilot period limited the ability to observe the decision-making and acting steps in the evaluation. A longer testing period would have allowed to include major software updates and measure their impact. Further, it needs to be noted that the feedback forms in the application focused on parking spot and route recommendations, and not on other aspects of the Smart City application and system. This focus could have held back participants from providing broader feedback.

Another concern is the construct of the interestingness of a situation. In the presented study, the interestingness was defined by asking developers for assumptions about what could go wrong, such as users not reaching the parking or being dissatisfied with it. This method depends much on human input, and it would be interesting to find methods to decide about interestingness in an automated manner. Using such triggers for the most "interesting situations" could allow reducing the need of disturbing the users, e.g. by reducing the number or frequency of feedback requests.

External Validity. So far, we have evaluated our concept in only one scenario with participants were interested in the scenario. Our results show the applicability of our method in systems that have a physical dimension, i.e. a city. They also show results that can be obtained with users that have a positive attitude, leaving the impact of neutral or negative users open. Generalization should be the subject of further evaluations.

7 Conclusion

We have presented an approach that combines system monitoring with proactive, autonomous user feedback collection. The approach offers automated collection of data from a runtime system and its users and analysis of that data to offer insights that support engineers in decision-making for system maintenance and evolution. We let our implementation of the approach be integrated in a pilot of a Smart City prototype application. The initial evaluation has shown that the approach was valuable for system evolution: the results were helpful for the Smart City Santander partners to adapt and improve their application as well as the IoT sensors deployed in the city. The evidence from the use case shows that our concept provides a systematic approach for gathering user needs, potential issues, and new requirements. Such an approach can be especially helpful for distributed systems and the IoT where it is difficult to localize the reasons for potential issues and weaknesses of the system.

Acknowledgment. Part of this work has been supported by the European Union's Horizon 2020 Research and Innovation Programme within the project WISE-IoT under the EU grant agreement No. 723156 and the Swiss SERI grant agreement No. 16.0062.

References

1. Kittlaus, H.-B., Fricker, S.: Software Product Management. Springer, Heidelberg (2017). https://doi.org/10.1007/978-3-642-55140-6
2. Stade, M., Fotrousi, F., Seyff, N., Albrecht, O.: Feedback gathering from an industrial point of view. In: IEEE 25th International Requirements Engineering Conference, Lisbon, Portugal (2017)
3. Maalej, W., Nyebi, M., Johann, T., Ruhe, G.: Toward data-driven requirements engineering. IEEE Softw. **33**(1), 48–54 (2016)
4. Guzman, E., Maalej, W.: How do users like this feature? A fine grained sentiment analysis of app reviews. In: 22nd International Requirements Engineering Conference (RE 2014), Karlskrona, Sweden (2014)
5. Oriol, M., Stade, M., Fotrousi, F., Nadal, S., Varga, J., Seyff, N., et al.: FAME: supporting continuous requirements elicitation by combining user feedback and monitoring. In: 26th International Requirements Engineering Conference (RE 2018), Lisbon, Portugal (2018)
6. Fotrousi, F., Fricker, S., Fiedler, M.: The effect of requests for user feedback on quality of experience. Softw. Qual. J. **26**(2), 385–415 (2018)
7. Chapin, N., Hale, J., Khan, K., Ramil, J., Tan, W.-G.: Types of software evolution and software maintenance. J. Softw. Maint. Evol.: Res. Pract. **13**(1), 3–30 (2001)
8. Fickas, S., Feather, M.: Requirements monitoring in dynamic environments. In: 2nd International Symposium on Requirements Engineering (RE 1995), York, U.K. (1995)
9. Ali, R., Dalpiaz, F., Giorgini, P., Souza, V.E.S.: Requirements evolution: from assumptions to reality. In: Halpin, T., et al. (eds.) BPMDS/EMMSAD -2011. LNBIP, vol. 81, pp. 372–382. Springer, Heidelberg (2011). https://doi.org/10.1007/978-3-642-21759-3_27
10. Bosch, J.: Building products as innovation experiment systems. In: Cusumano, Michael A., Iyer, B., Venkatraman, N. (eds.) ICSOB 2012. LNBIP, vol. 114, pp. 27–39. Springer, Heidelberg (2012). https://doi.org/10.1007/978-3-642-30746-1_3
11. Blank, S.: Why the lean start-up changes everything. Harvard Bus. Rev. **91**(5), 63–72 (2013)
12. Edison, H., Smørsgård, N., Wang, X., Abrahamsson, P.: Lean internal startups for software product innovation in large companies: enablers and inhibitors. J. Syst. Softw. **135**, 69–87 (2018)
13. Carreño, L., Winbladh, K.: Analysis of user comments: an approach for software requirements evolution. In: 35th International Conference on Software Engineering (ICSE 2013), San Francisco, CA, USA (2013)
14. Wellsandt, S., Hribernik, K., Thoben, K.: Qualitative comparison of requirements elicitation techniques that are used to collect feedback information about product use. In: 24th CIRP Design Conference, Milano, Italy (2014)
15. Leucker, M., Schallhart, C.: A brief account of runtime verification. J. Logic Algebraic Program. **78**(5), 293–303 (2009)
16. Knauss, E., Lübke, D., Meyer, S.: Feedback-driven requirements engineering: the heuristic requirements assistant. In: 31st International Conference on Software Engineering (ICSE 2009), Vancouver, British Columbia, Canada (2009)
17. Seyff, N., Ollmann, G., Bortenschlager, M.: AppEcho: a user-driven, in situ feedback approach for mobile platforms and applications. In: 1st International Conference on Mobile Software Engineering and Systems (MOBILESoft 2014), Hyderabad, India (2014)
18. Fotrousi, F., Fricker, S.: QoE probe: a requirement-monitoring tool. In: Requirements Engineering: Foundation for Software Quality (REFSQ 2016), Göteborg, Sweden (2016)
19. Maalej, W., Happel, H., Rashid, A.: When users become collaborators: towards continuous and context-aware user input. In: OOPSLA 2009, Orlando, FL, USA (2009)

20. Maalej, W., Nabil, H.: Bug report, feature request, or simply praise? On automatically classifying app reviews. In: 23rd International Requirements Engineering Conference (RE 2015), Ottawa, Ontario, Canada (2015)
21. Morales-Ramirez, I., Perini, A., Guizzardi, R.: An ontology of online user feedback in software engineering. Appl. Ontol. **10**(3–4), 297–330 (2015)
22. Elling, S., Lentz, L., de Jong, M.: Users' abilities to review web site pages. J. Bus. Tech. Commun. **26**(2), 171–201 (2012)
23. Pagano, D., Brügge, B.: User involvement in software evolution practice: a case study. In: 35th International Conference on Software Engineering (ICSE 2013), San Francisco, CA, USA, pp. 953–962 (2013)
24. Fotrousi, F., Fricker, S.A., Fiedler, M.: Quality requirements elicitation based on inquiry of quality-impact relationships. In: 22nd IEEE International Conference on Requirements Engineering, Karlskrona, Sweden (2014)
25. Dalpiaz, F.: Social threats and the new challenges for requirements engineering. In: 1st International Workshop on Requirements Engineering for Social Computing (RESC 2011), Trento, Italy (2011)
26. Cheng, B.H.C., et al.: Software engineering for self-adaptive systems: a research roadmap. In: Cheng, B.H.C., de Lemos, R., Giese, H., Inverardi, P., Magee, J. (eds.) Software Engineering for Self-Adaptive Systems. LNCS, vol. 5525, pp. 1–26. Springer, Heidelberg (2009). https://doi.org/10.1007/978-3-642-02161-9_1
27. Qian, W., Peng, X., Wang, H., Mylopoulos, J., Zheng, J., Zhao, W.: MobiGoal: flexible achievement of personal goals for mobile users. IEEE Trans. Serv. Comput. **11**(2), 384–398 (2018)
28. Ericsson, K.A., Simon, H.A.: Verbal reports as data. Psychol. Rev. **87**(3), 215–251 (1980)
29. Zowghi, D., Coulin, C.: Requirements elicitation: a survey of techniques, approaches, and tools. In: Aurum, A., Wohlin, C. (eds.) Engineering and Managing Software Requirements, pp. 19–46. Springer, Heidelberg (2005). https://doi.org/10.1007/3-540-28244-0_2

Open Source

Selecting Open Source Projects
for Traceability Case Studies

Michael Rath$^{(\boxtimes)}$ ⓘ, Mihaela Todorova Tomova, and Patrick Mäder ⓘ

Technische Universität Ilmenau, Ilmenau, Germany
{michael.rath,mihaela.todorova-tomova,patrick.maeder}@tu-ilmenau.de

Abstract. [**Context & Motivation**] Once research questions and initial theories have shaped, empirical research typically requires to select cases to study subsumed ideas. Issue trackers of todays open source systems (OSS) are a gold mine for empirical research, not least to study trace links among the included issue artifacts. [**Question / problem**] The huge amount of available OSS projects complicates the process of finding suitable cases to support the research goals. Further, simply picking a large number of projects on a random basis does not imply generalizability. Therefore the selection process should be carefully designed. [**Principle ideas / results**] In this paper we propose a method to choose OSS projects to study trace links found in issue tracking systems. Builds upon purposive sampling and cluster analysis, relevant project characteristics are identified whereas irrelevant information is filtered. Every step of the method is demonstrated on a live example. [**Contributions**] The proposed strategy selects an information-rich, representative and diverse sample of OSS to perform a traceability case study. Our work may be used as practical guide for other researchers to perform project selection tasks.

1 Introduction

Case study is a commonly conducted research strategy. It has been successfully applied in different domains including software engineering, medicine, political and social science [23]. A case study allows to test an individual hypothesis and can be viewed as a robust research method when performing an in-depth investigation [11,28]. To fully maximize the benefits of a case study, it is important to select samples in a systematic manner. However, time constraints, and lack of a well developed program theory often constrain grounded-theoretical approaches suggested in the literature. Therefore researchers fall back to basic selection (random) schemes, impressionistic evidence, or guesswork to aid them in making the critical decision of which cases to include in their study [28]. Further, simply increasing the sample size does not imply more generalizability of the performed study [18]. Nevertheless, different kinds of sampling methods and strategies exist to aid researchers in making decisions on how to perform the case sampling.

In this paper, we present a practical example how to select software projects to perform a case study in context of requirements traceability research. The

© Springer Nature Switzerland AG 2019
E. Knauss and M. Goedicke (Eds.): REFSQ 2019, LNCS 11412, pp. 229–242, 2019.
https://doi.org/10.1007/978-3-030-15538-4_17

presented approach is based on a qualitative method called purposive sampling followed by a clustering technique. For the outlined example, we formulate a research topic driving the project selection process and results in small yet information-rich and representative collection of projects. This collection is suitable to actually perform the case study, which itself is out of scope of this work.

The remaining paper is structured as follows. Section 2 presents related work concerning case studies. The next section, provides the background on purposive sampling and clustering algorithms, the main techniques used in our approach. Afterwards, in Sect. 4, we describe the approach starting with formulating the research topic, identifying relevant case characteristics and performing the clustering. Section 5 evaluates and interprets the created project clusters. Further is shows how to chose individual projects from the clusters in order to create the final set of projects for the case study. The paper ends with a conclusion.

2   Related Work

In Flyvbjerg [11], the author investigates five common misunderstandings about case studies. Common wisdom is that a case study is the detailed examination of a single example, which "cannot provide reliable information about the broader class". The author argues, that a case study *is* reliable and further is more than a pilot method to be used only in preparing the real study's larger surveys. The discussed misunderstandings center around concerns about the theory, reliability, and validity of a case study as a scientific method. The author shows, that case studies are generalizable. However, a strategic selection of cases is required, whereas a random or stratified sampling may not be sufficient. Therefore different information-related selection methods are presented.

Curtis et al. [8] examine samples for three different case studies and which are later evaluated based on six guidelines as suggested by Miles and Huberman [17]. Two guidelines check whether the sampling strategy can be considered as ethical and if it is relevant to the research question and conceptual framework. A third guideline considers factors such as accessibility, time, and cost. The remaining three guidelines examine if the sample generates rich information about the researched topic, enhances the generalizability of the findings, and produces believable explanations/descriptions. In their work, the authors acknowledge the importance of guidelines, but a "simple blueprint" for qualitative research is very hard to construct since each study depends on a different strategy. Depending on the researched topic misinterpretation of parts of the guidelines can arise. For example, researchers may have different opinions on what is considered believable and ethical.

Nagappan et al. [18] investigate diversity and representativeness and thus, whether phenomena found in few case (e. g. projects) are reflective of others. The paper introduces a measure called *sample coverage* combining the two concepts to access the quality of a sample. A sample is diverse, if it contains members of every subgroup of a population. On the other hand, a sample is representative, if the size of each subgroup is proportional to the size of the subgroup in the population, i. e. each sample in the population can be chosen with equal probability [12]. A better coverage can be achieved when the similarity between the candidate samples is smaller, and therefor the distance, defined by a similarity function, between projects is larger. Thus, new projects should be added to an existing sample set in order to maximize the sample coverage.

Another important step when performing studies is to find information-rich cases that can help researchers to better understand complex issues. While quantitative research methods, such as random sampling, concentrate on selecting unbiased, representative samples, qualitative research methods give researchers the opportunity to clarify or deepen their understanding about the phenomenon under study [13]. A widely used qualitative research method for identification and selection of information-rich cases is purposive sampling [19, 24, 25]. We discuss purposive sampling in more detail in Sect. 3.

Ryzin [28] uses hierarchical, agglomerative clustering to guide purposive selection of projects. After building the clusters, the author proposes to select projects randomly or by choosing projects most similar to the means of the whole cluster. The author highlights multiple benefits of using cluster analysis in project selection. Clusters can be easily build with different number of samples: small and large. After cluster creation, the assignment of projects to clusters can be integrated with judgmental criteria that provide additional information and insight to guide the selection process. At last, the results of a cluster analysis are a basis to decide about the extent to which the findings can be generalized to the population of projects.

3 Background

This section provides background of important concepts used in the paper.

3.1 Purposive Sampling

Purposive sampling, also known as *judgment* or *purposeful* sampling, is a non-probability sampling method. The samples are selected according to the objective of the study. Contrasting probability sampling, which leads to greater breadth of information from a larger number of units, purposive sampling leads to greater depth of information from a small number of carefully selected cases. Patton [20] examines 16 different purposive sampling methods. However, the precise understanding of what sampling methods are part of purposive sampling often differs in the literature.

Teddlie and Yu [25] categorizes purposive sampling methods, including those found in [20], based on the strategies they describe. The authors identified four categories:

1. Sampling to achieve representativeness or comparability
2. Sampling special or unique cases
3. Sequential sampling
4. Sampling using multiple purposive techniques.

The first category handles samples that represent a broader group of cases or sets up comparisons among different types of cases. Six types of purposive sampling procedures are present this category: typical case sampling, extreme or deviant case sampling, intensity sampling, maximum variation sampling, homogeneous sampling, and reputational sampling. This category concentrates on both representative (e.g. typical case sampling) and contrasting cases (e.g. extreme case sampling).

The second category deals with special and unique cases rather than typical ones. It consists of four types: revelatory case sampling, critical case sampling, sampling politically important cases, and complete collection or criterion sampling.

The third category is based on sequential selection. Here, the main objective is to select units or cases based on their relevance. Often such techniques are used when the goal of the project is to generate theories or the sample evolves during data collection (known as gradual selection). Theoretical sampling, confirming and disconfirming cases, opportunistic sampling and snowball sampling are examples of sequential sampling.

The last category represents combination of two or more purposive sampling techniques. Such an approach might be useful depending on the complexity of the research study.

Table 1 shows purposive sampling technics applied in this paper.

Table 1. Purposive sampling methods used in this paper.

Method	Pro/Con	Example
TYPICAL	+ Describes illustrative samples + Separates familiar from unfamiliar − Correctly identifying typical case	$R^\dagger$ Graduating students $S^\ddagger$ Schools where nothing unusual is found
MAXIMUM VARIATION	+ Covers cases that are extreme in one way and average in other ways − Depends on variety of the samples	**R** People listening to radio Participants must differ from each other as much as possible (age, gender)
HOMOGENOUS SAMPLING	+ Recruitment costs an efforts are low − Yields estimates that are not generalizable to the target population	**R** Leadership in villages after natural disaster **S** Cases where leader is present and examine his qualities

†Research, ‡Sample

3.2 Clustering Analysis

Clustering analysis is a multivariate classification technique used in quantitative research. The main idea of clustering is to group data into sets of related observations. Thus, observations in the same cluster are more similar to observations from other clusters. At the end of the analysis, every observation is part of a single cluster. The individual clusters are built by grouping observations based distance (linkage) function, which describes the similarity of the observations. Different linkage methods exist to measure the distance and dissimilarity between two clusters: minimal linkage, maximal linkage, average linking, or *Ward* linkage. The latter is based on sum of squares between all observations in the cluster and the centroid of the cluster. It aims to build homogeneous groups since clusters are joint based on the least variation [28].

The result of clustering is frequently presented as a tree like diagram called dendrogram. Each level of the dendrogram represents a segmentation of the data, and thus a different number of clusters. Finding the number of clusters is a manual step dependent on the specific research topic. Usually the most appropriate way to do this is by analysing the distances between the levels of the dendrogram and the resulting clusters [28]. The final number of clusters is then determined by the placing a *cut-off line*. When the distances between the levels is very high, i. e. a jump [27] exists, the cut-off line needs to be placed at a smaller distance.

4 Project Selection Approach

In this section we describe our project selection approach. Starting with the definition of a research topic, we derive characteristics describing the topic. Next, we calculate the characteristics for a large population of open source software (OSS) projects. By applying the introduced sampling techniques and clustering (see Sect. 3), we select a set of projects suitable to perform the case study defined by the initial research question.

4.1 Example Research Topic: Trace Links in Issue Tracking Systems

To demonstrate our approach, we first need to define a research topic for the case study. Usually, this initial step is not required and the topic is already at hand. As an example, we want to study trace links in open source issue tracking systems (ITS). In particular, we are interested whether existing trace links could be derived from properties of the linked issue artifacts or if the links introduce new information. For example, developers might link two issues because they share similar textual information or they belong to the same software component. In this situation, the links basically introduce no new information and could be potentially automatically created.

Research Topic: Do trace links in open source issue tracking systems introduce new information?

The goal of our approach is to identify a subset of open source systems suitable to perform the case study and provide answers to the research topic.

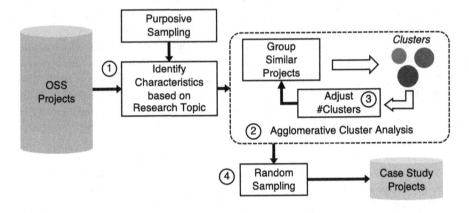

Fig. 1. Schema of the proposed approach to select projects for a case study.

4.2 Schematic Overview

The schema of the proposed selection method is depicted in Fig. 1. At first (①), characteristics that best describe the research topic need to be defined. Here, only relevant data should be included. Most analysts recommend the use of a limited number of clearly interpretable variables. If irrelevant information is not omitted, false interpretations can occur in later stages of the study or it can be much harder to analyse and interpret data. As we show, purposive sampling methods help in defining the characteristics. Next (②), a cluster analysis is performed to group similar projects. At this point, the number of clusters need to be determined. To ensure that the optimal amount of clusters, different placements of the cut-off (③) line as well as the validity of the results must be considered. The resulting clusters build a representative set of projects for the case study. To ensure diversity, projects from every cluster must be selected. Depending on the size of the clusters multiple projects can be chosen. The selection can be performed on a random basis (④).

4.3 Data Source

The defined research topic deals with open source projects using issue tracking systems. This topic defines the population, or *universe* [18], of the research. Based on popularity of ITS [15], we applied *homogenous case sampling* by selecting the Jira Issue Tracker [16]. Focusing on one ITS, further simplifies the data collection process described in the next section.

The Apache Software Foundation (AFS)[1] is the world largest open source foundation hosting 350+ projects [1]. Having Jira as a key tool, the ASF offers an Jira instance for every contained project. The projects have different sizes, use different programming languages, and stem from a variety of domains [1] resulting in an ideal source for searching for projects used in case studies.

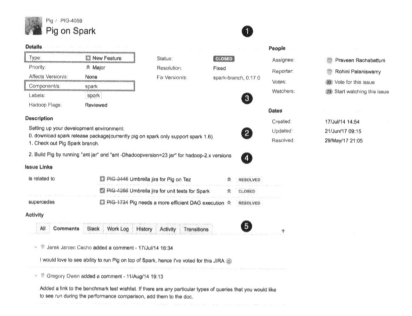

Fig. 2. Example feature and its properties as represented in Jira issue tracker.

4.4 Data Representation and Acquisition

Figure 2 shows an example issue `PIG-4059`[2] from project PIG. An issue is the fundamental artifact used in Jira ITS. It summarizes a variety of information including *summary/title* (❶), *description* (❷), *meta data* (❸), *issues links* (❹), and *comments* (❺). The meta data *type* specifies the artifact (issue) type. Jira has a predefined list of issue types containing *bug, improvement, new feature*, and *task*. The link property allows to create trace links between different artifacts within a projects. Similar to issues, trace links are typed and the predefined list of link types includes *relates*, and *clones*. Selecting projects based on the links is the purpose of our case study.

The Jira platform offers a RESTful web service, which allows to interact with the system programmatically. We used the data collection process defined in [21]

---

[1] https://www.apache.org.

[2] https://jira.apache.org/jira/browse/PIG-4059.

to retrieve the issues and trace links of the projects hosted by AFS. The captured data is locally stored within a database for further processing. The project data collection was performed early in May 2018.

4.5 Sampling Strategies

All 350+ AFS projects are potential candidates for the example trace link study. We apply different purposive sampling techniques and apply metrics based on diversity and representativeness to identify a smaller, yet still information-rich subset to be used in the study.

The projects hosted by AFS are at different maturity levels. The AFS defines a rigorous *incubation process* [2] for the projects, which enter the program as *candidates*, then become *podlings*, and ultimately lead to a new Apache *Top-Level-Project (TLP)*. One criteria to become a TLP is to setup a specific project infrastructure including an issue tracker. Aiming for mature projects which follow the AFS guide lines, we use *homogenous case sampling* and only consider TLP projects. At the time of data retrieval, 219 Top-Level-Projects[3] using Jira existed.

Next, we need to define characteristics (i. e. dimensions [18]) of the remaining projects. Later, the clustering is performed based on these characteristics.

When studying trace links, the most important characteristic is the amount of existing links in a project. Further characteristics are derived directly from the issues properties (see Fig. 2).

Textual artifact information, available in issue title and description, is often used in trace link analysis. It allows application of a wide range of textual similarity algorithms, such as TF-IDF [6], LSI [9, 22] or LDA [7, 10]. Thus we incorporate the existence of textual information in linked issues in the set of characteristics.

A previous study by Tomova et al. [26] identified the issue type as a relevant property when considering trace links. Especially the issue types *bug* (a problem which impairs or prevents the functions of a product), *feature* (a new feature of the product), and *improvement* (an enhancement to an existing feature) are of major interest.

To identify possible link patterns, i. e. combinations of issue types and link types, characteristics complementing textual analysis might be beneficial. As such, the component information is of special interest. Issues having the same type and component are similar to each other and may be more likely linked as duplicates or cloners. Further comments attached to issues are valuable, too. There, developers record additional details and collaborate with each other [3]. This activity might trigger the creation of trace links to other issues.

4.6 Data Preparation

After identification, the characteristics need to be calculated and prepared in order to apply the cluster analysis.

---

[3] https://projects.apache.org/projects.html.

At first, we built the set $I_{BFI} \subset I$ of all issue I representing the bugs, features and improvements and for every project. Projects without all three issue types were discarded. Next, we calculated the set $I_{lnk,BFI}$ containing all $i \in I_{BFI}$ that are linked to another issue $j \in I_{BFI}, j \neq i$. Next, we calculated the following values for every project:

- $n_{BFI} = |I_{BFI}|$: the number of bugs, features and improvements in a project. Its value estimates the size of a project. There is no such thing as *the* size of a (software) project. The standard ISO/IEC 14143/1 [14] defines functional size by quantify the functional user requirements (FUR). Counting the respective issues is one way reflecting the number of requirements what the software or product shall do.
- $n_{lnk,BFI}$: the total number of links between issues of type bug, feature and improvement. This value also reflects the size of a project, but from a linking perspective.
- $mean_{com,BFI}$: the average number of comments for an issue of type bug, feature and improvement. It captures the collaboration activity in the respective project.
- $lnk_{BFI} = \frac{|I_{lnk,BFI}|}{|I_{BFI}|}$ which represents the percentage of linked issues of type bug, feature, and improvements.
- $lnk_{desc,BFI}$: the fraction of linked issues $i \in I_{BFI}$, that have non-empty description.
- $lnk_{comp,BFI}$: the fraction of linked issues $i \in I_{BFI}$, that have an assigned component.

Aiming for many links, we filtered the projects on a link basis using lnk_{BFI}. Being a fractional quantity, the value accounts for different project sizes. We removed those projects having lnk_{BFI} lower than the average of 13% of all TLP. After this filtering step, 93 out of the initial 219 projects remained.

We applied *typical case sampling* by placing constraints on lnk_{BFI}. The remaining characteristics are left untouched, aiming for *maximum variation sampling*.

4.7   Clustering Analysis

The characteristics n_{BFI}, $n_{lnk,BFI}$, and $mean_{com,BFI}$ greatly vary in magnitude. In order to make the data less sensitive to the existing differences, they need to be scaled [28]. We applied a normalization scheme, such that the values have zero mean and unit variance. The other three characteristics represent percentages and thus are already in a closed range. The resulting transformed dataset is used as input for agglomerative clustering. We chose the common *ward* linkage to create homogenous clusters. The outcome of the clustering is shown as dendrogram in Fig. 3.

5   Evaluation

Analysing the dendrogram shown in Fig. 3, an important decision is to place the cut-off line, which ultimately defines the number of clusters. Trying different

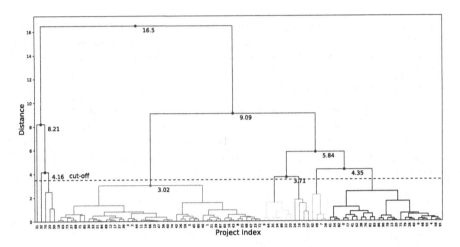

Fig. 3. Dendrogram resulting of hierarchical clustering with cut-off line at distance 3.5.

Table 2. Identified clusters, their size and example projects within the clusters.

Cluster	#Projects	Example projects
C_1	3	HIVE, LUCENE-CORE, SPARK
C_2	1	HBASE
C_3	1	HADOOP
C_4	47	ARCHIVA, APACHE COMMONS-LANG, SHIRO
C_5	7	CAMEL, DRILL, MAVEN, WICKET
C_6	4	CASSANDRA, CORDOVA, FLINK, OFBIZ
C_7	4	BOOKKEEPER, GORA, LOG4NET, ZOOKEEPER
C_8	26	GIRAPH, JENA, PIG, SUBVERSION

configurations, we finally settled to place the cut-off line at a distance of 3.5 and thus constructing 8 clusters. At this distance, no more major distance jumps are present in the tree. Additionally, the resulting clusters are well interpretable. Table 2 shows the number of projects (cluster size) as some example projects for each cluster. A common strategy to interpret the cluster meanings is to examine their differences compared to the grand means (macro averages) calculated from all 93 input projects [28]. The cluster mean values for all six characteristics along with the grand means are shown in Table 3. The interpretation of the clusters is as follows.

C_1 This cluster combines three projects, which have an equal size, i.e. minor variation, in terms of n_{BFI} and $n_{lnk,BFI}$, but are among the largest of all projects. The remaining characteristics are above average, except for the fraction of linked bugs, features and improvements ($lnk_{comp,BFI}$). The value is the lowest among all clusters.

Table 3. Cluster means of all projects. The color coding indicates, whether the respective value is greater or less then the grand mean (macro average).

Cluster	n_{BFI}	$n_{lnk,BFI}$	$mean_{com,BFI}$	lnk_{BFI}	$lnk_{desc,BFI}$	$lnk_{comp,BFI}$
			Cluster means			
C_1	16,536	3,619	11	0.28	0.92	0.21
C_2	15,274	2,547	25	0.22	0.95	0.12
C_3	31,073	10,407	18	0.39	0.96	0.25
C_4	1,225	172	5	0.21	0.92	0.14
C_5	6,781	948	6	0.21	0.94	0.18
C_6	9,626	1,288	12	0.18	0.95	0.13
C_7	1,116	197	17	0.23	0.97	0.18
C_8	2,610	390	10	0.20	0.94	0.14
Grand Mean	3,353	587	8	0.21	0.93	0.15

C_2 This cluster consists of APACHE HBASE, whose characteristics are above the grand means.

C_3 The third cluster represents the project APACHE HADOOP, which has by far the most issues and links. Further, HADOOP achieves the highest value in nearly all characteristics (except for $lnk_{comp,BFI}$).

C_4 Cluster four consists of 47 projects, making it the largest one. However, all other characteristics are below the grand averages.

C_5 The average characteristics of the seven projects in cluster C_5 are all above average, except for the low fraction of mean number of comments per bug, feature, and improvement.

C_6 The sixth cluster consists of four quite large (n_{BFI} and $n_{lnk,BFI}$) projects. However, the mean number of comments per issue is low in these projects. The remaining characteristics are above average.

C_7 This cluster combines four small projects. All projects have a high fraction of linked bugs, features, and improvements and thus $lnk_{desc,BFI}$ is the highest of all clusters. The remaining characteristics are also above the grand means.

C_8 The second largest cluster has 26 small projects in terms of n_{BFI} and $n_{lnk,BFI}$. The percentage of bugs, features, and improvements that are linked (lnk_{BFI}) and those with an assigned component ($lnk_{comp,BFI}$) is below average. The remaining two characteristics are above average.

The projects in the eight clusters represent the characteristics that describe the topic under study. The number of the samples, software projects in our exemplary study, within clusters can be very large, e. g. like clusters C_4 and C_8 which together represent 80% of all projects. Depending on the situation, not every observation of a cluster must be considered for further analysis. However, to ensure diversity, at least one project from each cluster must be selected. To guarantee unbiased selection random sampling can be used to pick more projects.

No imperative exists, to actually chose from each cluster [28]. This depends on the design of the research. In our example, special care should be taken of clusters C_2 and C_3, representing the two projects APACHE HBASE and APACHE HADOOP. Each cluster consists of only one project, and thus no actual grouping occurred. Further, the seven calculated values for each cluster are near the upper and lower bounds compared to grand means. Therefore the two projects could be seen as outliers and may not be included in the final project selection.

6   Threats to Validity

In this section, we discuss threats to the validity of our study and how we mitigated them.

A threat to internal validity exists by choosing only projects of the Apache Software Foundation (ASF). We used this setup, because the project host defines the concept of *project*, i. e. it needs to have an issue tracking system, a web page, documentation and thus a certain level of maturity defined by ASF. However, this does not limit the scope of our approach researching trace links among artifacts in the projects.

We only consider Jira as issue tracking system. In our approach, we calculate seven project metrics based on issue types, links between issues, and textual description/comments of issues. These properties are not specific for Jira. Basically every issue tracking system, whether open-source like Bugzilla, Github Issues, MantisBT, Redmine, and Trac, or proprietary including HP Quality Center, IBM Rational, Microsoft Team Foundation Server, and JetBrains YouTrack provides these basic features [5]. Therefore the presented metrics can be calculated for these issue tracking systems as well. We settled on Jira based on its popularity [15] and ease of accessing the stored artifacts via the RESTful web service.

Our approach focused solely on open-source projects. A potential threat to external validity arises when we want to generalize our findings to a wider set of projects, including commercial development. Jira is used by over 60.000 customers according to its owning company Atlassian, including many large and well-know commercial enterprises [4]. We expect similar usage of issue artifacts in these projects in respect to our calculated metrics, i. e. creating, typing and linking of issue artifacts.

Another threat exists when generalizing our approach outside of traceability analysis. As depicted in Fig. 1, performing steps ① and ③ is inherently tied to a specific research question by defining case characteristics and placing the cut-off line. Other research topics may require different characteristics and cluster adjustments. However, the overall idea of purposive sampling, clustering and random selection is generalizable. Depending on the initial size of projects to choose from, the clustering step is optional.

7   Conclusion

When conducting a case study it is important to gather information-rich samples, such as software projects, that well represent the researched topic and give scientists the opportunity not only to test hypothesis but also to learn from the selected samples. In this paper, we first investigated different strategies and important metrics when selecting samples for a study. Based on related work, we proposed an approach to select projects in a systematic way while taking into account important characteristics of the researched topic and metrics such as representativeness and diversity. As running example, we formulated a practical research question on the trace links in open source projects. We applied several purposive sampling techniques to describe trace link of the projects hosted by the apache software foundation. In this process, unnecessary information was filtered and characteristics characteristics strategically chosen. A hierarchical clustering algorithm was applied to identify patterns and group similar projects. Choosing projects out of the clusters via random sampling guarantees a variety of representative and diverse samples for later stages of the case study. Hopefully our work may be used as practical guideline to support other researchers for setting up their case studies.

In future work, we want to answer the stated research question, which only served as an interesting placeholder to drive the project selection method.

References

1. Apache Annual Report FY2018. https://s.apache.org/FY2018AnnualReport (2018). Accessed 29 Sept 2018
2. Apache Incubation Process. https://incubator.apache.org/policy/process.html (2018). Accessed 29 Sept 2018
3. Commenting on an Issue. https://confluence.atlassian.com/jira064/commenting-on-an-issue-720416302.html (2018). Accessed 29 Sept 2018
4. https://www.atlassian.com/customers (2019). Accessed 03 Jan 2019
5. Comparison of issue-tracking systems. https://en.wikipedia.org/wiki/Comparison_of_issue-tracking_systems (2019). Accessed 03 Jan 2019
6. Antoniol, G., Canfora, G., Casazza, G., De Lucia, A., Merlo, E.: Recovering traceability links between code and documentation. IEEE Trans. Softw. Eng. 28(10) 970–983 (2002)
7. Asuncion, H.U., Asuncion, A.U., Taylor, R.N.: Software traceability with topic modeling. In: Proceedings of the 32nd ACM/IEEE International Conference on Software Engineering, ICSE 2010, Cape Town, South Africa, 1–8 May 2010. vol. 1, ACM (2010)
8. Curtis, S., Gesler, W., Smith, G., Washburn, S.: Approaches to sampling and case selection in qualitative research: examples in the geography of health. Soc. Sci. Med. 50(7—8), 1001–1014 (2000)
9. De Lucia, A., Fasano, F., Oliveto, R., Tortora, G.: 20th IEEE International Conference on Software Maintenance (ICSM) (2004)
10. Dekhtyar, A., Hayes, J.H., Sundaram, S.K., Holbrook, E.A., Dekhtyar, O.: Technique integration for requirements assessment. In: 15th IEEE International Requirements Engineering Conference, RE 2007, 15–19th October 2007, New Delhi, India. IEEE Computer Society (2007)
11. Flyvbjerg, B.: Five misunderstandings about case-study research. Qual. Inq. 12(2), 219–245 (2006)

12. Foucault, M., Palyart, M., Falleri, J., Blanc, X.: Computing contextual metric thresholds, ACM (2014)
13. Ishak, N.M., Bakar, A.Y.A.: Developing sampling frame for case study: challenges and conditions. World J. Educ. **4**(3), 29–35 (2014)
14. ISO/IEC 14143/1: Information technology, software measurement, functional size measurement, Part 1: definition of concepts. Standard, International Organization for Standardization, Geneva (2007)
15. Issue management tools - popularity ranking (2017). https://project-management.zone/ranking/category/issue
16. Jira Issue Tracking System (2018). https://www.atlassian.com/software/jira
17. Miles, M.B., Huberman, A.M., Huberman, M.A., Huberman, M.: Qualitative Data Analysis: An Expanded Sourceboo. Sage, Thousand Oaks (1994)
18. Nagappan, M., Zimmermann, T., Bird, C.: Diversity in software engineering research, ACM (2013)
19. Palinkas, L.A., Horwitz, S.M., Green, C.A., Wisdom, J.P., Duan, N., Hoagwood, K.: Purposeful sampling for qualitative data collection and analysis in mixed method implementation research. Adm. Policy Ment. Health Ment. Health Serv. Res. **42**(5), 533–544 (2015)
20. Patton, M.Q.: Qualitative Evaluation and Research Methods. Sage Publications, Thousand Oaks (1990)
21. Rath, M., Rempel, P., Mäder, P.: The IlmSeven dataset. In: 25th IEEE International Requirements Engineering Conference, RE 2017, Lisbon, Portugal, 4–8 September 2017. pp. 516–519. IEEE Computer Society (2017)
22. Rempel, P., Mäder, P., Kuschke, T.: Towards feature-aware retrieval of refinement traces. In: 7th International Workshop on Traceability in Emerging Forms of Software Engineering, TEFSE 2013, 19 May 2013, San Francisco, CA, USA. IEEE Computer Society (2013)
23. Runeson, P., Höst, M., Rainer, A., Regnell, B.: Case Study Research in Software Engineering - Guidelines and Examples. Wiley, Hoboken (2012)
24. Suri, H.: Purposeful sampling in qualitative research synthesis. Qual. Res. J. **11**(2), 63–75 (2011)
25. Teddlie, C., Yu, F.: Mixed methods sampling: a typology with examples. J. Mixed Methods Res. **1**(1), 77–100 (2007)
26. Tomova, M.T., Rath, M., Mäder, P.: Use of trace link types in issue tracking systems. In: Proceedings of the 40th International Conference on Software Engineering: Companion Proceeedings, ICSE 2018, Gothenburg, Sweden, 27 May–03 June 2018. ACM (2018)
27. Tryfos, P.: Methods for Business Analysis and Forecasting: Text and Cases. Wiley, Hoboken (1998)
28. Van Ryzin, G.G.: Cluster analysis as a basis for purposive sampling of projects in case study evaluations. Eval. Pract. **16**(2), 109–119 (1995)

Managing Requirements Knowledge at a Large Scale

Crowd Intelligence in Requirements Engineering: Current Status and Future Directions

Javed Ali Khan[1], Lin Liu[1(✉)], Lijie Wen[1], and Raian Ali[2]

[1] Tsinghua University, Beijing 100084, China
`linliu@tsinghua.edu.cn`
[2] Bournemouth University, Poole BH12 5BB, UK

Abstract. Software systems are the joint creative products of multiple stake-holders, including both designers and users, based on their perception, knowledge and personal preferences of the application context. The rapid rise in the use of Internet, mobile and social media applications make it even more possible to provide channels to link a large pool of highly diversified and physically distributed designers and end users, the crowd. Converging the knowledge of designers and end users in requirements engineering process is essential for the success of software systems. In this paper, we report the findings of a survey of the literature on crowd-based requirements engineering research. It helps us understand the current research achievements, the areas of concentration, and how requirements related activities can be enhanced by crowd intelligence. Based on the survey, we propose a general research map and suggest the possible future roles of crowd intelligence in requirements engineering.

Keywords: Requirements engineering · Crowd intelligence · User feedback · Crowdsourcing

1 Introduction and Background

Software systems are engineered via interactive processes between multiple stake-holders in the developmental and operational environment. Depending on ones' command of design ability, and knowledge about the application domain, the creative process can happen either in the designer's mind or the user's mind or together [9]. The success of software product is measured by the degree it meets the intended design purposes and end-user needs [60]. Minimizing the cost and the speed in achieving that target is always desired. While conventional requirements engineering (RE) approaches often rely on limited number of stakeholders, e.g. through interviews and focus groups, it is made possible today to involve a large group of potential users and contributors distributed geographically and culturally. Therefore, RE for today's software, can benefit from novel techniques and tools to support converging crowd intelligence in requirements elicitation and decision [7, 70, 77]. Crowd intelligence arises from the cooperation, combined efforts, and competition amongst end users, who are interested to take part in requirements engineering activities.

© Springer Nature Switzerland AG 2019
E. Knauss and M. Goedicke (Eds.): REFSQ 2019, LNCS 11412, pp. 245–261, 2019.
https://doi.org/10.1007/978-3-030-15538-4_18

To cater for the diversity of the crowd in requirements elicitation, some effort has been made in term of persona and adaptive feedback acquisition [3]. The foci are on software systems being developed in open environment and offered in open market more than dedicated products for specific customers [3, 63]. But these techniques can only provide initial segmentation which needs further support to cater for the many facets of diversity in the crowd including those found in their comments and feedbacks [12, 19, 32, 42]. Therefore, more scalable mechanisms are needed where users can actively participate in different feedback channels thus contributing to the future system design decisions [72, 73].

Crowdsourcing has existed as a business paradigm long before the Internet era. However, its integration with the internet has brought great popularities and successful applications in many disciplines [10, 38, 76, 78, 84]. An extensive analysis to the crowdsourcing literature has led to a crowdsourcing taxonomy, which is composed of four major concepts: crowd, client, task and platform [30]. In recent years, crowd-sourcing has attracted much attention and was widely experimented in software engineering including requirements engineering [50]. One notable area is the engineering of crowdsourcing platforms to allow crowd intelligence to emerge, e.g. Wisdom of Crowd. The degree and focus areas of such crowd intelligence together with the facilities and algorithms built to allow it, are diverse. Also, it became apparent that activities like aggregation of crowd input and the derivation of collective decisions require the power of AI at the planning time and also production time.

In this paper, we explore such diversity and status of using crowd intelligence for requirements engineering and facilitating it through AI. We conduct a literature survey to evaluate the current status of the field of Intelligent Crowd-based RE. We describe our method in Sect. 2 and then our research findings in Sect. 3. We depict a map for the areas of research in Sect. 4, which fits the pieces into an integral picture and discuss possible future directions in Sect. 5.

2   Research Method

In this section, we describe our literature survey process including the research questions and the searching, filtering and analysis processes. In requirements engineering research, there is a growing interest in crowd-based RE. While crowd-based RE (CrowdRE) is considered promising, it is unclear what is the status of the research and practice in CrowdRE and what are the current challenges. Thus, we identified the main research questions of our literature survey as:

RQ1. What are the current foci of CrowdRE research?
RQ2. How traditional RE activities are mapped with CrowdRE activities and how crowd-based techniques support RE activities?
RQ3. What is a possible future role of intelligence in CrowdRE?

Search criteria required a paper title to meet the following search string and variations of it: ("CrowdRE" OR "Requirements Crowdsourcing" OR ("Crowd" AND "Requirements Engineering") OR "Crowd-based Requirements Engineering" OR ("Crowd intelligence" AND "Requirements Engineering"). The papers must be written in English and must have been published in peer reviewed conferences, journals, book chapters or be a refereed thesis. Snowballing approach was used to expand the search results.

Online libraries which were used for searching the research papers are: IEEE Xplore, ACM Library, ResearchGate, Springer Library, Elsevier Science direct and Google Scholar. The duration searched was between January 2010 and September 2018. Main conferences, workshops and journals whose title meet the search criteria were also searched in order to ensure important papers, while other major RE related conferences, workshops and journals are also included, e.g. IEEE RE conference, REFSQ, CrowdRE workshop, CAiSE, RCIS, REJ, IST and JSS.

The initial searching process led to 127 papers in total. Then a manual selection process was conducted and we excluded papers which were published in languages other than English, in unrecognized venues and meeting the search criteria but without being centered on the topic. For this, we read the title, abstract of each paper in order to check its relevance, if still relevant or uncertain, the introduction and even the whole paper is read. In total 97 papers where selected, out of which 77 papers are directly related to CrowdRE, while the remaining 20 papers are supportive papers to CrowdRE concepts like Crowdsourcing Taxonomy, books on crowd wisdoms, crowd motivations, software crowdsourcing companies case study etc. The final list of papers was validated again by the 2nd author of the paper, by looking at the title and reading the content if necessary. Also, the selection criteria were double checked, to ensure that no relevant papers were missed in the selection process. The major keywords from the title of the included papers were: requirements/requirement engineering, software, crowd, requirements crowdsourcing, mining, users/user, feature, reviews, case study, approach, online, elicitation, collaborative, and so on. Taking a closer look at the nature of the studies included in our survey, the surveyed studies included visions and previews, case studies, data analytics studies, tools and demos, domain-specific studies and applications. The survey papers included in our paper were studies which collected data about usage of crowdsourcing requirements elicitations [28]. We analyzed each paper to identify its nature of study and then grouped them into the categories. There are 34 technical solutions papers, 3 empirical study papers, 7 data analysis papers, 4 papers are about domain applications, 7 case studies, 7 papers about RE tools, there are also 4 surveys, 3 research previews, and 8 vision papers.

3   RE Activities: Crowd Support and Main Issues

CrowdRE is mainly founded on the assumption that it is important to collect up-to-date observations and experience of the "crowd" about a system and predict the future requirements. Also, CrowdRE is still developing, therefore there are exploratory studies on CrowdRE models, activities and validation with expert software engineers, end users and researchers through surveys and questionnaires in order to find some relationship between crowdsourcing features and requirements elicitation to better understand the needs of end users and overcomes human cognitive limitations by monitoring users at run time [2, 28, 29, 68]. In this section, the results of our survey around the status of the field and how this role has been fulfilled so far, including the support from AI, will be presented.

3.1   The Crowd in the Requirements Engineering Activities

Requirements is pivotal in software engineering as it is fundamental to ensure product quality and customer satisfaction. Major requirements engineering activities, such as requirements elicitation, modeling, analysis and validation, prioritization, and runtime adaptation and evolution are all serving these two ultimate goals. The role of the crowd can vary according to the RE activity and also the RE technique and model used. For example, while we would expect requirements expressed as User Stories to be understood fairly by the crowd, requirements validation may need advanced simulation and scenario building skills, and hence tools to engage and get meaningful input from the crowd. We try to answer RQ1 through this section by highlight current CrowdRE research focus through literature.

Table 1. Requirements activities that crowd are involved

RE. activities	Perspectives/activities		No. of studies
Elicitation	General requirements	[1, 13, 34, 39, 44, 50, 56–58, 70, 77, 84, 87]	70
	Features	[25, 49, 58, 69, 90, 91]	
	NFRs	[4, 5, 23, 51, 72]	
	Run-time feedback	[22, 31, 41, 71, 72, 96]	
	Emerging requirements	[15, 42, 57]	
	Design rationale	[37]	
Modelling and specification	Use cases [27, 46], process models [12, 26], Goals [61, 68], i* [59], feature models [19, 68]		8
Analysis and validation	By crowd [48, 54, 72], by textual data analysis [13, 20, 25, 33, 41, 42, 49, 51, 52, 62, 64, 80, 86, 88, 89], by prototyping [22], sentiment analysis [21, 79], image and unstructured data analysis [21, 73]		22
Prioritization	User rating and comments [14, 43], developer voting [72], crowd members vote [70, 72], statistical analysis [21], gamified approaches [36]		6
Run-time	Monitoring [2, 20, 73, 75, 93], adaption [3, 26, 55], evolution [25, 45, 66, 85], discovery [81], context [21, 42, 48]		16

Requirements Elicitation. Requirements elicitation is the process of gathering user demand and needs to be addressed by the software. As we can see from Table 1, 70 out of 77 paper covers requirements elicitation, using different approaches with different foci (type of requirements elicitation), where some of papers references are shown in Table 1. For this, we analysed each paper content to identify foci of requirements elicitation and grouped them into categories shown in Table 1. For example, there are works focusing on elicit general requirements, including: building personas for users profiling [3] and identify Personae Non Gratae (potential system attackers or abusers) [51], collecting runtime user feedbacks, or on extraction of novel or emerging functional or non-functional requirements [23], such as usability, user experience [4] and awareness [75], or security and privacy requirements [5, 8], or building elicitation tools for crowd.

Requirements Modeling. In requirements modeling, graphical models such as use cases, sequence diagrams, $i*$, goal, activity diagrams, etc. are typically used by developers and stakeholders to better understand and communicate about the requirements [1, 12, 27, 59]. Requirements modeling is considered as challenging for massive crowds, it is only possible to build collaborative modelling tools for small or medium sized groups [27], or competition platforms for the crowd to bid for an award for best requirements specifications [1, 64]. For example, Almaliki et al. [3] suggested clustering the crowd and their different styles of input, the crowd is being modelled linked to feedback acquisition process by a model-driven process. Specifically, linking the user's personas into associated goal models, then goal models are converted into use case models. Sherief et al. [68] proposed an architecture and ontology for acquiring crowd feedback and linking it to requirements models.

Requirements Analysis and Validation. Requirements analysis focuses on parsing and understanding the elicited requirements. During requirements analysis, inconsistences, ambiguities, and incompleteness in gathered and documented and possibly modeled requirements are identified. Hosseini et al. [31] propose a technique for feedback annotation, called CRAFT, which aims to harnessing the power and wisdom of the crowd. Stade et al. [73] argue that CrowdRE process cannot be implemented ad-hoc and that much work is needed to create and analyse a continuous feedback and monitoring data stream. Similarly, Liu et al. [46] propose to collect users click events in order to correlate user behavioral data with active feedbacks so that they can efficiently solves user issues. Almaliki et al. [3], proposed persona-based feedback acquisition technique using quantitative and qualitative analysis to help engineers understanding the diverse behaviors of the users. Maalej et al. [48] surveyed the state-of-the-art elicitation approaches of user input, and found that there is currently no unified model of user input. They proposed a development process enabling users to become "prosumers" of software applications and giving more continuous, direct and rich input. Requirements validation is the process of making sure that requirements gathered are aligned with the stakeholder's actual needs and are correct, consist and testable. As shown in Table 1, quite a few papers acknowledge that requirements validation in CrowdRE is challenging [28, 54, 68, 72, 73].

Requirements Prioritization. Requirements prioritization and negotiation play a pivotal role in CrowdRE [67]. A large number of stakeholders often result in a large set of requirements and preferences, but only a subset can be implemented in the software under design. Thus, prioritization and triage is required to solve this problem.

Researchers have used approaches such as, user rating and comments, developer voting, crowd member's votes, statistical analysis, gamified approaches [36, 61]. Lim and Finkelstein [43] developed tool named StakeRare, which uses social networking and collaborative filtering to elicit and prioritize large set of requirements.

Requirements Evolution. In CrowdRE, user feedback loops can be obtained iteratively throughout the lifecycle of the product. New requirements are gathered at run time and referred to when planning for the next release of the software system. Therefore, user's activities need to be monitored or reported to capture the usage context and users' intentions in the form of user's behaviors log. There are existing works on runtime adaptation or evolution in CrowdRE [2, 15, 20, 21, 26, 45, 55, 81].

3.2   Utilities in CrowdRE

Based on our survey in CrowdRE, we found that researchers focus was on the following aspects: the crowd, the tasks delegated to the crowd, and the design of mechanisms, such as those enabling crowd competition and collaboration, the media or channel for communication, the incentives for engaging the crowd, and ways to evaluate the quality of deliverables from the crowd.

Crowd. Crowd are the entities who will take part in the requirements processes. Crowds are mainly classified according to the following three properties: scale, level of skills, and roles. In the case of CrowdRE, we mainly deal with requirements approaches involving large crowd, but not necessarily unknown or random. *Level of knowledge and expertise* is the property representing the required skills of the crowd in a specific subject domain [65]. Stratified coverage could be specified to enable the acquisition of differences of viewpoints, e.g. from lowly and highly skills crowd. In the literature, there level of expertise of the crowd is one of the requirements of a crowdsourcing project. Techniques are proposed by Srivastava and Sharma [72], Levy et al. [39] and Groen [22], where macro user communities were involved to elicit requirements using different media channels (LinkedIn, users forums and research workshops). Munante et al. [55] gather preferences of both domain experts and end users in the form of personas and questionnaires about configuration requirements for adaptive systems. *Role* means which the remit and expectation of the crowd members involved in CrowdRE. In the literature, there are end users, domain experts, software engineers being involved for different purposes. Snijders [70], proposed a CrowdRE approach that gathered requirements are analysed and prioritized by involving crowd members. Similarly, in Groen et al. [21] requirements gathered are validated by developers or third-party experts.

Task. Task is the requirement activity in which the crowd participates. Tasks in CrowdRE are categorized according to their type and complexity, as shown in Table 3. Task *type* refers to the nature of the task for which crowd will participate. In Table 1, it can be seen that task type is extraction of raw requirements [34], provide feedbacks [39, 48], bugs identification [20, 21, 31, 73], feature request identification [29, 52], non-functional requirements [31, 72]. Task *complexity*: means whether the task is simple, medium, or complex to complete. Complexity is inter-related with crowd role, level of skills and the time needed by the crowd to perform it.

Mechanisms. Mechanisms are the means by which CrowdRE approaches achieve their intended goals of participation, including the media or sources used to reach out for the crowd, the incentives to motivate crowd for participating in RE activities and crowd collaboration or aggregation mechanisms. Mechanisms are further decomposed into the following sub-heading, as can be seen in Table 3, which is sketched based on literature.

Collaboration and Aggregation: Collaboration means that whether individuals in the crowd need to collaborate to complete a task. While aggregation means that individual's contributions are aggregated to present some useful information. In the literature, there are approaches requiring different types of collaborations to complete a task [3, 28, 39, 50, 83] and approaches to aggregate the individual contributions at the end [21, 43, 55, 73]. Groen et al. [20, 21] proposed theoretical models for CrowdRE using concepts of crowdsourcing where individuals' tasks are aggregated to provide a final list of identified requirements. Only few approaches adopted competition among crowds to yield optimal solutions [1, 22].

Media/Channel: In order to gain access to massive crowd, we need certain media. CrowdRE uses different channels to achieve this. Many existing work uses a general purpose media to access a community of crowd, online forums and mobile application marketplaces [29, 31, 35, 56], a few others uses social network tools to access crowd along with LinkedIn [22, 72], research workshops [39], mobile stores and twitter [6, 62, 79, 91], as in Table 3. Similarly, MuruKannaiah et al. [56, 57], developed their own crowd requirements research dataset to research user communities and other diverse characteristics of crowd members, which can be used for analysis and prioritization of requirements using Amazon Mechanical Turk, which is a crowd-based platform. Details of media/channel used in literature are depicted in Table 2.

Table 2. Types of media

Type of media	Researchers used media type
Twitter	Guzman et al. [22, 25], Williams and Mahmoud [79]
User forums	Bakiu et al. [4] (epinions.com), Do et al. [15] (Firefox, Lucene and Mylyn), Greenwood et al. [19], Kanchev et al. [34, 35] (Reddit.com), Li et al. [41] (sourceforge.net), Qi et al. [62] (Jd.com), Xiao et al. [80] (epinions.com), Shi et al. [69] (JIRA)
LinkedIn	Groen [22], Srivastava and Sharma [72]
Mobile stores	Groen et al. [23], Johann et al. [33], Maalej and Nabil [49], Williams et al. [87], Dhinakaran et al. [88], Liu et al. [91]
Amazon store	Groen et al. [23], Kurtanovic and Maalej [37]
Issue tracking	Merten et al. [52] (GitHub ITS & Redmine ITS)
MTurk	Murukannaiah et al. [56, 57], Breaux et al. [8], Gemkow et al. [89], Khan et al. [90]

Incentives/Motivation: To engage the crowd in feedback generation or requirements elicitation, certain motivation and incentives strategies are required. Most common motivations are rewards [1, 56] gamification and public acknowledgement [3, 70, 73] or multiple techniques in combination. Snijders et al. [71], propose REfine, a game-based requirements elicitation technique which use gamification to constantly motivate the crowd members for giving feedback and keeping them involved. Srivastava and Sharma [72], Levy et al. [39], Groen [22] and Munante et al. [55] propose that rewards and acknowledgements can be used to motivate experts and non-experts crowd members. Piras et al. [61] proposed to develop a framework for analyzing, modeling and accomplishing acceptance requirements for software application using gamification.

Quality. It is an important question to answer in CrowdRE to evaluate and ensure the quality of requirements obtained from the crowd either as individuals or as groups following some collective intelligence model. This problem remains largely uninvestigated in the literature. It is well argued in general crowd intelligence literature [94] that diverse, independent and decentralized crowd performs better than experts in certain circumstances and when communication and aggregation of knowledge is also done properly. We need to find out what are the necessary conditions and quality measures for crowd to deliver useful results. Getting knowledge from the crowd is by itself not a guarantee for quality knowledge. Indeed, as discussed in [92], quality is relates to the way the crowd is approached and organized, but not only to the quality of their input. One the other hand, ideal solutions from experts may be either biased towards their own expertise, or too ambitious in reality. Researcher's needs to explore this part further in future research, as up to date, according to our knowledge there is less research study and needs further exploration.

4 A Research Map for Intelligent CrowdRE

To support crowd intelligence in RE, we have developed a research map, described in Table 3, mapping the current research work in CrowdRE in response to RQ2 and RQ3. The map describes each requirements engineering activity with respect to Crowd activities covering: crowd tasks and mechanisms. The columns show the crowd-sourcing activities' while rows show RE activities. Possible techniques used for crowd motivation are given in Table 3 under the heading incentives/motivations.

There are diverse research efforts on crowd requirements engineering in the surveyed literature using AI techniques. For example, there are works on using natural language processing (NLP) techniques in classifying, clustering, categorizing users' feedback into feature requests, bugs, or simple compliments [16, 37, 41, 53, 69]. Analysis of user feedbacks and runtime human-computer interactions are experimented using NLP and text mining techniques. Maalej et al. also highlighted the issues and emphases to use automated techniques to categorize users' feedbacks into different categories in crowd-based requirements engineering [49, 58]. We adhere not the possibility that users may give feedback in the form of images, audio or video, thus analysis is required to deal with such unstructured data. Also, AI techniques such as *swarm algorithms*, *case-based learning* and *collaborative filtering* can be used with crowd-generated data to get useful insights. As more recently, Sarro et al. [86], used Case Based Reasoning (CBR) algorithm to predict mobile apps rating based on the features claimed for mobile apps in their description. Also, Gemkow et al. [89], applied AI techniques to a crowd-generated dataset, to extract the domain-specific glossary terms, and Seyff et al. [85], propose to use AI techniques together with crowd-generated data in order to observe the effects of requirements on sustainability. As CrowdRE generated a massive amount of candidate requirements, automated and AI techniques are required to validate the volume and diversity of test cases and contexts of use [85].

Table 3. Research map for CrowdRE

RE activities	Tasks		Mechanisms			
	Role/expertise	Types	Collaboration/ competition	Media/ channel	Incentives/ motivation	Quality of requirements gathered
Elicitation	System user/low	Feature requests, new requirements	Collaboration between crowd/aggregation in final outcome	Twitter, User forums, Facebook, websites, mobile app stores	Gamification vouchers, social recognition, cash	No individual guarantee, by statistical analysis
Modeling	Analysts & domain experts/logs analysed by development team/medium-high	Co-modelling, goal modeling, feature modeling, process modeling, argumentation	Direct/indirect collaboration	Platform-based	Gamification, assigned or obliged	Relying on individual expertise
Analysis & runtime adaptation/evolution		feedbacks on bugs, monitoring run time logs of exceptions, abnormal behaviors information retrieval, sentiment analysis, language patterns, recommender system	No collaboration between crowd/aggregation in final outcome	Manual or automated text analysis, speech act recognition tools, log analysis and mining tools	Gamification, social recognition, cash, assigned or obliged	Relying on individual expertise, fairly reliable
Validation	Developer or 3rd party/high	Annotation or walkthrough review		Validation need to check the influence		Relying on Individual expertise
Prioritization and negotiation	System user/low	Preference elicitation, win-condition elicitation	Direct/indirect group decision making	Voting or group decision making tools	Gamification, cash vouchers, social recognition	No individual guarantee, by consensus

To support our proposed framework, we have identified some related studies in the literature which also focus on using crowd intelligence. Dabrowski et al. [12] proposes that statistical techniques can be used to *maximize the capacity of crowd* in identifying new software requirements. Also, Liang et al. [42] use requirements mining from crowd user's behaviors data to *recommend services to crowd users*. Recently, Seyff et al. [85] proposed a crowd-based approach for *engaging stakeholders in a continuous cycle of negotiation* regarding the possible effects of requirements on sustainability. In their model, firstly, feedback regarding software services are gathered using crowd platform, then *machine learning techniques* are applied to *cluster and analyse feedback gathered*.

So far, there are few works been done in crowd *requirements modeling*. Khan et al. [90], propose semi-automated goal modeling approach to model features identified from CrowdRE. For requirements *analysis and validation*, Mead et al. [51] proposed that machine learning algorithms can be used to analyse individual Personae Non Gratae created by crowd users. To accommodate AI and exploit human intelligence in requirements analysis, Dhinakaran et al. [88] proposed an active learning approach to classify requirements into features, bugs, rating and user experience. Recently, Williams et al. [87] proposed that *automated social mining and domain modeling techniques* can be used to analyse mobile app success and failure stories to identify end-users' concerns of domain. Khan et al. [90], applied *AI techniques* to a crowd-generated dataset to cluster relevant features and then draw a *semi-automated goal model* from the extracted features. Stade et al. [73] proposed that automated approaches are required to combine monitored data with feedback data in crowd environment. To support continuous requirements elicitation Oriol et al. [93], proposed a framework to simultaneously collect feedbacks and monitoring data from mobile and web users. Gamification can be used to keep the crowd motivated and engaged. Kifetew et al. [36] developed gamification-based requirements prioritization tool to prioritize requirements. Moreover, our proposed framework is not final, that could be changed, and that, it needs verification and validation before being put into practice.

Recently, Williams et al. [87] proposed that automated social mining and domain modeling techniques can be used to analyse crowd-generated requirements. It can be seen in Table 3, possible AI techniques that can used for CrowdRE analysis, validation and modeling are, *information retrieval, sentiment analysis, language patterns, annotation, walkthrough, co-modeling, goal modeling, feature modeling and business process modeling, AI argumentation, CBR, Swarm algorithms and collaborative filtering* respectively. This lead to give answer to RQ2. These tasks are different nature but it can be overridden by introducing *automated algorithms* together with interactions with experts or knowledge base integrating crowd input and expert rules.

5   Discussion and Future Direction

Crowd participation are of potential aid for all RE activities. The size and significance of participation may vary but the added value is also the sense of participation itself where the crowd feel *relatedness* and *ownership* of the solutions all the way through the development process. *Relatedness* is a pillar of motivation as explained in self-determination theory (SDT) [11, 97]. Similar social principle can be adopted for motivating crowd members by integrating social media with crowd-based activities. Besides this, *fun and enjoyable* activities like visual effects, animations can be used to motivate and engage crowd members. *Aesthetics* in games are as important as level design and rewards. Continuous learning opportunities provided for user communities will also keep them interested in being involved. In fact, a one-size-fits all style for motivation would not work and personalization and cultural-awareness are needed [95, 96].

Much work has been done on requirements elicitation using the crowd. Requirements activities in CrowdRE are mostly focusing on user feedbacks. To cater for crowd intelligence, we can approach both experts (analysts, developers, domain experts) and non-expert users. Their input is then applied on the gathered feedbacks in different ways such as *sentimental analysis, information retrieval, co-modeling, goal modeling, usage mining, annotation, walkthrough reviews and prototyping*. User communities voluntarily contribute their data and intelligence by allowing run time monitoring of their behavior in order to identify recurring patterns. User logs are created from there feedback on usability issues, abnormal behaviors and run time exceptions, which are used as a media source. The nature of monitoring task is complex and required medium to high expertise.

For *requirements modeling*, we suggest direct or indirect collaboration support to incorporate crowd intelligence into requirements discoveries and decisions. Co-modeling scale shall be increased to cope with the volume and diversity of crowd. Semi-automated and fully automated goal-modeling techniques shall be used to model CrowdRE. Also, *Argumentation* can be used to model CrowdRE and capture requirements rationale. The current trend for collaborative modelling environments is more and more artefact-driven, as it embodied in the open software development platforms.

Our research map shows that multiple media channels are provided through which crowd input can be gathered. Different types of tasks can be delegated to the crowd using those media channels. The map suggests that for crowd intelligence to take effect, collaboration, competition or aggregation support is mandatory while there might be some projects which do not require collaborations amongst the crowd members. Mechanisms for collaborative tasks are provided to the crowd.

Similarly, input from different tasks can be aggregated to form the final outcome. For automated aggregation of individual contributions, data mining and analysis tools play an important role. To take maximum advantage of crowd intelligence in requirements gathering, certain incentives must be given to user communities in order to keep them motivated for actively and continuous feedback. For crowd intelligence to take effect, the crowd members have to be *independent, diversified* in terms of knowledge and skills [94]. Thus, we may look for differences rather than consensus when we collect raw requirements information, in particular, for paradigms like universal design and software product lines engineering (SPLE). When we analyse them and seek for creative ideas, we let the knowledge build up and form a continuation to better quality and better user experience by tracking and knowledge management tools [17, 18].

Harnessing the role of crowd in the validation is promising to cater for scalability and coverage of different user groups. In CrowdRE, raw requirements data come from end users are often massive in size, and are not generated by expert in RE, which leads to a threat. Therefore, automated requirements validation techniques are required for refining the set of requirements, reducing the complexity of task, or crowd sourcing the task back to the mass. Picking right requirements for the next release is important, which can be done through requirements prioritization and negotiation. *AI argumentation*, is best fit for eliminating ambiguity and decision making. Further work is required in CrowdRE for *preference elicitation* and *win-condition elicitation*. By considering the *users ranking, rating and comments* about current product features, adopt some *statistical analysis* could bring the state-of-the practice to a next level of success. Automated techniques, possibly supported by AI, are required to effectively prioritize the identify candidate requirements and keep as many stakeholders involved in the decision process as possible.

Once a list of candidate requirements is identified, they can be presented to the crowd members to elicit their preferences in prioritizing the potential requirements [80]. We can gather crowd intelligence in the form of preference elicitation and win-condition elicitation to support prioritization and negotiation. To support this, the proposed framework provides direct or indirect group decision making and voting mechanism. For requirements prioritization and negotiation, end users' participation is essential, thus it is necessary to keep them motivated by combining possible means, such as gamification, vouchers, social recognitions and monetary awards in order to achieve better user satisfaction and improved software usability.

Monitoring end users' behavior while interacting with the software system are very essential in CrowdRE. There is existing work in monitoring end user behavior by *mining user logs and mouse click events*. But it is only a start at a few minor points of the entire landscape. With the integration of crowd intelligence, we can collect feedbacks on usability issues, abnormal behaviors and run time exceptions. *Intelligent Mechanisms* are required to correlate monitoring data with user feedbacks, so that developers can better interpret the user's feedback. Although Monitoring tasks are very complex but its handling costs can be minimized with the introduction of *automated tools*. With the support of log analysis and data mining tools, it is easier for the development team in understanding the user feedback.

One open problem is in managing privacy of users which may deter users from participating, e.g. in discussion in an open forum for employees of a large-scale company. Privacy can be tackled by certain motivation mechanisms, including assurance by the organization policies, and data protection measures, including the right of the crowd to know how their individual input was judged and by whom. We note here that such measures can become a burden on the organization to adopt CrowdRE, e.g. in responding to Freedom of Information requests and the right of citizens to Automated Decision Making in the GDPR in Europe.

Acknowledgment. Financial support from the Natural Science Foundation of China Project no. 61432020 is gratefully acknowledged.

References

1. Adepetu, A., Ahmed, K.A., Abd, Y.A., Zaabi, A.A., Svetinovic, D.: CrowdREquire: a requirements engineering crowdsourcing platform. In: Proceedings of the AAAI Spring Symposium: Wisdom of the Crowd (2012)
2. Ali, R., Solis, C., Nuseibeh, B., Maalej, W.: Social sensing: when users become monitors. In: 19th ACM SIGSOFT Symposium and the 13th Conference on ESEC/FSE (2011)
3. Almaliki, M., Ncube, C., Ali, R.: Adaptive software-based feedback acquisition: a persona-based design. In. Proceedings of the IEEE 9th International Conference on RCIS 2015, pp. 100–111 (2015)
4. Bakiu, E., Guzman, E.: Which feature is unusable? Detecting usability and user experience issues from user reviews. In: RE Workshops, pp. 182–187 (2017)
5. Bano, M., Zowghi, D.: Crowd vigilante. In: Kamalrudin, M., Ahmad, S., Ikram, N. (eds.) APRES 2017. CCIS, vol. 809, pp. 114–120. Springer, Singapore (2018). https://doi.org/10.1007/978-981-10-7796-8_9
6. Bozzon, A., Brambilla, M., Ceri, S., Silvestri, M., Vesci, G.: Choosing the right crowd: expert finding in social networks. In: EDBT, pp. 637–648 (2013)
7. Brabham, D.C.: Crowdsourcing as a model for problem solving: an introduction and cases. Converg.: Int. J. Res. New Media Technol. 14(1), 75–90 (2008)
8. Breaux, T.D., Schaub, T.D.: Scaling requirements extraction to the crowd: experiments with privacy policies. In. Preceding of IEEE Requirement Engineering Conference (RE 2014), pp. 163–172 (2014)
9. Burnay, C., Horkoff, J., Maiden, N.: Stimulating stakeholders' imagination: new creativity triggers for eliciting novel requirements. In: Proceedings of IEEE RE Conference (RE 2016), pp. 36–45 (2016)
10. Byren, E.: Internal crowdsourcing for innovation development. Chalmers University of Technology, Sweden (2013)
11. Clifton, J.: State of the American WorkPlace (2013)
12. Dabrowski, J., Kifetew, F.M., Muñante, D., Letier, E., Siena, A., Susi, A.: Discovering requirements through goal-driven process mining. In: RE 2017 Workshops (2017)
13. Dalpiaz, F., Korenko, M., Salay, R., Chechik, M.: Using the crowds to satisfy unbounded requirements. In: Proceedings of CrowdRE@RE 2015, pp. 19–24 (2015)
14. Dheepa, V., Aravindhar, D.J., Vijayalakshmi, C.: A novel method for large scale requirement elicitation. Int. J. Eng. Innov. Technol. 2, 375–379 (2013)
15. Do, A.Q., Bhowmik, T.: Refinement and resolution of just-in-time requirements in open source software: a case study. In: RE Workshops 2017, pp. 407–410 (2017)
16. Ferrari, A., Donati, B., Gnesi, S.: Detecting domain-specific ambiguities: an NLP approach based on Wikipedia crawling and word embeddings. In: Proceedings of RE Workshops 2017, pp. 393–399 (2017)
17. Fricker, S.A., Wallmüller, E., Paschen, I.: Requirements engineering as innovation journalism: a research preview. In: Proceedings of RE 2016, pp. 335–340 (2016)
18. Fricker, S.A.: Systematic mapping of technology-enabled product innovations. In: RE 2016 Workshops (2016)
19. Greenwood, P., Rashid, A., Walkerdine, J.: UdesignIt: towards social media for community-driven design. In. Proceedings of the 34th International Conference on SE, pp. 1321–1324
20. Groen, E.C., Doerr, J., Adam, S.: Towards crowd-based requirements engineering: a research preview. In: Fricker, S.A., Schneider, K. (eds.) REFSQ 2015. LNCS, vol. 9013, pp. 247–253. Springer, Cham (2015). https://doi.org/10.1007/978-3-319-16101-3_16

21. Groen, E.C., et al.: The crowd in requirement engineering - the landscape and challenges. IEEE Softw. **34**(2), 44–52 (2017)
22. Groen, E.C.: Crowd out the competition gaining market advantage through crowd-based requirements engineering. In: IEEE Ist Workshop on CrowdRE, pp. 13–18 (2015)
23. Groen, E.C., Kopczynska, S., Hauer, M.P., Krafft, T.D., Dörr, J.: Users - the hidden software product quality experts?: A study on how app users report quality aspects in online reviews. In: RE 2017 Conference (2017)
24. Guzman, E., Alkadhi, R., Seyff, N.: A needle in a haystack: what do Twitter users say about software?. In: Proceedings of RE 2016 International Conference, pp. 96–105 (2016)
25. Guzman, E., Ibrahim, M., Glinz, M.: A little bird told me: mining tweets for requirements and software evolution. In: Proceedings of RE 2017, pp. 11–20 (2017)
26. Hamidi, S., Andritsos, P., Liaskos, S.: Constructing adaptive configuration dialogs using crowd data. In: ASE (2014)
27. Hu, W., Jiau, H.C.: UCFrame: a use case framework for crowd-centric requirement acquisition. ACM SIGSOFT Softw. Eng. Notes **41**(2), 1–13 (2016)
28. Hosseini, M., Shahri, A., Phalp, K., Taylor, J., Ali, R., Dalpiaz, F.: Configuring crowdsourcing for requirements elicitation. In: RCIS, pp. 133–138 (2015)
29. Hosseini, M., Phalp, K., Taylor, J. Ali, R.: Towards crowdsourcing for requirement engineering. In. 20th International Working Conference on Requirements Engineering: Foundation for Software Quality (REFSQ), Springer, Heidelberg (2014)
30. Hosseini, M., Phalp, K., Taylor, J., Ali, R.: The four pillars of crowdsourcing: a reference model. In: IEEE 8th RCIS (2014)
31. Hosseini, M., Groen, E.C., Shahri, A., Ali, R.: CRAFT: a crowed-annotated feedback technique. In. IEEE 25th International RE Conference Workshops, pp. 170–175 (2017)
32. Johann, T., Maalej, W.: Democratic mass participation of users in requirements engineering? In: Proceedings of the 23rd IEEE RE Conference, pp. 256–261 (2015)
33. Johann, T., Stanik C., Alireza, M., Alizadeh, B., Maalej, W.: SAFE: a simple approach for feature extraction from app descriptions and app reviews. In: RE 2017 (2017)
34. Kanchev, G.M., Murukannaiah, P.K., Chopra, A.K., Sawyer, P.: Canary: an interactive and query-based approach to extract requirements from online forums. In: RE 2017 (2017)
35. Kanchev, G.M., Chopra, A.K.: Social media through the requirements lens: a case study of Google maps. In: CrowdRE@RE 2015, pp. 7–12 (2015)
36. Kifetew, F.M., et al.: Gamifying collaborative prioritization: does pointsification work. In: RE 2017, pp. 322–331 (2017)
37. Kurtanovic, Z., Maalej, W.: Mining user rationale from software reviews. In: RE 2017 (2017)
38. Lakhani, K.R., Garvin, D.A., Lonstein, E.: TopCoder (A): developing software through crowdsourcing. Harvard Business School (2010)
39. Levy, M., Hadar, I., Teeni, D.: A gradual approach to crowd-base requirements engineering: the case of conference online social networks. In: IEEE 2nd CrowdRE, pp. 26–30 (2017)
40. Li, W., et al.: Crowd intelligence in AI 2.0 era. Front. IT EE **18**(1), 15–43 (2017)
41. Li, C., Huang, L., Luo, J.G.B., Ng, V.: Automatically classifying user requests in crowdsourcing requirements engineering. JSS **138**, 108–123 (2018)
42. Liang, W., Qian, W., Wu, Y., Peng, X., Zhao, W.: Mining context-aware user requirements from crowd contributed mobile data. In: Internetware, pp. 132–140 (2015)
43. Lim, S.L., Finkelstein, A.: StakeRare: using social networks and collaborative filtering for large-scale requirements elicitation. IEEE Trans. SE **38**, 707–735 (2012)
44. Linåker, J., Wnuk, K.: Requirements analysis and management for benefiting openness. In: RE Workshops 2016 (2016)

45. Liu, L., et al.: Requirements cybernetics: elicitation based on user behavioral data. JSS **124**, 187–194 (2017)
46. Lutz, R., Schäfer, S., Diehl, S.: Using mobile devices for collaborative requirements engineering. In: ASE 2012 (2012)
47. Maalej, W., Nayebi, M., Johann, T., Ruhe, G.: Toward data-driven requirements engineering. IEEE Softw. **33**, 48–54 (2016)
48. Maalej, W., Happel, H.-J., Rashid, A.: When users become collaborators: towards continuous and context-aware user input. In: Proceedings of the 24th ACM SIGPLAN Conference on Object-Oriented Programming Systems, Languages, and Applications (OOPSLA 2009) (2009)
49. Maalej, W., Nabil, H.: Bug report, feature request, or simply praise? On automatically classifying app reviews. In: Proceedings of the 23rd RE Conference (RE 2015), pp. 116–125 (2015)
50. Mao, K., Capra, L., Harman, M., Jia, Y.: A survey of the use of crowdsourcing in software engineering. J. Syst. Softw. **126**, 57–84 (2016)
51. Mead, N., Shull, F., Spears, J., Heibl, S., Weber, S., Cleland-Huang, J.: Crowd sourcing the creation of personae non gratae for requirements-phase threat modeling. In: RE 2017, pp. 412–417 (2017)
52. Merten, T., Falis, M., Hübner, P., Quirchmayr, T., Bürsner, S., Paech, B.: Software feature request detection in issue tracking systems. In: Proceedings of RE 2016, pp. 166–175 (2016)
53. Misra, J., Sengupta, S., Podder, S.: Topic cohesion preserving requirements clustering. In: RAISE@ICSE 2016 (2016)
54. Moketar, N.A., Kamalrudin, M., Sidek, S., Robinson, M., Grundy, J.C.: An automated collaborative requirements engineering tool for better validation of requirements. In: ASE 2016, pp. 864–869 (2016)
55. Munante, D., Siena, A., Kifetew, F.M., Susi, A., Stade, M., Seyff, N.: Gathering requirements for software configuration from the crowd. In: RE Workshops (2017)
56. Murukannaiah, P.K., Ajmeri, N., Singh, M.P.: Towards automating Crowd RE. In: Proceedings of IEEE 25th International RE Conference Workshops, pp. 512–515 (2017)
57. Murukannaiah, P.K., Ajmeri, N., Singh, M.P.: Acquiring creative requirements from the crowd: understanding the influences of personality and creative potential in crowd RE. In: RE 2016, pp. 176–185 (2016)
58. Nascimento, P., Aguas, R., Schneider, D.S., Souza, J.M.: An approach to requirements categorization using Kano's model and crowds. In: CSCWD 2012, pp. 387–392 (2012)
59. Niu, N., Koshoffer, A., Newman, L., Khatwani, C., Samarasinghe, C., Savolainen, J.: Advancing repeated research in requirements engineering: a theoretical replication of viewpoint merging. In: RE 2016, pp. 186–195 (2016)
60. Nuseibeh, B., Easterbrook, S.: Requirements engineering: a roadmap. In: FOSE 2000 (2000)
61. Piras, L., Giorgini, P., Mylopoulos, J.: Acceptance requirements and their gamification solutions. In: RE 2016 (2016)
62. Qi, J., Zhang, Z., Jeon, S., Zhou, Y.: Mining customer requirements from online reviews: a product improvement perspective. Inf. Manag. **53**(8), 951–963 (2016)
63. Regnell, B., Brinkkemper, S.: Market-driven requirements engineering for software products. In: Aurum, A., Wohlin, C. (eds.) Engineering and Managing Software Requirements, pp. 287–308. Springer, Heidelberg (2005). https://doi.org/10.1007/3-540-28244-0_13
64. Rooijen, L., Bäumer, F.S., Platenius, M.C., Geierhos, M., Hamann, H., Engels, G.: From user demand to software service: using machine learning to automate the requirements specification process. In: RE Workshops, March 2017

65. Saito, S., Iimura, Y., Massey, A.K., Antón, A.I.: How much undocumented knowledge is there in agile software development?: case study on industrial project using issue tracking system and version control system. In: RE 2017, pp. 194–203 (2017)
66. Salay, R., Dalpiaz, F., Chechik, M.: Integrating crowd intelligence into software. In: CSI-SE 2015, pp. 1–7 (2015)
67. Schneider, K., Karras, O., Finger, A., Zibell, B.: Reframing societal discourse as requirements negotiation: vision statement. In: RE Workshops 2017, pp. 188–193 (2017)
68. Sherief, N., Abdelmoez, W., Phalp, K., Ali, R.: Modelling users feedback in crowd-based requirements engineering: an empirical study. In: Ralyté, J., España, S., Pastor, Ó. (eds.) PoEM 2015. LNBIP, vol. 235, pp. 174–190. Springer, Cham (2015). https://doi.org/10.1007/978-3-319-25897-3_12
69. Shi, L., Chen, C., Wang, Q., Boehm, B.M.: Is it a new feature or simply "Don't Know Yet"?: on automated redundant OSS feature requests identification. In: RE 2016, pp. 377–382 (2016)
70. Snijders, R., Dalpiaz, F., Hosseini, M., Shahri, A., Ali, R.: Crowd-centric requirement engineering. In. IEEE/ACM 7th International Conference on Utility and Cloud Computing (2014)
71. Snijders, R., Dalpiaz, F., Hosseini, M., Ali, R., Ozum, A.: REfine: a gamified platform for participatory requirement engineering. In: 23rd IEEE RE Conference, pp. 1–6 (2015)
72. Srivastava, P.K., Sharma, R.: Crowdsourcing to elicit requirements for MyERP application. In: IEEE Ist International Workshop on CrowdRE, pp. 31–35 (2015)
73. Stade, M., et al.: Providing a user forum is not enough: first experiences of a software company with CrowdRE. In: IEEE 2nd International Workshop on CrowdRE, pp. 164–169 (2017)
74. Stol, K., Fitzgerald, B.: Two's company, three's a crowd: a case study of crowdsourcing software development. In: Proceedings of 36th ICSE (2014)
75. Sutcliffe, A., Sawyer, P.: Beyond awareness requirements. In: RE 2016, pp. 383–388 (2016)
76. Surowiecki, J.: Why the Many are Smarter than the Few and How Collective Wisdom Shapes Business, Economics, Society and Nations. Brown, Little, New York (2004)
77. Todoran, I., Seyff, N., Glinz, M.: How cloud providers elicit consumer requirements: an exploratory study of nineteen companies. In: 21st IEEE RE Conference (2013)
78. Wikipedia: Crowdsourcing (2017). https://en.wikipedia.org/wiki/Crowdsourcing. Accessed 28 Nov 2017
79. Williams, G., Mahmoud, A.: Mining Twitter feeds for software user requirements. In: RE 2017, pp. 1–10 (2017)
80. Xiao, S., Wei, C., Dong, M.: Crowd intelligence: analyzing online product reviews for preference measurement. Inf. Manag. 53(2), 169–182 (2016)
81. Xie, H., et al.: A statistical analysis approach to predict user's changing requirements for software service evolution. J. Syst. Softw. 132, 147–164 (2017)
82. Zhang, W., Mei, H.: Software development based on collective intelligence on the internet: feasibility, state-of-the-practise, and challenges. SCIENTIA SINICA Informationis (2017). (in Chinese)
83. Muganda, N., Asmelash, D., Samali, M.: Groupthink decision making deficiency in the requirements engineering process: towards a crowdsourcing model (2012)
84. Wang, H., Wang, Y., Wang, J.: A participant recruitment framework for crowdsourcing based software requirement acquisition. In: Conference on Global Software Engineering (2014)
85. Seyff, N., et al.: Crowd-focused semi-automated requirements engineering for evolution towards sustainability. In: Proceedings of 26th RE@Next Conference (RE 2018) (2018)

86. Sarro, F., Harmna, M., Jia, Y., Zhang, Y.: Customer rating reactions can be predicted purely using app features. In: Proceedings of 26 IEEE RE Conference (RE 2018) (2018)
87. Williams, G., Mahmoud, A.: Modeling user concerns in the app store: a case study on the rise and fall of Yik Yak. In: Proceedings of 26 IEEE RE Conference (RE 2018) (2018)
88. Dhinakaran, V.T., Pulle, R., Ajmeri, N., Murukannaiah, K.P.: App review analysis via active learning: reducing supervision effort without compromising classification accuracy. In: RE 2018 (2018)
89. Gemkow, T., Conzelmann, M., Hartig, K., Volesang, A.: Automatically glossary term extraction form large-scale requirements specifications. In: 26th IEEE RE Conference (2018)
90. Khan, J.A., Lin, L., Jia, Y., W, L.: Linguistic analysis of crowd requirements: an experimental study. In: Proceedings of 27th IEEE RE Workshop (Empri 2018), pp. 24–31 (2018)
91. Liu, X., Leng, Y., Yang, W., Zhai, C., Xie, T.: Mining android app descriptions for permission requirements recommendation. In: 26th IEEE RE Conference (2018)
92. Hosseini, M., Moore, J., Almaliki, M., Shahri, A., Phalp, K.T., Ali, R.: Wisdom of the crowd within enterprises: practices and challenges. Comput. Netw. **90**, 121–132 (2015)
93. Oriol, M., et al.: FAME: supporting continuous requirements elicitation by combining user feedback and monitoring. In: Proceedings of 26th RE Conference (RE 2018) (2018)
94. Surowiecki, J.: The Wisdom of Crowds. Anchor Books, New York (2005)
95. Shahri, A., Hosseini, M., Almaliki, M., Phalp, K., Taylor, J., Ali, R.: Engineering software-based motivation: a persona-based approach. In: The 10th IEEE Conference RCIS (2016)
96. Almaliki, M., Ali, R.: Persuasive and culture-aware feedback acquisition. In: Meschtscherjakov, A., De Ruyter, B., Fuchsberger, V., Murer, M., Tscheligi, M. (eds.) PERSUASIVE 2016. LNCS, vol. 9638, pp. 27–38. Springer, Cham (2016). https://doi.org/10.1007/978-3-319-31510-2_3
97. Ryan, R.M., Deci, E.L.: Self-determination theory and the facilitation of intrinsic motivation, social development, and well-being. Am. Psychol. **55**(1), 68 (2000)

Towards a Meta-model for Requirements-Driven Information for Internal Stakeholders

Ibtehal Noorwali[1](✉), Nazim H. Madhavji[1], Darlan Arruda[1],
and Remo Ferrari[2]

[1] Department of Computer Science, University of Western Ontario,
London, ON, Canada
{inoorwal,darruda3}@uwo.ca, madhavji@gmail.com
[2] Siemens Mobility, New York, USA
remo.ferrari@siemens.com

Abstract. **[Context & Motivation]** Providing requirements-driven information (e.g., requirements volatility measures, requirements-design coverage information, requirements growth rates, etc.) falls within the realm of the requirements management process. The requirements engineer must derive and present the appropriate requirements information to the right internal stakeholders (IS) in the project. **[Question/Problem]** This process is made complex due to project-related factors such as numerous types of ISs, varying stakeholder concerns with regard to requirements, project sizes, a plethora of software artifacts, and many affected processes. However, there is little guidance in practice as to how these factors come into play together in providing the described information to the ISs. **[Principle ideas/results]** Based on analyzed data from an action research (AR) study we conducted in a large systems project in the rail-automation domain, we propose a meta-model that consists of the main entities and relationships involved in providing requirements-driven information to internal stakeholders within the context of a large systems project. The meta-model consists of five main entities and nine relationships that are further decomposed into three abstraction levels. We validated the meta-model in three phases by researchers and practitioners. **[Benefits/Contribution]** The meta-model is anticipated to facilitate: (i) control and management of process and resources for providing requirement-driven information to stakeholders and (ii) communication among internal stakeholders.

Keywords: Requirements engineering · Requirements management ·
Requirements metrics · Meta-model · Internal stakeholders · Empirical study

1 Introduction

Context. The requirements engineering (RE) process and resultant requirements usually inform and interact with downstream (e.g., design and testing), upstream (e.g., contract management), and side-stream (e.g., project and quality management) processes in various ways. Each of these processes involves numerous internal stakeholders (e.g., managers, developers, architects, etc.) who, in turn, have different

© Springer Nature Switzerland AG 2019
E. Knauss and M. Goedicke (Eds.): REFSQ 2019, LNCS 11412, pp. 262–278, 2019.
https://doi.org/10.1007/978-3-030-15538-4_19

concerns with regard to the impact of requirements on their respective processes. In other words, the various stakeholders need different types of requirements information in order for them to manage, control, and track their respective process activities (e.g., requirements engineer: measures that track and monitor requirements growth; architect: requirement-design coverage information; systems manager: percentage of requirements dropped per release; etc.) [1–4]. The burden of providing this information (hereon, "requirements-driven information"), generally falls within the realm of the requirements management process [5, 6].

Problem. To this end, we conducted an action research (AR) study in a large systems project in the rail-automation domain to derive requirements-driven information that can be used by the project's internal stakeholders (IS) (see Sect. 3.2). However, we found it difficult for requirements engineers to derive and provide the various internal stakeholders with the correct requirement-driven information that addresses their various concerns due to a lack of understanding of: (i) the type of information that can be generated from system requirements, (ii) who the ISs are that would benefit from information generated from system requirements, (iii) the concerns of ISs which can be addressed by providing requirement-driven information, (iv) how the ISs use that information to address their various concerns, and (v) the type of artifacts needed to derive the requirements-driven information. This problem is also mirrored in the scientific literature (discussed in more detail in Sect. 2).

Principle Idea. To address the problem we experienced in industry we ask the following research questions: **RQ1:** What are the types of entities involved in the process of providing requirements-driven information to ISs in a large systems project? **RQ2:** What are the relationships that exist among the entities involved in the process of providing requirements-driven information to ISs in a large systems project? To answer the research questions, we performed a post-analysis on the data gathered from the AR study we conducted in industry (see Sect. 3.1). The result of the post-analysis is a meta-model that maps out the entities and relationships involved in providing requirements-driven information to ISs. The anticipated benefits of using the meta-model include (i) control and management of processes and resources involved in providing requirement-driven information to ISs and (ii) communication among ISs.

Contributions. The key contributions of this paper are: (i) descriptions of the entities involved in providing requirements-driven information to ISs, (ii) descriptions of the relationships among the identified entities, (iii) an empirically derived meta-model that combines the identified entities and relationships, and (iv) a discussion of the meta-model and its implications on industry and research.

Paper Structure. Section 2 describes related work; Sect. 3 describes the research methods; Sect. 4 presents the meta-model with a detailed description; Sect. 5 discusses the validation procedures and threats to validity; Sect. 6 discusses implications of the meta-model, and Sect. 7 concludes the paper and describes future work.

2 Related Work

This section focuses on three key issues in RE meta-models: (a) ISs and their concerns, (b) requirements-driven information, and (c) relationships among the preceding two items. With respect to IS, the literature lacks a comprehensive understanding of the types of ISs that can exist in large systems engineering projects and their concerns regarding requirements. Though the term "stakeholders" is well-known in RE, in-depth research has focused on external stakeholders (i.e., client/customer, business) and their concerns, which are usually translated into new requirements [7], while the concerns of ISs (e.g., project managers, architects, etc.) are rarely addressed [8]. In the rare cases in which ISs are addressed, the problem is two-fold: (1) they focus on developer concerns only (e.g., source code defect analytics) [8], or (2) the stakeholders are roughly divided into generic notions of "developer" and "manager" [1]. However, our observation is that ISs and their concerns exist at a finer granularity (e.g., different types of managers, technical stakeholders, and concerns).

In addition, requirements-driven information is usually limited to requirements quality metrics (e.g. use case completeness metrics) [9] and basic progress metrics (e.g., number of 'complete' requirements) [6, 10] that do not specifically address the concerns of the spectrum of internal stakeholders within a project.

Finally, the relationships amongst: (i) internal stakeholders, (ii) stakeholder concerns, and (iii) requirements-driven information have not yet received significant research attention. Thus, managing these elements to derive requirements-driven information from the correct sources and providing it to the correct ISs becomes a tedious task in practice.

From the above analysis, to our knowledge, a model to support the requirements management task of deriving and reporting requirements-driven information to internal stakeholders is currently lacking. The remainder of this paper addresses this gap.

3 Research Method

The meta-model presented in this paper is a result of a post analysis performed on data gathered from an AR study we conducted in industry. Figure 1 provides an overview of the research methods and data used in this study. The following subsections discuss the data gathering and data analysis stages in detail.

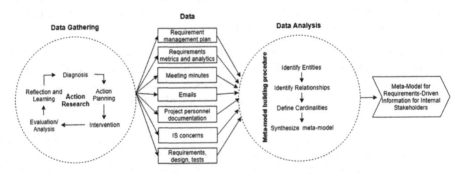

Fig. 1. Overview of study research methods and data

3.1   Data Gathering: Action Research Study

Action research (AR) is an iterative process involving researchers and practitioners acting together on a particular cycle of activities, including problem diagnosis, action planning, intervention/action taking, evaluation, and reflection/learning [11], where researchers identify problems through close involvement with industrial projects, and create and evaluate solutions in an almost indivisible research activity. We note that, because the goal of the AR study was to derive requirements-driven information (not reported in this paper) to be used by the ISs, we limit our description of the AR procedure to details relevant to the meta-model and its underlying constructs.

Our AR study, which followed the described approach [11], was conducted in a large-scale rail automation project in a multi-national company in the United States. The overall project (i.e., program) consisted of three sub-projects, each sub-project consisted of a product that had its own set of requirements, architecture design, test cases, and engineering team. Table 1 shows a breakdown of the software artifacts, number of requirements, design objects, and test cases per product that the first author worked with. Other official project documents that were analyzed included: requirements and change management plans and project personnel documentation that describe the roles and responsibilities of the ISs involved in the projects. The project adopted a waterfall software development approach. The internal project stakeholders included: systems manager, R&D managers, test mangers, developers, architects, testers, project managers, program managers, safety managers, quality mangers, financial managers, and project operations managers.

The AR study began in February 2017. The primary researcher (1st author) was onsite full-time for ten months and worked with the primary industrial partner (4th author) and secondary industrial participants (internal project stakeholders) in consultation with a senior researcher (2nd author).

In the diagnosis phase, the primary researcher, primary industrial partner and senior researcher, through a series of unstructured interviews, found that a central problem in the projects' RE process is a difficulty in tracking, monitoring, and managing requirements-driven information such as requirement growth (e.g., how many requirements so far), volatility (e.g., number of changed requirements over releases), and coverage (e.g., number of requirements that have been covered by test and design) and a difficulty in in accessing this information by ISs. To solve this problem, the industrial partner and researcher conducted several meetings, as part of the action planning phase, and decided to derive, define, and validate a set of requirements

Table 1. Software artifact breakdown per product

Product	# of req. spec. docs.	# of reqs.	# of design docs.	# of design objects	# of test cases
Product 1	40	59335	23	8373	1770
Product 2	13	25502	3	1199	960
Product 3	37	50051	28	24618	827
Total	90	134888	54	34190	3557

metrics and analytics that can be provided to ISs and used within the requirements management and software development processes. The requirements-driven information would include: measures on requirements size, growth, coverage, volatility, safety requirements distribution.

In the intervention phase, the primary researcher, with continuous feedback from the primary industrial partner, conducted a document analysis on the requirements, design, and test documents in which the meta-data were gathered in spreadsheets and the completeness and consistency of the data were ensured (see Table 1). The researcher then used the gathered meta-data to define a set of metrics using GQM+ [12] (not reported in this paper). The measures for the different products (see Table 1) were calculated and organized in spreadsheets and graphs. To familiarize the ISs with the derived information and to gather feedback from them, three iterations of focus groups were held. IS feedback included suggestions for new metrics and addition of descriptive information (e.g., dates) to the tables and graphs. After the three rounds of focus groups, the researcher provided the updated requirements-driven information to the ISs individually and upon request. Thus, the researcher received continuous feedback through direct engagement with the internal stakeholders and observation of the stakeholders' use of the information. Once the requirements metrics were inserted into the requirements management process, the primary researcher and industrial partner decided to add the requirements 'analytics' element by proposing a 'traffic-light' system that would provide insight into the projects' health. Such a system would utilize the derived requirements metrics in conjunction with other project artifacts such as project schedules, budget, resources, etc. The researcher evaluated the intervention effects of the derived metrics on the requirements management and system development processes through informal discussions with the primary and secondary industrial participants and observations of the processes. Issues such as improved requirement-design coverage, improved planning of time and effort per release, etc. were noted.

As part of the reflection and learning phase of the AR study, the primary researcher took on the task of eliciting the challenges and lessons learned during the study, which resulted in the identification of the problems in Sect. 1 (i.e., lack of understanding of: the types of requirements-driven information, the ISs and their concerns with regard to the requirements-driven information, IS usage of the information, the project artifacts needed to derive the information). This, in turn, led to the research questions posed in Sect. 1. In an attempt to answer these questions, and given the availability of data from the AR study, a post-analysis was conducted to construct the meta-model, which we discuss in the following subsection.

3.2 Data Analysis: Meta-model Building Procedure

To answer the research question posed in Sect. 1, we adopted the model construction process by Berenbach et al. [5] as we found it to be comprehensive. Berenbach states that a holistic understanding of the domain of interest is a prerequisite before commencing a model-construction process [5]. Our AR study allowed us to gain first-hand and in-depth knowledge of the overall context of the requirements engineering and software development processes in the project under study. Moreover, our continuous collaboration with our industrial partner allowed for live feedback throughout the AR study and model-construction process, thus supporting incremental validation of the resultant meta-model. The key steps of the model construction process are:

(i)   *Identify entities (RQ1):* The entities were incrementally identified and added to the meta-model by analyzing the data gathered from the AR study. First, the primary researcher extracted the metrics and the IS concerns they addressed from the metric spreadsheets and GQM+ document that was used to define the metrics during the AR study. The ISs were identified from the project's personnel documents and from meeting minutes that were gathered from the focus groups that were conducted during the AR. The project processes were extracted from the project's requirements management and change plans. We note that, up until this point of the entity identification process, the entities were concrete project data. We then began creating abstractions of the identified entities. For example, stakeholder categories in light of their requirements-related information needs (i.e., primary technical stakeholders, regular technical stakeholders, mid-level managers, high-level managers) were identified through analyzing the ISs' feedback and the primary researcher's correspondences with the ISs during the AR study. Specifically, the level of detail of the requirements-driven information requested by the ISs and the frequency with which they requested it were the main factors in determining these categories (see Fig. 1).

(ii) *Identify relationships among entities (RQ2):* We identified the relationships among the entities based on organizational rules such as the relationships between software artifacts and processes and their constituents. Other relationships were identified based on the metrics derived from the AR study such as the relationship between requirements metrics and their types. Finally, some relationships were identified based on our observations of the process and interactions between various elements in the project such as the relationship between ISs and their concerns.

(iii) *Synthesize the meta-model:* the identification of the entities and their relationships occurred iteratively and in parallel. Therefore, meta-model synthesis was an ongoing process since the beginning of the meta-model building procedure. For example, when we identified three main entities at the beginning of the process (i.e., requirements metrics, ISs, and IS concerns), we added the relationships between them and further entities and relationships were iteratively added as we gained better understanding of the entities and relationships involved. Moreover, the meta-model was incrementally updated in tandem with the feedback received from the reviews by the industrial partner, senior researcher and junior researcher, which resulted in the first version of the meta-model that did not include abstraction levels. After further evaluation and feedback at a workshop session [13] (see Sect. 5 for validation details), the abstraction levels were added, and the entities and relationships were updated accordingly.

We adopted Berenbach's [5] notation, for familiarity by the sponsor's organization, to depict the meta-model elements. An entity is represented by a rectangular box with the name of the entity. A relationship is represented by a line connecting two elements with a label to indicate the type of relationship between the elements.

4   A Meta-model for Requirements-Driven Information for Internal Stakeholders

The meta-model is intended to complement the organization's requirements engineering process, specifically, the requirements management process. The company's requirements engineering process consists of: requirements elicitation, analysis, validation and management. The requirements management process includes a number of activities: tracing, managing requirements workflow states, managing requirements change, deriving and reporting requirements measures and other relevant requirements-driven information; the meta-model is intended to support this latter activity.

The current version of the meta-model for requirements-driven information for ISs consists of entities and relationships organized across three abstraction levels as proposed by [14]. In this section we will discuss the entities, relationships among the entities, and abstraction levels. Figure 2[1] depicts the synthesized meta-model.

Entities. The meta-model consists of five main entities that are pertinent to the process of deriving and providing requirements-driven information to ISs: *requirements-driven information* consists of information mainly derived from requirements and requirements meta-data and that may be supported with other artifact data; *ISs* who are involved in the system development and use the requirements-driven information; *concerns* that the ISs have with regard to the requirements-driven information and that are addressed by that information; *artifacts* from which the requirements driven information is derived; and *processes* in which the IS are involved in. These entities are represented at abstraction **Level 1**, the highest level of abstraction in the meta-model. Entities and relationships at level 1 are abstract and generalizable enough to be applicable to any context regardless of domain, software development process, or organizational structure.

The decomposed entities constitute abstraction **Level 2** of the meta-model. Entities at Level 2 are also intended to be generalizable to different contexts. However, its applicability may differ from one context to another. For example, while in a large systems project, such as ours, the distinctions between managerial and technical ISs are well defined, the differences may not be so evident in a smaller, more agile project.

Thus, it is up to the project stakeholders to decide which ISs fall into which entity type. Table 2 consists of the entity descriptions at abstraction level 2. Due to space limitations, we restrict our discussion to entities that are not deemed self-explanatory.

The entities at abstraction level 2 are further decomposed into entities at abstraction **Level 3**. Level 3 is the project specific level in which the entities are tailored to represent the environment of a given project in a specific domain and development process.

For example, requirement metrics in our study consisted of size, growth, volatility, coverage, and maturity metrics. Another project's requirements metrics may include only volatility metrics. The same applies to other entities. Because entities at level 3 are

---

[1] High resolution images of Figs. 2 and 3 can be found at: http://publish.uwo.ca/~inoorwal/Uploads/Meta-Model_publish.pdf.

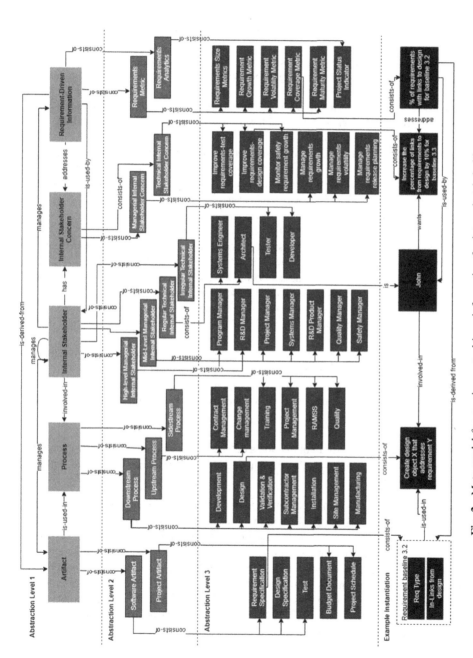

Fig. 2. Meta-model for requirements-driven information for internal stakeholders

Table 2. Descriptions of meta-model entities at abstraction level 2

Entity	Description
Requirements metric	A measurement derived from requirements to provide a quantitative assessment of certain requirements attributes
Requirement analytics	Analytics on requirements data in conjunction with other software artifacts (e.g., design, code, budget and schedule documents, etc.) that aims to gain insight about the state of the project from a requirements perspective
High-level managerial IS	Managerial stakeholders who manage at the project level or higher (i.e., program or regional levels) such as the program or regional R&D manager, etc.
Mid-level managerial IS	Managerial stakeholders who manage at the project level or lower (i.e., product level) such as test manager, product quality manager, etc.
Regular technical IS	Technical ISs who use requirement-driven information regularly such as architects and requirements engineers
Irregular technical IS	Technical internal stakeholders who use requirement-driven information less frequently such as developers and testers
Managerial IS concern	Managerial issues that ISs care about in relation to the requirements such as estimating time and effort for a software release
Technical IS concern	Technical issues that ISs care about in relation to the requirements such as increasing requirement-design coverage
Downstream process	Activities involved in system development and initiated after the requirements engineering process such as development, design, testing, etc.
Upstream process	Activities that are involved in system development and are initiated before the RE process such as contract/client management
Sidestream process	Activities involved in system development and initiated and executed alongside the RE process such as quality and project management, etc.

specific to our project, we did not include a detailed description of them. However, they can be seen in Fig. 1 and they illustrate how the meta-model can be applied within a large systems project.

Relationships. The following relationships are represented in the model: (1) is-used-by: represents the relationship when an inanimate entity (e.g., requirements metrics) is used by an animate entity (e.g., IS) to aid in technical or managerial tasks. (2) is-used-in: represents the relationship between entities when an inanimate entity (e.g., artifact) is used in another inanimate entity (e.g., process) to support the definition, execution, or management of the inanimate entity it is being used in. (3) addresses: represents the relationship between requirements-driven information and IS concerns. (4) consists-of: this relationship is used when an entity (e.g., requirements driven information) is composed of one or more of the related entities (e.g., requirements metrics and analytics). (5) is-derived-from: indicates that one entity (e.g., requirements size metrics) can be defined and specified from another entity (e.g., requirements specifications). (6) manages: indicates that an entity (e.g., ISs) can create, add, remove, modify the related entity (e.g., software artifacts). (7) involved-in: indicates that an entity (e.g., IS) actively participates in the related entity (e.g., processes). The participation can be in the form of execution, management, support etc. (8) has: indicates that an entity (e.g., ISs) possesses one or more of the related entities (e.g., IS concerns).

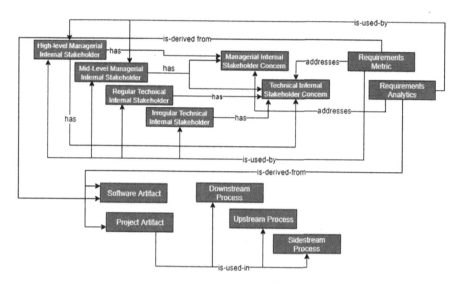

Fig. 3. A detailed overview of the relationships at abstraction level 2

The number of relationships among the entities increase as we go lower in abstraction level. This provides a more detailed picture of how the decomposed entities relate to one another [14] in different ways. For example, at **Level 1** there is one 'addresses' relationship between requirements-driven information and IS concerns. The 'addresses' relationships among the decomposed entities at **Level 2** increase in number and are more nuanced: requirements metrics 'addresses' managerial and technical IS concerns while requirement analytics 'addresses' managerial IS concerns only. Figure 3 shows the expansion of **Level 2** relationships. Similarly, the number of relationships among the decomposed entities at Level 3 increase in comparison to the relationships among the entities at Level 2. The relationships at Level 3 are project specific and thus can be tailored to project and organization rules. Due to space limitations and to preserve the readability of the model, we did not include project-specific relationships at level 3. Finally, the relationships that cross over the abstraction boundaries are *'consist-of'* relationships that connect the higher-level entities with their lower-level constituents.

Rationale. We believe that several entity and relationship choices in the meta-model warrant a discussion of their rationale. The identification of categories of ISs and IS concerns is based on their needs regarding requirements-driven information and therefore a discussion is warranted. The meta-model separates managerial and technical internal stakeholders because they have different *concerns* regarding requirements measures and information, and, therefore, require different types of requirements-driven information. For example, an architect is concerned with tracking and improving requirements-architecture coverage and, thus, needs to know the number of requirements with and without links to architecture. On the other hand, a R&D product manager is concerned with estimating time and effort for a product release. Therefore, s/he needs the number of allocated requirements for a specific release. However, our experience with a large–scale systems project revealed that managerial ISs may also have technical concerns. Then, how does the separation between managerial and technical ISs affect the generated requirements measures? We observed that even in the case when a technical and managerial IS share the same technical concern, the separation between managerial and technical ISs affected the level of detail of the relevant requirements-driven information. For example, both architect and a R&D manager may want to gain insight into the state of requirements-architecture coverage. However, while the architect is interested in detailed measures (e.g., the number of requirements that do not have links to architecture per feature, per release, and per requirements baseline), the R&D manager is interested in more big-picture measures (e.g., the overall percentage of requirements that have links to architecture per requirements baseline).

As for the separation between regular and irregular technical ISs, we observed that regular technical ISs need to be frequently updated with requirements-driven information while irregular technical ISs require the relevant information less frequently. For example, the architect requires a monthly report of requirement-architecture coverage measures and in detail. On the other hand, a tester requires requirement-test coverage measures only before a product release. Similarly, the separation between high-level and mid-level managerial ISs dictates both the frequency and level of detail of the relevant requirements information they need. These categorizations can aid the requirements engineer in knowing: *what* measures and information to generate and report from the requirements, to *whom* they should be reported, *how* to report it (i.e., level of detail), and *when* (i.e., how frequently), which, in turn, will facilitate the requirements management task of generating and reporting requirements relevant information.

Finally, the rationale for separating the meta-model into abstraction levels is to facilitate the tailoring of the meta-model to different contexts, and, thus, improving its generalizability.

Example Scenario. Figure 2 depicts an instantiation of the model based on our project data. For example, the measure '% of requirements with links to design for requirements baseline 3.2' is derived from the project's requirements specification and uses the attributes 'REQ Type' and 'In-links from design' in the requirements database to calculate the measure. The requirements measure is used in 'creating design objects that address the system requirements' that 'John' (architect) is involved in and who wants to 'increase requirements-design coverage by 10% for baseline 3.3'. Knowing that 'John' is a regular technical IS, the measure will be reported to him in detail, which includes the percentage and absolute value of requirements-design coverage for baseline 3.2. and a list of the requirements that do not have links to design is also provided.

5   Meta-model Validation

In [15], Shaw states that the form of validation in software engineering must be appropriate for the type of research result. For a qualitative model, validation through evaluation demonstrates that the study results (i.e., meta-model) describes the phenomena of interest adequately [15] and validation through experience shows evidence of its usefulness. Thus, the objectives of our validation are to: (i) ensure that the meta-model adheres to the scientific principles of model building, (ii) identify missing, superfluous, and/or incorrect entities and relationships, (iii) ensure that constructs (i.e., entities and relationships) represent their correct real-world meaning, and (iv) show preliminary evidence of its usefulness in practice.

To this end, the meta-model went through three phases of validation (see Table 3) by eight validators (see Table 4). The validators' areas of expertise include empirical software engineering, requirements engineering, quality and architecture, testing, software ecosystems, global and cross-organizational software development, agile methods, agent-oriented analysis, modeling, simulation, and prototyping of complex sociotechnical systems.

Table 3. Meta-model validation phases

Validation phase	Type of validation	Involved validators	Method	Output
Phase 1	Evaluation	V1, V2, V3	Expert opinion	Version 1 of the model (not included in paper)
Phase 2	Evaluation	V1, V4, V5, V6	Live study at workshop	Version 2 of the model (included in paper)
Phase 3	Evaluation, experience	V7, V8	Expert opinion	Evidence of meta-model usefulness

Table 4. Profile of meta-model validators

Validator	Research experience	Industry experience	Involved in studied project?
V1 Researcher	40 years	33 years of industry collaboration	No
V2 Practitioner	6 years	7 years	Yes
V3 Researcher	5 years	4 years	No
V4 Researcher	16 years	10 years of industry collaboration	No
V5 Researcher	44 years	30 years of industry collaboration	No
V6 Researcher	25 years	11 years	No
V7 Practitioner	2 years	17 years	Yes
V8 Practitioner	9 years	8 years	No

Phase 1. **V1** reviewed the meta-model for the soundness of its entities and relationships. He also brought to our attention the notion of 'change' in the meta-model. That is, who makes the changes to requirements metrics, software artifacts and stakeholders? This is in line with Berenbach's approach in which he states that the following questions must be asked when building a meta-model [5]: Who creates the entities? Who modifies them? How do they become obsolete? This feedback from V1 resulted in the addition of the '*manages*' relationship between: ISs and metrics, ISs and software artifacts, ISs and ISs (see Sect. 4 and Fig. 2). **V2** is the main requirements management figure in the project that we conducted our AR study. He manages the RE processes for all the products in the rail-automation project. He, therefore, is the most knowledgeable internal stakeholder on the RE processes. His validation consisted of feedback on the soundness of the meta-model constructs (i.e., entities and relationships) and ensured that the entities and relationships represented the project accurately. **V3** also reviewed the technical aspects of the meta-model to ensure the correctness of the meta-model. He also aided the first author in identifying proper relationship labels and reviewing the semantics of the meta-model.

Phase 2 consisted of a collaborative, live study at EmpiRE'18 [13] in which the meta-model from phase 1 was presented and explained to the audience. The participants were given questions to validate the meta-model, and then asked to write their answers on post-it notes that were pinned to their designated areas on the wall. 27 answers were provided in total and were used to enhance the meta-model. The main piece of feedback from the live study was the suggestion to divide the meta-model into abstraction levels.

Phase 3 is ongoing and consists of validating the meta-model for its usefulness in practice. To this end, we have sent out the meta-model to practitioners to gather their feedback on its usefulness. So far, we have received feedback from two practitioners (V7 and V8), who both asserted that the meta-model would be useful in practice with some modifications. V7, who has managed the project's quality management processes and is involved in the system architecture, says the meta-model would be very useful in managing the requirement-driven information that can be generated and disseminated among ISs. However, he suggests that "*this information get captured in modeling tools and thus tied to the system structure as opposed to chapters in a document*" for increased usability. V8 is from an external organization and states that "*I think the key are stakeholders. So taking the perspective of "WHO does/needs/provides WHAT?", this model would be a great way to elaborate what the stakeholder descriptions/roles are (for the internal stakeholders, and secondarily for the customer/upper management). In that respect, this model is a mental model that is used after having done stakeholder discovery (e.g., with the onion model) and gives some tools while documenting the stakeholder roles (e.g., when determining the importance & influence).*" Thus, phase three provides preliminary evidence for the anticipated practical benefits discussed in Sect. 1. V8 also suggested the replacement of the monochrome color scheme with different colors to facilitate reading and comprehension of the meta-model.

5.1   Threats to Validity

We discuss the study validity threats and how we mitigated them according to Runeson and Host's guidelines [16].

Internal Validity is concerned with the validity of causal relationships, typically in scientific experiments. Given that our study objective does not include investigation of causal relationships, this threat is not relevant to our study.

External Validity is concerned with the generalizability of the results to other contexts. The meta-model is based on the AR study conducted within the safety-critical, transportation domain, which may limit the meta-model's generalizability. Thus, readers must interpret and reuse the results in other contexts with caution. Despite this limitation, the results constitute an important data-point for making scientific progress. Further validation of the meta-model in different domains and project sizes is encouraged in order to improve its generalizability.

Construct Validity concerns the operationalized constructs of the study in that whether or not they accurately represent the real-world phenomena. It is possible that some meta-model entities (e.g., stakeholder concerns, metrics, etc.) might not have been captured accurately by the researcher. In order to minimize this threat, we validated the model constructs with our industrial partner and analyzed them against official project documentation to ensure that the constructs accurately reflect their real-world counterparts. In addition, given that the meta-model was not the main goal of the AR study, there is a risk that important data is missing from the meta-model. This risk was mitigated by obtaining feedback from a variety of sources on the meta-model entities and relationships during the workshop (see Sect. 5 for workshop details).

Reliability is concerned with the degree of repeatability of the study. The AR study followed AR principles for software engineering [17] to ensure rigor during the study. In addition, the AR and meta-model creation processes were documented to ensure traceability and analysis. Although a level of subjectivity is inevitable during the meta-model development process, our continuous involvement with our industrial partners and researchers inside and outside of the study helps to mitigate this threat.

6   Implications

Implications for Practice. The meta-model can aid in aligning internal stakeholder concerns with requirements-driven information that can be generated within the project [18]. It can also be an effective tool for enabling effective communication as well as controlling project complexity [18]. In our case, the complexity is the network of numerous internal stakeholders, stakeholder concerns, requirement metrics and analytics, downstream, upstream and side-stream processes, and a web of interactions amongst them. Therefore, mapping out the numerous elements and the relationships amongst them will equip requirement engineers with the understanding needed to effectively control and manage the requirements-driven information they are required to provide [18] and communicate to the right people (see Phase 3 of validation in Sect. 5). The meta-model could also aid incoming personnel (e.g., new requirements engineers) in understanding this complex web of interactions, which, in turn, will help them in their requirements management tasks.

The meta-model can also serve as a stepping-stone toward operationalizing the entities and relationships in the meta-model in the form of a tool (e.g., dashboard) that could aid practitioners in the requirements management process by implementing features inspired by the meta-model (see Phase 3 of validation in Sect. 5).

Implications for Research. The importance of requirements-driven information for internal stakeholders has been recognized by researchers [2, 8]. Some research efforts have targeted architects' and testers' information needs in relation to requirements and requirements specifications [2, 19] by proposing view-based solutions that would allow testers and architects to view the requirements specification in a format that will provide them with the requirements-based information they need. We take this work further by attempting to explicate the types of stakeholders in light of their needs with regard to requirements-driven information. Further research can be conducted to explore further questions addressing IS information needs with regard to requirements. Such questions could include: what are the types of ISs in an agile environment? What are their information needs with regard to requirements in an agile environment? In addition to requirements metrics and analytics, what other types of information can be generated from requirements and that can benefit internal stakeholders in their processes?

7   Conclusions and Future Work

Requirements is an information-rich software artifact that has the potential to provide ISs with information that can guide their respective processes. However, little is known about the types of ISs in light of their requirements-information needs, the information that can be generated from requirements, and how this information is used by ISs, all of which complicates the requirements management process. Based on empirical data that we gathered and analyzed from an AR study conducted in a large-scale rail automation project, we identified the main entities and relationships involved in providing requirement-driven information, which we assembled into a meta-model. The empirically derived meta-model depicts the internal stakeholders, internal stakeholder concerns, requirements-driven information, artifacts, processes, and relationships among them at three abstraction levels.

Our preliminary validation shows that the meta-model aids in understanding the complex network of entities and relationships involved in providing requirements-driven information to internal stakeholders. More specifically, the explicit identification of the types of internal stakeholders and their needs in relation to requirement-driven information (see Sect. 3) could facilitate: (i) communication among internal stakeholders and (ii) proper identification and presentation of requirement-driven information for the correct internal stakeholders (see Sect. 4).

For future work, we intend to extend the meta-model to include cardinalities, which will provide a more accurate representation of a project's rules and policies. For example, only one IS (i.e., requirements engineer) manages the requirements-driven information. This cardinality is a representation of the current project practices. Therefore, upon reading the meta-model, one would know that one person is in charge of managing the various requirements-driven information and so appropriate interpretation is facilitated. We also plan to incorporate the meta-model into the organization's requirements management plan to validate it empirically for its practicality, usefulness, and benefits within the project.

Acknowledgements. We thank Philipp Hullmann and Eduard Groen for their valuable feedback. This work is supported by the Ministry of Education of Saudi Arabia.

References

1. Buse, R.P.L., Zimmermann, T.: Information needs for software development analytics. In: International Conference on Software Engineering, Zurich, Switzerland, pp. 987–996 (2012)
2. Gross, A., Doerr, J.: What do software architects expect from requirements specifications? Results of initial explorative studies. In: 1st IEEE International Workshop on the Twin Peaks of Requirements and Architecture, pp. 41–45. IEEE, Chicago (2012)
3. Hess, A., DIebold, P., Seyff, N.: Towards requirements communication and documentation guidelines for agile teams. In: Proceedings of the 2017 IEEE 25th International Requirements Engineering Conference Workshops, REW 2017, pp. 415–418 (2017)
4. Doerr, J., Paech, B., Koehler, M.: Requirements engineering process improvement based on an information model. In: Proceedings of the IEEE International Requirements Engineering Conference, pp. 70–79 (2004)
5. Berenbach, B., Paulish, D.J., Kazmeier, J., Rudorfer, A.: Software and Systems Requirements Engineering in Practice. McGraw Hill, New York City (2009)
6. Wiegers, K.E.: More about Software Requirements: Thorny Issues and Practical Advice. Microsoft Press, Redmond (2006)
7. Sarkar, P.K., Cybulski, J.L.: Aligning system requirements with stakeholder concerns: use of case studies and patterns to capture domain expertise. In: Australian Workshop on Requirements Engineering, pp. 67–82 (2002)
8. Hassan, A.E., Hindle, A., Runeson, P., Shepperd, M., Devanbu, P., Kim, S.: Roundtable: what's next in software analytics. IEEE Softw. **30**, 53–56 (2013)
9. Costello, R.J., Liu, D.-B.: Metrics for requirements engineering. J. Syst. Softw. **29**, 39–63 (1995)
10. Berenbach, B., Borotto, G.: Metrics for model driven requirements development. In: Proceedings of the 28th International Conference on Software Engineering - ICSE 2006, Shanghai, China, pp. 445–451 (2006)
11. Susman, G., Evered, R.D.: An assessment of the scientific merits of action research. Adm. Sci. Q. **23**, 582–603 (1978)
12. Basili, V., Heidrich, J., Lindvall, M., Munch, J., Regardie, M., Trendowicz, A.: GQM^+ strategies – aligning business strategies with software measurement. In: First International Symposium on Empirical Software Engineering and Measurement (ESEM 2007), pp. 488–490 (2007)
13. Noorwali, I., Madhavji, N.H.: A domain model for requirements-driven insight for internal stakeholders a proposal for an exploratory interactive study. In: 2018 IEEE 7th International Workshop on Empirical Requirements Engineering, pp. 32–36 (2018)
14. Monperrus, M., Beugnard, A., Champeau, J.: A definition of "abstraction level" for metamodels. In: Proceedings of the International Symposium on Workshop on the Engineering of Computer Based Systems, pp. 315–320 (2009)

15. Shaw, M.: Writing good software engineering research papers. In: International Conference on Software Engineering, vol. 6, pp. 726–736 (2003)
16. Runeson, P., Höst, M.: Guidelines for conducting and reporting case study research in software engineering. Empir. Softw. Eng. **14**, 131–164 (2009)
17. dos Santos, P.S.M., Travassos, G.H.: Action research can swing the balance in experimental software engineering. Adv. Comput. **83**, 205–276 (2011)
18. Humphrey, W.S., Kellner, M.I.: Software process modeling: principles of entity process models. In: Proceedings of the 11th International Conference on Software Engineering, pp. 331–342. ACM (1989)
19. Hess, A., Doerr, J., Seyff, N.: How to make use of empirical knowledge about testers' information needs. In: IEEE 25th International Requirements Engineering Conference Workshops, pp. 327–330. IEEE Computer Society (2017)

In Situ/Walkthroughs (Research Previews)

Towards a Catalogue of Mobile Elicitation Techniques
Research Preview

Nitish Patkar$^{(\boxtimes)}$, Pascal Gadient$^{(\boxtimes)}$, Mohammad Ghafari$^{(\boxtimes)}$,
and Oscar Nierstrasz$^{(\boxtimes)}$

Software Composition Group, University of Bern, Bern, Switzerland
{nitish.patkar,pascal.gadient,mohammad.ghafari,
oscar.nierstrasz}@inf.unibe.ch
http://scg.unibe.ch/staff

Abstract. [**Context and Motivation**] Mobile apps are crucial for many businesses. Their reach and impact on the end users and on the business in return demands that requirements are elicited carefully and properly. Traditional requirements elicitation techniques may not be adequate in the mobile apps domain. [**Question/problem**] Researchers have proposed numerous requirements elicitation techniques for the mobile app domain, but unfortunately, the community still lacks a comprehensive overview of available techniques. [**Principle ideas/results**] This paper presents a literature survey of about 60 relevant publications, in which we identify 24 techniques that target mobile apps. We found that only every second strategy was evaluated empirically, and even worse, non-functional requirements were rarely considered. We provide an evaluation scheme that is intended to support readers in efficiently finding opportune elicitation techniques for mobile apps. [**Contribution**] The found literature characteristics may guide future research and help the community to create more efficient, yet better, apps.

Keywords: Requirements elicitation · Mobile applications · Literature survey

1 Introduction

Mobile applications have substantially gained traction since the two major distribution platforms and their operating systems came into existence a decade ago, *i.e.*, Google's Play Store (Android OS), and Apple's App Store (iOS OS). For example, the iOS platform encountered an increase in numbers of published apps from 2008 to 2018 of about 2 500 times, leading to 2M apps that are currently available in the store.[1] Similar numbers have been reported for the Android platform.[2] As a result, there exists a large base of users who demand seamless app experiences.

---

[1] https://www.statista.com/statistics/263795.
[2] https://www.statista.com/statistics/266210.

© Springer Nature Switzerland AG 2019
E. Knauss and M. Goedicke (Eds.): REFSQ 2019, LNCS 11412, pp. 281–288, 2019.
https://doi.org/10.1007/978-3-030-15538-4_20

The requirements elicitation phase of requirements engineering, which plays a critical role in the success of software applications, must take innovative forms to meet the individual needs of mobile app users. Typical difficulties are caused by the global variety of user affections, inconsistent device capabilities such as different screen size or battery life, and contextual factors such as user mobility. The research community has recognized this need, and since then has either proposed new elicitation techniques or modified existing ones to overcome these difficulties.

This paper aims to survey relevant literature, and to provide an initial step towards a comprehensive overview of requirements elicitation geared specifically towards mobile apps. Furthermore, we classify elicitation methods and propose an evaluation scheme for practitioners, based on our own criteria, which should provide invaluable immediate feedback to its users. Towards this aim, we pose the following three research questions:

- **RQ$_1$**: *What are the characteristics of current research in the field of mobile requirements elicitation i.e. requirements elicitation for mobile apps and use of mobile devices in requirements elicitation?* We elaborate on seven major properties found during the literature survey.
- **RQ$_2$**: *What are the existing techniques to elicit requirements for mobile applications?* We reviewed 60 publications shortlisted by well-defined inclusion and exclusion criteria, and we could identify 32 distinct elicitation methods.
- **RQ$_3$**: *How can developers be supported in the efficient selection of appropriate elicitation techniques?* We established an evaluation scheme that supports 19 parameters in six categories on which our elicitation methods can be evaluated successfully with little overhead for the practitioner.

The remainder of the paper is structured as follows: Sect. 2 outlines the research methodology we followed for conducting our literature survey. Section 3 presents an overview of the current research characteristics we found. In Sect. 4 we present several elicitation methods and propose a classification of these methods, leading ultimately to an actionable scheme for development leads. Finally, in Sect. 5 we report our conclusions.

2   Literature Survey

To carry out the literature survey we closely followed a well-known procedure from Kitchenham *et al.* [2]: conducting an initial search, screening the primary studies based on inclusion and exclusion criteria, before finally, the data are extracted and aggregated.

We performed three search iterations on five major digital libraries, *i.e.,* the ACM Digital Library, Springer Link, IEEE Explore, ScienceDirect, and Google Scholar. In the first iteration we used the search term "mobile requirements elicitation", and in the second the two terms "mobile requirement elicitation" and "mobile requirements engineering", as these terms lead to different results in some search engines. After carefully reviewing the results, we evaluated the cited publications of all relevant papers in the third iteration. We considered publications until October 2018, and did not apply any other filter to avoid incomplete results due to papers not closely following the publication guidelines, *e.g.*, using proper release dates. Ultimately, we collected 182 publications.

We then applied several inclusion and exclusion criteria to abstracts and introductions of the found literature. The inclusion criteria were: (i) the abstract or introduction should indicate a proposed elicitation method for mobile applications, or the use of a mobile device for eliciting requirements, (ii) the abstract is written in English, and finally, (iii) the study is accessible. In contrast, the exclusion criteria were: (i) languages other than English are used in the body of the paper, (ii) the paper is a short version of an extended paper, or (iii) the content is not relevant, *e.g.*, it presents a literature review rather than proposing a method.

In the end, 60 publications satisfied all criteria and were considered for the subsequent in-depth study. The complete list of the papers can be accessed online.[3]

3   Empirical Discoveries

We now present the seven major subjects that we identified while carrying out the literature survey in our investigation of RQ$_1$. We collected the properties by carefully reading each publication, while taking notes about specific peculiarities, *i.e.*, related to the *evaluation, meta* information, and *people*. Complementary information is only available online due to page limit restrictions. (See footnote 3)

Evaluation. 31 publications included an evaluation, while 29 did not report any evaluation. Of the 31 publications, 13 presented a case or field study, 16 described a controlled or industrial experiment, and two publications reported on evaluations with students. We clearly see that constrained (controlled or industrial) experiments prevail. Objective data-driven evaluation techniques were highly popular, *i.e.*, about 63%.

Effectiveness. Several different factors have a major impact on effectiveness; the ethnicity or cultural background of analysts being one of them. For example, the risk of misunderstood cultural differences is omnipresent when Indian citizens are working on requirements elicitation for a Swiss project. The literature proposes for such scenarios the *observation* technique that forces the subject to reason about localities. Another factor concerns data privacy obligations, which could substantially impede the effectiveness of traditional elicitation methods, *e.g.*, *interview*, if the client or stakeholder is not allowed to reveal the desired information. Unfortunately, the corresponding resolution strategy remains unclear from literature. In our study we found several factors that reduce effectiveness of requirements elicitation techniques, however, a resolution strategy has been proposed only for a few.

---

[3] http://scg.unibe.ch/download/supplements/REFSQ19_Supplementary_Materials. pdf.

Focus. Most of the methods are either human- or data-centric; only six publications propose an aggregation instead. Data-centric methods are useful to gather non-functional requirements (NFRs) or feature improvement requirements. They could cause severe privacy breaches, due to the availability of sensitive data. Furthermore, data-centric methods do not require stakeholders to be involved, but instead they rely heavily on natural language processing experts, and they require additional physical assets, such as computing hardware and workspaces, to analyze an enormous number of apps. In contrast, human-centric methods encourage creativity throughout the elicitation phase, and depend on the intensive use of human resources. We further discovered that benefits, drawbacks, and the evaluation of the proposed methods are frequently not the main concern of the authors, but rather they tend to focus on technical aspects of their solution.

Non-functional Requirements. While no method pays exclusive attention to NFRs, some methods do support the elicitation of certain NFRs, for instance, run time performance and user interface issues highlighted in app store reviews [1]. NFRs are crucial since they increase the app's usability for users, and answer special user needs, *e.g.,* the need for privacy and compatibility. Unfortunately, we did not find any guideline or evaluation scheme that would assist developers in choosing opportune methods for NFR elicitation.

Traditional Requirements Elicitation Techniques. Numerous traditional elicitation techniques such as *interview, brainstorming*, and *focus groups* have been adapted for mobile apps [4]. In addition, techniques based on data mining have also become very popular in mobile app requirements elicitation due to the extraordinarily large corpora used in app stores that provide a plethora of different features ready to use for requirements engineering, *e.g.,* end user review data and ratings. How to adapt a particular traditional requirements elicitation technique for mobile apps domain remains unanswered, as we did not find any guidelines or efforts put into this direction.

Collaboration Strategies. We found that about 68.3% of the reviewed publications, encourage active collaboration between analysts and stakeholders, 26.6% put the elicitation responsibility completely on the analysts' shoulders, and 31.6% suggest working only with data, avoiding any collaboration. Surprisingly, starting in the year 2004, 19% suggest that stakeholders should perform elicitation themselves. Furthermore, collaborative methods are frequently used in combination with methods targeting analysts, *e.g., interviews*. Unfortunately, clear patterns and guidelines are missing to help analysts choose a satisfactory combination.

End User Demographics. Eleven publications specifically focused on methods for children, the elderly, disabled people, and the illiterate. Of concern were elements that make apps delightful to use for them, or that match surprise factor to the audience, *e.g.,* gaining attention by audible notification is inaccessible to people suffering from deafness. All of the reviewed publications rely either on direct or indirect measures to gather contextual information and tacit knowledge. Direct measures, for example in app user feedback functionality, show a preference for eliciting requirements in the stakeholders' domain, which is especially helpful to capture functional requirements that are hard to formulate verbally. Indirect measures provide valuable insights without any end user interaction, for instance, data is collected autonomously while an app executes in the background (*e.g.*, location), or is gathered by observing user activities within the app.

4 Discussion

Here we present the found elicitation methods, classify them, and build a first version of an actionable scheme. RQ_2 and RQ_3 are briefly covered in Subsects. 4.1 and 4.2, respectively.

Table 1. Classification of methods

Analyst-centric category	Collaboration-centric category	Data-centric category	Stakeholder-centric category
Gamification	Activity theory	App description mining	Mobile feedback app
Interview/survey/questionnaire	Brainstorming	App log/ App usage data mining	User feedback on MVP
Modelling	CRC sessions	App store mining for similar apps	
Persona or User profiles	Crowdsourcing	Observation/Contextual data/Reflection	
Wizard of Oz	Focus groups	Opinion mining	
	Mobile requirements engineering app		
	Photo essay		
	Prototyping		
	Scenario		
	Story telling		
	Social networking sites/ Wiki		
	Viewpoints/ Six thinking hats		

4.1 Elicitation

A total of 24 elicitation methods were found in the 60 publications we studied. Due to space restrictions we only present an overview of the found methods in Table 1.

The classification of such methods is a non-trivial task as several parties with diverse interests are involved, *e.g.*, stakeholders, developers, and end users. Numerous solutions to this classification problem have been proposed, *e.g.*, based on the means of communication [4], or as suggested in our previous work, based on the commonalities between identifying problems and finding solutions [3].

As elicitation methods for mobile applications differ from traditional requirements elicitation methods, most evaluation schemes provide barely any help to mobile application developers. Hence we propose a novel evaluation scheme, where methods are classified according to data- and people-centric criteria, since one of the main purposes of current mobile apps is to provide access to a service-oriented infrastructure (*e.g.*, social media), that relies on a plethora of user data (*e.g.*, user feeds) to connect people (*e.g.*, friends).

We consequently grouped the elicitation methods into four categories as shown in Table 1: (i) *Data-centric.* Physical involvement of stakeholders is not required; these methods are intended to be used by analysts or requirement engineers. (ii) *Collaboration-centric.* Stakeholders and analysts have to physically work together in dedicated sessions. (iii) *Stakeholder-centric.* Stakeholders do not require the presence of analysts or requirement engineers to elicit requirements. (iv) *Analyst-centric.* These methods are intended to be used exclusively by analysts or requirement engineers; physical presence of stakeholders is not mandatory.

4.2   Evaluation Scheme

As it is important for practitioners to quickly select elicitation methods that best suit their organizational needs, we propose an evaluation scheme that provides immediate feedback regarding the selection of major requirements elicitation techniques in the mobile application domain. For each of the elicitation techniques we propose 19 evaluation parameters (*P01, ... , P19*) classified into six high level categories. Each category addresses a specific organizational resource.

The scheme is illustrated in Fig. 1 and supports various use cases: in the primary use case, the reader first determines the relevance of parameters or parameter categories in the topmost rows. Once the reader chooses the convenient parameters, the available methods are ready to explore in the respective columns. For example, if the reader is willing to convert an existing web application or a business process into a mobile app (*P18*), methods such as *Focus groups* or *Collaborative problem definition* will be efficient to apply as shown in Fig. 1a. Furthermore, the reader can exclude techniques by avoiding parameter combinations that are guaranteed to be unfeasible in the corresponding environment. For instance, if the reader can not afford to have personal collaborative interactions (collaborative-centric row category) with users or stakeholders (Stakeholders/Users column), all techniques that lie on the intersection of the row and the column are out of reach for the reader, however, the other techniques still remain available, *e.g.,* the elicitation method *App log/app usage data mining* would be a legitimate choice. We provide another motivating example for requirements engineers that already hold data assets, *e.g.,* data collected from app store reviews or social media platforms: These users can directly obtain all data-related methods by considering all methods available in the *Data-centric* row. Identical procedures, but with other parameters, can be performed with Fig. 1b.

In future work we plan to evaluate the utility of the evaluation scheme in practice, and to iterate its design to better support the selection of requirements elicitation methods for mobile apps.

Category	Methods	Data					Stakeholders and users					
		P01: Store reviews available?	P02: Social media feedback available?	P03: Similar apps available?	P04: Contextual data available?	P05: Complex app analysis possible?	P06: Are users known?	P07: Are users not known?	P08: Are users geographically distributed?	P09: Have beneficiaries special needs?	P10: Do beneficiaries lack literacy?	P11: Stakeholders ethnographic diverse?
Analyst-centric	Gamification						✓		✓			
	Interview						✓			✓	✓	✓
	Modeling			✓								
	Persona or user profiles							✓	✓			
	Wizard of Oz method						✓			✓		✓
Collaboration-centric	Brainstorming						✓					
	CRC sessions						✓					
	Crowdsourcing							✓	✓			✓
	Focus groups						✓			✓	✓	
	Mobile RE app						✓	✓				
	Photo essays						✓			✓	✓	
	Prototyping						✓					
	Scenarios						✓					
	Story telling						✓			✓	✓	
	Using social network sites or wikis						✓	✓				
	Viewpoint or six thinking hats						✓					
Data-centric	App description mining				✓	✓		✓				
	App log or app usage data mining				✓	✓		✓	✓	✓		✓
	App store mining for similar apps			✓	✓	✓						
	Observation/contextual data/reflection				✓		✓	✓	✓	✓	✓	✓
	Opinion mining	✓	✓	✓		✓		✓				
Stakeholder-centric	Activity theory						✓					
	Mobile feedback app						✓	✓	✓			
	User feedback on MVP						✓					

(a) data/stakeholder/user-based elicitation methods

Category	Methods	Communication channel		P14: Are NLP experts available?	Developers		Domain specificity	App specificity	
		P12: Is physical communication possible?	P13: Is digital communication possible?		P15: Are MVPs/prototypes feasible?	P16: Are developers geographically distributed?	P17: Is tacit knowledge involved?	P18: Does existing app, process, or web app exist?	P19: Is initial app idea present?
Analyst-centric	Gamification							✓	✓
	Interview	✓						✓	✓
	Modeling						✓		
	Persona or user profiles								✓
	Wizard of Oz method	✓							✓
Collaboration-centric	Brainstorming	✓					✓	✓	✓
	CRC sessions	✓					✓		✓
	Crowdsourcing		✓				✓	✓	
	Focus groups	✓					✓	✓	
	Mobile RE app		✓				✓		✓
	Photo essays	✓							✓
	Prototyping	✓			✓				✓
	Scenarios	✓					✓		✓
	Story telling	✓					✓		✓
	Using social network sites or wikis					✓			
	Viewpoint or six thinking hats	✓						✓	✓
Data-centric	App description mining			✓					
	App log or app usage data mining		✓					✓	
	App store mining for similar apps			✓				✓	✓
	Observation/contextual data/reflection						✓	✓	✓
	Opinion mining			✓					
Stakeholder-centric	Activity theory								
	Mobile feedback app		✓					✓	
	User feedback on MVP	✓			✓				✓

(b) communication/developer/domain/app-based elicitation methods

Fig. 1. Mobile requirements elicitation evaluation scheme

5 Conclusion

We have reviewed major relevant literature in the domain of requirements elicitation for mobile apps or using mobile devices, we extracted numerous elicitation methods, and derived categories suitable for easy selection. In addition, we discovered several different characteristics that have not yet been comprehensively covered in existing literature. Ultimately, we built an evaluation scheme which remains to be validated in practice, though we believe it is well-suited for all complex requirements elicitation scenario, as it is easy to apply and delivers immediate results. We are currently in the process of preparing an extended version of this literature survey.

Acknowledgments. We gratefully acknowledge the financial support of the Swiss National Science Foundation for the project "Agile Software Analysis" (SNSF project No. 200020-162352, Jan 1, 2016 - Dec. 30, 2018). We also thank CHOOSE, the Swiss Group for Original and Outside-the-box Software Engineering of the Swiss Informatics Society, for its financial contribution to the presentation of this paper.

References

1. Gebauer, J., Tang, Y., Baimai, C.: User requirements of mobile technology: results from a content analysis of user reviews. Inf. Syst. e-Bus. Manag. **6**(4), 361–384 (2008)
2. Kitchenham, B., Brereton, O.P., Budgen, D., Turner, M., Bailey, J., Linkman, S.: Systematic literature reviews in software engineering-a systematic literature review. Inf. Softw. Technol. **51**(1), 7–15 (2009)
3. Senft, B., Fischer, H., Oberthür, S., Patkar, N.: Assist users to straightaway suggest and describe experienced problems. In: Marcus, A., Wang, W. (eds.) DUXU 2018. LNCS, vol. 10918, pp. 758–770. Springer, Cham (2018). https://doi.org/10.1007/978-3-319-91797-9_52
4. Zhang, Z.: Effective requirements development - a comparison of requirements elicitation techniques. In: Berki, E., Nummenmaa, J., Sunley, I., Ross, M., Staples, G. (eds.) Software Quality Management XV: Software Quality in the Knowledge Society, pp. 225–240. British Computer Society (2007)

Towards the Next Generation of Scenario Walkthrough Tools – A Research Preview

Norbert Seyff[1]([✉]), Michael Vierhauser[2], Michael Schneider[3], and Jane Cleland-Huang[2]

[1] Institute for Interactive Technologies, FHNW & University of Zurich, Windisch, Switzerland
norbert.seyff@fhnw.ch

[2] Department of Computer Science and Engineering, University of Notre Dame, South Bend, IN, USA
{mvierhau,janeclelandhuang}@nd.edu

[3] Vocational School Baden, Baden, Switzerland
michael.schneider@bbbaden.ch

Abstract. [**Context and motivation**] With the rise of cyber-physical systems (CPS), smart ecosystems, and the Internet of Things (IoT), software-intensive systems have become pervasive in everyone's daily life. The shift from software systems to ubiquitous adaptive software-intensive systems not only affects the way we use software but further has an impact on the way these systems are designed and developed. Gathering requirements for such systems can benefit from elicitation processes that are conducted in the field with domain experts. [**Question/problem**] More traditional elicitation approaches such as interviews or workshops exhibit limitations when it comes to gathering requirements for systems of this nature – often lacking an in-depth context analysis and understanding of contextual constraints which are easily missed in a formal elicitation setting. Furthermore, dedicated methods which focus on understanding the system context such as contextual design are not widely adopted by the industry as they are perceived to be time-consuming and cumbersome to apply. [**Principal ideas/results**]. In this research preview paper we argue that scenario-based RE, scenario walkthrough approaches in particular, have the potential to support requirements elicitation for ubiquitous adaptive software-intensive systems through facilitating broader stakeholder involvement and enabling contextual requirements elicitation within the workplace of future system end-users. The envisioned on-site scenario walkthroughs can either be conducted by an analyst or by future end-users of the system themselves. [**Contribution**] We describe a research agenda including our ongoing research and our efforts to develop a novel framework and tool support for scenario-based RE.

Keywords: Contextual requirements elicitation · Scenario-based RE · Society

© Springer Nature Switzerland AG 2019
E. Knauss and M. Goedicke (Eds.): REFSQ 2019, LNCS 11412, pp. 289–296, 2019.
https://doi.org/10.1007/978-3-030-15538-4_21

1   Introduction and Motivation

Discovering, analyzing, and specifying requirements is of utmost importance for successful software- and systems engineering [10,12]. However, traditional requirements elicitation approaches (e.g., interviews and workshops) exhibit various limitations when it comes to the design and development of ubiquitous, adaptive software-intensive systems such as cyber-physical systems (CPS), smart ecosystems, cloud systems, and applications for the Internet of Things (IoT). There is a need for methods which are better-suited for gathering requirements from a large number of diverse stakeholders, require lower effort, and can be applied remotely [17]. Furthermore, a deep understanding of contextual issues is beneficial for the development of such systems [6] and contextual constraints can be easily missed in a more formal elicitation setting. Existing contextual requirements engineering methods such as contextual design [2] are often time-consuming to apply and are therefore not widely used in industry.

In this research preview paper, we argue that scenario-based RE, in particular, scenario walkthrough approaches have the potential to support requirements elicitation for ubiquitous adaptive software-intensive systems. We foresee different ways in which scenario walkthroughs can facilitate broader stakeholder involvement and create a more engaging requirements elicitation process. These include workshops with selected stakeholders as well as on-site scenario walkthroughs conducted either by an analyst or directly by end-users of the future systems. We furthermore envision that scenario tools would not only be applied during system design time, but could allow end-users and other stakeholders to continuously provide feedback and generate new ideas during system run time in order to support system evolution. These ideas are based on previous work and experiences in the field, as scenario-based RE has a long established tradition of using walkthroughs to support requirements elicitation and scenario validation within workshop settings and even on-site [1,7,8,15,19]. However, techniques developed a decade ago were based on technologies that simply were not mature enough at that time, rendering the successful, large-scale adoption of these approaches difficult if not infeasible.

In Sect. 2 we look back at seminal related work in the field of scenario-based RE, discuss limitations of previous scenario-based approaches, and identify new opportunities introduced by recent technological advances. Section 3 presents our research agenda and highlights research questions to drive future research in scenario-based RE. In Sect. 4 we present early research results in the form of a novel scenario tool prototype which will be the basis for evaluating scenario-based requirements discovery in different settings. Finally, Sect. 5 concludes this paper.

2   Looking Back a Decade: Earlier Tools and Limitations

Scenarios are used in diverse ways throughout the software system development life cycle, including requirements elicitation, negotiation, modelling, and specification [1]. The work presented in this paper focuses on scenario-based RE for the discovery of requirements – a field of research which has not received much attention from the RE community in recent years.

One of the leading tool environments, that was also applied in industrial projects, was ART-SCENE (Analyzing Requirements Tradeoffs – Scenario Evaluation) [7]. ART-SCENE was a simple-to-use tool environment which allowed the specification of Use Cases and the generation of normal and alternative course scenarios. ART-SCENE-based scenario walkthroughs were mainly conducted in workshop settings where a facilitator used the ART-SCENE Scenario Presenter to walk through the generated scenarios and to explore what-if questions with key stakeholders [7]. Additionally, ART-SCENE extensions also included multimedia representations of scenarios which were designed to improve the discovery of requirements [19].

ART-SCENE extensions also included an ART-SCENE variant for Personal Digital Assistants (PDAs) which enabled analysts to conduct scenario walkthroughs on-site, in the workplace of future system users [8,15]. These walkthroughs with the so-called Mobile Scenario Presenter (MSP) were successful in terms of requirements knowledge discovered [8,15]. However, at this time, mobile technologies were still in their infancy. Technological constraints, including the limited availability of suitable devices to run the mobile scenario-based tool, made it cumbersome for analysts to collect requirements on-site [8,15]. Furthermore, due to limited availability of mobile internet and the overall limited usability of software running on these devices, mobile scenario-based requirements elicitation remained a niche domain that did not gain broader attention.

Now, over a decade later, many of the previous hardware-imposed limitations have been resolved. Mobile devices, such as smartphones and tablets, are used on a daily basis, even by non-technical users, mobile internet is available almost anywhere, and cloud-based services allow fast access and storage of data.

However, due to the importance of contextual RE [6], other RE approaches making use of mobile devices have been developed. This for example includes the iRequire [14] approach, which focuses on end-users and allows them to take pictures of the system context and document text based requirements, but lacks end-user guidance and does not include underlying contextual models. Other approaches focusing on system evolution such as the ConTexter approach [18] use GPS positions of predefined objects to gather structured feedback on IT Ecosystems. In recent years several feedback approaches allowing end-users to give feedback on software systems have been developed (e.g., [5,11]). The evaluation of such approaches indicates that end-users are able to gather requirements for future systems. However, to the best of our knowledge, none of these existing mobile approaches are based on scenarios. Therefore, re-visiting (on-site) scenario-based requirements elicitation, which provides focus and structure in the form of scenarios and adopting it to today's environment and system needs is a timely, and worthwhile endeavor.

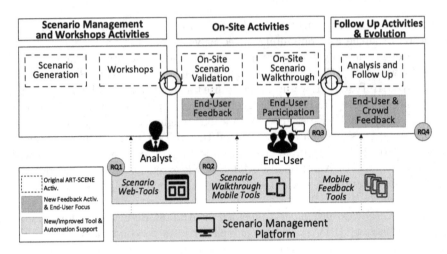

Fig. 1. Overview of the envisioned scenario-based RE framework.

3   Research Agenda

Our proposed research on scenario-based RE is driven by four key ideas: (1) the extension and reuse of scenario-based RE, making use of novel technologies (e.g., smartphones) and (2) its application within new domains. We further strive to (3) include end-users, who have previously been neglected, in the scenario-based requirements discovery process and (4) study the suitability of scenarios regarding new development paradigms (Fig. 1).

More specifically, we pursue the following research questions (RQ):

RQ1: To what extent can novel tools and techniques, built over current technologies, overcome the limitations of scenario walkthroughs as experienced in the past? With this first research question we focus on leveraging past experiences [8,15] and transition from old technologies such as PDAs to new up-to-date technologies such as smartphones, tablets and other mobile devices, as well as cloud-based computing. The research objective thus is to develop a framework and tool prototypes that leverage new technologies to address past limitations.

RQ2: What is the impact of using scenario-based approaches on the development of ubiquitous adaptive software-intensive systems from an analyst' point of view? We frame the second objective to investigate the suitability of the framework by applying it to different kinds of systems and by evaluating the usability and usefulness of the tools via user studies (e.g., using the cognitive dimensions of notations framework [3,13]). We present our initial prototype of the framework and tools alongside an initial application scenario in Sect. 4.

RQ3: To what extend can our novel scenario tools be used by non-RE experts such as (future) system end-users? In a second phase we will go beyond the initial scope and capabilities of scenario-based walkthroughs and actively involve end-users in the scenario generation and validation process.

RQ4: How can a scenario-based approach be integrated with modern development paradigms and support the ongoing evolution of software systems? Historical scenario-based approaches were designed at a time when more linear development processes, such as waterfall or the Unified Process (i.e., longer iterations), were common. However, we aim to explore integration of the scenario-based approach into new development paradigms, including rapid prototyping, agile software development, rapid release cycles, and DevOps. This will include to actively involve end-users and incorporating crowd-based feedback mechanisms [9,16] for existing features and also for iterative improvements to the overall systems.

4 NextGen Scenario-Based Requirements Discovery

As part of our initial effort to re-create and extend the previous scenario-based and mobile requirements tools [8,15] we developed an initial proof-of-concept framework supporting the generation, validation, and walkthrough of scenarios, for use in workshops and on-site. The prototype implementation currently includes key features available in the previous ART-SCENE solution. We developed a cloud-based web tool for generating new scenarios, and for managing existing ones, documenting individual steps for scenarios and generating "what-if" questions based on these scenarios. Secondly, a mobile application allows the on-site use of these scenarios by providing views that enable step-by-step walkthroughs of a scenario, commenting on individual steps, and adding diverse multimedia attachments such as images. A screenshot of the scenario management tool, alongside the mobile view is depicted in Fig. 2.

As part of our initial evaluation, we plan to use the tool-supported approach for understanding the system context and gathering requirements for

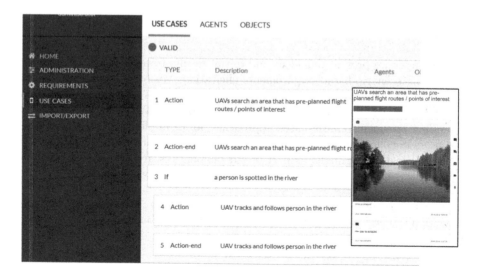

Fig. 2. Scenario management tool & mobile scenario tool prototype.

the Dronology system, a platform for managing, coordinating, and controlling unmanned aerial vehicles (UAV's) with support for collaborative tasks [4].

In a first pilot study the prototype tool was used by the authors to create initial scenarios for a community project which were validated in a workshop and used to capture requirements on-site. Workshop participants included city representatives, first-responders and firefighters, who discussed scenarios and necessary steps to use UAVs to support river-search-and-rescue and medical supply delivery. We found that the tool allowed us to create scenarios for the different UAVs use cases, and to capture requirements regarding their usage, deployment, and management on-site and in real-time.

Based on the feedback received during the pilot study and our ideas for how to further improve our prototype, we plan to redesign the user interface and improve the usability of the tool. A key goal is to develop a user interface which focuses on end-user needs, allowing them to use the tool without the help of an analyst. Furthermore, we are planning to make use of mobile positioning and tracking technologies (e.g., GPS) to trigger events automatically and document the geographic location of requirements. Another envisioned feature is to use the mobile device's sensors to capture contextual information (e.g., WiFi reception strength, proximity to other devices). This more advanced prototype will provide the basis for a fully fledged user study. In a first phase, we plan an evaluation of the prototype stakeholders of the Dronology project in workshops and on-site meetings. In a second phase, we will provide the prototype to future end-users of the Dronology system (e.g., firefighter) to document their requirements for the system.

In the more distant future, we plan to use the prototype in other projects and we will also explore new features such as integrating augmented reality or video-based approaches.

5 Conclusion

In this paper we present our ideas and initial results towards a new framework supporting scenario-based requirements elicitation. We build upon experiences from our previous work in this area nearly a decade ago and aim to overcome previous technical limitations by using new technologies. We further aim towards extending previous scenario-based approaches, for example by actively involving end-users in collecting requirements and providing feedback to existing or newly developed features. Finally, as part of our ongoing research we have started to evaluate the approach in context of smart- and cyber-physical systems.

Acknowledgments. This project has been funded by the Austrian Science Fund (FWF J3998-N319) and the US National Science Foundation Grants (CCF-1741781, CCF-1649448).

References

1. Alexander, I.F., Maiden, N.: Scenarios, Stories, Use Cases: Through the Systems Development Life-Cycle, 1st edn. Wiley, Hoboken (2004)
2. Beyer, H., Holtzblatt, K.: Contextual design. Interactions **6**(1), 32–42 (1999)
3. Blackwell, A., Green, T.: Notational systems-the cognitive dimensions of notations framework. In: Proceedings of the HCI Models, Theories, and Frameworks: Toward a Multidisciplinary Science, pp. 103–134. Morgan Kaufmann (2003)
4. Cleland-Huang, J., Vierhauser, M., Bayley, S.: Dronology: an incubator for cyber-physical systems research. In: Proceedings of the 40th International Conference on Software Engineering: New Ideas and Emerging Results, ICSE-NIER 2018, pp. 109–112. ACM (2018)
5. Doerr, J., Hess, A., Koch, M.: RE and society - a perspective on RE in times of smart cities and smart rural areas. In: Proceedings of the 26th IEEE International Requirements Engineering Conference (2018)
6. Knauss, A., Damian, D., Schneider, K.: Eliciting contextual requirements at design time: a case study. In: Proceedings of the 4th IEEE International Workshop on Empirical Requirements Engineering, pp. 56–63 (2014)
7. Maiden, N.: Systematic scenario walkthroughs with art-scene, pp. 166–178. Wiley (2004)
8. Maiden, N., Seyff, N., Grunbacher, P.: The mobile scenario presenter: integrating contextual inquiry and structured walkthroughs. In: Proceedings of the 13th IEEE International Workshop on Enabling Technologies: Infrastructure for Collaborative Enterprises, pp. 115–120. IEEE (2004)
9. Morales-Ramirez, I., Perini, A., Guizzardi, R.S.: An ontology of online user feedback in software engineering. Appl. Ontol. **10**(3–4), 297–330 (2015)
10. Nuseibeh, B., Easterbrook, S.: Requirements engineering: a roadmap. In: Proceedings of the Conference on the Future of Software Engineering, pp. 35–46. ACM (2000)
11. Oriol, M., et al.: FAME: supporting continuous requirements elicitation by combining user feedback and monitoring. In: Proceedings of the 26th IEEE International Requirements Engineering Conference, pp. 217–227 (2018)
12. Robertson, S., Robertson, J.: Mastering the Requirements Process: Getting Requirements Right. Addison-Wesley, Boston (2012)
13. Runeson, P., Höst, M.: Guidelines for conducting and reporting case study research in software engineering. Empirical Softw. Eng. **14**(2), 131 (2009)
14. Seyff, N., Bortenschlager, M., Ollmann, G.: iRequire: gathering end-user requirements for new apps. In: Proceedings of the 2011 IEEE 19th International Requirements Engineering Conference, pp. 347–348 (2011)
15. Seyff, N., Graf, F., Maiden, N., Grünbacher, P.: Scenarios in the wild: experiences with a contextual requirements discovery method. In: Glinz, M., Heymans, P. (eds.) REFSQ 2009. LNCS, vol. 5512, pp. 147–161. Springer, Heidelberg (2009). https://doi.org/10.1007/978-3-642-02050-6_13
16. Seyff, N., Todoran, I., Caluser, K., Singer, L., Glinz, M.: Using popular social network sites to support requirements elicitation, prioritization and negotiation. J. Internet Serv. Appl. **6**(1), 7 (2015)
17. Todoran, I., Seyff, N., Glinz, M.: How cloud providers elicit consumer requirements: an exploratory study of nineteen companies. In: Proceedings of the 21st IEEE International Requirements Engineering Conference, pp. 105–114, July 2013

18. Wehrmaker, T., Gärtner, S., Schneider, K.: ConTexter feedback system. In: Proceedings of the 34th International Conference on Software Engineering, pp. 1459–1460. IEEE (2012)
19. Zachos, K., Maiden, N.: Art-scene: enhancing scenario walkthroughs with multimedia scenarios. In: Proceedings of the 12th International Requirements Engineering Conference, pp. 360–361. IEEE (2004)

A Research Preview on TAICOS – Tailoring Stakeholder Interests to Task-Oriented Functional Requirements

Philipp Haindl[1]([✉]), Reinhold Plösch[1], and Christian Körner[2]

[1] Institute of Business Informatics - Software Engineering,
Johannes Kepler University, Altenbergerstraße 69, 4040 Linz, Austria
{philipp.haindl,reinhold.ploesch}@jku.at
[2] Siemens AG, Corporate Technology, Otto-Hahn-Ring 6, 81739 Munich, Germany
christian.koerner@siemens.com

Abstract. [**Context and Motivation**] Without a concrete functional context, non-functional requirements can be approached only as cross-cutting concerns and treated uniformly across the feature set of an application. This neglects, however, the heterogeneity of non-functional requirements that arises from stakeholder interests and the distinct functional scopes of software systems. [**Question/problem**] Earlier studies have shown that the different types and pursued objectives of non-functional requirements result in either vague or unbalanced specification of non-functional requirements. [**Principal ideas/results**] We propose a task analytic approach for eliciting and modeling user tasks with the software product. Stakeholder interests are structurally related to these user tasks and refined individually as a constraint in the context of each concrete user task. This individual refinement provides DevOps teams with important guidance on how the respective constraint can be satisfied in the software lifecycle and thus how the interest of the stakeholder can be satisfied sufficiently. [**Contribution**] We provide a structured approach, intertwining task-centered functional requirements with non-functional stakeholder interests to specify constraints on the level of user tasks. The results of a preliminary interview study with domain experts reveal that our task-constraint tailoring method increases the comprehensibility of requirements, clarity and quality of specifications.

Keywords: Stakeholder interests · Requirements negotiation · Task modeling · Constraint specification

1 Introduction

Intertwining functional and non-functional requirements is a challenging endeavor in software projects of any scale. We use the term *stakeholder interest* to represent our broader understanding of non-functional requirements ranging from development to operational aspects. As the complexity of satisfying an

© Springer Nature Switzerland AG 2019
E. Knauss and M. Goedicke (Eds.): REFSQ 2019, LNCS 11412, pp. 297–303, 2019.
https://doi.org/10.1007/978-3-030-15538-4_22

interest might differ between software features, the lack of precise specification often results in undetected non-functional dependencies between components and features in development, as well as increasing operational efforts throughout the DevOps cycle [15]. Focusing on concrete tasks that users will perform with a software system makes the individual relation between functional and non-functional requirements more tangible and facilitates negotiation [3], and assessment of tradeoffs in satisfying constraints [2].

In this paper we present the TAICOS *(Task-Interest-Constraint Satisfycing)* approach to eliciting and modeling user tasks based on a modified form of hierarchical task analysis [1], and tailoring stakeholder interests so that they can be refined into constraints and satisficed during the full software lifecycle. In contrast to existing approaches our approach methodically facilitates to derive constraints that *satisfice* the original interest, i.e. to *satisfy* an interest *sufficiently* and not better than required.

To give a better understanding of the terminology used in the TAICOS method, we want to clarify the meaning of the following terms used in this paper.

- **Satisfice:** is a portmanteau of *satisfy* and *suffice*. It expresses the intention to satisfy a requirement in a complex system only sufficiently and not optimally - so that a multitude of goals can be satisfied concurrently.
- **Task:** is a sequence of actions that people perform to attain a goal. Tasks differ in the goals they attain, their input modalities (e.g., software-based, in-person), and the actions they require for their attainment [1].
- **Constraint:** is a *"nonfunctional requirement that acts to constrain the solution"* [4] possibly more than it would need to satisfy functional requirements. Features and constraints cannot be seen isolated as constraints influence software design and architectural decisions [5].
- **Stakeholder Interest:** extends the primarily technical notion of constraints to also capture non-engineering interests such as customer value, legal or business aspects articulated by stakeholders of a software product.

2   Related Work

Goal-driven [9,12] approaches have proven to be effective for requirements elicitation. According to Fotrousi et al. [7], the key limitation of goal models is that the impact of an unsatisfied constraint is hardly comprehensible for stakeholders. Riegel et al. [11] elaborate on a requirements prioritization method which does also cover non-engineering related stakeholder interests such as customer value or implementation costs. Regnell et al. [10] presented a framework for visualizing and prioritizing interrelations between constraints. Yang et al. in [14] present approaches to resolve ambiguities between functional requirements and constraints based on architectural design patterns.

Our approach augments the computer-implemented development method outlined by US Pat. No. 15/661,498 [8] which aims to find suitable quantitative constraints for non-functional requirements through Monte-Carlo simulations.

The presented research preview explicitly facilitates to elicit, refine and specify constraints in the context of an individual functional requirement with quantitative measures. Also, it supports requirements engineers to evaluate possible trade-offs of contradicting non-functional requirements on the level of user tasks.

3 The TAICOS Approach

The TAICOS approach hierarchically decomposes functional blocks of software into user tasks and specifies concrete constraints for each task and stakeholder interest. This is done through relating user tasks and stakeholder interests in a tabular form and refining the interests to concrete constraints with the relevant stakeholders.

3.1 Eliciting User Tasks and Stakeholder Interests

Our approach defines multiple steps for eliciting tasks and is based on hierarchical task analysis [1] with some modifications to carve out the functional scope of the elicited actions. Initially, the objective, scope boundaries, and necessary data (e.g., about task execution, dependencies between tasks or constraints) for each task are defined. Based on its superordinate goal, the task is decomposed into subtasks to later allow a precise tailoring of the interests to each subtask. Finally, the *task details* are identified to explicate the users' pursued goal with the task and how the later software system shall support it. While hierarchical task analysis allows infinite refinement of tasks to the point that tasks are purely operational for a user, TAICOS only allows refinement of tasks by means of *task detail tables*. If the refinement of the task cannot be described in an operational manner, a separate model should be created for refinement. This assures that tasks and constraints are properly treated and described at the refined level.

Task Details. For the structured elicitation of task details, our approach offers two perspectives: (1) *user intentions*, the user's interactions during execution of the task; and (2) *system responsibilities* to support these user intentions through the system. Both perspectives are then compared with each other in tabular form and refined with *pre-* and *postconditions*, as well as *information objects*, which describe the information generated or required for task execution. The main objective of this refinement step is to map the fine-grained intentions of the user to suitable functional requirements by carving out the minimal and satisfactory technical solution which allows the user to execute the task effectively.

Stakeholder Interests. Based on existing frameworks [6,13] of interests influencing the software lifecycle, TAICOS aims to capture all stakeholders' interests that influence how the later software system needs to support users' tasks, as well as to identify what other objectives must be considered throughout the DevOps cycle from development and operation to decommissioning.

3.2   Tailoring Stakeholder Interests to User Tasks

In the last step of our method, stakeholder interests are individually analyzed in the context of a specific user task and eventually specified as a concrete constraint. The overall objective of this step is to specify constraints which *satisfice* the elicited stakeholder interest. As a practical example the performance of each user task might be subjected to different quantitative expectations. Table 1 shows how our approach explicitly tackles the different relevance of course-grained stakeholder interests among different user tasks.

Table 1. Exemplary task-interest-constraint matrix.

	User Tasks			
	Search for book	Update credit card information	Change shipping address	Write book review
The software must react quickly to user inputs.	Search results must be provided within 1 sec.	Card information must be updated within 2 sec.	Shipping address must be updated within 2 sec.	Review service must finalize within 3 sec.
Customer data must be deleted physically.	n/a	Delete primary, secondary and previous cards of the customer.	Delete current and previous shipping addresses.	Anonymize book review.
The software must be maintainable with moderate effort.	Technical debt must be below 1 day.	Technical debt must be below 2 days.	Technical debt must be below 2 days.	Technical debt must be below 2 days.
Assure that the software uses encryption when exchanging data.	n/a	Send encrypted security tokens to credit card billing system for authorization of credit card transactions.	n/a	n/a
The software must be resilient to external service outages.	Failover to alternative service implementation after 2 consecutive failures.	Rollback of transaction upon first service outage.	Failover to alternative service implementation after 3 consecutive failures.	Suspend and restart service implementation after 2 consecutive failures.

Our approach addresses the problem that stakeholder interests have variable relevance within the system depending on the functional scope within which these must be satisfied. Therefore stakeholder interests and user tasks are related in a two-dimensional matrix, and the relevance and concrete expression for each interest are evaluated and collaboratively specified among stakeholders. This also ensures that all elicited interests are thoroughly analyzed in the context of user tasks to identify whether they are relevant in each narrow task context and how they can be satisfied within that context. As an example, the generic interest *"The software must be resilient to external service outages"* must be differently treated depending on the security impact of the service outage and is thus reflected in the respectively refined constraints. As another example, the refinement of the interest *"The software must be maintainable with moderate effort"* shows that the maintainability requirements for each user task need to be differently *satisficed* depending on the importance of the task, the expected source code change frequency or the expected lifetime of the task.

4   Preliminary Evaluation Results

To validate our method, we conducted 11 expert interviews with senior software engineers, technical product and project managers, and requirements engineers from 11 different companies in Austria. The interviews were conducted face-to-face and comprised 20 open and four closed questions on a four-point Likert scale. One part of the interviews captured educational and company background, roles held by the experts and how the respective companies model functional requirements and constraints in software projects. The second part comprised questions to evaluate our approach to the task-centered modeling of functional requirements and tailoring multi-domain constraints to elicited user tasks.

4.1   Evaluation of Tailoring Stakeholder Interests in the Context of User Tasks

In the interviews we presented the experts with a selection of tasks from a well-known online book store and a list of generally understandable performance, privacy, and legal interests. Then, we illustrated how these interests can be used in our approach to derive constraints on the level of user tasks. Finally, we asked the experts four questions to evaluate our method for tailoring these interests in the context of individual user tasks.

Benefits and Weaknesses of the Interest-Tailoring Approach. We asked the experts two open questions to elaborate the benefits of our interest tailoring approach on the level of user tasks. Subsequently, we condensed their answers to these questions into eight categories, summarizing the main statements of the experts. Increased comprehensibility of the specification was expressed as a benefit by 82% of the experts, namely by increasing the clarity of objectives pursued through an interest. In 55% of the interviews, the experts mentioned the increased specification quality of constraints derived from interests, and 36% said it would help them to assess project risks by better understanding interests and their interdependencies.

In 18% of interviews, experts expressed the prioritization of interests, the time savings accrued by deriving constraints from interests, and the ease of documentation as benefits of the approach. Only 9% of experts mentioned that our approach could also help them to detect critical paths. Based on the open answers examining the weaknesses, we codified experts' answers into three groups. 45% of experts believed that the approach would introduce an additional specification effort but also expressed that the expected benefits outweighed these tradeoffs accompanying any structured method. 27% of experts mentioned the complexity of the approach as a drawback, and a further 18% anticipated that our approach would result in explicitly specifying standard industry constraints that usually need no special documentation. (e.g., a default availability, common security requirements).

Suitability of the Interest-Tailoring Approach. Finally, the experts were asked to rate the overall suitability of the approach on a four-point Likert scale. Again we received predominantly positive feedback, with 55% experts judging the approach as suitable and 36% as rather suitable. The 9% of experts judging the approach as rather unsuitable argued that a precise and comprehensive specification of constraints from interests should only be done for selected features and not on the level of user tasks. No expert judged the interest tailoring approach as unsuitable for their projects.

5   Threats to Validity

We see a threat to **construct validity** in the different interpretations of the questions by the experts, which is mainly due to their different roles and experiences. We addressed this threat by showing each expert concrete definitions of the terminology used in the interview and discussed any ambiguities. When summarizing the interview answers, we also considered the background and role of each expert to determine from what view and with what intention the statement was given. The foremost threat to **internal validity** can be seen in some experts' trend to answer in confirmation of our theories, which became evident when elaborating on the practice of eliciting constraints. This could have led to confirmation bias, but we regard this as negligible because in response to this trend to answer towards confirming our theories, we asked follow-up questions to capture experts' actual experiences. We addressed the threat to **external validity** by selecting experts who operate in different industry sectors, and we also selected only one expert per company. However, we see a threat to the generalizability of the results to other industries due to the different size and maturity of requirements engineering practices in the companies.

6   Conclusion and Future Work

Utilizing the proposed hierarchical task analysis approach to structurally decompose tasks into subtasks seems to offer a promising approach to clarify the core functionality needed to support the users' goals for involved stakeholders. Stakeholder interests can be effectively tailored to constraints within the context of a user task so that each interest can be fulfilled in a satisfying but not inevitably optimal way. Our approach explicitly addresses challenges arising from both the heterogeneity of stakeholder interests and the interdependences of functional requirements and constraints in software systems. Future work will concentrate on additional model elements for tagging tasks with contextual information and ensuring comprehensibility and applicability for large-scale software engineering projects. We also would like to improve the interest-tailoring method to reduce ambiguities which may occur when assessing the relevance and impact of each interest for each task. Finally, after having applied the TAICOS approach practically in different companies we also plan to conduct a more thorough validation comprising interviews and surveys with these companies to gather empirical evidence about its suitability and limitations.

References

1. Annett, J.: Hierarchical task analysis. In: The Handbook of Task Analysis for Human-Computer Interaction, pp. 67–82. Taylor & Francis, London (2003)
2. Berander, P., Andrews, A.: Requirements prioritization. In: Aurum, A., Wohlin, C. (eds.) Engineering and Managing Software Requirements, pp. 69–94. Springer, Heidelberg (2005). https://doi.org/10.1007/3-540-28244-0_4
3. Blaine, J.D., Cleland-Huang, J.: Software quality requirements: how to balance competing priorities. IEEE Softw. 25(2), 22–24 (2008)
4. Bourque, P., Fairley, R.E.: Guide to the Software Engineering Body of Knowledge, 3rd edn. IEEE Computer Society Press, Los Alamitos (2014)
5. Broy, M.: Rethinking nonfunctional software requirements. Computer 48(5), 96–99 (2015)
6. Chung, L., do Prado Leite, J.C.S.: On non-functional requirements in software engineering. In: Borgida, A.T., Chaudhri, V.K., Giorgini, P., Yu, E.S. (eds.) Conceptual Modeling: Foundations and Applications. LNCS, vol. 5600, pp. 363–379. Springer, Heidelberg (2009). https://doi.org/10.1007/978-3-642-02463-4_19
7. Fotrousi, F., Fricker, S.A., Fiedler, M.: Quality requirements elicitation based on inquiry of quality-impact relationships. In: 2014 IEEE 22nd International Requirements Engineering Conference (RE), pp. 303–312 (2014)
8. Gehmeyr, A., Höfler, W., Kochseder, R., Rettner, J., Horn, S.: Computer-implemented product development method, US Patent no. 15/661,498 (2018)
9. Lamsweerde, A.V.: Goal-oriented requirements engineering: a guided tour. In: Proceedings Fifth IEEE International Symposium on Requirements Engineering, pp. 249–262 (2001)
10. Regnell, B., Svensson, R.B., Olsson, T.: Supporting roadmapping of quality requirements. IEEE Softw. 25(2), 42–47 (2008)
11. Riegel, N., Doerr, J.: A systematic literature review of requirements prioritization criteria. In: Fricker, S.A., Schneider, K. (eds.) REFSQ 2015. LNCS, vol. 9013, pp. 300–317. Springer, Cham (2015). https://doi.org/10.1007/978-3-319-16101-3_22
12. Rolland, C., Salinesi, C.: Modeling goals and reasoning with them. In: Aurum, A., Wohlin, C. (eds.) Engineering and Managing Software Requirements, pp. 189–217. Springer, Heidelberg (2005). https://doi.org/10.1007/3-540-28244-0_9
13. Roman, G.C.: A taxonomy of current issues in requirements engineering. Computer 18(4), 14–23 (1985)
14. Yang, H., Zheng, S., Chu, W.C.C., Tsai, C.T.: Linking functions and quality attributes for software evolution. In: 2012 19th Asia-Pacific Software Engineering Conference, vol. 1, pp. 250–259 (2012)
15. Zowghi, D., Coulin, C.: Requirements Elicitation: A Survey of Techniques, Approaches, and Tools. In: Aurum, A., Wohlin, C. (eds.) Engineering and Managing Software Requirements, pp. 19–46. Springer, Berlin Heidelberg (2005). https://doi.org/10.1007/3-540-28244-0_2

Author Index

Printed in the United States
By Bookmasters